Gendered Modernisms

Gendered Modernisms

American Women Poets and Their Readers

EDITED BY

Margaret Dickie and
Thomas Travisano

University of Pennsylvania Press

Philadelphia

Permission is acknowledged to reprint material from published works. A complete listing can be found following the index in this volume.

Copyright © 1996 by the University of Pennsylvania Press

Library of Congress Cataloging-in-Publication Data

Gendered modernisms : American women poets and their readers / edited by Margaret Dickie and Thomas Travisano.
    p.   cm.
    Includes bibliographical references and index.
    ISBN 0-8122-3312-3 (cloth : alk. paper). — ISBN 0-8122-1550-8 (paper : alk. paper)
    1. American poetry—Women authors—History and criticism.   2. Modernism (Literature)—United States.   3. Women and literature—United States—History—20th century.   4. Authors and readers—United States—History—20th century.   5. Books and reading—United States—History—20th century.   6. American poetry—20th century—History and criticism.   7. Canon (Literature)   I. Dickie, Margaret, 1935–   .   II. Travisano, Thomas J., 1951–
PS310.M57G46   1996
811'.5099287—dc20   95-42906
                                                                            CIP

Contents

IV. Edna St. Vincent Millay (1892–1950)

V. Laura (Riding) Jackson (1901–1991)

VI. Elizabeth Bishop (1911–1979)

VII. Muriel Rukeyser (1913–1980)

VIII. Gwendolyn Brooks (1917–)

Introduction

The titles of these essays are long: "History as Conjugation: Stein's *Stanzas in Meditation* and the Literary History of the Modernist Long Poem," "Pornopoeia, the Modernist Canon, and the Cultural Capital of Sexual Literacy: The Case of H. D.," "'So As to Be One Having Some Way of Being One Having Some Way of Working': Marianne Moore and Literary Tradition," for example. Their length (matched also by the length of the essays, at least in their original form) suggests that the topics are fulsome, not easily contained nor readily indicated in abbreviated form, and highly original; in short, the essays perfectly reflect the work of the women poets themselves. The length of the titles points to the number and variety of issues that must be taken into account when women poets are added to literary history. Even the shorter titles, such as "The Elizabeth Bishop Phenomenon," cover a wide range of topics.

This collection of essays on eight modern American women poets is designed to reexamine the complex and still evolving relationship between these poets and their readers, not just those readers newly trained as feminist critics but also the poets' own contemporary readers—because they did have readers even when American poetic modernism was conventionally construed as a predominately white male phenomenon. Often, such readers treated even the most famous women modernists, such as those considered here, as little more than footnotes to the general literary histories they constructed. This collection provides another reading of these poets, placing them in the context of their times, examining the conditions that helped shape their vivid and diverse poetic careers, and reconsidering some of the assumptions that have led to their exclusion from the main narratives of modernist poetry and its aftermath. Ultimately, its aim is to enlarge the literary history of poetic modernism as a period that—with the addition of these women—can be extended both backward into the first years of the twentieth century and forward to the 1960s, overlapping with postmodernism.

The eight American women poets considered in this volume—Gertrude Stein, H. D., Marianne Moore, Edna St. Vincent Millay, Laura (Riding) Jackson, Elizabeth Bishop, Muriel Rukeyser, and Gwendolyn Brooks—have yet to find a settled place in critical and historical accounts of modernism or postmodernism, despite their considerable and varied achievements and their acknowledged significance. These eight are by no means unknown poets; but the process of reconsideration in recent literary histories and anthologies is incomplete. For example, *The Columbia History of American Poetry* (1993) includes only brief mention of (Riding) Jackson and Rukeyser, and even the second edition of *The Heath Anthology of American Literature* (1994) omits (Riding) Jackson and represents Stein as a poet only sparsely. The burgeoning work on Bishop during this period, the discovery of (Riding) Jackson, and renewal of interest in Rukeyser, among other developments, all suggest the urgency of a broader reconsideration of twentieth-century women poets.

This collection of essays is designed to raise some of the questions that women poets bring to the literary history of modernism, both as it has been written and as it might now be written in a fuller account that includes gender. In their own day, these poets were both well placed and prominent—Moore as an influential editor of a major little magazine; H. D. also as an editor; Gertrude Stein at the center of the avant-garde art world in Paris; Brooks as the first black woman poet to win a Pulitzer Prize; (Riding) Jackson as centrally located first among the Agrarians and then in England with Robert Graves; Millay as a popular success; Bishop as a protégée of Moore and perennial prizewinner; and Rukeyser as a political poet. This collection confronts the paradox that, despite their favor, they have been dismissed from literary history, frequently in so many words, as eccentric, as inessential, or as a special case.

It is true that they were notable for their individuality—not to say intransigence, at points—and their poetic careers were often marked by crafty evasions and blunt refusals to conform, by both quiet and aggressive gestures of decentering. But they were also productive and creative insiders in a movement we cannot fully understand unless we examine their role in shaping it. Gendered, modernism gives up its singularity and becomes more than the monolithic movement dominated by one important (and male) figure—whether it be Ezra Pound or Wallace Stevens, as traditional arguments have had it. Gendered, modernism becomes a diverse, disruptive series of movements, with a political left as well as political right, enacted in an arena where ideas of order contend with questions of sexuality, eroticism, and pornography, as well as domesticity and sentimentality. Gendered, modernism can configure issues of race and class from the position of the outsider, the dispossessed, the deracinated. Gendered, modernism emerges as sexier, more violent, more personal, more subversive.

These eight poets have no single story to tell. In fact, they were chosen because each one presents a distinct and different problem for literary history. Some of these poets are conservative in form and style, others are radical experimenters; some have been seen as excessively reticent and estranged, others as completely politicized. Each has been more or less misplaced. Moore and Bishop were, until recently, almost universally judged as good minor poets. (Riding) Jackson and H. D. have been dismissed as mere satellites of more important male figures. Despite, or perhaps because of, her popularity with readers, Rukeyser was regularly vilified by critics in the leading literary journals, from the right for her left-leaning politics and her highly personal aesthetic, from the left for her refusal to conform to a leftist political agenda and that same intransigent aesthetic. Stein, although certainly famous even in her own lifetime, has often stood, in both the popular and the critical imagination, as a figure for the more unreadable extremes of modernism. By contrast, Edna St. Vincent Millay was a popular poet, although after the triumph of modernism, she would live to see herself generally dismissed by critics as excessively conventional and sentimental. Her reputation is only now beginning to recover from an extended and precipitous decline. Brooks has chafed against the public desire to see her as *the* representative black woman.

Placing these writers more accurately in literary history is not an easy task. The essays here express something of the uneasiness the contributors have felt in trying to find a way to include everything that must be mentioned when women poets are included in literary history—new sensibilities, new definitions of genres, new ways of reading. In part, this uneasiness is with literary history itself; in part, too, it stems from the need to break new ground in an already cultivated field. But, in large part, it reflects the sense expressed by poet after poet that she alone does not fit into literary history, that she is a strange case, a special case, an original case, in short, that she is exactly what her detractors imagine her to be. From Gertrude Stein to Gwendolyn Brooks, women poets have considered themselves—in a variety of ways and for different reasons— to be unique. Surely every poet is unusually gifted; but these women poets seem more aware of their strangeness than their genius. And, unlike their male counterparts, they do not equate the two.

It may seem an obvious point: women poets felt unusual because, excluded from literary history, they were made to feel unusual. Less obvious is why so many women poets turned a public perception into their private sense of themselves. With the possible exception of Rukeyser, these poets did not see themselves as part of a group excluded by gender and placed outside the general boundaries of literary history (however much each poet may have considered that her own exclusion was related to her gender); rather, each poet imagined herself to be uniquely unassimilable as well as unassimilated.

Some of these poets were excluded from literary history because they were simply not in print or not readily available. Stein's poetry remained largely unpublished at her death, for example, and only now is some of it easily accessible. H. D.'s *Collected Poems: 1912–1944* came out in 1983. By contrast, Moore's endless revisions of her poetry made it available in so many versions that it is still difficult, as Robin Schulze argues, to establish her texts. Bishop's posthumous *Complete Poems* and *Collected Prose* produced work that changed the shape of her career. Brooks now publishes outside the mainstream press; (Riding) Jackson always did. In short, these poets present extraordinary textual, as well as critical and cultural, challenges to their readers. The essays here consider a variety of these challenges.

For some poets, this stand outside of the literary mainstream was, if not intentionally combative, at least an indication of the poet's resistance to easy inclusion. Others were complicit in their exclusion, taking issue with critics who might have placed them in literary history. Still others pursued their solitary ways, often heightening their eccentricity, without keen attention to their future or even their present audiences. The frequency with which the essays in this collection return to the idea that these poets imagined themselves to be unique is noteworthy and indicates the persistence of the idea that the woman poet is an oddity even to herself. Even more remarkable is the general agreement with the poets' self-assessments among the contributors to this volume. Far from attempting to regularize the careers of these poets and thus to fit them into even a newly devised historical construction, these contributors work to complicate and intensify our understanding of the poets' uniqueness. If anything, at the conclusion of these essays, the poets discussed will seem more strange and more compelling, and conventional literary history in need of more radical expansion and revision, than we had previously imagined.

Arranged in chronological order by the poet's birth dates, the essays reveal these women poets' growing awareness of their place in literary history, despite the fact that the contributors write from no single conception of literary history, articulate no common theory of literary production, and speak from no political consensus. The narratives they tell are varied, and, while it might seem that, moving from Stein to Brooks, this volume traces the gradual deepening of women poets' anger at being excluded from literary history, in fact, the story does not develop along such a straight line. Stein was as resistant to conventional literary history as Brooks (and Rukeyser more so), and Edna St. Vincent Millay and Laura (Riding) Jackson at midpoint in this chronology were more outrageously defiant than either Stein or Brooks. Together, these women poets form a continuing history of radical experiments in writing, extreme independence in their personal lives, and often impassioned involvement in the political and social issues of their time. From Stein to Brooks, these women poets have been committed to the woman's voice in poetry; in charting that commitment, the essays here also attempt to find a place for it in the culture of modernism.

Although the contributors to this collection set for themselves the task of addressing general questions about the social and political issues (including gender, race, and class) that generate conceptions of literary history, they focus chiefly on the poetry and return for their arguments' evidence to the poems. Since none of these poets is undiscovered or even unread, this insistence on offering readings of the poems suggests again and again how much has been elided or neglected in interpreting the works of these poets. Suppressed in H. D.'s image as an Imagist is what Dianne Chisholm calls her "pornopoeia," for example, and underestimated in the recent feminist reclamation of Stein is her conflicted feeling about her own sexuality, according to Margaret Dickie. This need to read the poems, then, is one indication of how little the readings of these poets have varied and of how much work they still require, although, even to this general rule, there are exceptions. Thomas Travisano, who does not provide readings of Bishop poetry, attests to the fact that critics have read that poet thoroughly in recent years.

The essays divide along two lines: The first line opens an examination of the ways in which the poet felt themselves to be unusual and perhaps even unready to fit neatly into the literary communities they knew or the history that might derive from them. The second line is a study of the phases of critical construction and reconstruction that have shaped and reshaped the readings of these poets. Contributors to this collection have pursued their own way in tracing these lines, and, by arranging them only in chronological order by poet, we have aimed to keep the issues as open and unresolved as modernism itself might be.

Starting with the oldest, Gertrude Stein, Mary Loeffelholz also makes the most radical case, arguing finally that Stein's resistance to her own completed long poem and to the very idea of writing poetry might best be honored by questioning the ground and effects of her placement in an anthology like this one, including the ground or effect that nominates Stein as a woman. Examining Stein's resistance to her own *Stanzas in Meditation* as a long poem, Loeffelholz first considers why it has not figured in literary histories of the modernist long poem; next, she sets it in the context of other modernist long poems, including those by women with which it might be compared; and, finally, she studies the risks of such readings of Stein.

Like this resistant Stein, H. D., in Dianne Chisholm's view, is a poet whose "metrical pulse, orgiastic intensity, violent affect, and visionary sadomasochism of her porno-, sometimes graphic, always hermetic, language," from *Sea Garden* (1916) to *Hermetic Definition* (1960), exceed the criteria of poetic difficulty for which her work has been valued as modernist literature. Not anxious to place a newer and sexier H. D. in literary history nor to correct modernist and feminist readings of her work by newly accredited queer ones, Chisholm wants rather to present H. D.'s bid for literary distinction as a bid for the authority to revitalize erotic language, and she wants to locate H. D.'s social efficacy in the field of cultural production, where she competes for the linguistic and symbolic capital that constitutes sexual literacy. Chisholm presents a poet who, writing against the grain of the sexual conservatism adopted by her closest modernist colleagues, persisted in developing a new sexual language.

Cultural and social issues are also at the center of Lisa Steinman's consideration of Marianne Moore, another poet who is presented as a special case. Aware that, as a woman, she would not easily fit into the list that T. S. Eliot imagined would constitute *the* literary tradition, Moore turned for a sense of community to visual artists and eventually to an accommodation with popular culture in her poems. Steinman sees Moore as self-conscious about the gendered nature of so-called universal culture. Opposed to a fixed tradition, Moore was, in Steinman's view, an eccentric collector of artifacts, one wedded to heterogeneity, miscellany, and energy. Steinman acknowledges that she herself expected to discuss the new and extraliterary sources for Moore's poetry and to suggest how such acts of inclusion shift the locus of intertextual references and finally the definition of a text; but, upon reflection, she found instead a Moore whose energies were not just lively but explosive as the poet became increasingly uneasy about the distribution of cultural capital and the fetishization of culture.

In considering Marianne Moore's multiple revisions of a single poem, "The Frigate Pelican," Robin Schulze turns her attention to the poet's habit of revising her work and thus of destabilizing her text; but Schulze too is concerned with the ways in which Moore's response to cultural issues changed her perception of her own poems. Focusing on the problem that most perplexes critics of Moore—the difficulty of developing an authoritative and stable list of the poet's own canon—Schulze sees the poet's revisions as themselves revising the modernist concept of an autotelic poem or a totalized and closed aesthetic. She shows Moore's response to different conceptions of both self and context as she worked over the poem dedicated to Wallace Stevens. In the 1934 version of "The Frigate Pelican," Moore, responding to the pressure of the Depression, posed the question of the poet's role in society. In revising the poem for the 1951 *Collected Poems,* she cut it dramatically and changed it into a much darker work—one that reflected the crisis of her creative imagination when faced with the horrors of World War II and the death of her mother.

Edna St. Vincent Millay was herself a cultural and social phenomenon in Suzanne Clark's estimation. She had a reputation for rebellious marginality, a commitment to the social causes of the bohemian left, from free love to support for the working masses, and yet she wrote poetry within the conventions of the dominant culture that had a sweeping success and an embarrassingly sentimental flourish. So resistant was Millay to any narrative of literary history that she still eludes classification. Clark presents a poet who is both a sentimental daughter, a child, and at the same time a woman who celebrates *jouissance.*

Muriel Rukeyser presents the quite different case of a poet who generated critical hostility partly because she could not be easily categorized or placed in literary history. Publishing in her first book poems that were tied to the apolitical and highly aesthetic tradition of "high modernism" along with politically committed poems, Rukeyser retained her independence from any literary tradition throughout her life, and for this stubborn resistance she was often personally attacked by critics. Kate Daniels views Rukeyser as no innocent victim of the critics' attacks, not even of the curiously personal venom in their commentary; rather, she reads Rukeyser as actively engaging them in a critical polemic, writing a parallel body of prose to promote and explain how her poetry might be fully appreciated and interpreted that remains intransigent in its insistence that it be taken on its own terms.

Richard Flynn takes up the case of Rukeyser's independence by considering her resistance to easy assimilation into the feminist movement, where in the mid-1970s she was heralded as a foremother only to be forgotten again by the 1990s. Although she wrote throughout her career from the experience of the female body, she rejects explicitly a poetics or a politics based on gender. Through a consideration of Rukeyser's commitment to processive and open forms and a close reading of "Double Ode," Flynn demonstrates the ways in which Rukeyser brought together the dualities of her experience: father and mother, parent and child, male and female, past and present, politics and poetry.

Gwendolyn Brooks, the first black woman to receive a Pulitzer Prize, was praised for a long time by the white liberal establishment as representative of her race and gender only to be attacked for aligning herself with the Black Power movement and what looks like the simply misogynist and nationalist Black Arts tradition. In Kathryne Lindberg's view, Brooks's career does not divide so simply. Rather, Lindberg argues, Brooks has always questioned the limits placed on representative black women writers, and she came increasingly to use her position as a respected artist to express her solidarity with young blacks and to resolve "the double bind of a black woman artist who would be heard as something other than victim of or exile from her race and class." Lindberg identifies Brooks's role as prophetic and provisional, writing a new (black) consciousness or, as Brooks writes, "New consciousness and trudge-toward-progress."

From Stein to Brooks, the essays here detail not only the poets' persistent self-consciousness about their places in literary history, but also their increasing willingness to make that self-consciousness a matter of public acknowledgment and debate. From Stein to Brooks, the poets voiced their resistance to literary tradition and history in open and abrasive terms. Stein, who may have been most angry at being excluded from a literary history in which she imagined herself to be central, cast up a wall of silence around her own literary production of the genre that most defined her generation, the long poem. Her resistance to her own poetry, as to naming in any form, may suggest the deepest conflict about tradition. In a more reserved way and yet nonetheless agitated by Eliot's establishment of a fixed literary tradition, Moore worked steadily as a poet and a critic to undermine or explode a tradition to which she as a woman would never belong. Millay and Rukeyser were, in different ways, flamboyant in their opposition to conventional literary tastes. One, the poetess, the other, the Marxist, each was committed to having it out on her own terms in poetry as in politics. Brooks rescued herself from the danger of being given too fixed a position in literary history as *the* representative Black Woman Writer by moving outside that history entirely to address a new audience and create a new consciousness among black young people and writers.

In addition to the poets' own resistance to the conventional formulations of literary history, this collection engages in another aspect of the problem generated by trying to place these women poets through essays that consider the critics' resistance to their work and the ways their reputations have fluctuated with an ever-wavering set of cultural and social values. Each of the poets in this collection has had a strange and varying critical reputation, moving in and out of favor. The group as a whole provides a compelling argument for the contingency of critical values and the instability of literary history.

The present moment in literary history and this collection as its product are, of course, no exception to this rule. Concentrating on poets whose works are now more easily accessible, whose careers have been the center of increasing critical attention, and whose significance is certified by these recent developments, this collection of essays has built on the discovery and recovery projects of feminist and cultural critics, such as Ulla Dydo, Susan Stanford Friedman, Sandra Gilbert and Susan Gubar,

Dianne Middlebrook, Alicia Ostriker, Emily Watts (and many of the contributors to this collection), among others. Not only has the pioneering
work of these critics created an audience for twentieth-century women
poets and new ways of reading individual poets, it has often made these
poets our contemporaries. That they are, in an important sense, and
some of them now have their first readers. But these poets had other
contemporaries, as well, and this collection of essays is designed to examine them in their own time.

Margaret Dickie views the feminist and postmodernist appropriations
of Gertrude Stein as a dehistoricizing of the poet, a reading that makes
her more attuned to the interests of the end of the century than to its
beginning when she wrote. In recovering Stein, the critics have exploited
the celebratory part of her erotic writing. Examining Stein's early experimental writing, from "Ada" (1907) and *Tender Buttons* (1911–13)
to "Lifting Belly" (1915–17), Dickie suggests that Stein used various
experimental strategies to disguise, encode, and naturalize the erotic
experience she wanted both to express and conceal. Her interest in naming without using the names was tied both to her radical experiments in
writing and to her conservative desire to hide from a too open revelation
of her lesbianism.

Cassandra Laity places her study of H. D.'s debt to the Aesthetes in the
context of her contemporaries, T. S. Eliot, William Butler Yeats, and
Ezra Pound, who owed a similar debt and distanced themselves from
it by various means—Eliot's objective correlative, Yeats's masks, and
Pound's personae. By contrast, H. D. was much more open in her use of
Decadent-Romantic masks and codes for sexual sameness in her poetics
of sympathetic love. Laity focuses particularly on H. D.'s use of the
recurring tableaux for the Platonic male-male continuum in Decadent-
Romanticism—the spectacle of an androgynous, beautiful young male
displayed before the discriminating male homoerotic gaze of his older
mentor—which she manipulated to articulate female homoerotic desire, as well as the equal relation between men and women, and the
power of mother-daughter eros. Because H. D. did not deny her debt to
the Victorian-Romantic past, she was frequently attacked by the anti-
Romantic male modernists and their critics. These attacks, as Laity
shows, concealed anxieties about the sexual "sameness" of Victorian-
Romantic Hellenism that Oscar Wilde's trial had rendered deviant.

A poet recovered for the 1990s is Edna St. Vincent Millay, that complex figure whom Cheryl Walker calls part vaudevillian, part Latinist,
whose reputation has ebbed and flowed in the tidal pools of literary history. Right now she is enjoying a resurgence of interest, as evidenced in
her emergence in new anthologies. One college textbook, Walker notes,
selects her work along with William Shakespeare's to represent the son-

net. But it has not always been so, and, as literary fashions change, the Millay we read today is not the one Edmund Wilson read. Claiming that complex cultural factors allow us to situate all poems in familiar and reusable contexts, Walker presents an antimodernist, a modernist, and a postmodernist Millay. Antimodernist in her use of traditional form, modernist in her feminism and political interests, postmodernist in her performative mode, Millay may fit all categories, or rather, in Walker's view, her changing reputation may suggest how changeable the construction of the usable past really is.

Also multiply identifiable in Jeanne Heuving's view is Laura (Riding) Jackson. She has been labeled a modernist, New Critical, and postmodernist poet, and yet none of these labels really fits her poetry, which itself points to the way these periodizing concepts only highlight the poetics of some poets over others. (Riding) Jackson fits more appropriately with poets such as Moore and Stein, whose innovative poetry also works to subvert gender relations and the "mirroring relations . . . critical to an art of the 'patriarchal leer,'" according to Heuving.

In his discussion of Elizabeth Bishop's critical reception, Thomas Travisano lays out five factors that influence a writer's rise or fall in literary status. He argues that a recent realignment in all five of these factors—a shift in the cultural perspective of the readership, a shift in the critical paradigm, the emergence of new evidence about the author, the clamor of influential advocates, and the assimilation of the intrinsic qualities of the work—has led to a dramatic revaluation of Bishop's status as a writer. Bishop's recent emergence at the center of intense critical and biographical study suggests the relevance of many of these factors to the critical and cultural evaluation of any of the poets studied here.

This group of poets and the particular problems they present to literary history do not exhaust the opportunities for revisionary readings of modernism. This collection marks a step toward a more comprehensively gendered reading of modern American poetry and the literary history it has made. It should open up the movement to a range of experiences, sensibilities, and crises—in short, to a wilderness of new possibilities for reading both familiar and entirely new texts.

Acknowledgments

In working on this book, we have divided the duties. Tom Travisano helped with the organization and prepared the index. Margaret Dickie did the rest. We have been immeasurably helped by the advice and skill of Jerry Singerman of the University of Pennsylvania Press. We wish to thank two graduate students at the University of Georgia, Leigh-Anne Urbanowicz Marcellin and Sylvia Henneberg, for their assistance on this project.

Margaret Dickie and Thomas Travisano

Part I
Gertrude Stein
(1874–1946)

Chapter 1
Recovering the Repression in Stein's Erotic Poetry

Margaret Dickie

Read today in the context of T. S. Eliot's *The Waste Land* or Wallace Stevens's "Le Monocle de Mon Oncle" or William Carlos Williams's "To Elsie," Gertrude Stein's "Ada," *Tender Buttons,* and "Lifting Belly" appear remarkably free from the anxiety, restraint, and misogyny that dominate the sexual attitudes of texts by the male modernists. So free has Stein's work appeared that Marianne DeKoven would release it from all interpretable meaning.[1] Stein's radically experimental form has encouraged Cary Nelson to argue that by 1914 she had "anticipated not only most of the linguistically experimental strain of modernism but much of postmodernism as well," and the Stein thus placed in the canon is a wonder woman, "quite impossible to naturalize and domesticate."[2] This view, held, curiously, by her admirers and detractors alike, first kept her at the margins of the modernist movement and now, with the rise of feminist and postmodernist criticism, moves her to an advanced position within modernism.[3]

In recovering Stein's work, critics have discovered a writer who seems more attuned to the interests of the last decades of the century than to those of the first decades when she wrote. In listing her achievements, DeKoven points out: "[h]er encoding of lesbian sexual feeling in her experimental work, her undoing of patriarchal portraiture in *The Autobiography of Alice B. Toklas,* the buried anger at female victimisation in *Three Lives,* and her overall, lifelong commitment to freeing language from the hierarchical grammars of patriarchy."[4] This list makes Stein a harbinger of the feminist movement of the 1970s and 1980s. That she may have been, but she was also a person of her own time, writing out of particular personal needs at a particular moment in history that neither DeKoven's feminist reading nor Nelson's postmodernist reading takes into account. Set back into her own time and examined in the context of her own development, Stein will appear less interested in freeing language from patriarchal strictures and more concerned with manipulating language to cover up meaning that might become too explicit for the taboo subject of lesbian eroticism, which was her central concern.[5]

Added to the literary history of her own time, Stein will contribute her own interest in the revolution of the word. Far from purifying the language of the tribe, as Ezra Pound claimed to be doing, Stein worked to find a way of locating within the language and structures available to her a means of expressing an erotic experience that she needed both to state and to conceal. Lesbian erotic poetry had to be written in code, as DeKoven suggests; but even within the code Stein struggled to come to terms with her sexual identity and experience as she worked to find a means of expressing it.

As one of the few modernists to write erotic poetry, Stein had little interest in the dissociation of sensibility that T. S. Eliot diagnosed as the problem of his generation. But, as a lesbian working in the first generation of writers who were self-consciously lesbian, she had certain reasonable reservations about revealing her feelings too directly and a deep anxiety about her sexual identity.[6] Even in her later theoretical writing, she was anxious to obscure the nature of her language experiments, presenting them as more abstract than they were. Thus, hiding behind the general experiments of the modernist movement, Stein uncharacteristically failed to take credit for her real and unique contribution to that period: an erotic poetry of considerable variety and power. In the work of Stein and eventually of Hart Crane, the modernist movement may lay claim to sensibilities in which imaginative and creative powers were perfectly aligned with emotional and erotic intensity.

Because writing for her was initially inspired by her love for May Bookstaver and later Alice B. Toklas, Stein's creative experiment may seem now to be an early example of *l'écriture féminine*, but it was first of all an effort to come to terms with a failed love affair and later to express, question, and celebrate a new love. Writing the female body, she was not engaged in celebrating a *jouissance* that was pre-verbal so much as she was enjoying a witty play with words. Behind it all, she was working through the conflicts of her own emotions and sexual identity. But, one might argue, so were Crane and even Eliot. Stein's experiments differ from theirs by refusing to cover themselves with aspirations to a cultural statement. She chose, rather, to hide within a radical experimentation in language in order to conceal the full nature of her subject. In her late lecture, "Poetry and Grammar," Stein claimed, "I too felt in me the need of making it be a thing that could be named without using its name."[7]

And so the radical experimentation of *Tender Buttons*, often theorized within the known parameters of modernist experimentation with non-referentiality and the absent subject, is not a style that abandons representation, but rather one that seeks to represent something that cannot be named.

In exercising this restraint, Stein was less anxious to pander to the taste of a large audience than to work her way through a complex of feelings that drove her simultaneously to celebrate her passion for Toklas publicly, to guard its secret in a kind of intimate and private code, to judge it, and to set it in the narrative of her life. Her description of her subject in *Tender Buttons* as "queer," "not ordinary," "dirty," are the clearest pointers to its nature for conventional readers who would make the same judgment.[8] They reveal Stein's ironic treatment of her audience, but they also indicate her own ambivalence about her experiment.

In recovering Stein's poetry then, we must recover the complete experiment, both her gaiety and her guilt. She had to find a way of saying both what had not been said before and what could not be said. She was as committed to the second experiment as to the first. She had few models, and she would have only the fit but few select readers who could decode her meanings. Yet, the double language of erotic lesbian poetry is not impossible to naturalize in a movement dominated by the modernist culture of despair, melancholy, impotence, or misogyny, even if it works to undermine the patriarchal structures of that culture.[9] It may be celebratory, subversive, and lively; but, like all erotic language, it has its own modes of despair and resistance not only to the dominant culture but to its own expression. Examining Stein's writing as it developed chronologically will make clear its connections to both the radical experimentation and the conservative impulse of the modernist movement.

In her first novel, *Q.E.D.* (1903), the character who represents Gertrude Stein's own position in the disastrous triangle of female lovers says: "As for passion . . . you see I don't understand much about that. It has no reality for me except as two varieties, affectionate comradeship on the one hand and physical passion in greater or less complexity on the other and against the cultivation of that latter I have an almost puritanic horror. . . ." (*FQED*, 59).

Some four years later, in "Ada," a portrait of Alice B. Toklas, Stein wrote, "Trembling was all living, living was all loving, some one was then the other one. Certainly this one was loving this Ada then. And certainly Ada all her living then was happier in living than any one else who ever could, who was, who is, who ever will be living" (*GP*, 16).[10] Telling about the composition of this portrait in *The Autobiography of Alice B. Toklas*, Stein records how excited she was in its creation, insisting that Toklas interrupt her supper preparations to read it immediately. She has Toklas comment: "I began it and I thought she was making fun of me and I protested, she says I protest now about my autobiography. Finally I read it all and was terribly pleased with it. And then we ate supper" (*SW*, 107). Then Stein admits, "This was the beginning of the long series of portraits" (*SW*, 107).

Thus, the composition of Toklas's portrait celebrates the decisive moment in Stein's development from a "puritanic horror" for passion to an acceptance of that passion and the "affectionate comradeship" of Toklas; in turn, that emotional development launched her on her life's project of writing portraits. This movement from the intimacy of her love for Toklas to the public world of portraiture is curious. After all, Stein had the example of her friends, the artists Picasso and Matisse, who could have launched her into portraits, and, as she theorized later, she was also inspired to experiment with a new way of looking by developments in the cinema. But her deliberate decision to emphasize Toklas as the person who launched her into portraits is an open declaration of the importance of passion, both as a source and as a subject, to her experiments in writing.

But Toklas was not the first person nor was she the first inspiration for Stein's creative imagination. Love and writing were intimately connected in Stein's life from the beginning, as her earliest writing suggests in its effort to find a form suitable to explore, explain, and express her unrequited passion for May Bookstaver. Bookstaver worked on Stein's imagination in a way quite different from Toklas's influence, leading Stein to explore character, hers and others', and, as Leon Katz has argued in discussing Stein's apprentice work (*FQED*, ii), to consider the "root problems—what is writing? what is knowing? what is describing?"

From early in her career and long before she met Toklas, Stein turned to writing in an effort to work out satisfactory answers to these questions. Trained as a scientist, Stein thought of "writing" as "describing" and "describing" as the way of "knowing" what she needed to understand about herself. In this project, she started—again as a scientist would—by classifying characters as types. Such a classification, an improbable method of describing her own identity, did allow her to express her differences from Bookstaver since, as she discovered, they were contrasting character types, "their pulses were differently timed," (*FQED*, 104). But classification posed problems in her narratives, as Katz has noted (*FQED*, xix). Character types and schematic patterns of relationships may be useful in distancing a writer from her personal troubles and disappointed love affairs; but they do not generate interesting narratives, and, as the contradictions of her method became more explicit, Stein began to abandon narrative for a different kind of composition and a completely different understanding of character. She began to see individual rhythms instead of types. Her new work began, as she explained some years later in "Portraits and Repetition," by "talking and listening . . . and in so doing I conceived what I at that time called the rhythm of anybody's personality" (*LinA*, 174).

The transition from character types to personal rhythms was gradual; but it began once Stein became interested in the rhythm of someone else's personality. "Ada," the first portrait of Toklas, belongs to a transitional moment when Stein was still writing narratives along familiar schematic patterns.[11] Although a number of critics have singled out "Ada" as marking a new beginning in Stein's writing (perhaps because it is about Toklas), the portrait is new only in its positive identification with Ada.[12] This "portrait" is of a character type that Stein does understand, a person whose pulse she wants to see as similarly timed.

But even here, or especially here, Stein retains something of the "puritanic horror" against physical passion that she expressed in *Q.E.D.* For example, however insistent "Ada" might be about the fact that "living was all loving," the portrait depicts "loving" as merely "listening to stories" and "telling stories" (*GP*, 16). At one level, of course, this emphasis signals the importance of Toklas's companionship to Stein's writing and the significance of the dialogue between them, as Harriet Chessman has argued. At another level, describing love as merely listening to stories reveals a kind of Victorian prudishness in writing about their relationship. This reticence is evident too in the identification of Ada's lover only as "some one" or "that one" or "this one." Chessman claims that identity is not important here because dialogue becomes a metaphor for "a certain form of relationship, where two 'ones' may be distinguished, yet where the boundaries may also become confused and even disappear." [13] And, it must be admitted, such confusion is evident even in Stein's account of this portrait in *The Autobiography*, which mixes up the pronouns so that the sentence "I protested, she says I protest now about my autobiography" is Toklas speaking both as "I" and as "she" (*SW*, 107).

But here there are two people, the lover and the beloved, and it might also be argued that identity is too important to be mentioned in "Ada." Stein wanted to identify neither herself nor Toklas in this portrait, even when she did want to announce the exaggerated claims of their happiness. The anonymity here is part of a pattern of secrecy that will screen Stein's imaginative treatment of their relationship throughout her life.[14] Although she embeds the subject in *Tender Buttons*, treats it more directly in "Lifting Belly," and certainly acknowledges it as a fact in *The Autobiography of Alice B. Toklas*, the need to write about her love for Toklas without stating it directly is the central impulse of her work in all its stages. This double-talk in her language reflects deeply divided feelings.[15] For all her interest in self-promotion, Stein kept something of herself hidden. She was worldly, that is, she lived in the public world, inhabiting the house of culture as a whole, and she was also extremely secretive.[16]

Hiding her desire behind words that are affectionate and generalized in "Ada," Stein moved on to try a much bolder experiment in *Tender Buttons.* Shifting her focus from Toklas to herself, she explored the pleasure, especially the erotic pleasure, of her relationship with her new companion. Stein began by asking how much she could write what she meant, how much she had to hide it. Again, it was a portrait—"Portrait of Constance Fletcher" (1911–12)—that signaled this new effort.[17] From gerunds to direct statements, the movement in the second half of "Portrait of Constance Fletcher" is to an exploration of meaning and especially of what is not meant. After abruptly changing style, Stein writes, "This has not any meaning" (*GP,* 159). But she goes on to explain the new way of writing: "This is all to prepare the way that is not the way to like anything that in speaking is telling what has come that like a swelling is inside when there is yellowing" (*GP,* 160). Later, she admits, "That is not a disclosure. That is not the way for all of them who are looking to refuse to see" (*GP,* 161). It is, rather, a way of seeing something quite different and differently. In *The Autobiography,* she describes the change: "hitherto she had been interested only in the insides of people, their character and what went on inside them, it was during that summer that she first felt a desire to express the rhythm of the visible world" (*SW,* 111–12). And again: "They were the beginning, as Gertrude Stein would say, of mixing the outside with the inside. Hitherto she had been concerned with seriousness and the inside of things, in these studies she began to describe the inside as seen from the outside" (*SW,* 147).

In all these explanations both in the text and years later in her autobiographical and theoretical works, Stein displays a concern about meaning or disclosure that is new to her. Her interest in the outside, even the rhythm of the visible world, was also an interest in how much of the inside Stein could make clear to the outside, how much she could come out where the rhythm of the visible world might impede the rhythm of her personality. In "Ada," she had identified the inside with emotions; in *Tender Buttons,* the inside is more closely connected with her erotic experience. Writing about emotions, she could be quite direct because she wrote in very general terms. But when she began to describe the erotic impulse behind those feelings, she had to change her style.

Her self-consciousness about this change of style is evident in "Rooms," the final section of *Tender Buttons* written in 1911 during the same period as "Portrait of Constance Fletcher." Here, Stein concentrates on her organization, as she begins to test the limits of her revelation. It opens, "Act so that there is no use in a centre" (*SW*, 498), and this idea runs through "Rooms" as Stein experiments with writing and simultaneously hiding what she means. The two efforts go on at once. On one level, Stein reworks the meaning of the center from its traditional association with stability to a new association with activity and free play.[18] On another level, she identifies the center of her passion for Toklas in the bedroom and writes a long warning to herself against exposing that fact. In this text, one meaning can cancel out or contradict another, even as it is reversing itself.

Stein writes, "Any change was in the ends of the centre" (*SW*, 498). She plays on that idea: "If the centre has the place then there is distribution. That is natural. There is a contradiction and naturally returning there comes to be both sides and the centre" (*SW*, 499). And suddenly the center becomes not the still point, but the place of division between two contradictory sides. It is a place of separating and ordering.

But, in a world where there is no contradiction, there is no need for such a center, and Stein suggests another way of positioning, as she creates this catalog: "A damp cloth, an oyster, a single mirror, a mannikin, a student, a silent star, a single spark, a little moment and the bed is made" (*SW*, 501–2). Here where the bed is made, as in the bedroom, this associative and contiguous grouping includes rather than separates things, as Stein explains: "This shows the disorder, it does, it shows more likeness than anything else, it shows the single mind that directs an apple" (*SW*, 502). Connecting it to the still lives of Cézanne and Picasso, Jayne L. Walker claims it is a "deliberate artistic model, not a naïve reproduction, of the 'real.' "[19] More than that, it is the creation of "the single mind," the mind that is not divided, the mind that reveals itself in "likeness," the mind that, in its "little movement," is willing to make its bed and lie in it, beginning to identify its lesbian desire.

Stein approaches that possibility by suggesting immediately that "it is not very likely that there is a centre, a hill is a hill and no hill is contained in a pink tender descender" (*SW*, 502). As if she has revealed too much here, she moves to a series of explanations that does not do much to clarify or describe its subjects, but starts suggestively: "A can is," "A measure is," "A package and a filter," and finally "A cape is." Each paragraph meditates on containment or covering and exposure, as if Stein had moved back in order to consider words themselves as containers, covering up as well as representing things. These paragraphs lead into a series of questions, including the question of the center: "Why is there a circular diminisher" (*SW*, 503).

Stein revises the meaning of "the centre," which she now claims is differently configured for "singularity":

the centre having spelling and no solitude and no quaintness and yet solid quite so solid and the single surface centred and the question in the placard and the singularity, is there a singularity, and the singularity, why is there a question and the singularity why is the surface outrageous, why is it beautiful why is it not when there is no doubt, why is anything vacant, why is not disturbing a centre no virtue. (*SW*, 505–6)

By stages, disturbing the center, Stein has moved the "centre" from a point of division to a place of "singularity." And, more explicitly, she makes singulars into doubles, reordering language to express a center that does not divide or distract but combines similar words as in "Sugar any sugar, anger every anger, lover sermon lover, centre no distractor, all order is in a measure" (*SW*, 506).

Having succeeded in translating divisive "centres" into unified "singularity," Stein advises: "Dance a clean dream and an extravagant turn up, secure the steady rights and translate more than translate the authority, show the choice and make no more mistakes than yesterday" (*SW*, 508). Showing her own choice, as she translates authority by assuming it, she sets the center in motion:

A willow and no window, a wide place stranger, a wideness makes an active center [*sic*].
The sight of no pussy cat is so different that a tobacco zone is white and cream. (*SW*, 508)

In this term of endearment and erotic pleasure, Stein uncovers her own desire to "translate the authority." "Rooms" is, in the end, one room— the bedroom, the center of a new found passion—and the section demands to be read again as an extended covering up of its subject or acting, that is, pretending, so that there is no use in such a center.

Read again, "Rooms" appears obsessed with the admission, early stated, that "There is a use, they are double" (*SW*, 498). And, then, the identities of Stein and Toklas in their bedroom come out from hiding: Stein, "the author of all that is in there behind the door and that is entering in the morning" (*SW*, 499), and Toklas, "this makes no diversion that is to say what can please exaltation, that which is cooking" (*SW*, 499). Again, as if to be more clear, Stein writes, "The sister was not a mister" (*SW*, 499).

Their bedroom activities include: "this which is no rarer than frequently is not so astonishing when hair brushing is added" (*SW*, 500– 501), "the bed is made" (*SW*, 502), "there is some use in not mentioning changing" (*SW*, 502), "lying so makes the springs restless" (*SW*,

503), "almost very likely there is no seduction" (*SW,* 503), "a window has another spelling, it has 'f' all together" (*SW,* 507), and "a pecking which is petting and no worse than in the same morning is not the only way to be continuous often" (*SW,* 509).

"Rooms" has often been overlooked in readings of *Tender Buttons* because the other two sections of the prose-poem appear to be more interestingly experimental. But "Rooms" has its own power as an early and quite successful effort to find a language that could both express and conceal lesbian eroticism. The text is multiply reversible; on one side, it appears to be about centering or rather decentering, translating the language of authority into a language of singularity. On the other side, it is a celebration of the center in the bedroom that Stein shared with Toklas. But these two sides are themselves always changing under our eyes so that the simple phrase, "act so that," can mean "go on so that" and "pretend so that" as well as "do not go on so that" and "do not pretend so that." The "centre," itself a point, a place, a moment, a table, a new place, is also a new moment.

Tender Buttons is a celebratory text that enjoys its private as well as its public celebrations. And it is an extremely witty example of Stein's continued interest in the inside even as she experimented with ways to turn the inside out, the outside in.[20] In this wordplay and quite apart from the idea of representation that any discussion of inside and outside entails, Stein is also entertaining the whole question of coming out, of what she could come out from or to, of where the outside begins and the inside ends. But within all this play, Stein expresses too her fear of a direct expression of eroticism. The wordplay itself allows her to take back as much as she reveals here of what goes on in the bedroom.

"Objects" and "Food," written simultaneously in 1913, appear to be more direct in their use of words, although they are, at the same time, more experimental. Opening with longer segments that look like the transitional style of "Rooms," these sections work toward a more radical deconstruction of language in brief segments composed of single lines. Still, the idea of the inside and outside—central to "Rooms," and important too in any referential use of words as well as in any expression of lesbian eroticism—persists. "Food" opens with a list of its separate segments and then moves to "Roastbeef," which appears to be set in the same bedroom as "Rooms," as Stein celebrates an "inside" of secret passion and an "outside" life of "meaning" or the writing that she did in the morning: "In the inside there is sleeping, in the outside there is reddening, in the morning there is meaning, in the evening there is feeling. . . . In feeling anything is resting, in feeling anything is mounting, in feeling there is resignation, in feeling there is recognition, in feeling there is recurrence and entirely mistaken there is pinching" (*SW,* 477).

Given the insistence here on "feeling," it is remarkable how much, even years later, Stein wanted to occlude the connection between her new life with Toklas and her writing.

In "Portraits and Repetition," writing about this period, Stein claims: "All this time I was of course not interested in emotion or that anything happened. I was less interested then in these things than I ever had been. I lived my life with emotion and with things happening but I was creating in my writing by simply looking" (*LinA*, 191). Although the book does include some commentary on looking, especially on how some people cannot see even when they do look, *Tender Buttons* appears to be much more interested in emotions, especially those that had entered her life with Toklas, than Stein is wiling to admit. If "Food" and even "Objects" describe, as Walker suggests, "a female world (circa 1912) of domestic objects and rituals—a world of dresses and hats, tables and curtains, mealtimes and bedtimes, cleanliness and dirt,"[21] it is a world especially and specifically devoted to Toklas. Food was her department, and her physical presence is celebrated everywhere in this section. "Certainly the length is thinner," Stein writes, acknowledging Toklas's body by contrast to her own, "and the rest, the round rest has a longer summer" (*SW*, 477).

It "is so easy to exchange meaning," Stein claims, as she introduces her term for orgasm, "a cow is absurd" (*SW*, 477–78). The passage rises to lyrical intensity where internal rhymes and repetition celebrate the passion of the two lovers: "Lovely snipe and tender turn, excellent vapor and slender butter, all the splinter and the trunk, all the poisonous darkening drunk, all the joy in weak success, all the joyful tenderness, all the section and the tea, all the stouter symmetry" (*SW*, 479). Here, references to size ("slender" and "stouter") and to food ("butter" and "tea"), mixed with feelings of both delirium and order, danger and pleasure, turn this passage into an encoded synesthesia of desire where the lilting iambic meter of traditional love poetry conserves Stein's own subversive tune.[22]

Against such passages as these runs the refrain, "It is not dirty," as if Stein had to convince herself of the acceptability of a passion she knew how to express in traditional meter. It made her uneasy, and she felt she had to explain it, seeing her role as "Lecture, lecture and repeat instruction" (*SW*, 483), even when she had to concede, "What language can instruct any fellow" (*SW*, 483). "What is the custom, the custom is in the centre," she claims, going back to her concern in "Rooms" (*SW*, 483). By contrast to "the custom," hers is "a bent way that is a way to declare that the best is all together" (*SW*, 484). Nonetheless, and again revealing her self-censorship, she admits, "it shows a necessity for retraction" (*SW*, 484), although she goes on to celebrate "wet crossing and a likeness," "a cow, only any wet place" (*SW*, 486), and urges "to pay and pet pet very much" or "cuddling comes in continuing a change" (*SW*, 486). Finally, "a cow is accepted"[23] (*SW*, 486).

But, however much "the difference is spreading," Stein's persistent use of the word "dirt" in "Objects" suggests that she had ambivalent feelings about her "not ordinary" life. In discussing *Tender Buttons* in an interview in 1946, Stein claims: "Dirty has an association and is a word that I would not use now."[24] But it is a word she uses throughout "Objects": "Dirty is yellow. A sign of more in not mentioned" (*SW*, 463); "Dirt and not copper makes a color darker" (*SW*, 464); "if they dusty will dirt a surface" (*SW*, 465); "If there is no dirt in a pin" (*SW*, 467–68); "If the chance to dirty diminishing is necessary . . . why is there no special protection" (*SW*, 468); "a disgrace, an ink spot, a rosy charm" (*SW*, 471), for example. And it seems to bring up the very associations she wants to cancel in her 1946 interview. Also, the persistence of "dirty" and "dirt" admits into the erotic experience of this text a severe, and unbalancing, judgment. If *Tender Buttons* is a celebration of lesbian desire, it is a celebration that is always being undercut.

As an erotic prose-poem, *Tender Buttons* is much more openly expressive than "Ada," however much it can conceal in its openness. Even its title appears to advertise the female body and to underscore the tenderness in her passion for Toklas. Freeing herself from narrative, Stein was able to celebrate here an erotic life that had, as yet, no plot, and, simultaneously, she was able to release language from its rigid referential bonds and display its polysemy.

Stein's many efforts to explain *Tender Buttons* in her later works emphasize its experiments in abstraction, in looking, and in ridding herself of nouns, finding words for a thing that was not the name of the thing. In "Poetry and Grammar," she writes: "And so I went on with this exceeding struggle of knowing really knowing what a thing was really knowing it knowing anything I was seeing anything I was feeling so that its name could be something, by its name coming to be a thing in itself as it was but would not be anything just and only as a name" (*LinA*, 242). She expresses the same idea differently in "Portraits and Repetition": "I became more and more excited about how words which were the words that made whatever I looked at look like itself were not the words that had in them any quality of description" (*LinA*, 191). Again in "Poetry and Grammar," citing the example of Shakespeare, who in the forest of Arden created a forest without mentioning the things that make a forest, she notes in a passage quoted earlier in this essay: "Now that was a thing that I too felt in me the need of making it be a thing that could be named without using its name. After all one had known its name anything's name for so long, and so the name was not new but the thing being alive was always news" (*LinA*, 236–37). Judy Grahn traces this effort to Stein's identity as a lesbian writer:

Writing out from the base of a woman to woman relationship considered taboo in the world, and translating this everyday personal experience into a literature that no longer overtly contains the taboo experience yet covertly contains it in great detail was a lifelong preoccupation of Gertrude Stein . . . she began perceiving and treating words as individual bricks that have a free-floating meaning of their own, unattached to the automatic cliched meanings they have in sentence form.[25]

As Stein became more distant from the text, for example in the 1946 interview, she became more general in her explanations, explaining, "PEELED PENCIL, CHOKE" as "That is where I was beginning and went on a good deal after that period to make sound pictures but I gave that up as uninteresting." [26] But "Rub her coke" picks up a number of other references to rubbing as sexual play or masturbation in *Tender Buttons* that prevents that phrase from being read merely as a "sound picture." So even as late as 1946 Stein still engaged in concealing the erotic nature of her language. Grahn is perhaps too optimistic in her assessment of Stein when she writes:

She removed all the expectation: this is good, this is bad, this is indifferent. In her sentences each word is indifferent, is good and is bad. Each word is evil, is a landlord, a heroine, is saving. And so she was able to use the substance of her inner life, her home life, her personal life and those of *all* her friends, not merely the socially acceptable ones. And because she had freed the language of all possible judgment there is no way to read her work and to judge her life in any terms except her own.[27]

Stein probably hoped that that would be true; but, as her very late theoretical comments suggest, she was never sure she had succeeded. Nor did she ever work free from her own expectation that some things were good, some bad. Over and over, in *Tender Buttons*, she moved from explicitness to unintelligibility and even authorial self-correction as she mused on how much she could say, how much she must obscure what she said. She entertained these possibilities not as an abstract idea; she was writing, after all, at a time when censorship was enforced and what was regarded as obscenity could be brought to trial. By generating a certain amount of nonsense in her sense, Stein opened herself up to caricature and critical attacks; but, like Virginia Woolf who was to pass off her study of bisexuality, *Orlando*, as a joke, Stein was also able to protect herself in this way from the public censure that, for example, Radclyffe Hall would suffer upon the publication of *The Well of Loneliness* a decade later.[28]

As a prose-poem, *Tender Buttons* owes something to the classifications of Stein's apprentice prose as it looks toward the expression of erotic experience that was to be more fully explored in her poetry. In making this transition, she works from a "no since" or nonsense or prohibition to discover what is "real" for her or, as she puts it, "Pain soup, suppose it is question, suppose it is better, real is, real is only, only excreate, only excreate a no since" (*SW*, 496).

This idea of relettering or excreating by providing a list of new definitions drives her next stage of writing in "Lifting Belly," which develops through a lengthy series of definitions, this time of that one phrase: lifting belly. Unlike the varied elements in "Objects" or "Food" that are defined in *Tender Buttons*, the single phrase calls up definitions that are so diverse and extensive that they defy explicit reference, play with all efforts to contain "lifting belly" in any single meaning and simultaneously create and "excreate" names for erotic experience in Stein's continuing effort to name it and to leave it unnamed.

Nonetheless, unlike the opacity of *Tender Buttons*, "Lifting Belly" is persistently referential, not just defining the activity of lifting belly, but commenting also on a whole array of daily events. In his notes to the poem, Virgil Thomson claims that the poem "is not a hermetic composition but a naturalistic recounting of the daily life" (*BTV*, 63). Written in Mallorca, Paris, Perpignan, and Nîmes during the years 1915, 1916, and 1917, according to Thomson, the poem records daily events and specific references to all these places: to Mallorca where Stein and Toklas went to sit out the war, to the Battle of Verdun, the purchase of the Ford car, the purchase of an antique Spanish desk imported to Paris with sausages in it, the photograph taken of Stein with her car, among other things. Thomson calls the poem "a diary" and "a hymn to the domestic affections" (*BTV*, 64).

Diaries and hymns have two quite independent purposes—the one to record events of the day and the other to celebrate special events—and Thomson is accurate in pointing out this double purpose. This odd combination in "Lifting Belly" reveals another effort on Stein's part to mix modes so that she will not be caught in the explicitness she obviously relishes.[29] The "hymn to the domestic affections" mixes the erotic and the everyday, sexual pleasures and the humdrum. Like the references to "dirt" in *Tender Buttons*, the daily events of "Lifting Belly" deflate, if they do not judge outright, the passion of the poem. For example, right after the declaration "Pussy how pretty you are," Stein writes: "That goes very quickly unless you have been there too long. / I told him I would send him Mildred's book. He seemed very pleased at the prospect" (*YGS*, 17). And then the refrain returns:

> Lifting belly is so strong.
> Lifting belly together.
> Lifting belly oh yes.
> Lifting belly.
> Oh yes.
>   (*YGS*, 17)

Stein states explicitly:

> Kiss my lips. She did.
> Kiss my lips again she did.
> Kiss my lips over and over and over again she did.
>   (*YGS*, 19)

Then she follows it with statements that blur the situation and relocate it in the idle chitchat of daily life:

> I have feathers.
> Gentle fishes.
> Do you think about apricots. We find them very beautiful. It is not
>   alone their
> color it is their seeds that charm us. We find it a change.
>   (*YGS*, 20)

Noting this rendering of an intimate situation that veers into a language of indirection, Chessman argues, "In this way, Stein attempts both to call into her writing the female body and love between women more directly than in *Tender Buttons*, and to avoid reproducing the structures of representation in which the female has been constrained." [30] But the conventional structures of representing women are reproduced here freely, in both the idealizing and the controlling of the beloved, in both the flattery and the commands. If Stein experiments at all in "Lifting Belly," it is not in the way she represents women but in the way she refuses to privilege sex over other activities. Lifting belly is there; so is the need to have a Ford.

Setting moments of intimacy in the routine activities of a life in this poem, Stein defies the conventional decorum of erotic poetry. [31] Absent from Stein's poem is the idealizing, even fetishizing, of sexual intercourse that marks Ernest Hemingway's style, for example. The earth does not stop turning for Stein's lovers. Sex is part of their daily life; like the "apricots," it is "beautiful," it has "charm," and it is a "change"; but, perhaps, this juxtaposition suggests, it is no more beautiful, no more charming, nor more different than apricots.

The persistence of a pattern of love talk followed by either specific and incongruous references to daily life or nonsense suggests Stein's uncertainty about the exaggerated and direct celebration of sex she was describing as an everyday reality. Even in this hymn where "lifting belly" starts line after line in an obsessive repetition and where the brevity of the lines would appear to set off the phrase as if it had special significance, the adjectives used to describe it flatten it out. Called "kind," "dear," "good," and even "my joy," "rich," and "perfect," "lifting belly" is given such a general description that it might refer to any experience. Normalizing "lifting belly" in this way, Stein lifts the taboo on the subject by repeated mention.

If the general adjectives she uses do not point in any particular direction, neither do the earnest declarations of passion lead to an erotic narrative.[32] The ongoing activity of lifting belly—kissing, cuddling, "Caesars" or orgasms, sexual contact, declarations of love—is the same at the beginning as at the end of "Lifting Belly." The poem has no intensity in its language, few verbal climaxes, and little quickening of details. And because the clutter of other concerns in this poem has the same value as sex, Stein appears to be making the case for the naturalness of lesbian eroticism, for its dailiness, its ongoing nature, its steadfastness. The only contrast to "lifting belly" is the war, as Stein writes:

> Lifting belly is so strong.
> I said that to mean that I was very glad.
> Why are you very glad.
> Because that pleased me.
> Baby love.
> A great many people are in the war.
> I will go there and back again.
> What did you say about Lifting belly.
> I said lifting belly is so strong.
>> (*YGS*, 8)

Again, Stein writes,

> Lifting belly is anxious.
> Not about Verdun.
> Oh dear no.
>> (*YGS*, 10)[33]

Placed in opposition to the war: "Lifting belly is peaceable" (*YGS*, 14), although it is consonant with patriotism as Stein writes:

> We used to play star spangled banner.
> Lifting belly is so near.
> Lifting belly is so dear.
> (*YGS*, 14)

And again,

> Lifting belly is so kind.
> She was like that.
> Star spangled banner, story of Savannah.
> (*YGS*, 29)

It fits into military life: "Lifting belly is notorious. / A great many people wish to salute. The general does. So does the leader of the battalion. In spanish. I understand that" (*YGS*, 19). And:

> What shall you say about that. Lifting belly is so kind.
> What is a veteran.
> A veteran is one who has fought.
> Who is the best.
> The king and queen and the mistress.
> Nobody has a mistress.
> Lifting belly is so kind.
> (*YGS*, 21)

Here it would seem that the war is linked to the heterosexual love triangle of "the king and queen and the mistress" and distinct from the passion celebrated in "lifting belly" as "kind." But the distinction does not hold, and, as the poem develops, the military and Stein's passion are brought together most notably in her use of "Caesar" as a code for orgasm:

> Big Caesars.
> Two Caesars.
> Little seize her.
> Too.
> Did I do my duty.

Did I wet my knife.
No I don't mean whet.
    (*YGS*, 22–23)[34]

The proximity of passion and war is underscored even in this amicable relationship as one letter of the alphabet is all that distinguishes the sex act from murder, love from duty. And soon, sex and war are not distinct at all. Making "Caesar" "plural" (*YGS*, 26), Stein fuses sex, patriotism, war, in "lifting belly say can you see the Caesars. I can see what I kiss" (*YGS*, 30).

The poem concludes in the declaration of "Lifting belly enormously and with song" (*YGS*, 54) and then the questions:

Can you sing about a cow.
Yes.
And about signs.
Yes.
And also about Aunt Pauline.
Yes.
Can you sing at your work.
Yes.
In the meantime listen to Miss Cheatham.
In the midst of writing.
In the midst of writing there is merriment.

Uniting "signs" of her passion ("cow") and of her war work ("Aunt Pauline"), Stein assures her interlocutor that she can include the full range of her experience in her song and that she can enjoy in all of it "merriment."

In the end, then, affirming her ability to sing about both a "cow" and "Aunt Pauline," Stein erases the division that she might have appeared to have drawn between her private passion and the public war. It is not that she cannot distinguish between the two, not even that they are similar; it is rather that Stein refuses divisions of all kinds in "Lifting Belly." She can play with divisions, even sexual ones, such as,

Darling wifie is so good.
Little husband would.
Be as good.
If he could.
        (*YGS*, 49)

She can divide war from passion, the everyday from the erotic, the public world from the intimacy of her relationship with Toklas; but, in the course of "Lifting Belly," she undermines all these divisions. The poem ultimately is a hymn to sameness and singularity, to lesbian eroticism that arises from, as it generates, "merriment."

Celebration is the dominant note in her early work inspired by Toklas from "Ada" through *Tender Buttons* to "Lifting Belly," but celebration that is often undercut, questioned, and censored. Stein's desire to simultaneously express and hide her passion for Toklas drives the constant experimenting with form that started with narrative and moved to poetry. First writing a prose-poem, she then moved on in "Lifting Belly" to poetry composed of short lines, which she explains,

Think of how you talk to anything whose name is new to you a lover a baby or a dog or a new land or any part of it. Do you not inevitably repeat what you call out and is that calling out not of necessity in short lines. Think about it and you will see what I mean by what you feel.

So as I say poetry is essentially the discovery, the love, the passion for the name of anything. (*LinA*, 234–35)

Describing a much later period in her writing that seems equally pertinent to her erotic poetry, Stein claims, "In writing this poem I found I could be very gay I could be very lively in poetry" (*LinA*, 243). She concludes, "I decided that if one definitely completely replaced the noun by the thing in itself, it was eventually to be poetry and not prose which would have to deal with everything that was not movement in space" (*LinA*, 245).

Although Stein carried her experimental writing beyond poetry into plays, mysteries, novels, her first experiments with finding a language to express her erotic experience led her to poetry where she could be not only "gay," but where she could simultaneously discover and hide the name of "anything." From the anonymity of "Ada" to the double language of *Tender Buttons* to the naturalizing context of "Lifting Belly," Stein worked deliberately both to express her erotic life and to censor it.

Feminist and postmodernist readers at the end of the century in which she began to write—perhaps Stein's first receptive readers—have been particularly alert to her experiments with *l'écriture féminine*, with writing the body, with undoing hierarchical relationships and language—in short, with the expression of her erotic life. They have been less aware of Stein's self-censorship, the sexual anxiety that drove her tireless experimental writing, the self-judgment that undercut even her most exaggerated celebrations of her sexual power.

Placed in literary history as the first of the modernists, Stein will appear a more complex, if no less revolutionary, figure. She was one of the few modernist poets of love and erotic experience. Along with Hart Crane, she demonstrates how important the modernist experiments in language were to the free expression of lesbian and gay desire even as these same experiments seemed designed to fragment the speaker and restrict the expression of heterosexual desire. But, even within that freedom, Stein was moved to question and undercut her own erotic expression. Like Crane and also like many lesbians of her time, she was given to self-erasure as often as to an open expression of *jouissance*.[35] In this, she seems more easily naturalized as a modernist than a postmodernist. Whatever her work may have anticipated for the postmodernists, Stein shares with her contemporaries both an interest in radical experimentation with language and a conservative reservation about a too open or personal expression of her experience.

Notes

1. Marianne DeKoven, *A Different Language: Gertrude Stein's Experimental Writing* (Madison: University of Wisconsin Press, 1983), 76.

2. Cary Nelson, *Repression and Recovery: Modern American Poetry and the Politics of Cultural Memory, 1910–1945* (Madison: University of Wisconsin Press, 1989), 179.

3. Marianne DeKoven has discussed this insider-outsider nature of Stein's reputation in "Gertrude Stein and the Modernist Canon," in *Gertrude Stein and the Making of Literature*, ed. Shirley Neuman and Ira B. Nadel (Boston: Northeastern University Press, 1988), 8–20.

4. Ibid., 9.

5. Discussing *The Autobiography of Alice B. Toklas* and *Everybody's Autobiography*, Catharine R. Stimpson takes a different interest in this subject, examining what she calls "a sub-genre we insufficiently understand: the lesbian lie" ("Gertrude Stein and the Lesbian Lie," in *American Women's Autobiography: Fea(s)ts of Memory*, ed. Margo Culley [Madison: University of Wisconsin Press, 1992], 152–53). Stimpson is anxious to explore what the lesbian lie does to the lesbian sense of herself and her autobiographical writing. Although Marianne DeKoven opens an essay with the statement, "Poetry, for Gertrude Stein, is painfully erotic," she develops that insight in a brief comparison of Stein to Ezra Pound ("Breaking the Rigid Form of the Noun: Stein, Pound, Whitman, and Modernist Poetry," in *Critical Essays on American Modernism*, ed. Michael J. Hoffman and Patrick D. Murphy [New York: G. K. Hall, 1992], 225).

6. Edmund Wilson was the first to note that Stein wrote of relationships between women that the standards of her era would not have allowed her to describe more explicitly (*The Shores of Light* [New York: Farrar, Straus and Young, 1952], 581). More recently, William Gass has explored what he identifies as the covert texts of Eve and Pandora that underpin *Tender Buttons*, arguing that evasiveness became a habit, a style, a method for Stein even when she was dealing with subjects where it was not necessary. See his discussion in *The World Within the Word* (New York: Knopf, 1978), 63–123.

7. "Poetry and Grammar," in *Lectures in America*, introduction by Wendy Steiner (Boston: Beacon Press, 1985), 236. Stein's writings will be quoted from this collection and *Bee Time Vine and Other Pieces: 1913–1927*, with preface and

notes by Virgil Thomson (New Haven, Conn.: Yale University Press, 1953), *Fernhurst, Q.E.D., and Other Early Writings,* edited with introduction by Leon Katz; appendix by Donald Gallup (New York: Liveright, 1971), *Geography and Plays,* introduction by Cyrena N. Pondrom (Madison: University of Wisconsin Press, 1993), *Selected Writings of Gertrude Stein,* ed. Carl Van Vechten (New York: Vintage Books, 1962), *The Yale Gertrude Stein,* selections with an introduction by Richard Kostelanetz (New Haven: Yale University Press, 1980). References will be to *LinA, BTV, FQED, GP, SW, YGS* in the text.

8. In an extremely fruitful reading of *Tender Buttons* that explains how Stein used and displaced the authoritative discourse of domestic guides to living (cookbooks, housekeeping guides, books of etiquette, guides to entertainment, maxims of interior design, fashion advice) in order to explain and justify her own idiosyncratic domestic arrangement with Toklas, Margueritte S. Murphy argues that Stein encoded lesbian intimacies and reconsidered what is "dirt" and what is "tender." For example, she parallels Stein's discussion of "dirt" near the beginning of the "Roastbeef" section of "Food" with a passage from *The New England Cook Book* on dirty tablecloths (" 'Familiar Strangers': The Household Words of Gertrude Stein's *Tender Buttons,*" *Contemporary Literature* 32 [1991]: 398).

9. In a discussion of *The Autobiography of Alice B. Toklas,* Leigh Gilmore argues that Stein displaces the function of the autobiographical "I" onto the lesbian couple, revealing her ambivalence about the self as a unified figure, and, I might add, in this respect at last revealing also her agreement with male modernists such as T. S. Eliot ("A Signature of Lesbian Autobiography: 'Gertrice/Altrude,' " in *Autobiography and Questions of Gender,* ed. Shirley Neuman [London: Frank Cass and Co., 1991], 56–75).

10. Ulla Dydo claims that Toklas and Stein joined hands by sharing the labor of copying the text from Stein's pocket notebook; but she claims that Stein wrote it (*A Stein Reader,* ed. Ulla Dydo [Chicago: Northwestern University Press, 1993], 100).

11. Sandra Gilbert and Susan Gubar have pointed out this schematic pattern fits Stein's own life in her effort to extricate herself from her brother Leo Stein (*No Man's Land: The Place of the Woman Writer in the Twentieth Century* [New Haven, Conn.: Yale University Press, II: 1989], 241).

12. For example, Jayne L. Walker argues that it starts "a new mode of rendering character, independent of the descriptive apparatus that absorbed individuals into 'kinds' in the novel" (*The Making of a Modernist: Gertrude Stein from Three Lives to Tender Buttons* [Amherst: University of Massachusetts Press, 1984], 75), and Harriet Chessman identifies its new mode as a movement from "nondialogic to dialogue, from narrative to circling nonnarrative" (*The Public is Invited to Dance: Representation, the Body, and Dialogue in Gertrude Stein* [Stanford, Calif.: Stanford University Press, 1989], 68).

13. Chessman, *The Public Is Invited,* 65.

14. Pertinent here is Diana Collecott's essay "What Is Not Said: A Study in Textual Subversion," in *Sexual Sameness: Textual Differences in Lesbian and Gay Writing,* ed. Joseph Bristow (London: Routledge, 1992). She notes: "The fear of being 'wiped out' is taken into much lesbian writing and may account for many of its self-contradictions and obliquities. But when this fear is counterbalanced by lesbian desire, in works like *Zami* or the poetry of Gertrude Stein, it accounts for the erotics of these texts: their word-play, subversion of grammatical rules, resistance to literal reading or single-minded interpretation" (96).

15. In *The Apparitional Lesbian: Female Homosexuality and Modern Culture* (New

York: Columbia University Press, 1993), Terry Castle claims that, given the way the lesbian is habitually expelled from the real world, "it is perhaps not surprising how many lesbians in real life have engaged in a sort of self-ghosting, hiding or camouflaging their sexual desires or withdrawing voluntarily from society in order to escape such hostility" (7). Castle is interested in the lives of lesbians; but we might apply her insights to Stein's writing in which, for all her self-vaunting, she engages in a self-ghosting as well.

16. Terry Castle uses the term *worldly*, which she extracts from Edward Said, to describe the lesbians she studies, and it seems certainly appropriate for Stein who always occupied center stage (*The Apparitional Lesbian*, 15–16).

17. See DeKoven's discussion of this change (*A Different Language*, 63–84).

18. The opening statement in "Rooms" would appear to identify Stein as a precursor to Derrida and the deconstructionists, and, in her chapter on experimental writing, DeKoven makes such a case for Stein as anticipating not only Derrida but Lacan and Kristeva (ibid., 3–26). But, as this discussion suggests, Stein is interested in redefining rather than negating the center. While she argues against certain kinds of conventional authority, she aims to assert her own authority.

19. Walker, *Making of a Modernist*, 135.

20. My reading of "Rooms" as a decentering of traditional authority and then a recentering of Toklas makes the subject, both Toklas and subjectivity itself, a central concern for Stein, and it agrees only partially with Walker's conclusion that "unseating both the subject and Western logic as privileged centers and guarantors of truth, this text deliberately flaunts the unlimited freeplay of substitution that is possible within the structure of language" (ibid., 141). Substitution was clearly important to Stein as she toyed with what she wanted to conceal, what to reveal about her relationship with Toklas. But she did not abandon entirely the idea of a center or of truth; rather it would be her own definition of an "active center" and her "Truth."

DeKoven's Kristevan reading cannot account for the wit of *Tender Buttons*, the wordplay that is not the same as language-as-play but much more like the deliberate attempt to release multiple meanings in words that is part of the seriousness of symbolic language. Catharine Stimpson has made the case against a Kristevan reading of Stein in "The Sonograms of Gertrude Stein," repr. in *The Female Body in Western Culture: Contemporary Perspectives*, ed. Susan Rubin Suleiman (Cambridge, Mass.: Harvard University Press, 1985), 30–43.

Chessman seems to capture the doubled efforts of *Tender Buttons* by admitting that it "entices us with all these potentially erotic objects and foods" but "it turns us around so that we become radically unsure of these metaphors" (*The Public is Invited*, 97). However, her claims about a female presence in *Tender Buttons* are more abstract than mine; she says, "Indirectly, in this new land we glimpse, not a specific woman or any clear representation, but a circuitously imaged idyll involving a 'wedding' and a 'near[ness]' to 'fairy sea'" (99).

By contrast to these efforts to resist interpretation, Lisa Ruddick's idea that in "Objects" and "Food" Stein "was engaging in a revisionary conversation with the dominant intellectual traditions of Western culture," specifically the sacrificial origins of partriarchal culture, is perhaps too tied to identifiable patterns of thought in interpreting these sections (*Reading Gertrude Stein: Body, Text, Gnosis* [Ithaca, N.Y., and London: Cornell University Press, 1990], 192). It is interesting that "Rooms" does not have the same status in her discussion because "Rooms" contains few references to sacrifice.

21. Walker, *Making of a Modernist*, 127.

22. Elizabeth Fifer notes that "'Butter,' like cake and water, appears frequently as part of Stein's special food imagery for sex," in her discussion of the erotic language of her early work "Is Flesh Advisable: The Interior Theater of Gertrude Stein," *Signs* 4 [Spring 1979]: 479).

23. In commenting on the opening sections of "Objects," Chessman suggests that Luce Irigaray's theorizing a new form of speculation sheds light on Stein's project here: "Instead of being seen and named as object, the woman may begin to take the 'speculum' in her own hands, to 'press on' into herself, and to find, not the certainty of the named, but the fiery, uncertain, lively, and unlocatable place of the unnamed" (*The Public is Invited*, 95). In the course of "GLAZED GLITTER," Chessman claims "vision has become replaced by a modality of touch" (96). Stein's insistence that the change of style in *Tender Buttons* came from a new way of looking would argue against Chessman's conclusion here.

24. "A Transatlantic Interview: 1946" in *The Gender of Modernism: A Critical Anthology*, ed. Bonnie Kime Scott (Bloomington: Indiana University Press, 1990), 510.

25. Judy Grahn, *The Highest Apple: Sappho and the Lesbian Poetic Tradition* (San Francisco: Spinsters, Ink, 1985), 62–63.

26. Scott, *The Gender of Modernism*, 511.

27. Grahn, *The Highest Apple*, 64–65.

28. Yet it is Stein's apparent ambivalence toward the text that makes it resistant to theoretical interpretations. Although *Tender Buttons* experiments freely with expressing the erotic, it does not lend itself easily to feminist theories about women's writing. It does not fully respond to Kristevan reading, as we have seen. Nor does Irigaray's theory of a new form of speculation in women's writing serve to open a text that is so quick to retract or cover up its most daring statements. Even attempting to locate Stein in her period, as Shari Benstock does in describing her as the philosopher-theorist of what she calls "Sapphic Modernism" vital in Paris and London at the turn of the century, is not very helpful since Stein was resistant both to other lesbian writers in the Paris community and to Sappho as a model ("Expatriate Sapphic Modernism: Entering Literary History," in *Lesbian Texts: Radical Revisions*, ed. Karla Jay and Joanne Glasgow [New York: New York University Press, 1990], 183–203). Nor can Sandra Gilbert and Susan Gubar, who note the need in her generation—the first fully self-conscious generation of lesbian writers—for a kind of literary double-talk and the literal doubling of writers as in *The Autobiography*, do justice to this period of her work, finding her writing "tenaciously, even boringly incomprehensible and self-serving" (*No Man's Land*, 245).

29. Chessman argues that "Stein attempts to present, as immediately as possible, a sense of an ongoing intimacy, yet she carefully refuses to make her representations of this intimacy stable or certain. She achieves this resistance to direct representation partly through the absence of one narrative or lyrical voice speaking throughout the poem from a position of authority, able to describe the figures who speak and make love" (*The Public Is Invited*, 101).

30. Ibid.

31. Penelope J. Engelbrecht argues that Stein signifies the lesbian sex act with the verb "say," claiming that for Stein, "to speak *is* to act; she conflates text and reality, makes the flesh word/makes the word active flesh. Then she asks if 'you,' the reader can 'read' it, understand it" ("'Lifting Belly Is a Language?': The Postmodern Lesbian Subject," *Feminist Studies* [Spring 1990]: 99).

32. Discussing "Lifting Belly" in the context of other lesbian writing such as

Nicole Brossard's *The Aerial Letter*, Engelbrecht comments, "Back and forth and back, the language of lesbian Desire con/fuses two women, as in Stein's text, each one Desiring to 'tak[e] pleasure in knowledge' and to give knowledge in pleasure." Engelbrecht quotes Brossard's claim that "there is no more plot" in her fiction, acknowledging that the resulting immense calm is not static, but quite the opposite—full of constant movement (ibid., 103).

33. In her excellent study of women poets and second world war (*A Gulf So Deeply Cut: American Women Poets* [Madison: University of Wisconsin Press, 1991]), Susan Schweik includes a brilliant reading of Elizabeth Bishop's "Roosters," concluding: "it is not that 'Roosters' is ostensibly a war poem but actually a love poem; it is that the two here are impossible to tell apart" (233). She notes "a distinct tradition of women's lyrics which use war as metaphor for conflicts in the home or bedroom or psyche (looking backward to Dickinson, forward to Cooper and Plath); but here, as elsewhere in that tradition, the war is also more than metaphor, not only mask" (234). Against this tradition, Stein appears to distinguish love and war, to set love apart from the hazards of war.

34. See Chessman's treatment of "Caesars"; she claims that Stein reclaims the name for peaceable purposes (*The Public Is Invited*, 106–8).

35. See Terry Castle's *The Apparitional Lesbian* for a discussion of this tendency.

Chapter 2
History as Conjugation: Stein's *Stanzas in Meditation* and the Literary History of the Modernist Long Poem

Mary Loeffelholz

In "Poetry and Grammar," the final piece printed in her 1935 collected *Lectures in America*, Gertrude Stein addressed herself to what was by then, of course, a familiar literary-historical question about the historical possibility or impossibility of the long poem in English. Noting that she had recently "found in longer things like Operas and Plays and Portraits and Lucy Church Amiably and An Acquaintance With Description that I could come nearer to avoiding names in recreating something," Stein then observes:

> That brings us to the question will poetry continue to be necessarily short as it has been as really good poetry has been for a very long time. Perhaps not and why not.
> If enough is new to you to name or not name, and these two things come to the same thing, can you go on long enough. Yes I think so.[1]

Curiously, Stein's own catalog of her recent longer works—seen, in light of the concerns of the 1934 lecture, as experiments in poetry—omits to note (or to issue advance advertisement for) her most recently completed long poem, *Stanzas in Meditation*. Finished, probably, in 1932, but not published until it appeared in Volume 6 (1956) of the posthumous Yale edition of Stein's unpublished writings, *Stanzas in Meditation*, at 150 pages, is surely the longest among what Richard Kostelanetz classifies not quite unequivocally as poems, but as "works that Stein meant to publish as poems."[2]

Stanzas is also, as Neil Schmitz has persuasively argued, intimately in dialogue with the theoretical concerns of "Poetry and Grammar."[3] Its circling and endlessly recirculated pronouns—"I," "she," "they"—perform what "Poetry and Grammar," in a much-cited passage, describes and performs as poetry's everlasting resistance to, love for, and displacement of nouns as the names of things:

> Poetry is concerned with using with abusing, with losing with wanting, with denying with avoiding with adoring with replacing the noun. It is doing that always doing that, doing that and doing nothing but that. Poetry is doing nothing but using losing refusing and pleasing and betraying and caressing nouns. ("P&G," 231)

If this is poetry, then arguably Stein wrote nothing more poetic than *Stanzas in Meditation*. And if, as Stein also goes on to say in "Poetry and Grammar," the primal scene of "adoring and replacing the noun" is— as "anybody knows"—"how anybody calls out the name of anybody one loves" ("P&G," 232), then the biographical occasion of *Stanzas in Meditation* returned Stein to that scene of writing or vocation, in every sense of the word, in several painful ways.[4] Written in tandem with *The Autobiography of Alice B. Toklas* and in the wake of a crisis in the relationship with Toklas produced by the discovery of Stein's manuscript of her early novel *Q.E.D.* (which recorded Stein's 1901–3 love affair with May Bookstaver), *Stanzas in Meditation* performs the crisis in the love affair as a crisis of nomination: not only in its abstract waltz of pronouns, but also, as Ulla Dydo's study of the manuscript has shown, in its partially repressed variations on the name "May": may, many, marry.[5]

When Stein asked herself, in "Poetry and Grammar," "can you go on long enough," naming and not naming, to write a long poem, she had ample reason, with *Stanzas* behind her, to say "I think so." But again, as I noted earlier, "Poetry and Grammar" does not name or directly hint at Stein's own recent composition of *Stanzas in Meditation*. Nor do I think this is entirely a matter of Stein's courteously restricting her lecture to works her audience could have read (although she is scrupulous and, no doubt, politic in quoting her work where she can from the editions of her newly enthusiastic publisher, Bennett Cerf at Random House). Stein's evasion of nomination in "Poetry and Grammar" rather, I think, indicates something of Stein's resistance to her own completed long poem and of her protracted, prolific resistance to the very idea of writing poetry—the resistance to naming that is exactly what, as she says, makes it possible for her to "go on long enough."

Stein's own resistance to—or as—poetry has been more than repaid by most critics. Gertrude Stein is seldom received as a poet in critical works about or in anthologies of modernist poetry—including major feminist works on women's modernist poetry.[6] Still less often is she credited as an author in the genre of the modern long poem or poetic sequence. The *MLA Bibliography* has indexed a category of "poetry" for

Stein since 1982; the work that most often appears in that category, however, is her earlier and shorter *Tender Buttons*. Her longest and, I have suggested, most "poetic" (according to Stein's own theoretical musings) poem, *Stanzas in Meditation* has been relatively neglected even by Stein's most able readers, and neither Stein nor *Stanzas in Meditation* appears in canonical studies of modernist long poems, such as M. L. Rosenthal and Sally M. Gall's *The Modern Poetic Sequence: The Genius of Modern Poetry*.

The aims of this essay are threefold: first, to account for Stein's failure to figure in particular literary histories of the modernist long poem; second, to offer some possible "canonizing" (in Marianne DeKoven's ambivalent sense of the word) readings of *Stanzas in Meditation* as a modernist poetic sequence, readings focused not only on the poem itself, but on the comparisons that may be drawn between *Stanzas* and other long poems by canonical modernist writers; and finally, to assess what seem to me (as to DeKoven) the limitations and risks of such "canonizing" readings where Stein, and perhaps other women modernists, are concerned.[7] Rather than simply urge that resistance to "canonizing" Stein as a poet, or *Stanzas in Meditation* as a long poem, be overcome, I want to read these several, related forms of resistance: Stein's resistance to naming her own *Stanzas* in "Poetry and Grammar"; how "Poetry and Grammar" figures poetry as resistance to nomination; and how some ways of writing the literary history of the twentieth-century long poem in English, including recent feminist literary histories, resist considering Stein's work, especially *Stanzas in Meditation*. I hope less to fix a reading of *Stanzas in Meditation* than to inquire into what makes it so opaque to existing critical accounts of the modernist long poem, or indeed accounts of modernism as a literary-historical period often critically defined by a series of heroic long poems, beginning with *The Waste Land* and ending with Pound's *Cantos*, Williams's *Paterson*, or even H. D.'s more recently celebrated *Trilogy* and *Helen in Egypt*. And in the end, I think it may even be necessary—if Stein's extraordinary resistance to being conjugated in a historical series is to be honored—to wonder about the grounds and effects of her placement in an anthology like this one. Including the ground, or effect, that nominates Stein as a "woman."

Surveying the grounds of modernist poetry and some of its most influential critics in 1982, Marjorie Perloff asked herself and her readers, "Pound/Stevens: Whose Era?"[8] Although the critical landscape has certainly changed since 1982, the form of Perloff's question, along with the critical dichotomies underlying it, remain reasonably familiar. Choosing one alternative or the other, for Perloff in 1982, leads to different ways of answering her two major questions: "What do we mean when we talk of Modernism in poetry? And, more important, what are our

present norms for the 'great poem'?" (504). The school of Stevens, principal champion Harold Bloom, holds that "the best twentieth-century
poetry . . . carries on the great tradition of Romantic visionary humanism. . . . Such poetry takes the lyric paradigm for granted" (504). Pound,
by contrast, models the great poem as metonymic, encyclopedic collage,
and for the critics of "his" era, modernism "is the era when the norms
of the Romantic crisis poem as of the Symbolist lyric were exploded,
when poetry found that it could once again incorporate the seemingly
alien discourses of prose without losing its identity" (505).

Perloff's own evaluation of the relative interest and persuasiveness of
these alternatives is undisguisedly in Pound's favor; moreover, the sixties,
she thinks, saw "the balance begin to tip" more generally in favor of
"constructivist" as opposed to "expressivist" versions of modernist poetry.[9] What interests me, however, is the silence this essay preserves on
Stein's poetry in relation to the alternative figures it picks out to frame
the era—especially in light of Perloff's own earlier, extended discussion
of Stein, "Poetry as Word-System," in *The Poetics of Indeterminacy*, also
dedicated to mapping out what Perloff calls "the other tradition"—
stretching from Rimbaud through Williams, Stein, and Pound.[10] My
point is not to chastise one of the best critics ever to have written on Stein
for not carrying through her interest in one particular essay; however,
that Stein disappears under this essay's particular *way* of encapsulating
the tensions of modernism is striking for at least two reasons.

For one, her disappearance foregrounds the liabilities of framing periods as lineages organized under the sway of one or another father—a
problem more obvious after a decade more of feminist criticism than in
1982, to be sure, but one that (as I will argue) more recent, feminist
criticism of modernism has not itself altogether exorcised. For another,
the very terms of this essay irresistibly invite, at least to me, consideration
of Stein, and more specifically still of *Stanzas in Meditation*. Is Stein's longest poem a modernist "great poem," or was it intended to be, and by
what standards of value? Is it "encyclopedic" in Pound's sense; if not, is
it "lyric" in Stevens's sense? If neither, how to place it under the familiar
poles (whatever their names) governing our readings of modernism? As
readers for many years have noted, *Stanzas in Meditation* foregrounds its
claims on the lyric doubly in its title (songs and subjectivity), and in its
very first line—"I caught a bird which made a ball"—throwing out an
initial lyric "I," coupled with the familiar lyric song-bird, whose odd
song-ball may recall the strength and sweetness rolled "into one ball" in
Marvell's "To His Coy Mistress" (like Marvell's speaker, Stein's unnamed
"they" are "in a hurry yet / In a kind of way they meant it best").[11] But
if ever there were a long poem organized as a metonymic lyric, *Stanzas
in Meditation* is it. If, as Perloff argues, Pound does not in any simple way

abandon lyric, rather places it within collage-forms of "metonymic link-ages"—"the juxtaposition without explicit syntactic connection of disparate items" (499)—perhaps Stein's *Stanzas* could be read as offering a still different modernist way of breaking or metonymizing while yet preserving aspects of lyric form, one whose strategies of "refusing the noun" might fracture or fractalize (in the mathematical sense) the "thingy" boundaries and juxtapositions of collage.

Or at least these are the thoughts provoked by Perloff in company with another critical work on modernist poetry that curiously omits Stein, and more particularly *Stanzas in Meditation*. M. L. Rosenthal and Sally M. Gall's *The Modern Poetic Sequence* appeared in 1983, the year after Perloff's essay and, it would seem, directly to counter Perloff's evaluation of the relative current standings of expressivism versus constructivism in critical configurations of modernism (if nevertheless to confirm rather closely Perloff's sense of what is at stake in this opposition). For Rosenthal and Gall, the "modern poetic sequence" is what we mean, again to recall Perloff's questions, by "modernism in poetry," and by the modernist "great poem." And the "modern poetic sequence" is the long poem written as a sequence of lyrics; or, in Rosenthal and Gall's aggressively ahistorical, organicist dictum, "*A poem depends for its life neither on continuous narration nor on developed argument but on a progression of specific qualities and intensities of emotionally and sensuously charged awareness.*" [12] Rosenthal and Gall manage to bend all the major modernist sequences, including those of Perloff's "other tradition" (Pound's *Cantos*, Williams's *Paterson*), along with an impressive range of later works, to this description.

But not Stein, who is mentioned nowhere in *The Modern Poetic Sequence*, and not *Stanzas in Meditation*, despite the abundant provocation the title, structure, and seeming ambition of Stein's poem offer to their account of the modern poetic sequence. Not to mention Stein's own personal attraction to the word "genius," which Rosenthal and Gall so anxiously defend: "It may strike some readers as curious or naive to speak of the 'genius' of modern poetry. . . . Yet we must insist—whatever the theoretical attractions of exalting intellectual systems and ennui-generated positions over living works—that the individual work of genius is our one touchstone of value in the arts" (17). Or, as Stein writes in *Stanzas*, repeating the more famous opening of *The Autobiography of Alice B. Toklas*:

> She knew that she could know
> That a genius was a genius
> Because just so she could know
> She did know three or so
> So she says and what she says

No one can deny or try
What if she says.

(*SIM*, 77)

Stein's rhymes seem proleptically to smile at Rosenthal and Gall's rather desperate efforts to expand sheer tautology, genius is genius, into the space of a logic or reference somehow grounded outside of language (in the "touchstone"). Indeed, the whole of *Stanzas in Meditation* seems exactly pointed at the vulnerabilities of Rosenthal and Gall's project: it is the work that *The Modern Poetic Sequence* could least afford to acknowledge. Displaying its marks of lyricism exactly *as* marks, *Stanzas in Meditation* makes the expressive lyric subject the effect rather than the cause of its grammar; what "thickens" into subjectivity in its pages, triggering the wonder of its speaking, "I," is "black on white," ink on the page (*SIM*, 130).

For all its pointing to lyric effects—in the sense of "because" as well as "in spite of" its pointing to them— *Stanzas in Meditation* thus falls out of these two influential literary histories of modernism's most ambitious poems, both Perloff's, in which lyric is one pole of modernist production, and Rosenthal and Gall's, in which sequences of lyric intensity are definitive of the period. *Stanzas in Meditation* seems opaque to other conventional literary-historical ways of placing long poems in the context of poetic careers. Written, as I have noted, primarily in 1932 (with some work continuing perhaps as late as 1935), *Stanzas in Meditation* was first issued in 1956 in the Yale edition of Stein's unpublished writings. This hiatus between composition and publication may have deprived *Stanzas* of certain forms of canonical legibility characteristic of other modernist long poems. Unlike Pound's *Cantos*, Williams's *Paterson*, or H. D.'s *Trilogy*, all of which emerged in significant partial publications before assuming their final forms, *Stanzas* was published in its entirety well after Stein's death, and then as part of one volume in a series; Stein's poem was not eagerly awaited and interpreted as the ongoing, culminating project of an important modernist poet's career. Nor, given the gap between 1932 and 1956, was *Stanzas in Meditation* easily assimilable as a long poem in relationship to its historical circumstances: the "heroic" pattern of legibility given by war to Pound's and (differently) to H. D.'s major works, as feminist critics recently drawn to both *Trilogy* and *Helen in Egypt* have insisted, was signally missing here, both in terms of the timing of publication and *Stanzas'* apparent lack of concern for historical particularity. Stein's longest poem seems to offer little purchase to critical readings that look to engage the ambition of modernist long poems with historical contexts.

As Marianne DeKoven has argued, Stein's entire career and reception seem notably to lack this sort of history-making, "heroic" single work, the summative career-making work a long poem is usually assumed to represent. Placing Stein

next to any of the consensually accepted modernist (to take the "central" twentieth-century canon) heroes—Conrad, Joyce, Lawrence, Faulkner; even Woolf; Yeats, Pound, Eliot, Stevens, even HD or Moore—the difference comes into sharper focus. The *oeuvre* of each of those writers can be organised into a hierarchy of great and not-so-great, mature and apprentice. . . . It is impossible to order Stein's *oeuvre* into such a hierarchy, not only because everything in her writing works to undermine hierarchy, but because there is no principle of "the same" running through her writing, no spinal column along which her works could be arranged from head to bottom.[13]

This seems extraordinarily useful as both observation about and prescription for how Stein's reception may differ from those of other now-canonical modernists. It is nevertheless striking to me that, as DeKoven goes on in this essay to demonstrate the incompatibility of various of Stein's texts with the usual moves of canonization, *Stanzas in Meditation*, Stein's longest single "poem" and a relatively late work, never enters the catalog of substantial but somehow not "heroic" works that evade the canonizing narrative, a catalog that includes *The Making of Americans, Three Lives,* and *The Autobiography of Alice B. Toklas* as the more obvious possible candidates and *Tender Buttons, The Geographical History of America, Four Saints in Three Acts, The Mother of Us All,* and "Patriarchal Poetry" as the limit cases for canonization among "Stein's great writings." (And DeKoven's catalog fairly represents the selections, I think, most recent feminist critics of Stein would make if faced with the question DeKoven raises here.)[14] Why no *Stanzas in Meditation*?

One possible answer, paradoxical as it may seem, is that *Stanzas in Meditation* comes uncomfortably *too* close, in certain respects, to these career-making ambitions of modernist long poems—for readers who think to engage *Stanzas* in this context. As most of the critics who have looked at the poem agree, beginning with Richard Bridgman, the poem repeatedly raises the problem of Stein's ambition—for whom she thought she was writing, for what motives, and to what results—and does so in ways that double and question the terms of authorship and fame Stein set out at the same time in *The Autobiography of Alice B. Toklas.*[15] Judging from the relative amounts of critical attention garnered by the paired texts, *Stanzas* and *The Autobiography,* feminist readers (along with other readers) not only may have found *The Autobiography* more accessible than *Stanzas;* they may have found—or made—the displaced and doubled voice of *The Autobiography* more attractive, more permissible, as a paradigm of female authorship and ambition. The picture of the relationship between Stein and Toklas in *The Autobiography* may also, as Ulla Dydo observes, have contributed to their relative popularity: "In the *Autobiography* she renders the appearance and the public image, with the sort of peace-loving statements an audience likes to hear. In the stanzas she depicts the war, in all its disparate pieces. It is neither easy nor pretty." [16]

It is just possible that *Stanzas in Meditation* has fallen unassimilably between several different sorts of canonizing stories, including the one in which feminist readers set out to level all hierarchies in Stein's work by selecting particular texts—canonical antimatter, as it were—to demonstrate Stein's incompatibility with canonicity. (Of course, this is the very [anti] canonizing story my own essay is repeating with *Stanzas*.) In this new climate of reception, perhaps it is becoming harder rather than easier to answer to DeKoven's question of "Why, if [Stein] is so central, is she so generally perceived as marginal?" with the reply, "We know, thanks primarily to Catharine Stimpson, how much of the answer to that question is that Stein was a woman and a lesbian." [17] The problem is not that Stimpson's answer is any less valuable, under many critical circumstances, than it was in 1977. Rather, it is that this question-and-answer does not, perhaps cannot, fully account for the circumstances of its own enunciation,[18] nor for how the gesture of centralizing Stein's dual status as "woman and lesbian" canonizes some constructions of both terms while displacing others—to judge from the different critical fates of *The Autobiography of Alice B. Toklas* and *Stanzas in Meditation*. Similarly, to say, with DeKoven, both that "everything in [Stein's] work undermines hierarchy" and that "there is no principle of the same running through her writing" is to trap an important line of feminist criticism within a self-undoing situation of enunciation: once you've stated that "everything undermines hierarchy" throughout Stein's writing, you have made yourself enunciate a principle of the same.

But, as Stein herself writes of the relationship, it would seem, between *The Autobiography* and *Stanzas*: "Now that I have written it twice / It is not so alike as once" (*SIM*, 145). This self-undoing is not a failure of logic on DeKoven's part but a productive crisis of nomination (of "same" and "everything" as nouns and replacements for nouns), one that returns us to Stein's own way of framing her resistance to poetry and poetry as resistance to naming in both "Poetry and Grammar" and the *Stanzas in Meditation*. It is also an exemplary performance of some of the feminist critical dilemmas that Ellen E. Berry, in her 1989 essay "On Reading Gertrude Stein," brilliantly anatomizes as "two feminist narratives of the reading process—the modernist judicial plot of struggle against the father; the postmodernist relational plot of 'escape' from the law to an intersubjective space of perfect mutuality."[19] "Undermining hierarchy," in DeKoven's words, Stein's writing undermines the father, while delivering us at the same time to the utopia organized without a "principle of sameness" ("Oh yes I organise this. But not a victory," Stein says [*SIM*, 29]), the place of utter difference-without-subordination. What Berry observes about these readings of Stein sums up my sense of the place of *Stanzas in Meditation* in much of the existing criticism on Stein, even feminist criticism, even Berry's own essay, in which *Stanzas* is not mentioned: "The limitation here being that if narrative privileges a certain form of evolution and resolution, then points of resistance to that evolution, elements which are contradictory, inexplicable, excessive—sites of difference may all disappear" (4).

As an alternative to such narratives of reading, whether modernist or postmodernist, feminist or not (and her analysis acutely observes how readings on one side or the other of these divides nevertheless mirror one another), Berry proposes a set of what she calls "reading moments"—a series of heterogeneous positions, "as flexible as those she assumed," that readers may take up in response to Stein's writing; Berry labels them (and numbers them in sequence) "collaboration," "watchful distance," "claustrophobia," and "resolute privacy" (7–15). And indeed, Berry's characterization of another very little-read Stein text, *A Novel of Thank You*, as a "moment four" work of "resolute privacy" might be applied directly to *Stanzas in Meditation* as well. As in *A Novel of Thank You*, "words and phrases suggesting attachment and those relating to separation recur repeatedly, as do numbers and naming"; likewise, "the most consistent stylistic feature in the text is pronouns lacking clearly specifiable antecedents, suggesting the speaker's desire to both disclose (it) and to conceal (it)" (15). Berry suggests that the special value of such "'unreadable' or limit texts" as *A Novel of Thank You* and, if we add it, *Stanzas in Meditation*, is that they "may help to reveal the 'unknown' of our feminist theories, leaving open the way for the construction of new theories" (17).

One difficulty I have with Berry's provocative sequence of "reading moments," however, is that they seem to frame an implicit narrative no less insistently than do the modernist and postmodernist narratives of reading, a narrative proceeding from old to new, from relative closeness to relative distance, achieved or desired, and from relative readerly pleasure to displeasure in the text. In this implicit narrative, the current reception—or lack of reception—of *Stanzas in Meditation* would be charged to its tendency to prompt readers toward the far end of this spectrum of response; by the same token, the poem's value-to-be-realized would lie in its power to deliver readers into a utopian future that tropes on similarly utopian, earlier feminist readings of Stein's pleasures without altogether broadening or changing their terms of reference.

By way of alternative to Berry's acute but narrowly psychologized analysis of the narratives through which we read or avoid reading various of Stein's texts, I would like to suggest ways of turning the question of reading *Stanzas in Meditation*, at least for a time or as an experiment, back out to a more external or comparative history of the modernist long poem. Doing so perhaps goes against the grain not only of previous histories of the modernist long poem that do not include Stein, or of feminist readings of Stein's works that do not include the *Stanzas*, but also, perhaps, against the grain of Stein's own insistence on her uniqueness. It may be a sort of "resistant" reading that resists aspects of Stein herself. I would rather resist Stein in this way, however, than resist her through the more "Oedipal" narrative—and Berry is surely right about the persistent lure and entrapment of this readerly plot—of trying to uncover Stein's uniquely generative "secret," whether the secret is (dis)figured as Stein's dirty little mechanical trick on a gullible reading public (as in B. F. Skinner's notorious article on Stein's automatic writing, "Has Gertrude Stein a Secret?")[20] or as the secret knowledge of life and language as those might exist beyond patriarchy or history itself. In a way, I want to issue a call for "historicizing" Stein's contribution to the modernist long poem, but without foreclosing in advance the problems Stein raises for anyone's call to "historicize."[21]

Although I have already suggested that *Stanzas in Meditation* offers little for historically minded critical readings of the long poem to grasp, Stein herself writes in *Stanzas*, however equivocally, "There can be said to be all history in this" (*SIM*, 29). What "history" means in *Stanza*, however, in context, is exactly the question, as is the question of "context" itself; far from standing security against arbitrariness of meaning or interpretation, quotation in context widens the noun's possible scope.

> There can be said to be all history in this.
> They can be often opposite to not knowing him
> Or they can be open to any impression
> Or even if they are not often worried
> They can be just bothered
> By wondering do they often make it be alike afterward
> Or to continue afterward as if they came
> It is useless to introduce two words between one
> And so they must conceal where they run
> For they can claim nothing.
>   (*SIM*, 29)

The writing of literary history may well be an enterprise of making it be alike afterward, as interpretation is a business of introducing two words between one. Both may be antithetical to what Stein says of poetry in "Poetry and Grammar": that poetry "has to do" with "natural counting, that is counting by one one one one one," "the natural way to count is not that one and one make two but to go on counting by one and one as chinamen do as anybody does as Spaniards do as my little aunts did. One and one and one and one and one. That is the natural way to go on counting" ("P&G," 227–28). Pure series, without pattern or addition, pure nomination, might then be pure poetry to Stein; and if so, it would be as resistant to history and as wedded to timeless essence as Stein's potentially racist or primitivist invocations of "chinamen," Spaniards, and her aunts imply. Such a pure series is not what happens consistently, however, in either *Stanzas in Meditation* or "Poetry and Grammar"; look at the difference between "one one one" and "one and one and one and one and one," or "One is not one for one but two / Two two three one and any one" (*SIM*, 41). Stein herself time and again "puts two words between one"—literally, graphically, as part of the strategy that generates her characteristic repetitions and variations—and interrupts poetry's "natural," pure series of nonadditive counting with the minimal scraps of pattern: two, three.

In this highly abstracted, minimalist way, then, *Stanzas in Meditation* frames its achievement as a long poem in terms of protracted resistance offered by pure series to the repeated intrusion of sequence: minimal lyric meeting minimal epic, to recall the terms of Perloff's division of Stein's "era." One currently available critical response to this way of resisting history in "Poetry and Grammar" and *Stanzas* would be to frame and historicize it as the performance of a particularly modernist sense of a crisis or failure in the traditional meanings of history.[22] Whether readers see such a performance as a culpable evasion of human responsibility or as the harbinger of our liberation from the dead hand of the master narratives, I do think that Stein generally, and perhaps *Stanzas* particularly, should figure more often and conspicuously in such ambitiously general readings of modernism's relation to history, especially those oriented to the genre of the long poem with its traditionally privileged relationship to history. The most feminist thing some schools of historically minded criticism could do for Stein and for *Stanzas in Meditation*, in other words, might be to extend to her seriously the hermeneutics of suspicion or negativity they bring to the evaluation of other modernist poets.[23] And reciprocally, some feminist ways of understanding modernism and placing Stein as a heroic or proleptically utopian figure within it—what Ellen Berry, as we have seen, calls the "modernist" and "postmodernist" narratives of reading Stein—might benefit from being moved to reply to literary-historical narratives in which Stein was taken seriously, but *not* as a figure of perfect anticipatory knowledge or pleasure, *nor* as "the mother of us all, nor—in Astradur Eysteinsson's phrase—as "the deconstructive angel" of feminist criticism of modernism.[24]

This is not in any way to suggest that gender be thought of as irrelevant to some supposedly more universal problem of what "history" is for Stein's longest poem and for Stein's *oeuvre* as a whole. Rather, it is to plead for more nuanced comparative readings, on the grounds of history, among modernist women as well as between modernist women and men: for comparisons between H. D.'s, Moore's, and Stein's longer poems as well as between Stevens, Pound, Williams, and Stein.

Here I can only sketch briefly some of the comparisons *Stanzas in Meditation* could invite in a more broadly comparativist history of the modernist long poem. Like Pound's *Cantos, Stanzas in Meditation* maps a certain Mediterranean world selectively in terms of perception and action. Where *The Cantos*, however, layers this world densely through quotation and allusion and informs quotation and allusion with the Oedipal plot of male poetic ambition, its erection and chastening, *Stanzas* grinds its literary-historical references (largely, as critics have noted, to lyric topoi) so fine as to disperse any historical plot or depth to its author's ambition, leaving Stein's "I" to announce itself in a willfully present-tense performative: "I think I know I like I mean to do" (*SIM*, 36). If, on the other hand, Stein's *Stanzas* were compared to the "norm of lyric" established, according to Perloff, in histories of modernism centered on Stevens, it could be observed that like the Stevens of "Notes Toward a Supreme Fiction," Stein in *Stanzas* is concerned with what is abstract, what must give pleasure, and what must change—or, in Stein's less impersonal construction, "They could have pleasure as they change" (*SIM*, 4). But again, the "fat girl" both summoned and deferred "by name, my green, my fluent mundo" in the conclusion of Stevens's "Supreme Fiction" would also bear contrasting with Stein's

It is the day when we remember two.
We two remember two two who are thin
Who are fat with glory too with two
With it with which I have thought twenty fair
If I name names if I name names with them . . .
(*SIM*, 9)

Unlike Stevens's supreme fiction, as well as the era-defining, male-authored "encyclopedic poems," to recall Perloff's terms— *The Cantos*, looked on by the eyes of Aphrodite, or Williams's *Paterson*, discovering the "beautiful thing" in the bowels of the modern industrial city—Stein's *Stanzas* eschews figuring its access either to encyclopedia history or to lyric intensity of vision through woman as "other" and muse. Stein's speaker "names names" *with* the other, contiguous woman, rather than casting names after her in order to stop her revolutions, "Check your evasions, hold you to yourself." [25]

Turning to possible comparative contexts for *Stanzas in Meditation* among longer works by other women poets, it is suggestive that, like H. D.'s *Trilogy* and *Helen in Egypt, Stanzas in Meditation* revisits in poetry an autobiography (of a marriage, among other things) also told in prose. It matters, however, and seems typical of so many other differences in their approaches to writing that the prose and poetry autobiographies are synchronically related in Stein's career, diachronically or genetically related in H. D.'s. Like H. D.'s *Helen in Egypt*, Stein's *Stanzas* insistently configures desire in triangular or structural terms, and figures history itself in terms of this structure of desire. But again, the comparison points just as much to how different Stein's deliberate, grammatical, abstracted conjugation of this structure is from the psychoanalytically informed, mythic depth-history of H. D.'s *Helen in Egypt*. Or like Marianne Moore in "Marriage," a poem whose "he says / she says" rhetorical form anthologizes historically disparate fragments of writing to try marriage "by the tooth of disputation," [26] Stein in *Stanzas in Meditation* positions herself skeptically but lovingly vis-à-vis a "he," "she," and "they" who together conjugate history in the language of " 'Liberty and union / now and forever' " (Moore ["Marriage"], quoting Daniel Webster). "They find it one in union. In union there is strength," says Stein; but also, "Mine often comes amiss / Or liking strife awhile" (*SIM*, pp. 30, 4). Set next to one another, these poems present a striking comparative triptych on how three important women poets represent the subject of history: as palimpsest, as the staging space of rhetorical conflict, as a place staked in a circulating network of pronouns.

As these fragmentary readings may suggest, positioning Stein's *Stanzas in Meditation* centrally within a comparative history of the modernist long poem might help us to explicate further the relationships and cross-figurations, for both male and female modernists, between crises of historical narratives or representations and crises of gender systems and representations. What else might such comparative readings of Stein's longest poem in the context of other modernist long poems accomplish for the way we write the history of modernism as a whole? Clearly, I hope they would disrupt the master narrative that takes the question of modernism to be "whose era?"—whether such narratives are generated by oppositions between titanic male figures (Pound's "encyclopedic poem" versus Stevens's "norm of lyric," for Perloff) or, in a feminist narrative perhaps beginning to emerge more recently and more hesitantly, between women poets (Moore at home versus H. D. in Egypt). However such contests for possession are framed, Stein generally falls out of them, ontologically *uncoupled* with an opposite in terms of which she can be made a voice for one pole in a dialectic.[27]

And beyond this, I hope that reading *Stanzas in Meditation* would productively complicate the most lively oppositional history of modernism currently in critical play, that between male- and female-authored modernisms. Is *Stanzas in Meditation* authored by a woman? And how do we know? Marianne DeKoven and Ellen Berry, as we have seen, between them have done the most creative work in raising questions about Stein's lack of fit into canonizing narratives, even feminist narratives. Yet even for DeKoven, it makes sense to begin her closing discussion of a passage from Stein's *Tender Buttons*, in her book *Rich and Strange: Gender, History, Modernism*, with the words: "Because Stein wrote as a woman . . ." And DeKoven proposes to "use" this passage "in the same paradigmatic way for the female modernists that I used 'In a Station of the Metro' for the male modernists."[28] For Berry, too, the question to be explored in feminist readings of Stein is what kinds of relation they allow us to imagine between women as readers and the "other woman" of the text—rather than the more fundamental question of *how* the "other" of the text is construed as "woman" to begin with.

Is Stein a woman? And how do we know? This is a familiar issue, if assumed more often than foregrounded in the professional constitution of an anthology like this one. We may be on surer ground in deciding that the object of Stein's desire in *Stanzas in Meditation* is a woman, given the insistence of the poem's references to "she"; but the pronoun also signals the absence of a common or proper noun, "woman" or "Alice" or, perhaps, "May"—gender, as well as desire, the shifting pronouns suggest, being the effect of emplacement in a grammar rather than the expression of essence. (*Stanzas* does not play much with nicknames like "Caesar" and "wife," so conspicuous in the writing from earlier and probably happier periods of Stein and Toklas's marriage, although Caesar's ghost appears in the poem by quotation in a lovely evocation of that time: "She said she knew we were the two who could / Did we who did and were and not a sound / We learned we met we saw we conquered most"— *SIM*, 7.) Curiously, it is sometimes Stein's biographical lesbianism that today seems to guarantee her critical status as a woman, in an inversion of what we are accustomed to thinking of as the proper relationship between the two identities. The unexpressed logic of this identification seems almost to go: Stein loved women; Stein was a lesbian;

therefore Stein is a woman. And once understood as a woman and a lesbian, her exclusion from canonical histories of modernism becomes legible, as does the "coding" of her erotic life in her writing.

But understanding the logic of Stein's exclusion in this way tends to narrativize her being a lesbian as the generative "secret" of her career and reception when surely nothing was less secret, considering the blaze of publicity that accompanied *The Autobiography of Alice B. Toklas*, in anticipation of which she wrote *Stanzas in Meditation*. It would be the project of another essay or another anthology, perhaps, to reimagine this narrative of secrecy and disclosure for modernist women and lesbians, with its intricate and reversible implications of sexual and gender identities, in terms as complex as those generated by Eve Kosofsky Sedgwick for male homosexuality at the turn of the century.[29] This project would try to see Stein's production and reception not in terms of the repressive hypothesis—the secret—but the epistemology of the closet: the open secret.[30] It is not that I think the literary-historical enterprise of nominating Stein as a woman, or a lesbian, should simply stop; rather I want it to return at last to Stein's own description in "Poetry and Grammar" of the possible long poem she does *not* choose to name there as *Stanzas in Meditation*, to *go on long enough*.

Notes

1. Gertrude Stein, "Poetry and Grammar," in *Lectures in America*, intro. by Wendy Steiner (1935; repr. Boston: Beacon Press, 1985), 240. Hereafter cited parenthetically as "P&G."

2. Gertrude Stein, *Stanzas in Meditation and Other Poems [1929–1933]*, vol. 6 of the Yale Edition of the Unpublished Writings of Gertrude Stein (New Haven, Conn.: Yale University Press, 1956). Hereafter cited parenthetically as *SIM*. On the composition date of *Stanzas*, see Richard Bridgman, *Gertrude Stein in Pieces* (New York: Oxford University Press, 1970), 214.

3. Neil Schmitz, "The Difference of Her Likeness: Gertrude Stein's *Stanzas in Meditation*, in *Gertrude Stein and the Making of Literature*, ed. Shirley Neuman and Ira B. Nadel (Boston: Northeastern University Press, 1988), 124–49; see especially pp. 134–37.

4. See Marianne DeKoven's comment on Stein's anecdote, in "Poetry and Grammar," of finding her brother's love poems: "a comic and ambivalent parable that narrates a literary primal scene," issuing "from private act to generic definition of poetry." "Breaking the Rigid Form of the Noun: Stein, Pound, Whitman, and Modernist Poetry," in *Critical Essays on American Modernism*, ed. Michael J. Hoffman and Patrick D. Murphy (New York: G. K. Hall, 1992), 225.

5. Ulla E. Dydo, " 'Stanzas in Meditation': The Other Autobiography," *Chicago Review* 35, no. 2 (Winter 1985): 4; see especially pp. 11–14.

6. A catalog of works in one way or another on modernist poetry that did not include Stein at all, or that mentioned her only in passing, would be too long and uninformative to compile here. A recent piece of particular relevance to this argument, however, might be Lynn Keller's essay on "The Twentieth-Century Long

Poem," in *The Columbia History of American Poetry*, ed. Jay Parini and Brett C. Millier (New York: Columbia University Press, 1993), which mentions Stein and *Stanzas in Meditation* only parenthetically in the context of possible influences on the Language writers (p. 561).

7. See Marianne DeKoven, "Gertrude Stein and the Modernist Canon," in Neuman and Nadel, *Gertrude Stein and the Making of Literature*, pp. 9–20, especially 14–18.

8. Marjorie Perloff, "Pound/Stevens: Whose Era?," *NLH* 13, no. 3 (Spring 1982): 485. Subsequent references to this work are given parenthetically in the text.

9. These terms for the "Pound/Stevens" poles of modernism, along with Perloff's evaluation of the current balance between them, appear in the version of the essay published as chapter 1, "Pound/Stevens: Whose Era," in Marjorie Perloff, *The Dance of the Intellect: Studies in the Poetry of the Pound Tradition* (Cambridge: Cambridge University Press, 1985), 23.

10. Marjorie Perloff, *The Poetics of Indeterminacy: Rimbaud to Cage* (Princeton, N.J.: Princeton University Press, 1980), 67.

11. On the lyricism of *Stanzas in Meditation* and Stein's growing interest in lyric during the years leading to its writing, see Donald Sutherland's preface to *SIM*, especially pp. ix–xiii, and Neil Schmitz's more antilyric reading of the birds, flowers, and other commonplaces of lyric language distributed through *Stanzas* in "The Difference of Her Likeness."

12. M. L. Rosenthal and Sally M. Gall, *The Modern Poetic Sequence: The Genius of Modern Poetry* (New York: Oxford University Press, 1983), p. 6. Emphasis in the original.

13. DeKoven, "Gertrude Stein and the Modernist Canon," 14–15.

14. To glance at two recent feminist books on Stein's career: Harriet Chessman's *The Public is Invited to Dance: Representation, the Body, and Dialogue in Gertrude Stein* (Stanford: Stanford University Press, 1989), cites *Stanzas* only in passing, as evidence of Stein's and Toklas's troubled relationship in the early 1930s (p. 152). Chessman cites as Stein's (anti)heroic works *Ida, Three Lives, Tender Buttons*, and *Blood on the Dining-Room Floor. Stanzas* makes no appearance in Lisa Ruddick's *Reading Gertrude Stein: Body, Text, Gnosis* (Ithaca, N.Y., and London: Cornell University Press, 1990), in which Stein's (anti)heroic works are *Three Lives, The Making of Americans*, and *Tender Buttons.*

15. See Bridgman, *Gertrude Stein in Pieces*, 214–17; also Schmitz, "The Difference of Her Likeness," 128–29.

16. Dydo, "'Stanzas in Meditation': The Other Autobiography," 18.

17. DeKoven, "Gertrude Stein and the Modernist Canon," 11; citing Catharine Stimpson's "The Mind, the Body, and Gertrude Stein," *Critical Inquiry*, 3, no. 3 (Spring 1977): 489.

18. Astradur Eysteinsson makes a similar observation in *The Concept of Modernism* (Ithaca, N.Y.: Cornell University Press, 1990), 91: "It is easy to agree with Marianne DeKoven that as a whole Stein's work 'fits neatly nowhere,' But . . . in order to discern her as a modernist writer, we have to 'fit' her into a canon. The recently surging Stein criticism, much of it feminist and post-structuralist, has found her to be representative for an aesthetic or literary relation to modernity."

19. Ellen E. Berry, "On Reading Gertrude Stein," *Genders* 5 (Summer 1989): 4.

20. See Neil Schmitz's discussion of Skinner's and others' approaches to Stein's "secret" in "The Difference of Her Likeness," 126–29.

21. For an excellent discussion of what history meant to Stein herself, focused

on her earlier fiction, see Jayne L. Walker, "History as Repetition: *The Making of Americans*," in *The Making of a Modernist: Gertrude Stein from Three Lives to Tender Buttons* (Amherst: University of Massachusetts Press, 1984), 43.

22. See Eysteinsson, *The Concept of Modernism*, 12–46, for a cogent survey of critical disputes over modernism's relationship to history.

23. Andrew Ross's sweepingly titled *The Failure of Modernism*, to take just one example, might have been more interesting if Stein had really figured in its diagnosis; she appears only once, in a laundry list—otherwise all male—of modernists said to be "concerned in some way with the need to confront the body in new ways, and each governed by a formal imperative to 'make it new' on behalf of language and humanism." *The Failure of Modernism: Symptoms of American Poetry* (New York: Columbia University Press, 1986), 87.

24. Eysteinsson, *The Concept of Modernism*, 92. Marianne DeKoven, in her early book on Stein's experimental writing, *A Different Language*, registered her uneasiness with unqualified utopian celebration of Stein's achievement, proposing to "distinguish[] between what deserves admiration and what perhaps does not" by virtue of going "too far" into indecipherability. *A Different Language: Gertrude Stein's Experimental Writing* (Madison: University of Wisconsin Press, 1983), xxi. This is not quite the same, however, as a critical approach to which the fascinations of Stein's experiments would be historically and analytically inseparable from their particular opacities or ignorances.

25. Wallace Stevens, "Notes Toward a Supreme Fiction," *The Collected Poems of Wallace Stevens* (New York: Alfred A. Knopf, 1978), 406.

26. Marianne Moore, "Marriage," in *The Complete Poems of Marianne Moore* (1967; repr. New York: MacMillan, 1981), 66.

27. I tried staging such an opposition myself, setting Stein versus Djuna Barnes, in *Experimental Lives: Women and Literature, 1900–1945* (New York: Twayne Publishers, 1992), 117–28—unconvincingly.

28. Marianne DeKoven, *Rich and Strange: Gender, History, Modernism* (Princeton, N.J.: Princeton University Press, 1991), 198.

29. See Eve Kosofsky Sedgwick, *The Epistemology of the Closet* (Berkeley: University of California Press, 1990).

30. In the lead essay of the recent special issue of *Modern Fiction Studies* devoted to Virginia Woolf, Brenda Silver does a brilliant job of exploring the vicissitudes of Woolf's reception (which does not exactly follow a linear plot of increasing and then lessening repression) and of showing how Woolf's writing and image have been used in postmodernity to designate open secrets of sexuality and feminism. See Brenda R. Silver, "What's Woolf Got to Do with It? or, The Perils of Popularity," *Modern Fiction Studies* 38, no. 1 (Spring 1992): 21. Woolf's case parallels Stein's in interesting ways.

Part II
H. D. (1886–1961)

Chapter 3
H. D., Modernism, and the Transgressive Sexualities of Decadent-Romantic Platonism

Cassandra Laity

In 1931, the *Manchester Guardian* tersely dismissed H. D.'s "romanti-ciz[ed]" classicism for "neither reflect[ing] the Greek nor giv[ing] the effect of it on the modern mind."[1] Douglas Bush's sweeping book-length repudiation of Romanticism, *Mythology and the Romantic Tradition in English Poetry* (1937), scathingly denounced H. D.'s "fundamentally romantic and precious conception both of Greece and poetry," contend-ing that her escapist, "wax[en]" "unhuman" "world of the feminine eye and the feminine heart" derived rather from the implicitly deca-dent "Greece of Pater and Wilde."[2] These critical assaults on H. D.'s Decadent-Romantic "effeminacy" summarized the often hostile anti-Romanticism of male modernists and their critics, which concealed, among other things, anxieties about the sexual "sameness" of Victorian-Romantic Hellenism that Oscar Wilde's infamous trials had rendered de-viant.[3] Indeed after his guilty verdict was announced, Wilde began his impassioned defense of male-male desire with a reference to the Greek ideal of Platonic love that characterizes Romantic Aestheticism—the "pure," "perfect" and "intellectual" bond between men "such as Plato made the very basis of his philosophy."[4]

While H. D. was stung by the critical attacks on her Romanticism, she never denied her debt to the Victorian-Romantic past. In order to "speak adequately" of her "poetry and its aims" she assented wearily in a "note" on her poetry (1938), "I must drag in a whole deracinated epoch."[5] Far from dissociating herself from Wilde, in H. D.'s fictional autobiography, *Asphodel* (composed 1921–22), her aspiring poet-heroine regards the Aesthetes, headed by Wilde, as a parental tradition of sexually transgres-sive artists. Hermione begs her woman lover to live with her in London by sentimentally invoking the Aesthete community and their classical code of "Greeks and flowers": "We are children of the Rossettis, of

Burne Jones, of Swinburne. We were in the thoughts of Wilde when he spoke late at night . . . to a young man named Gilbert. They talked of Greeks and flowers. . . . We belong here."[6] And H. D.'s most lesbian novel, *Paint It Today*, relies heavily on the Platonic search for the mother/sister twin of early Romanticism to configure the lesbian coupling that concludes Midget's quest to join physical and spiritual love. Most notably, the novel is framed by discourses on Plato and Shelley, or suggestive conflations of the two—as in *Paint It Today*'s early allusion to Midget's search for a twin-love via Shelley's translation of Plato in the epigraph to *Adonais*:

> Thou wert the morning star among the living,
> Ere thy fair light was shed,
> Now having died thou art as Hesperus giving
> New splendor to the dead.[7]

Victorian critics are currently discovering that the Aesthetes, early and late, summoned the authority of Platonic "sameness" to affirm their experimentation with outlawed forms of love and desire. In the first half of the century, Platonic love sanctioned the incestuous male ties to a mother/sister "twin" that pervade Romantic and Gothic literature. By the 1890s, Wilde, Swinburne, Pater, and others skillfully maneuvered Platonic twinning to encode male same-sex love and mother-son eroticism, summoning in particular the Greek system of mentoring associated with Plato, whereby the higher love between the boy and his adult instructor reconciles both intellect and eros. Recent critical inquiries into the impact of Trinity College professor the Reverend J. P. Mahaffy and his discourses on Greek homosexuality agree that this ideal formed the basis of Wilde's and others' codes for masculine desire in the Hellenist poetic.[8] Using this model, Wilde elaborated a "continuum" of male-centered relationships; in his Commonplace Book, Wilde wrote approvingly, "the refinement of Greek culture comes through the romantic medium of impassioned friendship."[9]

However, as H. D.'s sometimes adverse critical reception indicates, male modernist schemes of sexual masking did not embrace the sexual codes of Victorian-Romantic Hellenism. Theorizers of modern poetry such as Eliot, Yeats, and Pound focused rather on killing off the Aesthete poet and his Platonic doctrine of symbiosis with a spiritual/erotic twin. Perhaps the most urgent polemic against Romantic "effeminacy"[10] issued from the poets who had lionized the late-Victorian Romantics in their youths and now faced the task of erasing the feminine Aesthete from modern memory and reinventing a more acceptable sex/gender image of the poet and his poetics.[11] As Yeats records in his *Autobiographies*, although the literati had originally viewed Oscar Wilde as a "triumphant figure," their approbation turned to expressions of contempt (which Yeats claimed not to have shared) following the revelations made by his trials. Yeats notes Lionel Johnson's obvious "bitterness" and quotes from a letter in which Johnson furiously denounces Wilde's treachery and imposture: "He got a 'sense of triumph and power, at every dinner table he dominated, from the knowledge that he was guilty of that sin which, more than any other possible to man, would turn all those people against him if they but knew.' "[12]

This essay argues that unlike her male contemporaries, H. D. openly embraced the Decadent-Romantic Aesthete mask and its attendant Platonic philosophy to articulate sexual sameness in her poetics of sympathetic love. Critics have extensively explored H. D.'s philosophy of erotic/spiritual twinship encompassing mother-daughter eroticism, love between equal men and women, and homoerotic love.[13] Here I focus particularly on H. D.'s encodings of transgressive "female" desires through the Victorian Hellenists' principal icon for Platonic male-male love—the nude male bodies of Greek statuary that poets such as Swinburne, Pater, and Wilde summoned frequently as objects of the male, homoerotic "gaze." H. D.'s adaption of Victorian Hellenist "statue love" as well as the variety of trace-images it spawned for the loved male body such as whiteness, white light, and the transparently veined white body, enabled her to write the elusive body of mother-daughter eros and homosexual (male and female) desire in works such as "Hyacinth" and her play *Hippolytus Temporizes*.

Before discussing H. D.'s Romantic revisionism, however, I begin by surveying the ways in which anti-Romantic, male modernist theories of poetic identity created a hostile environment for feminine desire and language.[14] Eliot's objective correlative, Yeats's masks, and Pound's personae deliberately countered the Aesthete mask and neo-Platonic sexual "sameness," serving rather, at times, to divine the symptoms if not provide the curative for the typically Romantic sexually/textually ruinous "pathologies" of mother-son fixation or, more covertly, male-male desire. At the same time, these theories often suppressed linguistic indeterminacy and textual deferrals of desire—which we have come to associate with *écriture féminine*[15]—for what I will call a poetics of "consummation," a linear, male heterosexual/textual narrative that, among other things, deliberately sealed off the free play of desire in open-ended narratives of Romantic quest. Yeats and Pound in particular repeatedly referred to the trap of sexual frustration issuing from the Romantic search for a spiritual twin, which lost the Aesthete poet in "excessive" "sensuous" language and psychic distress.

Male Modernist Gender Masks:
The Death of the Aesthete Poet

Pound, the male modernist poet who was closest to H. D., judged his earlier Aestheticism to be, as one critic remarks, "a masturbatory phantasmagoria."[16] Pound's later theory of multiple personae enabled him to act out the lyric homicide of his former Romantic self in *Hugh Selwyn Mauberley*, the poem most frequently cited as an example of his dictum to cast off multifarious personae in "each poem." Pound himself described the volume in which *Mauberley* appears, *Personae*, as the testing ground for his new theory: "I began the search for the real in a book called *Personae*, casting off, as it were, complete masks of the self in each poem."[17] Further, Pound's decision to adapt his theory of personae probably crystallized after 1916 when he began composing *Mauberley*. In that poem, Pound killed, buried and inscribed the epitaph for his Aesthete self, thus emblematically laying waste to the cult of the effeminate Aesthete.

Pound, however, initially identified with the Romantic Aesthetes. H. D. recalled that Pound shared her passion for Swinburne and introduced her to Rossetti and Morris. Although H. D.'s early novel, *HER* (composed 1927)[18] deliberately played down Pound's role in her own Romantic phase of poetic development, H. D.'s later memoir of Pound, *End to Torment* (composed in 1958), resurrects an exuberantly Romantic young Pound who resembled the red-haired Swinburne, "read me [Morris's] 'The Haystack in the Floods' with passionate emotion," and "literally shouted Morris' 'The Gilliflower of Gold.'"[19] Pound's collected love poems to his then fiancée, H. D., *Hilda's Book* (published in *End to Torment*), is unabashedly influenced by the Victorian Romantics they read to one another and particularly by Swinburne. The young Pound unquestionably shared the Romantic/Dantean conception of the beloved as a twin soul. In "La Donzella Beata" from *Hilda's Book* the lover addresses his beloved (H. D.) as "Soul / caught in the rose hued mesh / of o'er fair earthly flesh."[20]

In *Mauberly*, however, the effeminate Aesthete and his mother/sister twin are included among those nongenerative forms of sexuality, such as celibacy and homosexuality, which Gail McDonald remarks of *The Cantos*, Pound "condemned in some of the most vitriolic language in American poetry."[21] Pound's Mauberley is the flaccid, self-absorbed Aesthete, capable only of

> maudlin confession,
> Irresponse to human aggression,
> . . . Lifting the faint susurrus
> Of his subjective hosannah.

Turning against his former enthusiasm for the Pre-Raphaelite twin soul, Pound now pictured a listless, barren, and ravaged Elizabeth Sidall, absorbed by "sterile" languor, with a "half-ruin'd face," wasted body, "thin like brook water" and "vacant gaze."[22] As Ronald Bush observes in *The Gender of Modernism* of Pound's subsequent relation to the feminine, Pound conceived woman as "a chaos"[23] controlled by male principles of form and order, an image that rejects Romantic twinning for the inequality implied by the nature/culture binary of gender stereotypes.

Pound's aversion to male sexual difference in any form is apparent in his ridicule of the progressive debates about sexuality in Britain. He jibed, "In England . . . if any man be abnormal or impotent . . . if he be in one of a number of known ways pathological, he sets to writing books on the matter and to founding cults and collecting proselytes. And he seems to expect society to reform itself according to his idiosyncrasies."[24] The Vorticist movement shared Pound's demolition of the Victorian Aesthete in *Mauberley*. Their collective desire to explode their stuffy, unmanly, and sexually idiosyncratic precursors is evident in the following "Blast" written by Wyndham Lewis:

BLAST
Years 1837 to 1900 . . .
BLAST their weeping whiskers—hirsute
RHETORIC OF EUNUCH AND STYLIST—
SENTIMENTAL HYGIENICS
ROUSSEAUISMS (wild Nature cranks)
FRATERNIZING WITH MONKEYS.[25]

While Eliot appears to have acknowledged the male-male erotic dynamic of literary influence—"we experience" "a genuine affair" "with the writers that most move us"[26]—Eliot's depiction of his early Romanticism shifts from the "homosocial"[27] eros of "Tradition and the Individual Talent" to what might be interpreted as a homophobic fear of sexual thralldom:

I took the usual adolescent course with Byron, Shelley, Keats, Rossetti, Swinburne. . . . At this period, the poem, or the poetry of a single poet, invades the youthful consciousness and assumes complete possession for a time. We do not really see it as something with an existence outside ourselves; much as in our youthful experiences of love, we do not so much see the person as infer the existence of some outside object which sets in motion these new and delightful feelings in which we are absorbed. The frequent result is an outburst of scribbling which we may call imitation. . . . *It is not a deliberate choice of a poet to mimic, but writing under a kind of daemonic possession by one poet.*[28]

Elsewhere I discuss this passage in the context of my argument that Eliot and other male moderns experienced Romanticism as an all-encompassing "foremother" rather than forefather.[29] However, the passage might also suggest recoil from excessive self-identification with a sexually ambiguous male precursor. Eliot's characterization of his early Romantic intimacy both as a "daemonic possession" and as an "invasion" places the young poet in a suggestively erotic, feminine, victimized relation to his forefather. Among the ill effects of this all-encompassing bond on the young ego is a blurring of boundaries between self and other characteristic of Romantic twinning—"we do not so much see the person as infer the existence of some outside object which sets in motion these new and delightful feelings in which we are absorbed." Eliot cautions that Romantic influence should be nothing more than an adolescent phase of erotic and linguistic experimentation that the young poet properly renounces in his passage to a mature manhood, "we must not confuse the intensity of the poetic experience in adolescence with the intense experience of poetry."[30]

Eliot's definition of the antidote to the sexual/textual pathology of Romanticism, the objective correlative, occurs tellingly in "Hamlet and His Problems" (1919)[31] as the missing literary device that condemns the Shakespeare of both *Hamlet* and the sonnets to the related "effeminate" Romantic debilities of son-mother fixation and, Eliot suggests, male-male homoeroticism.

Contextualized mainly in terms of the mother-son psychological narrative of *Hamlet*, Eliot's objective correlative takes on the problematics of male sexual identity. Eliot's device is presented here as a buffer against such "pathologies" as "the feeling of a son toward a guilty mother" (124). Eliot acknowledges in the first paragraphs that his essay is conceived in reaction against poets who focus vicariously on the psychology of the protagonist, of which Coleridge and the German Romantic Goethe are exemplars: "Such a mind had Goethe, who made of Hamlet a Werther: and such had Coleridge who made of Hamlet a Coleridge" (121). Indeed, Eliot's essay may be read as an attempt to kill Coleridge's Romantic conception of Hamlet. For while Eliot contends that the play should be approached historically, his essay fixes both on the psychology of Hamlet and on a Coleridgean Hamlet whose excessive inwardness and effeminacy he blames for the play's "artistic failure."

Eliot repeatedly pronounces "the essential emotion of the play" to be "the feeling of a son toward a guilty mother"—a "feeling" he describes as so "inexpressibly horrible," that he wonders "under compulsion of what experience" (126) Shakespeare undertook the theme of *Hamlet*. Throughout the essay Eliot suggests that, lacking the intervention of an objective correlative, *Hamlet*'s theme of mother-son eros remains unredeemably "pathological": "The intense feeling, ecstatic or terrible, without an object or exceeding its object, is something which every person of sensibility has known: it is doubtless a subject of study for pathologists. It often occurs in adolescence . . ." (126). The creator of Hamlet may therefore be said to have been overwhelmed by the pathological and adolescent imagination Eliot attributes to his own forfeited Romanticism. Indeed, Eliot concludes that "Shakespeare tackled a problem which proved too much for him" (126).

Further, Eliot's vague allusion to the perversity of the sonnets would seem to target Shakespeare's (and Wilde's) appeal to the Greek Platonic model of male-male love. Eliot accuses Shakespeare of beclouding the text of *Hamlet* with the implicit perversions of his sonnets: "*Hamlet*, like the sonnets is full of some stuff that the writer could not drag to light, contemplate, or manipulate into art. And when we search for this feeling, we find it, as in the sonnets, very difficult to localize" (124). This insidious "stuff," Eliot asserts, contrasts with Shakespeare's exposition of other themes (in *Othello*, and so on) that are "intelligible, self-complete, in the sunlight" (124). Eliot's rhetoric of sexual morality—"light" and "dark"—further impugns Shakespeare's sometimes sexual deviance. The "problems" besetting Shakespeare's sonnets and the character of Hamlet are thus defined as unmitigated by the universalizing operations of the objective correlative that might have supplied a "formula [for a] particular emotion; such that when the external facts are given, the emotion is immediately evoked" (124). (Although Eliot praised Djuna Barnes's lesbian/gay *Nightwood* as a study of "universal" human suffering, Nancy Gish notes that his editorial cuts in his edition of the novel focus largely on Dr. Matthew O'Connor's speeches "about his transvestism and homosexual experience." [32]

Similarly, Yeats's theory of the "anti-self," which he developed in reaction against his early Aesthete mask and its attendant "womanish introspection," [33] served, among other things, to lessen or counteract Romantic effeminacy, "morbidity" and the pathology of mother-son symbiosis. The shift in Yeats's aesthetic toward a more virile persona has been attributed to many things;[34] however, I would add that the sexual panic sweeping through the modernist movement in the wake of Wilde's trials and other incidences of gender trouble contributed to Yeats's personal crisis and alerted him to the gender-implications of his early work.

Yeats's disenchantment with the Aesthete pose and his subsequent gendered doctrine of the opposing self was reflected in his attitude toward the tragic generation, whom he now pictured as glutted Aesthetes yearning for the simplicity of a more manly era: "The typical young poet of our day is an aesthete with a surfeit, searching sadly for his lost Philistinism, his heart full of an unsatisfied hunger for the commonplace. He is an Alastor [*sic*] tired of his woods and longing for beer and skittles." [35] Further, like Eliot's objective correlative in "Hamlet and His Problems," the (female) "anti-self" Yeats would prescribe to cut the sensuous excess of the "aesthete with a surfeit" prevented the "pathology" of Romantic sameness or twinning. Yeats's scheme of sexual masking displaced his former Shelleyan, doctrine of sympathetic attachment to a mother/sister twin—"I had gathered from Shelley and the romantic poets an idea of perfect love"—with an image of the beloved as "the exact contrary rather than the Shelleyan counterpart to his normal self." [35] Yeats's oppositional redefinition of love often posited the heterosexual act of coitus as the privileged moment of reconciliation between warring male and female contraries: as

> a kiss
> In the mid-battle, and a difficult truce
> Of oil and water, candles and dark night . . .
> A brief forgiveness between opposites
> That have been hatreds,[37]

Yeats's new conception of love left little room for the spectrum of desires encoded by Platonic sameness—passionate celibacy, homoeroticism, and love between androgynous male and female spirits.

Linguistically, the male modernists' bias against Romantic twinning, among other things, compelled them to displace the "excessive," "sensuous" and "morbid" body/language of Romantic love poetry in favor of a closed and self-referential textuality. If, as William Ulmer describes Shelleyan quest-romance, the characteristically Romantic, "rapid, destabilizing passage from image to image" of the beloved which "subjects desire to an open-ended process . . . giv[ing] value no place to rest," "seeks to incarnate unrealized desires" [38]—to which I would add, "other" desires—then the modernists' deliberation to halt the Romantic onrush of signifiers in freeze frame for the single "word-picture" might be said to interrupt the flow. Eliot's objective correlative as defined in his essay on Hamlet strives, I suggest, to close, "consummate," or fill the gaps engendered by the free play of desire he claims Shakespeare could not concretize, "drag to light, contemplate or manipulate into art." To Eliot, the textual and sexual spaces created by Shelley's cascading imagery constituted a *lack*: Eliot praised the precision of Pound's doctrines in 1917 for making it "impossible to write like Shelley, leaving blanks for the adjectives" as in "what is called the 'music' of Shelley." [39] Both Eliot and Pound suggestively attacked Swinburne's preoccupation with "unusual and gorgeous words" for its sexual/textual fetishism and failure to "aim straight for the object": "the word . . . gives him the thrill not the object." [40] And Yeats would come to view the beloved at the center of Romantic quest as the ruling image that had submerged his generation in linguistic fragmentation, "morbidity," sexual deprivation, and malaise. Yeats placed the poets he associated with the Decadent-Romantic cult of the woman, Baudelaire and Ernest Dowson, at the thirteenth phase of *A Vision*, the phase of "the Sensuous Man," where "sensuality . . . without the intermixture of any other element" stimulates linguistic morbidity: "There is almost always a preoccupation with those metaphors and symbols [that are] most strange and most morbid." Here, "happy love is rare" and "the woman" and "every beloved object" "grows harder to find." [41]

By contrast, feminist transpositions of Victorian-Romantic neo-Platonism pervade twentieth-century women's literature. Indeed, although the Greek system classified women's love as inferior and bounded, the Aesthete's adaptation of the Greek continuum formed, for women writers, an earlier male example of Adrienne Rich's famous "lesbian continuum." [42] Like Rich's continuum of sexual and nonsexual relationships, the Greek system is based on nurturing romantic friendships that do not necessarily include sexual intimacy but rather define eros, in Rich's words, as "a diffuse and omnipresent energy" not limited "to any single part of the body or solely to the body itself." [43] Marilyn Farwell acknowledges that Adrienne Rich's "lesbian continuum" of women-centered relationships and creative reciprocity resembles, "admittedly, a Romantic/Aesthetic relationship." [44]

According to Sydney Janet Kaplan, Katherine Mansfield's early fascination with Pater and Wilde was linked to their "elevation of the Greek ideal of male friendships." Kaplan speculates that Mansfield used this model to articulate "her sexual attraction" to women such as her friend Maata and "in her early attempts to write about her sexuality" toward men. An early journal entry (1906) describes her erotic feelings for "a Dorian-like young man." [45] H. D. also frequently positioned herself imaginatively on a male continuum with her male mentors/instigators in poems such as "Hyacinth," "Toward the Piraeus," "The Charioteer," or "Red Roses for Bronze" where the male-male relation surpasses a limited and predatory heterosexuality. Further, H. D. and Frances Gregg, her first woman lover, appear to have expressed their "sister love" through self-identification with the Greek male hermaphroditic or androgynous bodies of Swinburne's *Poems and Ballads*. Barbara Guest notes that on the flyleaf, back pages, the title page of H. D.'s first copy of *Sea Garden*, Frances Gregg had inscribed several love poems to H. D., including a Swinburnian ode to H. D.'s androgynous beauty, entitled after

Swinburne's poem to the Greek statue of the *Hermaphrodite,* "Hermaphroditus." [46]

H. D.: Writing the Male Continuum

Yeats, Eliot, and Pound rejected the male Aesthete and his poetics of
erotic/spiritual sameness, preferring a poetics of consummation that
prevented the "morbid" images and symbols of Romantic quest from
diverting the linear narrative of male desire. Throughout the 1920s, however, H. D. assumed the Aesthete mask/text at its most transgressive. Her
so-called "crystalline youth" clearly derived from the Victorian Hellenists' "scene" of male homoerotic desire and the boy-man continuum in
which the erotic "gaze" of the male artist fixes on Greek statuary of
young male nudes. In works such as *Hippolytus Temporizes* and *Hedylus,*
poems from *Hymen, Heliodora,* and *Red Roses for Bronze,* and novels such
as *HER* and *Paint It Today,* H. D.'s adaptations both of "statue love"
and its metonymic spin-offs of whiteness, crystal, and the transparently
veined human body enabled her to write the vanishing sexual/textual
body of maternal eros and homoeroticism absented from her contemporaries' poetics of the single "concrete" image/object. [47]

The familiar tableau of a boy model's androgynous, Greek, "sculpted"
beauty displayed before the adoring, aesthetically discriminating, and
sensuous gaze of the older male artist recurs in various Aesthetic documents ranging from the opening of Wilde's *Dorian Gray,* in which the
young Dorian poses for the infamous painting "with a beauty such as old
Greek marbles," [48] and Pater's appreciation of art historian Winckelmann fingering "those pagan marbles" of nude Greek statuary "with
no sense of shame or loss," [49] to Swinburne's tender lament on the
Greek statue of the *Hermaphrodite* in "Hermaphroditus." Indeed, the
only "real" love in the otherwise "perverse" couplings of Wilde's *Dorian
Gray*—that of the artist Basil Hallward—is represented through allusions
to famous male artists who projected the Greek ideal on their beloved
boy models: "for it was really love," Wilde comments, "had nothing in it
that was not noble and intellectual. . . . It was such love as Michael Angelo
had known . . . and Winckelmann and Shakespeare himself." [50] Further,
Pater implicitly associated female beauty with the lesser beauty of nature,
and male beauty, exemplified by Greek statuary, with the homoerotic
male gaze at a more refined male beauty in a quote from Winckelmann,
"[To those who are observant of beauty only in women] . . . the beauty
of Greek art will ever seem wanting, because its supreme beauty is rather
male than female. But the beauty of art demands a higher sensibility than
the beauty of nature." [51]

Unlike her male contemporaries, H. D. appears to have frequently ma-

nipulated the Platonic male-male code of "statue love" to articulate female homoerotic desire, the equal relation between men and women,
and mother-daughter eros. Poems such as "Toward the Piraeus," which
reimagines H. D.'s relationships with her male mentors on a male-male
Greek continuum, reenact the Decadent Aesthetic "scene" of the homoerotic male gaze at Greek statuary. An apology to Pound for her
early chastity, "Toward the Piraeus" argues that if its female speaker
"had been a boy" she might have "worshipped" him, but as a woman
she feared sexual/creative obliteration—"you would have broken my
wings." [52] Purposefully assuming the boy-man eroticism of the Greek
ideal, H. D. fantasizes both male bodies as luminous spectacles/statuary
in alternating scenes of transgressive Aesthetic art/desire. Watching
male beauty is desire as the boy-H. D., "rent with an ecstasy," describes
how he would have "stood, / and watched and watched / and burned,"

> glad . . .
> to watch you turn
> your great head, set on the throat,
>
> . . . .
> burned and wrought like the olive stalk,
> and the noble chin
> and the throat.
>
> (*CP*, 178)

And by the same token, Pound as loving mentor, the speaker elaborates,
would have

> found my hands,
> beyond all the hands in the world,
> cold, cold, cold,
> intolerably cold and sweet.
>
> (*CP*, 179)

The metonymy of cool hands recalls the eroticism of the "chill" statue
while drawing on the popular synecdoche of white hands for the Decadent body (to be discussed shortly). Evoking the love between actual
brothers and the power of the (Greek) sculpted male body to surpass the
beauty of women in "Charioteer," H. D.'s speaker, a brother, "taut with
love, / more than any bright lover," mourns the loss of his charioteer
brother and vows to "fashion a statue / of him" "to embody this image;
an image to startle, / to capture men's hearts." [53] H. D.'s most overt debt

to the Aesthete's scene of transgressive desire occurs in a reference to H. D.'s lesbian narrator in *Paint It Today* as a "sister" of Charmides, the beautiful youth in Wilde's poem "Charmides" who falls in love with a statue. (Richard Ellmann argues that the mother-son eroticism between Charmides and his sculpted Artemis in Wilde's poems is actually a mask for male-male love.) Chapter 6 of H. D.'s *Paint It Today*, entitled "Sister of Charmides," puts a feminist spin on the Aesthetes' code of statue-love while acknowledging H. D.'s sister-brother bond with her Wildean precursor by designating Midget as a twin sister to Wilde's fair youth. H. D. is well aware of the homoerotic implications of this exchange: earlier, Midget had imaginatively become "a sister of Charmides" (or of Pater's Winckelmann) as she gazed at the *Venus de Milo* with eyes that longed to trace like fingers "the curve of the white belly and short space before the breasts brought the curve to a sudden shadow." But she "dared not" betray "the whitest passion" while in the company of the uncomprehending Basil (a type of H. D.'s husband Richard Aldington).[54] And in H. D.'s other homoerotic fictional autobiography, *HER*, Hermione's physical attraction to Fayne (based on H. D.'s woman lover, Frances Gregg) is conveyed in part through the "luminous" mask of marble boy statuary. As the women kiss, Hermione's aroused sensibilities recreate Fayne's approaching face in the image of Greek sculpture, "the mouth was straight," she fantasizes, ". . . marble lifted from marble and showed a boy" (*HER* 162–64).

Further, consciously erotic male-male poetic narrations of Aestheticism in Wilde, Swinburne, Pater, and others often inscribed the higher aesthetic / sexual appreciation for the boy androgyne through references to his whitely transparent skin (often of the hands) whose delicately veined tracery and blood-response—red, violet, and pulsing—can be seen beneath its surface translucence. The tracery of scarlet or violet venation on the white body is a familiar mark of the male or female Decadent body; however, at times, it functions as a metonymy for the Aesthete's fantasy of male romantic friendships in which the animate statue, a marble phantasmagoria of cool white boy statuary burns with the energies of the male-male continuum; creativity, life, eros, spirit, or intellect. Swinburne's ode to the boy-girl of "Fragoletta," for example, suggests an erotically charged, scarlet, and pulsing specter of the Greek ideal. Although "Fragoletta" may refer affectionately to a diminutive of the Italian *fràgola* (strawberry), the name also points to the luminous fragility of the boy's body, "I dreamed of strange lips yesterday," the male narrator extols, "And cheeks wherein the ambiguous blood was like a rose's—yea, / A rose's when it lay / Within the bud."[55] In a lesbian version of the Decadent body trope, Swinburne's Sappho ("Anactoria") dwells lovingly on her beloved's "flowerlike fingers . . . roseleaf colored shells / and blood with purple blossom at the tips / quivering."[56] And in Wilde's *The Picture of Dorian Gray*, Lord Henry's "cool, white, flower-like hands" that seem to "have a language of their own" gesture toward the finely tuned sensibilities of the "higher" love.[57]

H. D.'s "Hyacinth" in particular presents the Decadent synecdoche of diaphanous white, delicately veined hands for the body of male homo-erotic desire. As I have written elsewhere,[58] "Hyacinth" may be described as a revenge poem in which H. D. assumes the mask of the boy Hyacinth beloved by Apollo (who accidently slew him in a discus contest) to figure the spiritual twinship she believed she had shared with Richard Alding-ton before he abandoned her for the conventionally feminine, sexually vital Dorothy Yorke. Apollo, the speaker of the poem whom I have sug-gested is a type of Richard Aldington, contrasts the vulgar, scarlet eros of the femme fatale (a type of Dorothy Yorke) with the more spiritual and intellectual "white" desire of the slain boy Hyacinth (a type of H. D.). Apollo's confrontational address to the basely passionate, russet-haired siren is immediately followed by a wistful meditation on the red-veined glowing intricacies of Hyacinth's white hands:

> Your anger charms me,
> and yet all the time
> I think of chaste, slight hands,
> veined snow;
> snow craters filled
> with first wild-flowerlets;
> glow of ice-gentian,
> whitest violet;
> snow craters
> and the ice ridge
> spilling light;
> dawn and the lover
> chaste dawn leaves bereft—
> I think of these
> and snow-cooled Phyrgian wine.
>   (*CP*, 201)

Unlike the male modernist poetic of erotic and linguistic "consumma-tion," neither the loved body of Apollo's desire nor the body of the text is neatly bounded off by means of a single image/object. The passage's rapt cascade of differential images subjects both hands and text to rapid shifts and decenterings that resemble the above-mentioned description of Shelley's similar technique of spewing metaphoric surrogates for the beloved, giving "value no place to rest." The free play of an open-ended desire is further replicated by successive acts of permeation through transparency after transparency, which are themselves progressively deferred as the tightly contained binaries of "ice-gentian" or "whitest violet" spill over in the loosely joined chiasma, "ice ridge / spilling light"; or when transparency becomes absence in the penultimate "dawn and the lover / chaste dawn leaves bereft."

H. D. creates a similarly open space for androgyny in her novel *Hedylus* from the loosely formed transparencies or visual play occurring between mother/son erotic bodies. There the Oedipal son, Hedylus, is a specular white reflection of his mother, Hedyle: "uncanny in their likeness," Hedylus's face is "a live blue star reflected in a chill pool, a flaming red-lotus that sees its face pale and removed in a marble-oblong of fresh water." Together mother and son present a spectacle of "red" veined and "white" transparencies, exotic and "pale," "flaming" and "chill." Entranced, Hedyle murmurs to her son, "I don't believe any man begot you. There's no man in you." [59]

H. D.'s maternal erotic quest-romance, *Hippolytus Temporizes*, perhaps best exemplifies H. D.'s deployment of the sexually ambiguous "white" Aesthete androgyne or "crystalline youth" and the open sexual narrative of quest-romance and Decadent-Romantic mother-son twinning her contemporaries deplored.

Hippolytus Temporizes

Unintentionally recalling Eliot's chief example of Romantic excess, John Walsh's afterword to *Hippolytus Temporizes* describes H. D.'s Hippolytus as a version of Hamlet, pronouncing the play's ruling emotion to be "the madness of mother-obsession." [60] As I attempted to demonstrate above, male modernist theories of masking often rejected the slippery, unrequited maternal erotic narrative of the male androgyne. However, H. D.'s argument to her verse drama, *Hippolytus Temporizes*, indicates immediately that her attraction to Euripides' play lies in its fatal mother-son erotic pairings. H. D. asserts that the plots of *Hippolytus*—Phaedra's ill-conceived obsession for her beautiful stepson and Hippolytus's distant, Oedipal worship for the goddess Artemis—have gained the play legendary status as "the prototype of unrequited love for many centuries." "Hippolytus is his mother again," H. D. continues in the argument, "frozen lover of the forest which maintains personal form for him in the ever-present vision, yea, even the bodily presence of the goddess Artemis" (*Hipp. Temp.*, 7). In H. D.'s version of "the familiar story," therefore, Phaedra's famous sexual deception of Hippolytus in the guise of Artemis is secondary to Hippolytus's roving passion for the goddess-shade of his mother.

Unlike Eliot's interpretation of Hamlet or his own "Prufrock," H. D.'s modernist quest-romance does not perceive unrequited love as a symptom of emasculation or psychic collapse, but of the necessarily unrequited maternal eroticism that animates H. D.'s tale of female desire. Each character in the various mother-son twinnings of *Hippolytus Temporizes* searches for a mysterious "she" whose only identifiable trait is a maternal presence: Hippolytus longs for the elusive warrior goddess Artemis who hunted beside his dead mother, Hippolyta, and who has become "the mother," "the nearest," "a spirit even as she" (*Hipp. Temp.*, 29); Artemis reluctantly desires this beautiful boy-shade of her beloved warrior twin, Hippolyta; and even the "scarlet" Phaedra who would appear to be lusting only for a boy lover, actually perceives in Hippolytus the ghost of a lost female "sister."

H. D.'s transformation of Euripides' play into a maternal erotic quest-romance, unlike the masking narratives of Eliot and Yeats, seeks rather than repels symbiosis with the mother twin. The sexual embrace that lies at the center of the play's plot—Phaedra's elaborately contrived ruse to trick Hippolytus into sexual intimacy by posing as Artemis—becomes, by contrast, a striking emblem for the maternal eroticism that necessarily "exceeds" its object: the love requited or otherwise that is always already a ruse, a substitution, a replacement for the lost maternal presence. Far from a languishing narrative of frustrated desire, however, H. D.'s tale of the crystalline youth is a vital tracing of erotic stratagems. Both sides of the mother-son pairings are alternately agent and object of this sexual history in the making and the creators of an erotic presence (their own and that of the beloved's) spun from a mutual, ongoing quest to capture, affix, read one another. Indeed, H. D.'s *Hippolytus* is also a more interactive and female version of Shelley's Alastor-poet's search for the wood-spirit who flees him through the forest. Compelled separately by his/her love for the elusive "she," each character in *Hippolytus Temporizes* finds "her" and a former self momentarily in one another—a temporary stay against the belated desire that drives and forms them. Their union, sexual or otherwise, resembles Rich's definition of sexuality as "a diffuse and omnipresent energy," which H. D. evokes poetically as an effusion of the white phosphorescent body that is the height of an androgynous and sympathetic eros in Romantic/Victorian poetics.

Further, H. D.'s play finds a compelling source in Pater's "Hippolytus Veiled: A Study from Euripides." Like H. D.'s, Pater's Romantic mythology bears little resemblance to Euripides' tale of a hearty Hippolytus and his merry band of worshippers, but uses the Greek play to explore the intensity of the "crystalline" Hippolytus's fixation on Artemis's all-embracing maternity. Although Pater's Hippolytus possesses a service-able mother, he dedicates himself to the worshipful study of the goddess who is his "new mother," "his great mother," an eroticized presence that "glides through [his dreams] with abundance of salutary touches." [61] H. D. was probably directly influenced by Pater's androgynous depiction of the delicate youth and austere, statuesque Artemis. In H. D.'s play Artemis notes Hippolytus's "fragile and imperious length, / your pale set features / and your woman's grace." Hippolytus exalts at his first sight of Artemis, "O fair, like . . . / some rare young warrior / with his glitter-ing arms and spear" (*Hipp. Temp.*, 27, 13). Pater's Artemis and Hippoly-tus provide models for H. D.'s diaphanous pairings of "white" crystalline erotic bodies. In "Hippolytus Veiled," Hippolytus is a "crystal" youth, a "star flashing" and Artemis, the familiar crimson/white, hot/cold eros he gathers each dawn with the flowers of "purple and white frost" he places "against [her] ancient marbles [shrines]." [62]

The mother-son configuration of H. D.'s *Hippolytus Temporizes*, how-ever, further transforms Pater's masks for "forbidden" desire into a code for the mother-daughter bond. Like Wilde's "Charmides," Pater's "Hip-polytus Veiled" arguably encodes the Greek ideal of a boy-man mentor-ship in which the older man nurtures and educates the younger. While Pater's Phaedra is the type of the femme fatale, associated not only with "sickly perfumes" and gaudy attire, but also pejoratively linked with the heterosexual institutions of marriage and procreation, Artemis is the fatherless boy's appointed mentor—an austere and masculine figure whose sylvan ways he literally studies (he is a scholar of Artemisian lore) and strives to emulate. As Eileen Gregory observes, however, H. D.'s Hip-polytus "mirrors and bespeaks the female body." [63]

Sharon O'Brien suggests that possible interpretive strategies for determining when a male character comprises a female mask rather than an opposite sex character include "textual clues" that contradict the protagonist's assigned gender, such as the "over-identification" be-tween mother and son. [64] The Oedipal dyads of H. D.'s early work—Hedyle-Hedylus, Hippolyta-Hippolytus—are frequently spiritual and erotic twins, each projecting an androgynous mirror of the other. Cho-dorow's model of the prolonged Oedipal attachment between mother and daughter is discernible in Hedylus's (*Hedylus*) struggle to separate from the all-powerful mother who "encloses me as if I never were born." [65] Similarly, Hippolytus believes that his mother, Hippolyta, "lives in me," "her white soul lives in me" (*Hipp. Temp.*, 27).

Although the scope of this essay does not permit me to discuss *Hippoly-tus Temporizes* at length, I conclude with a close examination of H. D.'s proem to the play, Hippolytus's prefatory prayer, which Eileen Gregory lucidly locates as the moment when Hippolytus "temporizes," "in the aftermath of Hippolytus's lovemaking with one he assumes to be Artemis" in which "he prays to her and imagines he holds her, seeing her luminous bones beneath the flesh." Here, as Gregory observes, "love of the absent mother [is] inextricably associated with the "white" erotic body, which, I add, finds a source in Decadent-Romanticism.[66] In this highlighted scene of postcoital eroticism, Hippolytus's dream of the maternal white body does not differ from his earlier virginal quest, but serves as an appropriate preface to a tale of deferred desire in which sexuality is an "omnipresent energy" that is not entirely "of the body." Since desire for the mother is always already on the run, unrequited love (chastity) and sexual consummation are not in opposition, nor do they form a linear, progressive narrative, but give on to a sexual/textual chase of signifiers.

Even after he has, presumably, possessed his beloved, Hippolytus summons the white body of displacement, doubling and dissolving grounds that always elude him. The proem is worth quoting in full:

I worship the greatest first—
(it were sweet the couch,
the brighter ripple of cloth
over the dipped fleece;
The thought: her bones
under the flesh are white
as sand which along a beach
covers but keeps the print
of the crescent shapes beneath:
I thought:
between cloth and fleece,
so her body lies.)

I worship first the great—
(ah sweet, your eyes—
what God, invoked in Crete,
gave them the gift to part
as the Sidonian myrtle-flower
suddenly, wide and swart,
then swiftly,
the eye-lids having provoked our hearts—
as suddenly beat and close.)

I worship the feet, flawless,
that haunt the hills—

(ah sweet, dare I think,
beneath fetter of golden clasp,
of the rhythm, the fall and rise
of yours, carven, slight
beneath straps of gold that keep
their slender beauty caught,
like wings and bodies
of trapped birds.)

I worship the greatest first—
(suddenly into my brain—
the flash of sun on the snow,
the fringe of light and the drift,
the crest and the hill-shadow—
ah, surely now I forget,
ah, splendor, my goddess turns;
or was it the sudden heat,
beneath quivering of molten flesh,
of veins, purple as violets?)

(Hipp. Temp., 4–5)

Isolated as the proem to *Hippolytus Temporizes*, this open-ended quest-poem haltingly remembers the sexual embrace through a process of displacement and forgetting, articulating the height of desire, like Swinburne's "Fragoletta" or H. D.'s "Hyacinth," as an elusive visual trek through the transparencies of the eroticized body. The successive acts of forgetting, remembering and displacement thus shape Hippolytus's poem, which fades in and out from formal utterance to the associative dream of a white, vanishing body, and back again. The infinite regress of phosphorescent prints and erasure writes his ecstasy of sexual requital while replicating the chaste but desiring Hippolytus's search for a Hippolyta/Artemis through clues in the wooded landscape that will open the play.

In the proem, Hippolytus's gaze at the imagined "white" body sets a forbidden and infinitely deferred maternal eros in motion as he looks through and thereby illuminates its coverings only to experience further coverings. Traveling easily through fleece, cloth, white flesh, and the "print" of white bones under the coverlet, which like "sand" along a beach "covers" yet "keeps the print / of the crescent shapes beneath," Hippolytus engages in an ongoing search for the trace "of one long since forgotten," a conflation of his mother and Artemis.

In the proem's concluding stanza, the poem's already erratic glimmers of the white body are interrupted by a further loss of orientation and a heightened eros: "suddenly into my brain— / the flash of sun on the snow." This seizure or abrupt epistemological shift in which Hippolytus's dream of Artemis becomes shockingly vivid begins with distractions of white light. Sun reflects and deflects wildly off snow, the "dips," gaps, and opacities of "crest" and "hill-shadow," signaling a more profound obliteration than the associative shifts of before. The brain's sudden erasure—"Ah, surely now I forget"—is abruptly displaced by Hippolytus's almost painfully acute awareness of Artemis's physical presence—"my goddess turns"—which as suddenly becomes in Hippolytus's imagination the hallucination of the passionate and transparently veined Decadent body: "Or was it the sudden heat, / beneath quivering of molten flesh, / of veins, purple as violets?"

After the sexual deception occurs in the play itself, Phaedra's and Hippolytus's retellings of their night of passion do not differ significantly from the dream of the white body in the play's proem. Although Phaedra had formerly been designated as the vulgar, crimson femme fatale, she recounts her night of love by way of the phosphorescent trace emitting from the white body, seen, heard, and embraced:

O night, luminous with phosphorescence
and more bright
than day-star
climbing heaven's stair at noon.
>   (*Hipp. Temp.*, 81)

Hippolytus replies,

Lady,
I know your dream,
I feel your thought,

   . . . .
last night, I too, lay bathed in phosphorescence
like white dew

   . . . . . .
O her hands were cool.
>   (*Hipp. Temp.*, 93)

H. D.'s reference to "cool hands" recalls the body of homoerotic love in "Hyacinth." That Phaedra is in fact a fraud makes little difference. When the battered and nearly dead Hippolytus—object of his father's jealous wrath—in the final act at last encounters an embodiment of the "real" Artemis, he fails to recognize her. Her memory displaced by the Artemis-Phaedra-Hippolytus that gave him rest, Hippolytus longs for the Decadent detail that marked the eros of that night, the border of pink roses on the hem of Phaedra's white dress, which is absent from Artemis's more spare and severe attire.

Phaedra, perhaps, speaks most poignantly for H. D.'s female sexual narrative of an infinitely deferred maternal eroticism: wistfully correcting Hippolytus in the midst of rhapsodically lamenting the departure of the woman he believes to have been Artemis, she protests,

> say rather in some other arms,
> you'll feel her shape,
> that in some other form
> count her heartbeat.
> (*Hipp. Temp.*, 79)

H. D. never abandoned her Romantic philosophy of twinship, however in her later work she would drop the mask of the crystalline youth for the more passionate, abject body associated with the cult of the femme fatale. Although for both modernist women writers and Decadent Aesthetes alike, the vanishing body of the Greek male androgyne might have cleared a space for difference and erotic/linguistic play, the curiously hygienic male youth with his participation in discourses of purity and whiteness also exhibited the cultural somatophobia (misogynist or heterosexist) that denies sexually transgressive men and women writers a gendered, sexualized, affective, and interactive body.[67] From the thirties onward, in poems such as *Trilogy* and *Helen in Egypt*, H. D. would increasingly summon the power of the brazenly sexual, profuse, and horrific maternal body of the Pre-Raphaelite fatal woman.

Notes

1. *Manchester Guardian* (1931).
2. Douglas Bush, *Mythology and the Romantic Tradition in English Poetry* (London: Oxford University Press, 1937), 501–6.
3. Critics have attributed the ongoing debates about sexuality in literary modernism to such historical or social phenomena as the New Woman, Havelock Ellis's theories of female inversion, and Oscar Wilde's trials. See Sandra Gilbert and Susan Gubar's *No Man's Land: The Place of the Woman Writer in the Twentieth Century*, vol. 1, *The War of the Words* (New Haven, Conn.: Yale University Press, 1988), which describes a literary "battle of the sexes" originating from the proliferation of women writers, the New Woman and other phenomena. Esther Newton's "The

Mythic Mannish Lesbian: Radclyffe Hall and the New Woman," *Signs* 9 (1979): 178–203, considers the impact of Ellis's "Sexual Inversion in Women" in his *Studies in the Psychology of Sex*, 4 vols. (New York: Random House, 1941), 195–263. Eve Kosofsky Sedgwick's *Epistemology of the Closet* (Berkeley: University of California Press, 1990) first argued extensively that the twentieth-century crisis in homo/ heterosexual definition informing male literary modernism (among other discourses) was provoked by the Wilde trials.

4. Linda Dowling, *Hellenism and Homosexuality in Victorian Oxford* (Ithaca, N.Y.: Cornell University Press, 1994), 10.

5. H. D., "A Note on Poetry," *The Oxford Anthology of American Literature*, ed. William Rose Benet and Norman Holmes Pearson (Oxford: Oxford University Press, 1938), vol. 2, p. 1287.

6. H. D., *Asphodel*, ed. Robert Spoo (Durham, N.C.: Duke University Press, 1992), 53–54.

7. H. D., *Paint It Today*, ed. Cassandra Laity (New York: New York University Press, 1992), 12.

8. For important studies of Victorian Hellenism and the Platonic codes for homosexuality, see: Richard Jenkyns, *The Victorians and Ancient Greece* (Cambridge, Mass.: Harvard University Press, 1980); Richard Ellmann, *Oscar Wilde* (New York: Knopf, 1988); Richard Dellamora, *Masculine Desire: The Sexual Politics of Victorian Aestheticism* (Chapel Hill and London: North Carolina University Press, 1990); Linda Dowling, *Hellenism and Homosexuality in Victorian Oxford*; and Eve Kosofsky Sedgwick, *Between Men: English Literature and Male Homosocial Desire* (New York: Columbia University Press, 1985).

9. Quoted in Ellmann, *Oscar Wilde*, 29.

10. For a summary of the ways in which poets and philosophers equated Decadent-Romanticism with feminine or effeminate writing, see my essay, "H. D. and A. C. Swinburne: Decadence and Modernist Women's Writing," *Feminist Studies* 15, no. 3 (1989): 465–470.

11. Gail McDonald's *Learning to Be Modern: Pound, Eliot and the American University* (Oxford: Oxford Clarendon Press, 1993) argues that Eliot and Pound (and the American academy) fashioned a more virile image of the poet and poetry in response to the fall of the feminized gentry and the emerging culture of professionalism.

12. W. B. Yeats, *Autobiographies* (New York: Collier Books, 1965), 189.

13. Studies that examine H. D.'s maternal eros and aesthetics of twinship include Deborah Kelly Kloepfer, *The Unspeakable Mother: Forbidden Discourse in Jean Rhys and H. D.* (Ithaca, N.Y., and London: Cornell University Press, 1989); Susan Stanford Friedman, *Psyche Reborn: Reading H. D.* (Bloomington: Indiana University Press, 1981) and *Penelope's Web: Gender, Modernity, H. D.'s Fiction* (Cambridge: Cambridge University Press, 1990); Susan Stanford Friedman and Rachel Du-Plessis, "'I Had Two Loves Separate': The Sexualities of H. D.'s *HER*," repr. in *Signets: Reading H. D.*, ed. Susan Stanford Friedman and Rachel Blau Duplessis (Madison: University of Wisconsin Press, 1990); and Rachel Blau DuPlessis, "Romantic Thralldom and the 'Subtle Genealogies' in H. D." in *Writing Beyond the Ending: Narrative Strategies of Twentieth-Century Women Writers* (Bloomington: Indiana University Press, 1985).

14. At this writing there are very few scholarly examinations of gender and theories of male poetic modernism. Bonnie Kime Scott's edition *The Gender of Modernism: A Critical Anthology* (Bloomington: Indiana University Press, 1990) contains selections from Eliot and Pound and introductions by, respectively,

Nancy Gish and Ronald Bush, which consider the sexual politics of Eliot's doctrine of "impersonality" and Pound's attitude toward the feminine (139–43, 353–59). Shari Benstock briefly discusses the masculinist theory of language behind Pound's insistence on the image's correspondence between the word and its referent in *Women of the Left Bank* (Austin: Texas University Press, 1986), 327–31. My "H. D. and A. C. Swinburne" also discusses Pound's and Eliot's condemnation of Swinburne's evasive signification in their definitions of the image/object (469–70). Elizabeth Butler Cullingford's pathbreaking study of Yeats and gender in *Gender and History in Yeats's Love Poetry* (Boston: Cambridge University Press, 1993) is largely devoted to uncovering the feminist aspects of Yeats's poetics.

There are, however, several reassessments of the political implications (social, personal, linguistic) of the modernist poetics of impersonality formulated by Eliot and/or Pound. These include Lyndall Gordon's two literary biographies of Eliot, *Eliot's Early Years* (Oxford and New York: Oxford University Press, 1977) and *Eliot's New Life* (New York: Farrar, Straus, Giroux, 1988), Gail McDonald's *Learning to Be Modern*, Andrew Ross's *The Failure of Modernism: Symptoms of American Poetry* (New York: Columbia University Press, 1986), Louis Menand's *Discovering Modernism: T. S. Eliot and His Context* (New York: Oxford University Press, 1987), and Maud Ellmann's *The Poetics of Impersonality: T. S. Eliot and Ezra Pound* (Boston: Harvard University Press, 1987).

15. Hélène Cixous's "The Laugh of the Medusa" perhaps best summarizes the French feminist notion of women's writing, in *New French Feminisms*, ed. Elaine Marks and Isabelle de Courtivron (Amherst: University of Massachusetts Press, 1980).

16. McDonald, *Learning to Be Modern*, 82.

17. Ezra Pound, *Gaudier-Brzeska* (New York: New Directions, 1970), 85.

18. H. D., *HERmione* (New York: New Directions, 1981) (hereafter cited as *HER*).

19. H. D., *End to Torment: A Memoir of Ezra Pound*, ed. Norman Holmes Pearson and Michael King (New York: New Directions, 1979), 22, 23.

20. Ibid., 70.

21. McDonald, *Learning to Be Modern*, 24.

22. Ezra Pound, *Personae* (New York: New Directions, 1971), 202, 192.

23. In Scott, *The Gender of Modernism*, 353.

24. Ezra Pound, "Patria Mia," in *Selected Prose: 1909–1965*, ed. Norman Cookson (New York: New Directions, 1983), 119.

25. Wyndham Lewis, "Blast," *Blast*, no. 1 (1915): 18.

26. T. S. Eliot, "Reflections on Contemporary Poetry," *The Egoist* (July 1919): 39, 40.

27. Eve Sedgwick discusses her theory of "homosocial" desire in *Between Men*, whereby the scapegoating of women either as foul body or "gift" effects cultural and erotic bonds between men. Sedgwick derives her configuration from René Girard's literary theory of "mimetic desire" and the love triangle in *Deceit, Desire and the Novel: Self and Other in Literary Structure*, trans. Yvonne Freccero (Baltimore: Johns Hopkins University Press, 1981) and Gayle Rubin's anthropological exploration of the cultural "traffic in Women" in "The Traffic in Women: Notes Toward a Political Economy of Sex," in *Toward an Anthropology of Women*, ed. Rayna Reiter (New York: Monthly Review Press, 1975), 157–210.

28. T. S. Eliot, *The Use of Poetry and the Use of Criticism* (London: Faber and Faber, 1964), 33, 34. Emphasis mine.

29. In my "H. D. and A. C. Swinburne," 467.

30. Eliot, *The Use of Poetry*, 34.

31. T. S. Eliot, "Hamlet and His Problems," in *Selected Essays: 1917–1932* (New York: Harcourt Brace, 1932), 121–26. Subsequent references to this work are given parenthetically in the text.

32. In Scott, *The Gender of Modernism*, 141.

33. W. B. Yeats, *The Letters*, ed. Allen Wade (New York: Macmillan, 1955), 434.

34. Many critics agree that Yeats underwent a crisis in his sexual identity at the turn of the century that led him to dub his former Aestheticism as "effeminate" and to evolve a more "virile" conception of the poet and poetry. Richard Ellmann in *Yeats: The Man and the Masks* (New York: Norton, 1978), which first studied this shift as a critical turning point, attributes it largely to Maud Gonne's marriage. Most recently, Elizabeth Cullingford (*Gender and History*) revalues the early "feminine" phase, dismisses the manly "posturings" of his middle phase as provoked by his reading in Nietzsche, and discovers a third "feminine" phase at the end of Yeats's career when he became interested in lesbian women and the "woman in me."

35. W. B. Yeats, *Letters to the New Island*, ed. Horace Reynolds (Cambridge: Cambridge University Press, 1934), 147.

36. Quoted in George Bornstein's *Yeats and Shelley* (Chicago: University of Chicago Press, 1970), 142. *Idem*, 141.

37. W. B. Yeats, *Variorum Edition of the Plays*, ed. Russell Alspach (New York: Macmillan, 1966), 489.

38. William Ulmer, *Shelleyan Eros: The Rhetoric of Romantic Love* (Princeton, N.J.: Princeton University Press, 1990), 137–40.

39. T. S. Eliot, *To Criticize the Critic* (New York: Farrar, Straus, Giroux, 1965), 169, 170.

40. Ezra Pound, *Literary Essays of Ezra Pound*, ed. T. S. Eliot (New York: New Directions, 1935), 293, 294. T. S. Eliot, *Selected Essays*, 284.

41. W. B. Yeats: *A Vision* (New York: Collier Books, 1965), 129, 130.

42. Dellamora equates Victorian models of Platonic male-male desire with Rich's lesbian continuum (*Masculine Desire*, 196).

43. Adrienne Rich, "Compulsory Heterosexuality and Lesbian Existence," *Signs* 5, no. 4 (1980): 632.

44. Marilyn Farwell, "Toward a Definition of the Lesbian Literary Tradition," *Signs* (Autumn 1988): 117.

45. Sydney Janet Kaplan, *Katherine Mansfield and the Origins of Modernist Fiction* (Ithaca, N.Y., and London: Cornell University Press, 1991), 54, 39.

46. Barbara Guest, *HERself Defined: The Poet H. D. and Her World* (New York: Quill Press, 1984), 231.

47. Richard Jenkyns's *The Victorians and Ancient Greece* first began to uncover "the complex pattern of imagery," which includes whiteness, white light, and nude male statuary that Aesthetes such as Pater associated with Hellenic male homoeroticism. More recently, Richard Dellamora explores the codes and tropes of male-male transgressive desire in several Victorians. See particularly chapter 3 of *Masculine Desire*, "Pater at Oxford in 1864: Old Morality and *Diaphaneitè*" (58–68), which argues that Pater's discussion of his crystal or diaphanous male ideal in his essay "*Diaphaneitè*" anticipates his later homoerotic commentary on Winckelmann and Greek sculpture. Linda Dowling's essay "Ruskin's Pied Beauty and the Constitution of a 'Homosexual' Code," *Victorian Newsletter* (1989), discusses the term *poikilos* ("pied," "dappled") as part of the Aesthete's homosexual vo-

cabulary. She expands this discussion of Victorian "codes" in her recent book, *Hellenism and Homosexuality in Victorian Oxford.*

48. Oscar Wilde, *The Picture of Dorian Gray,* in *Complete Works,* ed. and intro. Vyvyan Holland (London and Glasgow: Collins Press, 1973), 41.

49. Walter Pater, *The Renaissance,* ed. Donald Hill (Berkeley: University of California Press, 1980), 177.

50. Wilde, *Dorian Gray,* 97.

51. Pater, *Renaissance,* 153.

52. H. D., *Collected Poems, 1912–1944,* ed. Louis L. Martz (New York: New Directions, 1983), 175–79 (hereafter cited as *CP*).

53. H. D., "Charioteer," in *CP,* 190–97.

54. H. D., *Paint It Today,* 60.

55. A. C. Swinburne, *Poems and Ballads,* first series (London: Chatto and Windus, 1914), 85–87.

56. *Ibid.,* 68.

57. Wilde, *Dorian Gray,* 31.

58. In "H. D.'s Romantic Landscapes: The Sexual Politics of the Garden," *Sagetrieb* 6, no. 2 (1987): 57–75.

59. H. D., *Hedylus* (Redding Ridge, Conn.: Black Swan Books, 1980), 31.

60. H. D., *Hippolytus Temporizes* (Boston: Houghton Mifflin, 1927), 144 (hereafter cited as *Hipp. Temp.*).

61. Walter Pater, "Hippolytus Veiled: A Study of Euripides" in *Greek Studies,* repr. in *Selected Writings,* ed. Harold Bloom (New York: Columbia University Press, 1974), 241–62.

62. Ibid., 255, 252.

63. Eileen Gregory, "Virginity and Erotic Liminality: H. D.'s *Hippolytus Temporizes,*" *Contemporary Literature* 31, no. 2 (1990): 141.

64. Sharon O'Brien, *Willa Cather: The Emerging Voice* (New York: Oxford University Press, 1987), 217.

65. H. D., *Hedylus,* 68.

66. Gregory, "Virginity and Erotic Liminality," 153.

67. Thus, as Thaïs Morgan demonstrates in her essay, "Male Lesbian Bodies: The Construction of Alternative Masculinities in Courbet, Baudelaire, and Swinburne," *Genders* 15 (1992): 37–57, the Decadents also gave body to male-male passion in the often violent, visceral songs of their lesbian femmes fatales ("Anactoria," "Faustine," etc.).

Chapter 4
Pornopoeia, the Modernist Canon, and the Cultural Capital of Sexual Literacy: The Case of H. D.

Dianne Chisholm

> But O, it goes further than that
> further than that;
> as I am swept away
>
> in the orgy of your poetry
> —H. D., "Grove of Academe"

The first premise of this essay is that H. D.'s poetry is pornographic,[1] and, more particularly, porno *poeic*. Her lyrics are charged with the incantatory charisma of offshore sirens, harbor whores, courtly hetaerae, frenzied bacchantes, Eleusianian initiates, Sapphic ecstatics, avatars of Aphrodite. It is to the elemental power of pornographic imagism that her meditations sing their highest praises. Speculating on the mythic genealogy of poetry in *Notes on Thought and Vision*, H. D. finds roots in the Greek epigrammatist Meleager, whose tendrils of genius draw their source, in turn, from the soiled, seaport slum of emigrant prostitutes: "What God of the Hebrew, what demon of the islands had presided at his ill-omened begetting? Heliodora, Zenophile, what were they but names? Greek prostitutes—branded by Syrian traders and Jew merchants alike. . . . Heliodora, Zenophile—no Attic hetairas."[2] Such thinking hardly conforms to a prevailing modernist adherence to Aristotle's *De generatione animalum*, its privileging of transcendental phallic form over the corruptible "demon" of chthonic matter. But for H. D.'s Meleager, prostitute material is the richest soil for the flowering of his "garland" of epigrams.[3]

Elsewhere in these *Notes*, H. D. argues more directly:

There is plenty of pornographic literature that is interesting and amusing.
If you cannot be entertained and instructed by Boccaccio, Rabelais, Montaigne, Sterne, Middleton, de Gourmont and de Régnier there is something wrong with you physically.
If you cannot read these people and enjoy them you are not ready for the first stage of initiation. (30)

According to H. D.'s *abc of reading*, initiation into cultural literacy and spiritual fulfillment begins physically with pornographic literature. Only when the mind has been sensitized to the ecstasies of a joyful body will it acquire the capacity for vision. Yet, rooted in the pornographic, these higher faculties never transcend the carnally elemental: drawing from sources in the body, the intellect illuminates the cosmic in an aura of sensual wisdom.[4] Such loose and sweeping pronouncements, resonating with aesthetic predilections more Decadent than classical, decree H. D.'s lifelong pursuit of a hybridized language we might more accurately tag as "porno-hermetic," a bodies-language, which sees the mind and the word as instrumental in raising the pornographic to the epiphanic in a sensual and sexualizing lyricism.

My second premise is that with this porno-hermetic language H. D. adopts a tactic of writing for distinction within the literary field—a tactic that contributes to the history of the struggle over what constitutes cultural and sexual literacy, but that escapes the recognition of institutions responsible for consecrating her inclusion in the modernist canon. In terms of cultural capital, H. D. has been awarded the distinction that goes with the canonization of modernist discourse and texts, including its hermetic "difficulty," the "paradox, irony, and ambiguity" of its decipherability as once practiced by New Critical pedagogy, and more recently its feminist difficulty, its rhetoric of gender troubling and "theorization" of sexual difference. But the metrical pulse, orgiastic intensity, violent affect, and visionary sadomasochism of her porno-, sometimes graphic, always hermetic, language exceed the criteria of poetic difficulty and gender troubling for which her writing has been valued as "modernist literature."

What do we make of the sexual excess to be found throughout H. D.'s writings from *Sea Garden* (1916) to *Hermetic Definition* (1960), in the earliest erotically animated poems where gender is missing; in the satyric dithyrambs of the middle period where "hymen" figures as orgiastic rupture exploding gender in a grotesque and inflammatory parody of the modern marriage rite; in the "becoming-woman" of Achilles and the sexual flowering of his myrmidons as they undergo a sea-change in the labile incantations of *Helen in Egypt*; in the hermeticism of the later period where the literary academy and the canon itself (personified by Saint-John Perse) are sexualized beyond recognition in the "Grove of Academe"? Once convinced of the pervasiveness of H. D.'s pornopoeia, how do we value it? And what prompted H. D. to value the pornographic so devotedly, if eccentrically, in the first place? What transvaluation of H. D. as cultural producer of modernist and feminist discourses ensues, if any?

My purpose is not to canonize a newer and sexier H. D., or conversely, to validate a noncanonical, unmarketably subversive H. D. Nor is it to "correct" modernist and feminist evaluations of her discourse with newly accredited queer ones. I propose to look beyond the canon and its continual reformation to the larger field of social struggle between agents of cultural production in which the canonization of poets is but a singular, mystifying instance. I understand H. D.'s literary aspirations as, in part, a bid for the legitimacy and authority to revitalize erotic language, and I locate her social agency not in the canon of the pedagogical imaginary but in the field of cultural production where she and her critical advocates must compete for the linguistic and symbolic capital that constitutes cultural and sexual literacy.

From where, what sector of the literary field, does H. D. find the encouragement in terms of cultural capital to pursue the production of "pornographic literature"? This question is especially compelling when considered in light of powerful antagonism from close quarters, including: Ezra Pound's injunction "NO Pornography,"[5] D. H. Lawrence's insistence on woman's sexual silence before man's superior eloquence, and T. S. Eliot's severely sublimated, devoutly desexualized *Definition of Culture.* Did she find alternative capital from feminist avant-gardes and lesbian bohemia? Not likely, since she shied away from the Parisian salons of Gertrude Stein and Natalie Barney, preferring asylum with (and without) Bryher in the Swiss Alps. It is even less probable that she found the necessary literary capital in her erotic liaisons with Frances Josepha Gregg or with Bryher herself, whose distinction could hardly compete with that of Pound, Lawrence, or Eliot.

Liberated from real economic burdens by support from the wealthy Bryher, H. D. was indeed free to authorize her literary autonomy and to expand her own idea of canonical literature. To the list of "Boccaccio, Rabelais, Montaigne, Sterne, Middleton, de Gourmont and de Régnier," she might have added those pornographic sources, A. C. Swinburne and Count Zinzendorf, to which she would ultimately be most indebted. But if a revitalized sexual language is her goal, why should she not work for the freedom of speech, elaborating a dialect of openness and frankness or democratizing sexual discursivity by writing and publishing in the erotic vernacular? In our attempt to understand the hermetic "difficulty" of H. D.'s sexual language, it is essential to identify those powers, not only legitimizing like those behind canonization, but also delegitimizing like those that administered the enforcement of the Postal Act ("Comstock Act") and the Publication of Obscenities Law, which censored the "obscene" writing of modernists and sexual activists in the late nineteenth and early twentieth centuries.

My third and final premise is that in cultivating her "pornopoeia" H. D. attempted a revolutionary symbolic act. To understand this radical element of her writing and sexual practice as a precursor to *écriture féminine*, gender trouble, or queer theory, we might ask how to value it for what it was worth in its day, and what it means to a history of sexuality that documents the formation of disciplinary discourse to the exclusion of "obscene" artistic language that contests and supplements (if not actually changes) the dominant form of sexual literacy. That is, how do we value H. D.'s efforts to sexualize, eroticize, pornographize, behind a mask of hermeticism, the most prized institutions of Western culture: maternity, masculinity, Christianity, the academy, and literacy itself?

H. D.'s Pornopoeia

I adapt the term "pornopoeia" from the nomenclature Pound uses to categorize poetry in general and to review the poetry of Marianne Moore and Mina Loy in particular. Poetry, he says, can be categorized into three sorts: melopoeia ("poetry which moves by its music"), imagism or phanopoeia ("certain men move in phantasmagoria"), and logopoeia ("a dance of the intelligence among words and ideas." [6] With these categories, he proceeds to judge the poets according to their versatility in all three: Pope and the eighteenth-century writers were "limited" in their use of this medium, whereas Browning, Laforgue, and T. S. Eliot have made the widest possible use. Moore and Loy, however, are excessively limited: they write only logopoeia.

Pound either refrained or neglected to review H. D.'s poetry in such explicit categorical terms; but he promised her "imagism" as exemplary material for a new avant-garde aesthetics. Certainly in the first book of poems, *Sea Garden* (1916), the accent falls less heavily on logopoeia than on phanopoeia, which Pound describes more fully as "poetry wherein the feelings of painting and sculpture are predominant (certain men move in phantasmagoria; the images of their gods, whole countrysides, stretches of his land and forest, travel with them)." [7] "Pornopoeia," however, might best describe that obscene lyrical intensity that casts and shatters the image in sensual excess.

Reading *Sea Garden* might be likened to taking "the first step in the Eleusinian mysteries" toward elemental sensualization, which in modern contexts can only be simulated by "walking through the pornographic chamber at the museum at Naples" (H. D., *Notes*, 29). But the images figured in this "chamber" are orgiastic *sans* ritual, less representational than expressive. Spray-born sea plants and swelling fruiting bodies do not allegorize human sexual organs or reproductive relations so much as animate a brute feeling of sexual potency in tense and voluptuous images of kaleidoscopic lust and wildly oscillating passion.

Genderless part-bodies populate these poems with splitting membranes, battered flesh, and fermenting sap; fluid and rigid bodies couple with elemental earth (sea, fire, wind), the fertile medium of desire; fleshly or stony vegetable bodies are beaten, lacerated, and whipped into an orgy of sensual intensity; bodies disemboweled, beheaded, and impaled are swept away in disfiguring vertiginous intoxication; all bodily commotion and emotion is orchestrated to the dissonant and accelerating drumbeats of single syllables. Unless singularly devoted to the interpretive techniques of New Criticism, psychoanalysis, or gender analysis, the reader might feel exposed to and affected by the eroticizing mysteries of an incantatory superpositioning of corporeal images.

The poems that move me most include "Sea Lily," whose "great heads," "reed," "myrtle bark," "scales," "stem," and "petal" are tortured into vivid animation by such violently stimulating actions as slashing and turning, shattering, dashing, cutting, furrowing, and lifting.[8] "Sheltered Garden" personifies an eroticism unbound by conventional (gardened) beauty and prudish (sheltered) domesticity: "I have had enough- / border-pinks, clove-pinks, wax-lilies, / herbs, sweet-cress," the lyrical subject protests, gasping for a scent of a sublime "wind-tortured place" beyond "border on border of scented pinks" (*CP*, 19–20). What is particularly striking about this desire, and what distinguishes it from the sublime agonism and/or nihilism of Romanticism,[9] is its "sadism":

I want wind to break,
scatter these pink-stalks,
snap off their spiced heads,
fling them about with dead leaves—
spread the paths with twigs,
limbs broken off,
trail great pine branches,
hurled from some far wood
right across the melon-patch,
break pear and quince—
leave half-trees, torn, twisted . . .

(*CP*, 19–20)

As is often the case with Imagist poetry, the poems of "Sheltered Garden" have been read allegorically. But I am persuaded by *Notes on Thought and Vision* to read them as expressions of an unidentifiable eroticism whose voluptuous obscenity recalls Meleager's epigrams. If there is an allegory here, it is tortured and twisted like its literal content of flowering bodies. It is a peculiarly perverse Isis, who, as the "I" of the poem, invokes a titan-cyclone to break and scatter the limbs of Osiris, the vegetal god whose modernist domestication fails to fertilize her imagination.[10] Like the "pornographic chamber" of Eleusis, the sea garden's "terrible, wind-tortured place" envelops the senses in elemental feeling and initiates the soul in ecstatic mysteries.

"Orchard" (originally "Priapus") figures fruiting bodies in grotesque, overripe excess ("fallen hazel-nuts," "pomegranates already broken," "grapes, red-purple / their berries / dripping with wine," "shrunken figs") that seduce us into savoring fecundity's fleeting transience, corruptible materiality, and intoxicating degeneracy more than the flowering of beauty or fruitfulness itself ("spare us from loveliness") (*CP*, 29). "Sea Rose" also brings us down to earth, where eros not only flowers and fruits but also seeds, roots, wilts, ferments, drips, hardens, and petrifies. The sea rose is a "harsh," "marred," "meagre," "thin," "sparse," "stunted," "hardened," "acrid" borderline bloom, which rises not to the touch of the sun but to the grating caress of "crisp sand" compelled by the turbulent "drives" of off-shore winds (*CP*, 5).

H. D.'s *Sea Garden* not only imitates and exaggerates Meleager's *Garland* but also conflates it with Baudelaire's *Fleurs du mal* and anticipates Bataille's "Language of Flowers" in its predilection for the grotesque and obscene. H. D.'s flowers figure morphological flux and upheaval rather than formal perfection; they are voluptuously earthy and contrarily carnal, hence unbeautiful: at once, prickly and soft, static and vertiginous, strong and vulnerable, broken and mobile, bruised and luscious, sterile and overripe, harshly frigid and dripping wet. The paradoxical language of flowers is a transgressive medium, hyperbolizing the sensuality of decomposition in an attempt to free desire from aesthetic idealism. To quote Bataille:

desire has nothing to do with ideal beauty, or, more precisely, that it only arises in order to stain and with the beauty that for many sad and well-ordered personalities is only a limit, a *categorical imperative.* The most admirable flower for that reason would not be represented, following the verbiage of old poets, as the faded expression of an angelic ideal, but, on the contrary, as a filthy and glaring sacrilege.[11]

As if in philosophical agreement, H. D. writes: "Flowers are made to seduce the senses: fragrance, form, colour. If you cannot be seduced by beauty, you cannot learn the wisdom of ugliness" (*Notes*, 32).

After *Sea Garden,* H. D.'s flowering eros puts on the masks of mythic personae: but this shift to the Apollonian does not subdue their Dionysian or "satyric"[12] potency. The language of flowers prevails, becoming arguably more pornographic as desire acquires a human form. Her deities are frequently draped in the color of fleshly passion and fructifying desire.

For instance, in "The God," the poem that first greets the reader in the book of poems collected under that title, the marble visage of the deity is too sculptured, too aesthetically remote, "far distant from my sense." But, under the bacchante's lingering gaze, his stony stasis becomes animated presence, his ebony solidity flushes with florid color, as "the god" becomes the wine-god, as his idealism becomes Dionysian. Earthbound, he draws rootlike upon the essence of fertile life, bathing his beholder in an aura of intoxicating

cyclamen-purple,
cyclamen-red, colour of the last grapes,
colour of the purple of the flowers
cyclamen-coloured and dark
(*CP*, 47)

Since, according to H. D.'s *Notes,* these are the colors that decorate the "pornographic chamber" of the lower stage of the Mysteries ("there were images set up in a great room, coloured marbles and brown pottery, painted with red and vermilion and coloured earthen work or clay images" [29]), we can guess we are back in "Eleusis."

H. D. also locates "Eurydice" in this pornographic chamber, where the reader is positioned to witness the mysterious transcendence of desire from its infernal exile in hapless romance. The poem's final stanzas mark the beginning of Eurydice's first step toward Eleusinian enlightenment. In these stanzas, Eurydice finds herself in the deepest layer of hell, possessing nothing but "the flowers of myself," "the fervour of myself for a presence" and "my own spirit for light" (*CP*, 55).

The rest of the poem testifies to the infernal ordeals of romantic love or "thralldom,"[13] protesting in particular, the sexual politics of the look, or "specularization" to use Irigaray's term to describe speculative, self-projecting, practices of patriarchal colonization:

what was it you saw in my face?
the light of your own face,
the fire of your own presence? . . . So for your arrogance
and your ruthlessness

> I have lost the earth
> and the flowers of the earth
> and the live souls above the earth.

> (*CP*, 52–53)

Although the sexual imperialism to which Eurydice feels subjected is harrowingly triumphant, and although she struggles to express her deepening sense of betrayal in a redemptive language of flowers, it is not mystery but agony that finds its voice here. Eurydice anguishes over the effacement of her desire in light of the self-illuminating gaze that her lover casts upon her. Assuming a masculine position of subjective domination in the battle for recognition in love, Orpheus banishes her to abject anonymity. The desire she denounces she cannot redeem by eroticizing. As her speech becomes self-consciously despairing, Eurydice gathers the emotional momentum to enter another realm of eroticism. This is the realm of "thought and vision" where a darkening lust excavates and eclipses Orpheus's solar will to power. Part VI and VII of "Eurydice" deterritorializes and pornographizes the spirit of romance.

> Against the black
> I have more fervour
> than you in all the splendour of that place . . .
> and the flowers,
> if I should tell you,
> you would turn from your own fit paths
> toward hell,
> turn again and glance back
> and I would sink into a place
> even more terrible than this.

> (*CP*, 54–55)

Retreating to the abysmal depths of hell, where her "fervour" burns without Orpheus's light of troubadorial self-glory, Eurydice declares erotic sovereignty. "At least I have the flowers of myself, / . . . I have the fervour of myself for a presence" (55). Beyond this emotional and libidinal threshold, romantic love has never ventured, and so here, at the far edge of psychic and poetic being, she stakes her survival in boundless, furious passion. Should the spectral dead of her denounced erotic past attempt to enter this new imaginary space, the gates of hell must break open, like the lips/petals/flames of a fiery, incinerating vulva:

my spirit with its loss
knows this;
though small against the black,
small against the formless rocks,
hell must break before I am lost;

before I am lost,
hell must open like a red rose
for the dead to pass.

(*CP*, 55)

Primal erotic self-affirmation must displace and defeat the sophisticated despotism of romance: if not itself an elusive (Eleusinian) manifesto, this poem should be read in the context of such contemporary productions as Valentine de Saint-Point's "Manifesto of Lust" (1913) and Mina Loy's "Feminist Manifesto" (ca. 1914). These manifestos call for the cultivation of lust as "the carnal quest of the unknown," [14] as well as the destruction of romanticism and, in particular, for woman's destruction of her desire to be loved.[15]

While H. D.'s struggle with thralldom does not end with "Eurydice," she continues to foreground pornopoeia as a counterpractice to romantic or troubadorial lovemaking. The title piece of *Hymen* (1921) presents a sexual initiation rite for modern times, sharing with Edith Sitwell's *Façade* (1922) a bacchanalian accent on the bucolic, the satyric, and the obscene. The lyrical, musical, and dramatic elements of "Hymen" are choreographed with melodramatic excess and voluptuous hyperbole. Throughout the procession of vestal virgins, flower girls, wood nymphs, and amazons, maids of honor, the "hymen" appears center-stage as a "curtain" of fleshly anticipation: "the curtain—a dark purple hung between Ionic columns—of the porch or open hall of a palace" (*CP*, 101). "Love" enters as a supplicating eros with flaming hair and "wings, deep red or purple," bearing "black-purple cyclamen" (108) and singing laurels to hymen's immanent ru/apture:

The crimson cover of her bed
Is not so rich, nor so deeply bled
The purple-fish that dyed it red,
As when in a hot sheltered glen
There flowered these stalks of clyclamen . . .

> Crimson, with honey-seeking lips,
> The sun lies hot across his back,
> The gold is flecked across his wings.
> Quivering he sways and quivering clings
> (Ah, rare her shoulders drawing back!)
> One moment, then the plunderer slips
> Between the purple flower-lips.
>
> (*CP*, 108–9)

With that, " *love passes out with a crash of symbols. There is a momentary pause and the music falls into its calm, wave-like rhythm* " (109). Sexuality in this ceremony is neither gendered nor propertied; desire is processional but the climax does not end in marriage in any territorial sense. Ecstatic, not phallic, "Hymen" celebrates the colors, aromas, arias, motions, commotions of orgiastic capability: the "plundered" shares with the "plunderer" the crescendo of vibrating lips, scattered light, rapture of rupture.

There are passages throughout *Hymen* and *Heliodora* (1924) that radiate with pornopoeia, particularly the sapphic fragments: "shall I turn and slake / all the wild longing? / . . . So shall I take you?" ("Fragment Thirty-Six," *CP*, 166); to sing love, / love must first shatter us" ("Fragment Forty," *CP*, 175);

> . . . though my flesh is scorched and rent,
> shattered, cut apart,
> slashed open;
> though my heels press my own wet life
> black, dark to purple,
> on the smooth, rose-streaked
> threshold of her pavement.
>
> ("Fragment Forty-One," *CP*, 182)

After H. D.'s analysis with Freud in 1933–34, however, the cue to narrate autobiographical investigations subdued her pornographic eloquence. There are moments in *Helen in Egypt* when her obsessional tracking of Egyptian and Olympian family romance gives way to pornopoeia, where epic narration breaks into ecstatic lyricism, foregrounding a language of flowers reminiscent of the *Sea Garden* poems. But only for a moment, and the strain of transition is reflected in the overdetermination of symbols: for instance, where Achilles' orgiastic dismemberment before Helen on the Trojan battlefield figures interchangeably with Isis's scattering of the limbs of Osiris, or where the flowering of the multipetaled Egyptian sea-lotus figures interchangeably with the dissemination of Achilles' Myrmidons across the water in their many battle ships. All of these moments are quickly reterritorialized by the poet's impulse to genealogize, to ground her roots in a lineage of hermetic distinction among the pharaohs, prophets, scribes, and muses of Egypt.

Yet, H. D.'s pornopoeia continued to star or stain her writing, even the most hermetic, until the end of her career. Most remarkable is that she would award particular prominence to the pornographic in "Grove of Academe," Part 2 of *Hermetic Definition,* which she composed after receiving the gold medal for poetry from the American Academy of Arts and Letters. On this occasion she met the widely famed French poet, Saint-John Perse, to whose poetry she pays tribute in the lines at the head of this article:

> But O, it goes further than that
> further than that
> as I am swept away
> in the orgy of your poetry.[16]

And she does indeed take it further than *that,* sexualizing not only his poetry, but also his person, through the mediation of her/their muse:

> I touch his head and his throat
> where your hands have fondled him,
>
> my hands run along his proud length,
> filled with milk from your cup
> and honey from your rocks . . .
> (*HD,* 34)

This is not just the displaced and fantastical desire of an aging hermetic pornographer; in these and surrounding passages, we can read the wider, institutional context of H. D.'s pornopoeia. Acutely aware of her location in academe (not a comfortable one: she failed or dropped out of literary studies at Bryn Mawr) and shy of Saint-John Perse's intellect, she regards him nonetheless with the highest possible esteem. What she desires from him is his recognition, not for that with which she cannot compete ("I do not compete with your vast concept") but for that in which she feels she excels—pornopoeia, an unacademic poetics of ecstasy, mysterious lusts, and desires. What she recognizes in him, where he touches her, in turn, is "the orgy of [his] poetry." There is a place for competition after all:

> . . . you draw me out
> to compete with your frenzy;
> there are other roses . . .
>
> I am alive in your recognition.
> (*HD*, 33)

Saint-John Perse too knows the flowers, the fervor. There are other roses; but she takes the laurel for recognizing and fondling the divinity in him, the deity of creative libido, who, in this case, is Athené Hygeia because there is "healing" as well as "ecstasy" (*HD*, 33) in this grove. Clearly it is not the Academy's recognition, nor Saint-John Perse's academic reputation, that H. D. values; her poetry may be worth its weight in gold, but only the poet who shares her desire and solicits her gods can award her consecration. Ultimately she finds consecration in the verse she quotes from Saint-John Perse's *Anabase*, wherein she savors the essence of her own verse, feeling hailed by the eros embodied in a fellow poet:

> surely he speaks to me,
> *toute parfumée*—your *mélisse?*
> it is you he incorporates,
> and his speech is the poet's speech,
> *j'aviverai du sel*
> *les bouches mortes du désir.*
> (*HD*, 34)

She waives all academic credentials aside in her canonization of the erotic poet, but how? Why? Do the academy and the poet agree on the value of pornopoeia, and if not, what account can we make of the discrepancy?

Cultural Capital and the Canonization of H. D.

The poet in H. D.'s "Grove of Academe" reflects a form of mystification specific to the autonomous literary agent that Pierre Bourdieu's notion of "cultural capital" goes a long way in helping to explain. What then remains to be understood is the mystique in which academia itself cloaks H. D.; can her "emergence" as a major writer be attributed simply to ideological pressures to revise the canon, as if the social and cultural transvaluation of values is mobilized directly by achieving minority representation in the field of literary reproduction?

The hermetic and erotic aura with which H. D. casts academia and Saint-John Perse can be explained by how she locates herself in the "field of literary production" and how she judges her capacity to compete for literary distinction or cultural legitimacy. According to Bourdieu, the literary world comprises a "field" that is

neither a vague social background nor even a *milieu artistique* like a universe of personal relations between artists and writers (perspectives adopted by those who study "influences"). It is a veritable social universe where, in accordance with its particular laws, there accumulates a particular form of capital and where relations of force of a particular type are exerted.[17]

Bourdieu stresses that the literary field is a "separate social universe" with "laws of functioning independent of those of politics and the economy" (164), whose historical development toward autonomy began in quattrocento Florence (113) and culminated in nineteenth-century Paris with the "art for art's sake" school of cultural production.

One of the principle struggles of the literary field, according to Bourdieu, concerns "the question of knowing who is part of the universe, who is a real writer and who is not" (164). Writerly distinction derives not simply from the quality of the literary product but more specifically from the legitimacy awarded the literary producer who then sets the value of literary production.[18] It is not surprising that H. D. should honor above all the poet in recasting the academy awards ceremony; in Saint-John Perse, she recognizes the writer as the "*creator* of value" (Bourdieu, 164) and uncontested judge from whom alone she accepts distinction:

I read of initiations, adepts, neophites,
masters and imperators,
but this isn't it,

nor angels' names, nor right or wrong,
nor intricate *sentiers* or paths,
it's that you write,

even that I have written; . . .

it wasn't that I was accepted
by the State, the Office, the Assembly,
but by you . . .

(*HD*, 24)

But whereas Bourdieu understands the writer to be "the end of a collective enterprize," a historical invention whose existence "as a fact and
as a value, is inseparable from the existence of the literary field as an
autonomous universe endowed with specific principles of evaluation of
practices and works" (162–64), H. D. envisions an autonomous *being*
whose "pre-occupation with stylus and pen" (*HD*, 26) derives ultimately
from the Egyptian demigod Thoth.[19] Why should H. D. honor the writer
and discredit the academy? Because she locates herself at that pole of the
literary field where the value of art, its cultural capital, is strictly artistic,
as established by artists alone and by "gifted" artists whose genius is self-
evident and beyond institutional recognition.

Bourdieu explains that, while the literary field is a separate social field,
it does not occupy a social vacuum; it is located in the larger field of
power of economic and political relations, which in turn occupies the
field of class relations. The bourgeois middle class dominates the late
nineteenth and early twentieth century's fields of class relations and economic power, so that within the field of literary and cultural production,
even the most autonomous artistic agents are politically and economically *dominated*, even though they participate in the domination of culture at large. All agents competing for the cultural capital of artistic
distinction must exploit a position of relative freedom between the poles
of autonomy and heteronomy that define the field.

A hermetic modernist and disciple of Mallarmé, H. D. is disposed to
occupying that place in the field to which Bourdieu assigns the Symbol-
ists, namely "the most perfectly autonomous sector of the field of cultural production, where the only audience aimed at is other producers"
and where "the economy of practices is based . . . on a systematic inversion of the fundamental principles of all ordinary economies: that of
business (it excludes profit . . .), that of power (it condemns honours
and temporal greatness), *and even that of institutionalized cultural authority
(the absence of any academic training or consecration may be considered a virtue)*" (39, emphasis added). Although H. D. is perfectly aware that it is
the Academy of Arts and Letters that has awarded her the gold medal for
poetry and that an assembly of critics and teachers, as well as writers, have
gathered in support of that recognition, as an autonomous cultural
agent she receives consecration only from the poet. She acts on faith—
not good faith, perhaps—but with the form of belief specific to her po-

sition in the literary field.[20] Hermeticism is particularly serviceable to literary agents who value their writing on faith that it will be valued independently of heteronomous (market) principles that, according to Bourdieu, dominate the field of power (72–73).

Bourdieu might help explain why H. D. hermeticizes the academy as the "Grove of Academe," but why does she eroticize Saint-John Perse as an orgiastic poet? Why does she choose pornopoeia as a medium and style with which to "compete" (to use her word) for artistic recognition? Perhaps because she perceives pornopoeia to be her special "gift," meaning, in terms of cultural capital, a unique contribution to the market of symbolic goods that distinguishes her writing from other literary agents, even other hermetic modernists like Saint-John Perse, while deserving comparable, transcendental distinction.

As Bourdieu advises, to know the work of any writer, it is "absolutely crucial" that we take into consideration their "structurally contradictory position" (164) as autonomous artistic agents in a largely heteronomous, market-driven, and state-organized society. H. D. may write in the belief that her artistic legitimacy derives from her gender authority, her Moravian ancestry, her muse/divinity, or from visionary sources extracted from experimental sex, but she is awarded cultural capital according to the rules of consecration instituted and administered by legitimate social and institutional agencies, including the academy.

She has a stake in denying this: First, as a twentieth-century disciple of the late nineteenth-century "art for art's sake" schools of (hermetic) Symbolism and (fleshly) Decadence, H. D. was disposed to producing the form of writing that merited no other distinction than "pure art." She wrote "pornographic literature," not as a commercial venture on the side of more serious writing, as did Anaïs Nin, but as a form of "pure art," which, "like pure love," to quote Bourdieu, "is not made to be consumed" (169). Second, she shares with Pound a disposition toward well-rounded poetry, surpassing him in her taste for the categories of enchantment—melopoeia and phanopoeia—to which pornopoeia is added; she privileges these categories at the expense of logopoeia, whose "arid clarity" in the writings of Moore and Loy, Pound had mockingly credited as having the merit of American "graduates or post-graduates."[21]

If we were to follow Bourdieu in an attempt to understand "the emergence of H. D." as a writer, we must ask "not how a writer comes to be what he is, in a sort of genetic psycho-sociology, but rather how the position or 'post' he occupies—that of a writer of a particular type—became constituted" (162). Moreover, we must ask what institutional investments are at stake in the canonization of H. D. as a modernist and particularly as a modernist who has received the recognition of late twentieth-century academic feminism. Bourdieu's sociological advice does not call into question biographical scholarship such as Susan Stanford Friedman's *Psyche Reborn: The Emergence of H. D.* (1981), the first major critical study of H. D. that championed the way for future studies, but it does call for a shift in attention from the self-making of the writer to the writer's cultural economy, to the fields of cultural production, reproduction, and consecration.

It is a more radical shift than the one made by Rachel Blau DuPlessis in *H. D.: The Career of That Struggle* (1986), even though DuPlessis writes at the cutting edge of feminist criticism, directing new understanding toward "the formation of a woman writer and her writing career" with analyses of those "'conceptual' and 'linguistic' acts" which prepare her for "actual literary production" and "seal" her literary success.[22] DuPlessis approaches the writer in terms of her bid for cultural legitimacy and with remarkable astuteness charts H. D.'s contradictory and changing dispositions over the course of her "career." But having confined her study to the field of restricted production, she limits her understanding of how the writer's tactical positions are constituted to "authoritative" acts of writing itself.

But neither the author nor the canon nor even "those particular authors who happen to be canonical" play a major role in this system of reproduction; as John Guillory instructively suggests, "the far larger role belongs to the school itself, which regulates access to literary production by regulating access to literacy, to the practices of reading and writing."[23] The school's primary means of (re)production is the literary syllabus through which, Guillory says, two forms of cultural capital are constituted: "first, it is *linguistic* capital, the means by which one attains to a socially credentialed and therefore valued speech, otherwise known as 'Standard English.' And second, it is *symbolic* capital, a kind of knowledge-capital whose possession can be displayed upon request and which thereby entitles its possessor to the cultural and material rewards of the well-educated person" (ix).

Together, these two forms of capital constitute the social meaning of "literacy." "Literary language" is not an aesthetic category, Guillory suggests, but a category marking socially differentiated speech (66); it incorporates a linguistic difference by which the upper classes have historically marked their cultural distinction.[24] The "canon," Guillory says, has always functioned in the schools as a pedagogic device for producing an effect of linguistic distinction (62). Authors themselves do not produce the effect of linguistic differentiation, according to Guillory, but they "confront a monumentalized textual tradition already immersed as speakers and writers in the social condition of linguistic stratifaction that betrays at every level the struggle among social groups over the resources of language, over cultural capital in its linguistic form" (63). For instance, in spite of Pound's efforts to authorize a canon of his own,[25] Pound himself was eventually canonized and hence neutralized by the academy (though not "until the early seventies"[26]).

H. D.'s inclusion in the canon marks the outcome of a shift in the constitution of "literacy" in society at large; canon reformation is due less to the ideological campaigns of activist scholars than to the domination of university by a new class of professional managers who oversee the restructuring of the syllabus to accommodate the demand for graduates who are "literate" in the prevailing form of social currency. According to Guillory, "Canons of texts belong to the *durée* of the school as both an objectification of tradition and as a list of texts (syllabus, curriculum) continuously changing in response to the frictional relations between institutional and social reproduction" (59).

H. D.'s canonization as a modernist reflects in the first place the cultural capital of New Criticism, whose graduate school syllabus prevailed, for a duration in the fifties and sixties, as the primary access to what was then the most prized form of cultural literacy—"literary language." Distinguished by the "difficulty" of its canon of modernist texts and by its ordination of a secular class of "priests" to decode and disseminate the "paradox, irony, and ambiguity" of the hieratic knowledge inscribed there, this particular school of interpretation was in position to exploit the advantage of being recognizable in the larger technobureaucratic world as marketably "technical." H. D.'s further canonization as a feminist modernist/postmodernist reflects the academy's domination by, in Guillory's words, a "newly constituted professional-management class, no longer exclusively male or white" (38) and its ordination of a theory syllabus that privileges deconstructive "theory," reflecting a continuing demand for highly technical "rigour," and a cultural studies syllabus to accommodate proliferating numbers of "sociolects" (80), including "women's writing," which has fractured and displaced the "literary language" of the older New Critical syllabus as the dominant form of cultural literacy.

Bourdieu and Guillory help explain the mystery of H. D.'s "success," which Meryl Altman recently assessed in the terms of its marketable reproduction. "Her books are in print: even some material she was unable to, or chose not to, publish during her lifetime is available or forthcoming, and one can buy a comprehensive *Collected Poems* in paperback. Even undergraduates know who she is."[27] Surveying a new list of critical studies on H. D.,[28] Altman is willing to attribute this success to feminism at work in the academy but is troubled and mystified at H. D.'s appropriation by the feminist agenda.

As Altman reviews it, the "case of H. D." exposes the growing concern of feminist critics to reflect the image of feminist criticism itself: that is, its current obsessions with biography, which privilege H. D.'s fiction over poetry, and with postmodernity, which argue anachronistically for a futurist H. D. who "anticipates" the strategies of *écriture féminine*. But beyond feminism's pedagogical imaginary, we can see that this critical focus derives in part from the larger concerns of the university academy to remain competitive in the socioeconomic world. The "H. D." of academic feminism reflects its current investment in those discourses that have the linguistic and symbolic capital to constitute today's form of cultural literacy—as established by the outcome of (mostly unconscious) negotiations between institutional and social reproduction.

Altman is particularly concerned to call into question the *sexual* agenda of feminist criticism, which, she says, persistently misrecognizes H. D.'s writing as an instance of "gynopoetics" and her sexuality, however queer and esoteric, as decidedly "maternal" (39). What "gynocritics" read as H. D.'s Eleusinian "exaltation of the mother goddess," Altman reads as the "validat[ion]" of "sexual ecstasy as religious and aesthetic experience" (39). The critical issue here is not about the true meaning of Eleusinian sexuality but about the role the academy plays in "the legitimate exercise of symbolic violence";[29] the legitimization of one form of sexuality, or of several forms (lesbian, bi, pre-Oedipal) under the rubric of one ("maternal"),[30] serves at the same time to delegitimize or prevent the legitimization of others ("sexual ecstasy").

But the matri- and bisexuality that H. D.'s feminist critics privilege on their agenda do not represent their own ideological predilections so much as the strategy of the institution, which is not the direct expression of any "university community" but an issue for constant renegotiation with the norms and powers that safeguard social reproduction. The sexualities of academic feminism are not sexualities, in the sense that they might refer to sexual practices, sexual pleasures, sexual bodies, sexy languages, *ars erotica*, but instead primary figures of gender discourse. Also known as *écriture féminine*, gender theory, gender performativity, and gender troubling, gender discourse is one of the latest forms of theoretical rhetoric to acquire the linguistic and symbolic capital to amount to a valued form of cultural literacy. Other factors also contribute to the institutional incorporation of this discourse: the restructuring of the sexual division of academic labor (reflected by growing numbers of women in the newly constituted class of professional managers), and a more diversified booksellers' market (writing by women still acquiring appreciable marketability). As queer sexuality gains more legitimacy in real social terms so is it bound to gain in the academy, where it will bear the specific value signs of rhetorical/theoretical "rigour." A "queer H. D." is already competing for ascendancy.[31]

H. D.'s pornopoeia, however, remains eccentric to the "sexualities" of the modernist/feminist syllabus but not outside the institution's legitimate exercise of symbolic violence. My purpose is not to challenge "gynopoetics" by anticipating a market for lesbian literacy or by recalling a taste now past for pure poetics (as Altman does). I consider "the case of H. D.'s pornopoeia" to be, first, an instance in the history of sexuality worth exploring, since it marks the development of a sexual language that speaks unlike any sexual discourse legitimized in the field of cultural reproduction and hence, second, an occasion for determining new ways of reading sexuality that undo the effects of symbolic violence and that privilege precisely those eccentric features of sexual language that have not warranted enough linguistic and symbolic capital for reproduction and/or that have been reterritorialized as the sexuality of gender.

Cultural Activism and the Struggle for Sexual Literacy

Had H. D. been in her prime in late nineteenth-century America, she may have joined the Free Lovers' movement and written for their obscure monthly newspaper, *The Word*.[32] Spearheaded by Angela and Ezra Heywood, the Free Lovers waged battle on Victorian prudery and what they viewed as its direct consequences—sexual ignorance, venereal disease, male dominance, and the atrophy of erotic imagination. Their chief weapon was "the word," the invention and deployment of a frank and refreshing sexual dialect. In Bourdieu's terms, the Free Lovers elected to overcome prevailing powers of legitimization by creating sufficient linguistic and symbolic capital to reconstitute *sexual literacy*.[33]

H. D.'s penchant for pornopoeia might partly be explained by her early training in American transcendentalism. With the Free Lovers she shared a "transcendentalist conception of language," including a familiarity with Whitman's, which "insisted that the reconnection of words to things would only occur after the 'forbidden voices . . . of sexes and lusts' had been freed from the censors' grip."[34] But unlike Angela Heywood and the Free Lovers, H. D. did not write for the general public. H. D.'s intended audience was closed to an imaginary procession of Eleusinian initiates or "companions of the flame" (*Trilogy*, 21); if she addressed any temporal body at all, it was the pure poetry sector in the field of restricted production, which advocated art/eroticism for art's/eroticism's sake, a more hermetic than democratic form of transcendentalism.[35]

Heywood's pursuit of "Fleshed Realism" led her to champion the use of "'Anglo-Saxon' designation[s]" such as "c[ock], c[unt] and f[uck]." Deploring the prevailing practice in literary and scientific discourse of employing "Latin names and devious phrases," she "urged Americans to incorporate 'plain English' designations of the 'sexual organs and their use' into everyday speech and writing." [36] Conversely, H. D.'s invocation of "spiritual realities" and mythic presences (most often "Venus"), endorsed the use of Latinate English to "venerate" (Venus-ize) desire and thereby transcend the language of modern prudery in which it was condemned as "venery," "impurity," "venereous," "lascivious" (*Trilogy*, 74). But the difference between these transcendentalist sex radicals is not simply aesthetic or ideological; it is complicated by the social history of obscenity.

Between the time the Heywoods were most active (in the 1880s and 1890s) and the time H. D. began her Eleusinian forays into pornographic literature (the late 1910s), the development of freer, franker sexual language as promoted by the Free Lovers was aggressively suppressed by symbolic and legal violence at the hand of "social elites." The attempts of Victorian moralists "to eradicate linguistic and artistic forms of 'obscenity' . . . began with local, extralegal actions of vice societies in the 1830s and culminated in the enactment of the Postal Act of 1873 (known as the Comstock Act)." [37] A powerful lobbyist for the YMCA, Anthony Comstock pressured state powers to police and punish activities that the Heywoods and others mobilized through the mail and eventually the Free Lovers were expelled to "the margins of social discourse, both in their own day and in the decades that followed." [38] Meanwhile, in England, Victorian moralists were busy administering "the Obscene Publications Act of 1857." [39] It was under the *Hicklin* reading of this act that the sexual language of Havelock Ellis, Radclyffe Hall, and D. H. Lawrence was brought to trial and tested for obscenity. [40]

Of course not all modernists suffered in this battle over sexual literacy. Pound recruited Emerson's notion of "spermatic man" to elaborate a phallic idealism for an emasculated contemporary culture. His translator's introduction to Rémy de Gourmont's *Natural Philosophy of Love* collapses the sexological discourses of Emerson and Gourmont in a compound ideogram whose pornoglyphics, since dedicated ostensibly to the service of a *scientia sexualis*, escaped the patriarchal censor:

It is more than likely that the brain itself, is, in origin and development, only a sort of great clot of genital fluid held in suspense or reserve. . . . It would explain the enormous content of the brain as a maker or presenter of images. Species would have developed in accordance with, or their development would have been affected by the relative discharge and retention of the fluid. . . . Even oneself has felt it, driving any new idea into the great passive vulva of London, a sensation analogous to the male feeling in copulation. [41]

Pound proceeded to develop his seminal ideas on human evolution and libidinal economy in *The Cantos*, adapting Dante to cast powerful, damnable images of sodomy-usury, a fictitious coupling that supposedly aspired to "fight against the natural reproduction of species." [42] Part of Pound's cultural ambition was to prescribe the forms of sexuality that would constitute the literacy of well-educated generations in the future.

On the other hand, H. D. puts little cultural investment in the libidinal economy of future generations. From hermetic materials of the past, she cultivates pornopoeia for the ecstatic pleasures of the moment. Her idea of procreation privileges the perverse production of joy and vision at the expense of phallic legacies; the "Child" born to her allegorical personae is always the product of an illegitimate, often incestuous union of spiritual longing and fleshly lust (e.g., "Espérance" of "Winter Love," *Hermetic Definition*).

Against Pound's spermatic brain, it is tempting to interpret H. D.'s speculations in *Notes on Thought and Vision* on "womb or love-vision" (20–21) as a language pitched for gender warfare on the battlefield of literary production. But the autoerotic and pornohermetic excesses of her lyricism question and transcend the categorical oppositions of sexual difference: "Is there none left / can equal me / in ecstasy, desire?" ("Cassandra," *CP*, 169). Her pursuit of the pornohermetic is not merely attributable to a carefully disguised articulation of a forbidden lesbian and/or bisexuality. The sadomasochistic shatterings of *Sea Garden*, the bacchanal rapture of "Hymen," the flowering fervor of "Eurydice," the narco-electro lusts of *Nights*, and the orgiastic consecrations of *Hermetic Definition* exceed in intensity and fluidity the categories of sexuality defined by the gender of their object, however perverse.

In the face of legitimate social violence mounted by the dominant class against all attempts to expand sexual free speech, H. D. occupies (consciously or unconsciously) the highly autonomous—art for art's sake— position in the literary field as the most tactical site to produce pornographic literature. Writing in the oppressor's language with a sense of having been exiled from her native language/mother tongue, she contributes to the making of what Gilles Deleuze and Félix Guattari call "minor literature."

Like her modernist contemporaries, H. D. deplores the cultural desert of standardized, commercial English; of the strategies open to the minoritarian writer (perhaps the most autonomous agent of the dominated class of cultural producers), she chooses to "artificially enrich this [English], to swell it up through all the resources of symbolism, of oneirism, of esoteric sense, of a hidden signifier." [43] But she also chooses a poetry of destitution. The pornographic supplement to the hermetic works more directly on the senses through a sexualized language of flowers stripped of gender, romance, object-love, so that "nothing remains but intensities." [44]

If H. D. produces a minor literature and is therefore not disposed toward setting a standardized English, then how, finally, do we understand her role in the struggle for sexual literacy? We must understand this minoritizing function as a strategy that differs from the Heyworths' majority one of sexualizing public discourse, and that also differs from the minority strategy of speaking out as a woman or coming out as gay. A minor pornographic literature, H. D.'s pornopoeia advocates neither a majority nor a minority sexuality, reflects neither a body politic nor even a body, and is thus bound to be lost in the reterritorializing process whereby H. D.'s literature is canonized as "woman's writing." The radical value of H. D.'s pornopoeia will be discovered when read as a tactical contestation of the norms of sexual literacy, which, while competing for distinction within the restricted field of cultural production and struggling to revitalize the exhausted tradition of *ars erotica*, sets no stake in becoming the norm itself.

Notes

1. From the *Shorter Oxford English Dictionary* (1973): "Pornography. Description of the life, manners, etc. of prostitutes and their patrons; hence the expression or suggestion of obscene or unchaste subjects in literature or art."

2. H. D., *Notes on Thought and Vision* (San Francisco: City Lights Books, 1982), 33. Hereafter cited as *Notes.*

3. I allude to the *Garland of Meleager*, which Richard Aldington (then H. D.'s husband) translated for the Egoist Press, 1920. In his foreword, Aldington contrasts Meleager's "exceedingly rich, voluptuous poems" with Anyte's "chaste, almost Spartan simplicity of morals." Of the 141 poems attributed to Meleager in the Greek Anthology, he omits 13 from translation, including V.208, XI.223, and XII.86, which he describes as "obscene." H. D. uses an epigram from the *Garland* to preface her novel *Hedylus* (1928), a psychological novel that attempts to narrate the flowering of the boy-poet's eroticism from the omniscient but dissociated perspective of his prostitute mother. Since it is a projection of the hetaera's "oriental" and incestuous desire, the narrative subject's "Greek" is not boyish or Greek at all but uncannily, charismatically "voluptuous" and "obscene."

4. "One must understand a lower wisdom before one understands a higher." H. D. insists. But the higher wisdom (with which you "look into things with your intellect, your sheer brain") is neither more noble nor more ethereal than the lower wisdom. "To understand dung chemically and spiritually and with the earth sense, one must understand the texture, spiritual and chemical and earthy, of the rose that grows from it. . . . Is the earth greater or less than the white rose it brings forth?" (*Notes*, 31–32).

5. E.g., the advertisement for *Blast* in *The Egoist* (15 April 1914).

6. Ezra Pound, "Marianne Moore and Mina Loy" in *Selected Prose 1909–1965*, ed. Norman Cookson (London: Faber & Faber, 1973), 394–95.

7. Ibid., 394. It is not historically accurate to say that H. D.'s poetry *conforms* to Pound's "imagism" since, as Cyrena Pondrom persuasively argues ("H. D. and the Origins of Imagism," *Sagetrieb* 4, no. 1 [1985]: 75–100), the latter *derives* its aesthetic doctrine from H. D.'s poetic practice.

8. H. D., *Collected Poems 1912–1944*, ed. Louis L. Martz (Manchester: Carcanet, 1984), 14. Hereafter cited as *CP*.

9. For an informative and persuasive discussion of H. D.'s revision of the "Romantic Landscape" in *Sea Garden, HER,* "Hyacinth," and *Murex,* see Cassandra Laity, "H. D.'s Romantic Landscapes: The Sexual Politics of the Garden," *Sagetrieb* 6, no. 2 (1987): 57–75.

10. A mockery perhaps of Pound's *ars poetica* entitled, "I Gather the Limbs of Osiris" (1911–12), in *Selected Prose*, 21–43.

11. Georges Bataille, *Visions of Excess: Selected Writings 1927–1939,* trans. Allan Stoekl (Minneapolis: University of Minnesota Press, 1985), 13.

12. In Meleager's language of flowers H. D. translates the main premise of Nietzsche's *Birth of Tragedy,* namely, that the satyric dithyramb staged in the spirit of the orgiastic god, Dionysus, is the primal and generative form of Attic tragedy supposed to have been inspired by the sun god, god of enlightenment, Apollo—

> Euripides is a white rose, lyric, feminine, a spirit. Aristophanes is a satyr.
> Is the satyr greater or less than the white rose it embraces? (H. D., *Notes*, 32)

13. One of H. D.'s favorite leitmotifs, romantic thralldom runs throughout her poetry and prose. According to Rachel DuPlessis,

> romantic thralldom is an all-encompassing, totally defining love between unequals. The lover has the power of conferring self-worth and purpose upon the loved one. Such love is possessive, and while those enthralled feel it completes and even transforms them, they are also enslaved. The eroticism of romantic love, born of this unequal relationship between the sexes, may depend for its satisfaction upon dominance and submission. Thralldom insists upon the differences between the sexes, encouraging a sense of mystery surrounding the motives and powers of the lover: thus it begins and ends in sexual polarization. Viewed from a critical, feminist perspective, the sense of completion or transformation that often accompanies thralldom in love has the high price of obliteration and paralysis, for the entranced self is entirely defined by another. ("Romantic Thralldom in H. D.," *Contemporary Literature* 20, no. 3 [1979]: 178–9)

14. Valentine de Saint-Point, "Futurist Manifesto of Lust, 1913," *Women's Art Journal* (Fall-Winter 1987): 13.

15. Mina Loy, *The Last Lunar Baedecker* (Manchester: Carcanet, 1985), 271.

16. H. D., "Grove of Academe," in *Hermetic Definition* (New York: New Directions, 1972), 33.

17. Pierre Bourdieu, *The Field of Cultural Production* (Cambridge: Polity Press, 1993), 163–64. Subsequent references to this work are given parenthetically in the text.

18. "Cultural production distinguishes itself from the production of the most common objects in that it must produce not only the object in its materiality, but also the value of this object, that is, the recognition of artistic legitimacy. This is inseparable from the production of the artist or the writer as artist or writer, in other words, as a creator of value. A reflection on the meaning of the artist's signature would thus be in order" (Ibid., 164).

19. H. D., *Trilogy* (Manchester: Carcanet, 1973), 17, 48. Subsequent parenthetical references are to this edition.

20. Since "the literary field is the economic world reversed," but at the same time does not displace the economic world, it must operate in the *belief* of its transcendence: "the artistic field is a *universe of belief*" (Bourdieu, *Cultural Production*, 164).

21. Pound, *Selected Prose*, 394.

22. Rachel Blau DuPlessis, *H. D.: The Career of That Struggle* (Brighton: Harvester Press, 1986), xiv.

23. John Guillory, *Cultural Capital: The Problem of Literary Canon Formation* (Chicago: University of Chicago Press, 1993), ix. Subsequent references to this work are given parenthetically in the text.

24. "Thus, while the standard or 'common' language seems to efface social stratification by making language itself the vehicle of a common national identity, the 'literary' language reinstates at another level a linguistic difference by which the upper classes can continue to mark their cultural distinction" (Ibid., 78).

25. For example, with his *ABC of Reading* and his anthology, *From Confucius to Cummings*, edited with Marcella Spann.

26. Marjorie Perloff, *Poetic License: Essays on Modernist and Postmodernist Lyric* (Evanston, Ill.: Northwestern University Press, 1990), 32.

27. Meryl Altman, "A Prisoner of Biography," *Women's Review of Books* 9, nos. 10–11 (1992): 32. Subsequent references to this work are given parenthetically in the text.

28. Susan Stanford Friedman, *Penelope's Web: Gender, Modernity, H. D.'s Fiction* (Cambridge: Cambridge University Press, 1990); Susan Stanford Friedman and Rachel Blau DuPlessis, eds., *Signets: Reading H. D.* (Madison: University of Wisconsin Press, 1990); Donna Krolik Hollenberg, *H. D.: The Poetics of Childbirth and Creativity* (Boston: Northeastern University Press, 1991); and Claire Buck, *H. D. and Freud: Bisexuality and a Feminine Discourse* (New York: St. Martin's Press, 1991).

29. Bourdieu, *Cultural Production*, 121.

30. Altman laments that Claire Buck's focus on H. D.'s lesbian and bisexuality should present such a "formidable theoretical apparatus" that "ultimately" serves a notion of "maternal discourse" (40).

31. See Cassandra Laity's introduction to H. D.'s *Paint It Today* (published in the "Lesbian Life and Literature" series by New York University Press, 1992).

32. Jesse F. Battan, " 'The Word Made Flesh': Language, Authority, and Sexual Desire in Late Nineteenth-Century America," in *American Sexual Politics*, ed. John C. Fout and Maura Shaw Tantillo (Chicago: University of Chicago Press, 1993), 101.

33. Battan expresses it differently, in Foucaultian terms, as a conflict over discursive power and control:

> Nowhere was the struggle between linguistic purity and vulgarity more evident than in the conflict over words used to describe sexuality. Although the contending voices in this dialogue supported diametrically opposed ideas on the nature of sexuality and the role it should play in the creation of their vision of the ideal society, all were convinced of its power and sought to monitor and guide it. Linking consciousness to conduct, the participants in this struggle believed that the erotic imagination it inspired could be controlled if the words used to describe sexuality were carefully chosen. They all believed, in short, that language could be used to regulate the expression of sexual desires. (Ibid., 104)

34. Ibid., 111.

35. Angela Heywood believed that a *frank* revitalization of sexual language could radically democratize gender and class relations. Whereas H. D. believed that the route to sexual and social liberation lay in a hieratic excavation of the universal language of dreams. Nonetheless these differences are obscured by a common transcendentalism; each testifying to the linguistic/literary transformation of society, the radically different positions these women take on democratization paradoxically warrants close comparison. Consider these statements of Heywood's, quoted by Battan:

> "When fit words please the ear as physical-human beauty pleases the eye, when sentences are quick with warm, throbbing life; when LANGUAGE, in original power and charming surprise, is the perennial miracle Spontaneity allows it to be; when souls know bodies, and mind informs matter well-enough to help us meet and work in the realm of ethical possibility," the millennium will be at hand. A "new literature," she argued, would create "new social harmonies, a new heaven and a new earth." ("The Word Made Flesh," 116)

And this statement of H. D.'s:

> The picture-writing, the hieroglyph of the dream, was the common property of the whole race; in the dream, man, as at the beginning of time, spoke a universal language, and man, meeting in the universal understanding of the unconscious or the subconscious, would forgo barriers of time and space, and man, understanding man, would save mankind. (H. D., *Tribute to Freud*, [1961; repr. Manchester: Carcanet, 1985], 71)

36. Battan, "The Word Made Flesh," 113–14.
37. Ibid., 115, 104.
38. Ibid., 122. "More than sixty years later," Battan writes, "the radical ideas and activities of Free Lovers such as Moses Harman and Angela and Ezra Heywood still remain largely unexplored" (122).
39. See Leigh Gilmore, "Obscenity, Modernity, Identity: Legalizing *The Well of Loneliness* and *Nightwood*," *Journal of the History of Sexuality* 4, no. 4 (1994): 606:

> The Obscene Publications Act was introduced in 1857 in England by Lord Campbell as a stopgap against "European pornography." The act designated obscenity as an effect rather than a cause or an inherent wrong; it did not define obscenity, prohibit specific representations, or take into account authorial intention. It indicated, instead, that state control would be exercised at the point of circulation in order to protect audiences for whom the materials were most probably not intended or likely to reach, but who might be influenced by them.

40. Gilmore writes:

> The rule of obscenity law emerged a decade after the act's introduction when, in 1868, the *Hicklin* doctrine was defined by Queen's Bench. In *Regina v. Hicklin*, obscenity was defined as a "test" rather than as a quality in the material: "The test of obscenity is this, whether the tendency of the matter charged as obscenity is to deprave and corrupt those whose minds are open to such immoral influences and into whose hands a publication of this sort may fall." Given this vague definition of obscenity, magistrates could target any pub-

lished material, including the novels that would later constitute the modernist canon. (Ibid., 606).

41. Ezra Pound, introduction to *The Natural Philosophy of Love* by Rémy de Gourmont, trans. Ezra Pound (1934. Repr. London: Quartet, 1992), viii.

42. Jean-Michel Rabaté, *Language, Sexuality and Ideology in Ezra Pound's Cantos* (London: Macmillan, 1986), 73.

43. Gilles Deleuze and Félix Guattari, *Kafka: Toward a Minor Literature,* trans. Dana Polan (Minneapolis: University of Minnesota Press, 1986), 19.

44. Ibid.

Part III
Marianne Moore
(1887–1972)

Chapter 5
"So As to Be One Having Some Way of Being One Having Some Way of Working": Marianne Moore and Literary Tradition

Lisa M. Steinman

As T. S. Eliot wrote in "Tradition and the Individual Talent," the past is "altered by the present as much as the present is directed by the past." [1] While Eliot's further description of a whole or universal tradition of "monuments" suggests contemporary critical theory might have appalled him, I want to revisit his remarks in light of comments by two recent theorists. In particular, I am interested in Raymond Williams's description of the selectivity of cultural traditions, suggesting how "that which . . . is always passed off as '*the*' tradition . . . is continually active and adjusting," and in John Guillory's examination of the relationship between what we read, especially in educational institutions, and literary tradition, which Guillory describes as a necessarily imaginary totality, one that "never appears as a complete and uncontested list in any particular time and place." [2] Although both Williams and Guillory call into question Eliot's imagination of some ideal list to which the best poets add themselves, both also acknowledge that we read, as Eliot suggests, intertextually and contextually. This fact about reading poses problems for writers who will not, or cannot, easily claim the avenue to literary authority Eliot envisioned. Such writers need to reimagine the texts and contexts within which readers will make sense of their work.

Eliot himself forms part of the context in which Marianne Moore framed her thinking about literary tradition. His view is one she would have read in either in *The Egoist* of 1919 or in the 1920 volume, *The Sacred Wood*. As Jeanne Heuving has pointed out, Moore's engagement with such modernist attempts to construct a universal poetics was necessarily subversive; her awareness of the constructed nature and—for her—the limited nature of subject positions within poetry stems from what Heuving calls the psychosexual pressures Moore faced. [3] Moore's consciousness of the role of gender in announcing one's literary ambitions was linked, early, specifically to her relationship with Eliot, both "the guiding spirit in . . . Moore's search for community" and a locus of resistance, given Moore's need to "write her own history as a poet," as John Slatin has argued in his book on Moore, pointing out that Moore's first review of Eliot's *Prufrock and Other Observations* adopted a male persona, an indication that Moore saw the problematics of being a woman attempting to write (and to join) literary history.[4] I want to suggest further that Moore's sense of herself not only as a woman but also as an American informed her skepticism about any singular literary tradition; moreover, in Moore this self-consciousness, while fostered by her particular historical circumstances, finally led her to anticipate something very like Williams's and Guillory's awareness of the contingent and multiple nature and function of literary traditions.

Thus, it is not simply that the intertextuality so evident in Moore's poems offers readers a newly configured list of predecessors—Traherne, Goldsmith, Gray, and above all Emerson and an American literary tradition—or that her poems are in turn reinscribed in a tradition by those seen as her heirs, poets like Josephine Miles and Elizabeth Bishop. It is also that the concerns and construction of Moore's poetry force a more general reassessment of what a literary tradition might be. After all, Moore's reading diaries make clear the range of discourse echoed in the poetry, as her reading skipped from the poems of Alice Meynell to baseball to Shakespeare to newspaper articles on Prohibition to the poetry of Traherne to the invention of the typewriter. Like the notes to her poems, such catholicity requires a reconsideration of what kind of a "whole" literature may form. Certainly, literature is no longer arranged by genres (as James, Burke, Longinus, and Maria Edgeworth enter Moore's poetry and poetics). Nor is there a distinction between major and minor writers; or between "high" literature and popular literature or "less serious" forms of writing. As the 1919 "Poetry" puts it, quoting Tolstoy's diary (and so enacting its point), poetry cannot "discriminate against 'business documents and / school-books.'"[5]

I will to return to Moore's statements about selectivity and inclusiveness (as well as to her construction of lists that seem to foil any attempt by readers to project some whole). But first I want to trace some of the nuances of how readers of Moore are made to rethink ideas about intertextuality and tradition as well as to make some proposals about how Moore's thinking on such issues seems to have evolved. In particular, I want to examine how Moore's insistence on energy and, increasingly, her inclusion of commercial culture mark her sometimes vexed attempts to dismantle any post-Romantic Wordsworthian reverie of poets "connected in a mighty scheme of truth," forming a privileged band something like a transhistorical chain of major poets holding hands across the centuries.[6]

From her earliest published work, it is clear that Moore's relationship to past, especially male, authority was fraught. For example, by 1915–16, she was writing poems like " 'He Wrote the History Book,' " in which she adopts a child's voice in order to shed

> . . . a ray
> of whimsicality on a mask of profundity so
> terrific, that I have been dumbfounded by
> it oftener than I care to say.
>> (*CP*, 89)[7]

While the poem voices an admiration for the man who taught Moore history at Bryn Mawr, it is not accidental that profundity is identified as a "mask," nor that "terrific" can mean both wondrous and terrifying, nor that the result of her confrontation with an authority on history is described as a kind of silencing or being "dumbfounded" (indeed, ultimately a self-silencing in that the speaker does not "care to say" how often she has been silenced by awe).

This sly poem goes on to poke fun at the notion of some singular or universal account of the past—"*The* book? Titles are chaff," Moore writes of the son's description of his father as writing "the history book." The poem concludes:

> Authentically
>> brief and full of energy, you contribute to your father's
>>> legibility and are sufficiently
> synthetic. Thank you for showing me
>> your father's autograph.

William Doreski argues that here Moore is "[un]concerned with tonal unity," and "deconstructing her own thank-you by expressing her delight at the child's simplicity in a language of mock-profundity, . . . in doing so [she] mocks herself for her Latinate expression."[8] One can go further, noting that the poem is aware of the gendered nature of masks of profundity; to make the father "legible" is to unmask the authority of the father and to replace it with a glimpse of a man writing himself (in that an autograph is a writing of the self, etymologically). It is, on first reading, the child's "energy" and "brevity" that help the speaker move from awe to amusement; part of the joke is that the child is in fact giving a shortened version of his father's title: Charles McLean Andrews was the author of *The History of England for Schools and Colleges.* But "Dr. Andrews" (as Moore's letters home from college refer to him) is also in the poem transformed from a monument—"He is the 'biggest' man I've had [in class] yet. I wish I could have Major History with him"—to a mortal, and a sexual being, at that: the child shows the speaker his father's "autograph" in the flesh, or in his person, in other words.[9] The poem may, as Doreski proposes, mock the speaker for her "mock-profundity," but finally the point may be that as a woman Moore cannot adopt the father's mask.

The question raised then is how, even if masks are rejected, a woman writer can become legible or write her own autograph? In " 'He Wrote the History Book,' " the problem is already raised of how to be part of a book, and so "legible," without being "dumbfounded" or silenced. For Moore, part of the solution to this problem was forged in the context of American modernist art circles, and specifically among the practitioners of what is now called American precisionism. Situating herself within the precisionist movement in America served an already felt need both for a community in which she could see herself working and for a strategy by which to position her work outside of some exclusive notion of literary authority.

The community to which Moore turned was a loose association of visual artists, photographers, and writers in early twentieth-century New York. Although the period from about 1909 through the 1930s was one of manifestos and self-conscious movements, there were also more casual exchanges among artists and between artists and writers. As Paul Strand described interchanges between the visual artists: "We all talked the same language. . . . We each had our own way. We didn't sit down and have discussions." [10] Yet if no formal discussions took place, there were more casual conversations. Indeed, the sense of a shared language and common project was in part a result of interpersonal relations, as William Carlos Williams reveals in titling one chapter in his *Autobiography,* "Painters and Parties." [11]

Moore obviously wanted to participate in this sense of an informal and intimate group. In 1909, when she was still in college at Bryn Mawr, she wrote Alfred Stieglitz's name and the address of his gallery in her college notebook and slightly later she wrote Ezra Pound that there was "more evidence of power among painters and sculptors than among writers" in America, indicating her understanding of how the New York art community could provide a context—a sense of power—and perhaps using this understanding to resist Pound as the self-designated impresario of literary authority.[12] In *America & Alfred Stieglitz: A Collective Portrait,* Marsden Hartley describes Stieglitz's gallery, 291, the gathering place for American modernist artists, which Moore finally visited on one of her first trips to New York in 1915: the gallery was a small room, ringed with a shelf, "and below . . . curtains of dark green burlap," with a central platform "also hung with burlap, and in the center of this . . . a huge brass bowl." Part of the excitement for Hartley, as for Moore, was the gallery's function as a gathering place: "A morning in this room with the brass bowl was revealing, for a smart array of stylish personages appeared and stood about, for there was no place to sit except on the edges of the brass bowl and few there were who felt courage enough to disturb this very awesome symbol." [13]

Moore's 1923 poem "Bowls" seems at first reading to be about the game played on a bowling green:

> on the green
> with lignum vitae balls and ivory markers,
> the pins planted in wild duck formation,
> and quickly dispersed—
>
> (*CP*, 59)

But given Moore's interest in Stieglitz and his circle, her usual method of literary collage, and the subject matter of poems written within the same two-year period (like "New York" [1921] and "People's Surroundings" [1922]), one suspects Stieglitz's brass bowl on green burlap, perhaps conflated with Strand's *Abstraction—Bowls, 1915*, informs Moore's poem. [14] In "Bowls" the pins "quickly dispersed," like ducks in transit, become emblems of Moore's style in the poem, where images are presented in precise and vivid detail, but quickly replaced. In "Bowls," as in "'He Wrote the History Book,'" energy and motion become ways of being able "to look playwrights and poets and novelists straight in the face" (*CP*, 59); in other words, artists are redefined as living producers rather than dead (and intimidating) monuments of literature. "Bowls" goes on to images of Pompeii, of etymology, of magazine publication, and of letter writing, all of which juxtapose permanence with ephemera, a juxtaposition captured etymologically in "lignum vitae" or the wood of life, a substance, like language itself, that is hard and yet also in the process of growth. Further, Moore's style—precise, juxtaposed images that suggest and describe motion—is one that invokes her understanding of much of the American art she admired and so allies her with the visual artists.

It is not easy to characterize a precisionist style, especially a precisionist literary style. There were a number of different influences that converged in places such as 291. Early in the century, Stieglitz, among others, had introduced European modernists to the United States. Stieglitz's special number of *Camera Work* (1912) was especially important, in that it included reproductions of French modern art, as well as two prose pieces on Picasso and Matisse by Gertrude Stein. Stieglitz announced that in Stein's writing "the Post-Impressionist spirit is found expressing itself in literary form," offering his readers her prose as "a decipherable clew to that intellectual and esthetic attitude which underlies and inspires the movement upon one phase of which they are comments and of the extended development of which they are themselves an integral part."[15] Like Stieglitz, Moore seems to have identified Stein's style with the new modernist movement, and in 1926 she commented specifically on what she called Stein's "*precisely* perplexing verbal exactness" (*CPr*, 121, emphasis added). She then included herself among the practitioners of a modernist style when she wrote in "Bowls": "I learn that we are precisians— / not citizens of Pompeii arrested in action."[16]

In fact, Moore revised "Bowls" for her 1951 *Collected Poems*, where she replaced her original reference to "precisians" with a reference to "precisionists," and so retrospectively confirmed her claimed alliance specifically with the visual artists who had by 1951 come to be known as precisionists.[17] The word Moore first used, "precisians," meaning "one who is precise, especially in religious observance; Puritan," already links the early version of "Bowls" with Hartley's description of Stieglitz's "awesome" bowl and, further, with a distinctively American style or practice, although one filtered through Stein's interpretation of painters like Matisse and Picasso. In both versions of her poem, Moore sends her readers to an etymological dictionary to find the root of her work in the Latin *praecidere*, "cut short" or "abridged," further relating to the modernist emphasis (through Pound and the painters) on economy of expression.

Moore's verbal equivalent of a visual style helps reveal how rich and complex her use of literary and extraliterary traditions was; moreover, her practice suggests the headiness of the exchange between people who wanted to be part of a vaguely defined new, modern movement, and who like Moore found or located themselves in the places associated with this movement, with a further alchemy taking place as the vocabulary of one art was translated into another and as European developments were transmuted and claimed in the rather different cultural context of early twentieth-century America.

Most specifically, as I have been suggesting, Moore associated herself with the visual artists in order to find a sense of community that would avoid some of the problems literary modernism, and Eliot in particular, posed for her. However, this association posed its own challenges. Having once engaged herself in this more open group conversation, a conversation including Stein as well as Stieglitz, Moore was "not arrested in motion" (to quote from "Bowls"). That is to say, the exchange between American and European, visual and literary artists yielded new questions about what it would mean to reconstruct the tradition to include various arts, finally including popular or mass culture, and also questions about the nature of representation.

The complexity of the exchange can be suggested by returning to Stein's portrait of Picasso, which Hartley's tribute to Stieglitz in *America & Alfred Stieglitz* recalls as Stein's "One, One, One" portrait (240). Stein's piece begins: "One whom some were certainly following was one who was completely charming"; it also invokes action or process (like Moore's poem) in the grammatical variations and use of verb forms: "This one was one who was working and he was one needing this thing needing to be working so as to be one having some way of being one having some way of working." [18]

As Stieglitz said, Stein's portrait is not only "about" Picasso, but itself can be taken as a cubist work of literature. The genre of abstract portraits practiced later by visual artists in fact stems largely from Stein's pieces, although Stieglitz's promotion of American artists and an American subject matter also influenced the artists.[19] For example, the style of one abstract portrait (of Stieglitz by Francis Picabia), *Ici, C'est Ici Stieglitz*, echoes mail-order catalog illustrations, and the schematic realism invites a camera bellows also to be read as a staircase; a bulb (or gearshift), as a lamppost; a rod (or brake), as a walking stick.[20] Both in its style—drawing on American commercial art—and in its reflections of American subjects characteristic of Stieglitz's or Charles Sheeler's by 1917 (as in Stieglitz's images of New York or Sheeler's *Stair Well*), the image pays homage to the aesthetic of "clean lines" Stieglitz was helping to promote.[21]

Picabia's portrait betrays literary as well as artistic influences. Stein's verbal portrait works in part by force of repetition and off-rhyme as well as by shifts of grammatical function so that, for instance, one clause ("one having some way of being") exactly parallels the next clause ("one having some way of working") even while the fact that the second clause is technically the object of the first shifts the emphasis from an equation between "being" and "working" ("some way of being"/"some way of working") to a more distanced perspective; "so as to be one having some way of being one having some way of working" suggests the pose of someone trying to be a person who knows how to work, as it were, although to paraphrase is to destroy the delicacy of Stein's near pun.

In that puns involve many meanings in one space, Stein's multiplication of perspectives echoes verbally Picasso's manipulation of space as well as his play of signs.[22] One suspects that for Moore reading Stein (as for Stein herself) this fracturing of a single perspective point underlines a sense of the gendered nature of perception, as does the emphasis on how to position one's self as a producer of art, so as to have "some way of being one having some way of working." There is certainly a similar self-consciousness about gender, production, and perception in Moore's work, not only in "'He Wrote the History Book,'" but also in her 1921 poem "A Grave," which opens with an address to a male figure: "Man looking into the sea, / taking the view from those who have as much right to it as you have to it yourself" (*CP*, 49–50).[23] Stein's prose further calls attention to the conjurings of grammar; although suggestive of multiple meanings, the prose is legible because it always remains grammatically respectable. Picabia's schematic realism echoes Stein in that it too, for all its resonance, is legible in part because it respects the conventions of commercial illustration.[24] One might say that Stein's verbal equivalent of Picasso's painting was transmuted to pieces like Picabia's visual equivalents of Stein's prose, and the painters' work was in turn verbally reinterpreted by poets like Moore. As Moore said in a late (1964) interview, borrowing a metaphor from Stieglitz: "Talent should go on, attempting equivalents" (*CPr*, 689).[25]

What uses Moore made of this idea of "equivalents" is worth examining. She in part drew on both Stein and the visual artists to find ways of making her own work "legible," replacing an Eliotic sense of literary history with new contexts (such as those of the modernists and the American precisionists) in light of which her work could be read. Yet at the same time, Moore shifted the nature of the artistic context in which she invited readers to place her poems. For example, Strand described his own work as a "crystallization" or capturing a "moment" when forces become "physical and objective."[26] The remark suggests he saw his own work as involving stillness, not motion. Moore, on the other hand, reviewed the 1925 "Seven Americans" exhibit, a show of precisionist work assembled by Stieglitz at the Anderson Galleries, and described Strand's photographs as follows: "We welcome the power-house in the drawing-room when we examine his orientally perfect combining of discs, parabolas, and verticals . . . the depth of tone upon the anaconda-like curves of central bearings" (*CPr*, 151). Typically, Moore's language emphasizes the motion of Strand's working (his "combining") and adds life to his subject matter ("anaconda-like curves"). A similar move happens in Moore's retrospective essay on her years at *The Dial*, where she emphasizes Sheeler at work, that is, in action or, in Stein's terms, "being one having some way of working." Moore's Stein-like description of Sheeler "coping with the difficulty of photographing" Lachaise's work is full of verbs and gerunds: "these scientifically businesslike proceedings reminding one of the wonderfully mastered Bucks County barn and winding stair turn" (*CPr*, 362). In short, whatever Strand or Sheeler intended,

Moore understood or reinterpreted their work as indicating motion in her "equivalents," which are finally neither identities nor copies.

Why Moore reinterpreted precisionist works in order to emphasize motion is a question without a single answer, but surely was related both to her reading of Stein and to her earlier emphasis on "energy" in poems like "'He Wrote the History Book.'" Energy and motion were also, for Moore, part of her self-identification as an American writer. By the twenties, references to speed or motion were further informed by cultural debates, and especially by the commonplace association between America, speed and activity, an association like that between America and industrial design, which Moore transvalued and claimed.[27] Moore's review of the "Seven Americans" exhibit, for example, opens with a negation of national stereotypes: "'Action, business, adventure, discovery' are not prerogatives exclusively American; and obversely creative power is not the prerogative of every country other than America" (*CPr*, 150). Motion was also something Moore's own work brought to her readers' attention, as evidenced for instance in Williams's description of her ability to achieve a result like that of abstract painting "by rapidity of movement."[28]

Moore's redefinition of both American "action" and American art was then a way of insisting on and claiming for Americans the creativity found in the process of production. Moreover, although Moore positioned herself in a more open-ended, less literary community to evade, with Stein's help, contending with a male tradition, it was at least as important to her to define a tradition that was not exclusively European, as her 1926 statement on Williams suggests in praising his work for making his readers realize "how little poetry—or prose—depends on definitions, or precedents" (*CPr*, 156). Moore thus surely understood her use of images and language drawn from American culture as part of a celebration of American democracy as well as a way of aligning herself with the American precisionists. Despite this, precisionist representations of American industrial landscapes or products raised questions about American culture more generally. And Moore was well aware of how celebratory representations of modern American culture, especially commercial and industrial culture, posed their own set of problems.

In the twenties and even more pointedly in the thirties, this indeed was an overt topic of conversation for American modernists. Williams, for instance, came to feel that Sheeler's work was too "impersonal . . . too much [a] withdrawal from life"; ultimately Williams wrote that he "wanted more of a comment . . . [and that] someone should smash [Sheeler's] camera and open his brain."[29] The judgment is related to Williams's sense that Sheeler, who worked for Condé Nast and—through the N. W. Ayer and Son advertising agency—for Ford, did not have sufficient suspicions of commercial and industrial America whose products he so painstakingly documented.[30] Williams's own work increasingly called attention to the socioeconomic world glossed over by a machine aesthetic.

But what of Moore's position? After all, she also eventually worked for Ford, which hired her to name what finally became, despite her, the Edsel.[31] That both Sheeler and Moore were featured in *Life* presents a similar ambiguity: The magazine's 1938 spread on Sheeler was arguably a matter of publicity and commerce, in that the piece appeared due to pressure from Harcourt, who wanted to promote Constance Rourke's book on Sheeler, while Moore's difficult poems—mostly drawn from printed sources—were domesticated as lines taken out of context were used to illustrate pictures of Moore posed with zoo animals.[32] Moore's relationship to commercial culture was not as unmixed as Sheeler's. But she did voice admiration for the work of commercial artists and writing; for example, she praised advertising for its "energy" (*CPr*, 193).

Earlier, in "'He Wrote the History Book,'" energy seemed to be that which could reanimate but also reduce to life-size (as the child "full of energy" helps to make the father legible to the speaker). These are not contradictory motions. To revivify something is to show its human proportions. In the poem, there is further the child's assumption that everyone will know who his father is, an assumption that, presumptuously voiced, becomes a parody of the father's mask. The child in Moore's poem, then, enacts a double-edged drama, showing, first, the life that Moore insists is central to all creative work. Like the canonized past or museum artifacts or those who lives were arrested by the eruption at Pompeii (who are compared to the snapshots of ourselves captured in "a cross-section of [our] correspondence" in "Bowls"), lack of energy is disparaged not simply because it makes literature a dead letter, but also because it allows the formation of an imposing, apparently unchallengeable, edifice. Energy, for Moore, then, is both a good in itself and an instrument of self-defense for her as an American and as a woman writer.

As such, an insistence on energy enabled Moore's revision of Eliot's injunction for the poet to live in "the present moment of the past," a bid for a place in the tradition that Eliot negotiated in "Tradition and the Individual Talent" with his image of the poet as a kind of impersonal medium or catalyst.[33] In Moore's view, as with the son of Dr. Andrews in "'He Wrote the History Book,'" this act of making present can also be a way of making legible—and of signing the name of—the father. In other words, to use Eliot's image of the tradition, living in the present moment of the past can simply mean to reopen the closed structure of the past long enough to allow the properly positioned writer to sign his name in the book and so reimagine a whole, a canonical list, culminating in his signature. As I have already suggested, this was a concept Moore came to challenge, both with her idea of energy (whereby having written was less the issue than the present act of working) and by the twenties with her inclusion (along the lines of Picabia's "portrait" of Stieglitz) of commercial culture. The space thus opened, as her 1921 poem "New York" insists, is "not the plunder, / but 'accessibility to experience'" (*CP*, 54). One might add that Moore's use of American culture and American energy not only opens a space in which she can work, but also makes her work accessible to readers that Eliot did not envision.

"New York," for example, quotes from a variety of sources: Henry James provided the poem's final line (an enactment of Moore's willingness not to have the last word and of her reanimation of other voices in what is once again a decidedly un-Eliotic manner). The use of quotations like the one that ends "New York" is a strategy with which Moore experimented from at least 1915. The poem she consistently reprinted just before "He Wrote the History Book" was originally titled "So far as the future is concerned" and retitled to appear in the 1924 *Observations* so as to echo Eliot's 1919 statement: "The Past Is the Present." [34] Like "'He Wrote the History Book,'" the original poem opened, as Margaret Holley has noted, with a titular epigraph, an "emblem of the poem's enclosure of past voices within its present text":

So far as the future is concerned,
"Shall one not say with the Russian philosopher,
'How is one to know what one doesn't know?'" [35]

In its final form, "The Past is the Present" enters a discussion of rhymed and unrhymed verse by claiming Habakkuk as a predecessor and announcing: "Ecstasy affords / the occasion and expediency determines the form" (*CP*, 88). "Ecstasy," as Moore, given her fascination with etymology, surely knew, comes from Greek roots meaning "out of place." The whole poem, then, revisits Eliot's notion of an individual serving as a mouthpiece for (and in the process transforming) "the" tradition to offer instead a notion of emotional (and spiritual) energy that is not placing or in place as the origin and end of poetry.

By the twenties, this open-endedness was clearly linked in Moore's mind not only with inclusiveness or "accessibility to experience," but also with education in a democracy (through her readings of people like Dewey) and with mass culture. It is not coincidental that this period also marks a shift in Moore's style, with a growing use of lists like the one that makes up most of "New York." Unlike Sheeler, Moore did not dismiss the idea that representations of the products or landscapes of commercial American involved social commentary; her turn (in "New York," for instance) to include not only James but a list or catalog formed in part of quotations from *Forest and Stream, The Literary Digest,* and *The Psychology of Dress* is itself a form of social commentary, insisting as it does not only on a democratic inclusiveness and on a democratic accessibility for readers, but also on the rapid replacement of any given item on the list (*CP*, 269).[36] Increasingly, staying in motion is a way for Moore to disclaim possessiveness within the extraliterary culture that forms part of the context making her poems legible.

All this, then, is to say something quite different than that Moore sends a scholarly reader to a wider range of source materials than most poets. In her published collections of poetry, Moore always included notes to her poems that provide readers with her polyglot and often unscholarly sources, a mark of her democratization of Eliot's ideas about the poet's relationship to culture and, indeed, a redefinition of culture itself. Moreover, Moore's poems are "ecstatic" in that they decontextualize or temporarily recontextualize what they contain; everything, in short, is out of place. Just as Moore redefines the cultural space in which *she* can work, so too *her readers* need not have so absorbed the past as to make it present; the poem itself becomes a sufficient introduction to its sources, which in any case are not designed to dumbfound anyone. In this way, Moore markedly changes what the ear hears in and as literature to include any use of language or image. Further, the very process of selection—the process by which traditions are formed, as traditions are always formed by the act of intertextual reading—is called into question and redefined insofar as selection (or "Picking and Choosing" [1920]) becomes one of Moore's central thematic concerns.

Following debates like the one between Williams and Sheeler over the uses of American cultural icons—and from 1935 to 1955, debates about mass culture generally—Moore was aware of some of the issues involved in so clearly placing her own (and others') cultural productions within commodity culture.[37] For Moore, at first, the use of mass or commercial culture allowed her to insist on the local American culture as a viable stage for artistic work (as with the precisionists) and to solve the problem Eliot and others posed of how to open tradition to individuals who could not assume the mask of profundity. Nonetheless, by the twenties, debates about mass culture did raise a difficult series of problems about the values of such a culture. Moore shows her awareness of the problematic nature of American commercial culture in poems such as "New York," where she deflects the idea that poetic commerce is a form of "plunder," or "When I Buy Pictures," which insists that the speaker's lists of images

are of things "of which [she] may regard [her]self as [only] the imaginary possessor" (*CP*, 48).

However, it is not simply that Moore resists possessiveness in order to
take a moral stand against greed. Her collections of images quite purposefully are designed in their heterogeneity, their diverse origins, and
the rapidity with which they are replaced to resist an Eliotic totalization.
A 1927 review of a series of poetry anthologies, for instance, states that
"[a]cademic feeling, or prejudice possibly, in favor of continuity and
completeness is opposed to miscellany—to music programs, composite picture
exhibitions, *newspapers, magazines*, and anthologies" (emphasis added);
the review continues:

Persons susceptible to objects of "extreme significance" may remember with
gratitude in the late Lieutenant Commander William Barrett's Naval and Marine
Collection at the Anderson Galleries, an albino tortoise shell decorated in scrim-
shaw with an American clipper ship in full sail; and in the Spanish collection of
Señor D. Raimundo Ruiz, at the American Art Galleries in December, a remarkable Gothic forgéd iron gate and "some small objects." (*CPr*, 182)

The review then ends with the question of to "what degree diverse sub-
ject-matters lend themselves to association" and finds that in anthologies
the unity provided is "of the mind which brought the assembled integers
together" (*CPr*, 183). Moore's own commitment to miscellany is obvious
in her inclusion of "some small objects," presented as a piece of found
prose, rather than as a reference to any actual things, thus marking her
investment in that which resists any sense of completion. But miscellany
is finally reunified with the idea of the *assembler's* energy. Especially given
that the review is of poetry anthologies, Moore's concern with literary
tradition and with the need to make legible one's own "autograph" without writing others out of the tradition seems clear.

Moore consistently warned that what is assembled "must not wish to
disarm anything" (to quote the 1921 "When I Buy Pictures") and attempted to distinguish between conspicuous consumption and active, or
energetic, self-fashioning (*CP*, 48). In a similar vein, in a late (1965) essay
on "Dress and Kindred Subjects" Moore pronounces: "I am not a collector, merely a fortuitous one," and then follows this with a paragraph-long
list of things: a silver rat, a teak mouse, an embroidered bird, an amber
fly, a Dresden leopard, among other things (*CPr*, 598). Most of the objects in the list are identified either by place of origin (Japan, Austria,
China, Alaska) or by the person who gave it to Moore. The essay thus
presents the objects in Moore's curiosity cabinet as marks of activity; as
she says in "The Pangolin" (1936), "To explain grace requires / a curious hand" (*CP*, 118), and her late essay similarly emphasizes the "fortu-

itous" nature of her collection, a mark of curiosity or collecting (not self display), a sign of grace rather than of self.

But "Dress and Kindred Subjects" may also betray an increasing anxiety over what such lists signal, ending as it does with an explicit warning that happiness is more likely "if one wants to *do* something than if one wants to *have* something," and with disavowals of greed or claims to "superiority" (*CPr*, 600). Indeed, Moore's list of multicultural curios is perilously close to a fetishized list. Moreover, the essay itself was written for *Women's Wear Daily* and thus starkly poses the dangers inherent in Moore's strategy for how to speak publicly as a woman and for a popular audience. If she dismantles any notion that serious literature does not appear in magazines like *Women's Wear Daily* (a matter of both class and gender), still she places her voice in a forum designed to represent women in its own formation of fetishized commodities.[38]

If Moore's alteration of the past, partly in response to Eliot, partly in response to her association with the American precisionists, is thus problematic, nonetheless it is self-conscious about these problems and conscious, too, of the importance of making culture a matter of *how* as well as *what* to read. By the twenties this shift of emphasis and self-consciousness seems to stem from an awareness of the larger social issues involved in the uneven distribution of cultural capital. Indeed, one suspects it already mattered to Moore in 1915 that the "he" of "'He Wrote the History Book'" was the author of a college textbook. As John Guillory notes, universities and colleges are not representative places, but they are the locus of real power, namely the distribution of cultural capital.[39]

In "The Student," as first published in 1932 in *Poetry*, Moore describes paired fruit trees ("tree-of-knowledge—/ tree-of-life") and then lists the mottoes of four colleges, including Yale, which did not admit women in 1932.[40] Moore comments: "these apple-trees should be for everyone." As in the list of words for which the same poem says thoughtful pupils should have two thoughts (words like "bachelor" and "damsel"), Moore's lightness of tone hardly masks her ironic awareness of the gendered nature of so-called universal culture or of the role institutions play in the construction and accessibility of such culture, particularly in the case of literary traditions. Bachelors and damsels were originally both young, unmarried people, but the former stems from the medieval term for young men aspiring to knighthood (the modern equivalent being college graduates). "Damsel," on the other hand, is a word that originally, to quote the *Oxford Dictionary of English Etymology*, "had no implication of rank or respect." The *Oxford Dictionary* further notes that academia altered the medieval Latin *baccalarius* by a jocular (or false) association with *bacca lauri*, or laurel berry. Thus academic institutions

appropriated the traditional materials of the poet's crown by a false association between upper-class *men*, college graduates, and literary laurels. Moore's humor does not so much attempt to replace bachelors with
damsels as to rethink who owns knowledge or the respect (her word is
"immortality") such knowledge might confer. In the same vein, "The
Student" focuses on redefining education, originality, and representation, suggesting especially that the last is a word for which a thoughtful
reader should have two thoughts.

Moore's 1944 essay on Anna Pavlova gathers together many of the
ideas I have been tracing. The essay concentrates on Pavlova's autobiographical statements, moves to describe a photograph of Pavlova and to
cite a chorus of voices on the dancer. Moore focuses on the conditions
for writing one's self, and in particular for a woman writing herself, including, once again, ecstasy and energy as she notes Pavlova's problem
with "her simulacrum," and adds that "Nothing . . . so eludes portraiture
as ecstasy"; the contrast is with Degas, whose works are said to delineate
"attitudes not movement" (*CPr*, 387–88). Expanding some of the insights presumably first drawn from Stein's and the precisionists' "portraits," as opposed to Eliot's "Portrait of a Lady," this essay on portraiture
and self-expression is also a meditation on and an education in the
theory of representation; the objectified dancers of Degas, for Moore as
for Pavlova, are not only static, but they place women as the objects of
culture rather than the agents or representatives of culture.[41]

Moore, then, leads her readers to see and to question the relationship
between representation and representativeness. The political implications are especially clear when Moore contrasts Degas's dancers with
those for whom Pavlova choreographed—she insisted that her dances
"be within the ability of the average dancer"—and reiterates her distinction between process and product, underlining that for Pavlova's audience, it was not important "what she did . . . [but] how she did it" (*CPr*,
387, 391). It is for this reason that representations of Pavlova, especially
advertisements, are simulacra; indeed, the essay ultimately suggests no
representation is adequate, not Malvina Hoffman's wax statuettes, not
even good photographs or moving pictures, and, by implication, not
Moore's essay either (*CPr*, 388, 391). The images of democratic leveling
or action, then, although they are characteristic virtues in Moore's poetics, do not simply make Pavlova a representative woman, "a statuette of
ivory on ivory," as the 1923 "Marriage" describes "the logical last touch"
of self-representation within the social institution it explores (*CP*, 68).

In a late (1965) interview, Moore voiced admiration for pieces of criticism that "stimulate *resistance*" (emphasis added); encountering her
claim, in the same interview, that Emerson's "Representative Men" was a
piece of criticism she also admired, the reader of Moore finds that Em-

erson has been altered (*CPr*, 593). More importantly, though, Moore's reader finds herself not only questioning that literary tradition is composed of representative *men*, but also asking: "Representative of *what?*" And "*How?*" And "*At what cost?*"

One might carry these questions further in light of John Guillory's skepticism about what representation takes place in lists, syllabi, or canons, and his suggestion that texts are not authors and authors do not stand in for social identities so that simply to rewrite or revise lists is to reinscribe mass culture's dream (undreamed before the eighteenth century) of some cogent and homogeneous totality. In this light, Moore's impossible self-assigned task might be seen as the destabilization of lists and the unmasking of any act of list-making as potentially staking out imaginary boundaries in order to lay claim to some territory. That Moore's work contains such recognitions has everything to do with her own, local circumstances as a woman and a poet in early twentieth-century America, but this is not, on her own account, necessarily to say that including Moore's writings on our reading lists tells us about the characteristics of American women poets any more than Moore's Pavlova is offered as representative. "Does imagination care to look upon a sculptured fairy? . . . It would seem that Pavlova was obliged to overcome her roles," Moore writes, suggesting that "Pavlova" cannot or should not be reduced to what she can represent, nor to any representations of her (*CPr*, 391).

When I was asked if I would like to write an essay on Moore for a book on American women poets and literary history, I imagined I would discuss her inclusion of new and extraliterary sources and how such acts of inclusion shift for us the locus of intertextual references and finally even the definition of a "text." But in the course of thinking about how and why Moore moved from her exchange with Eliot and her association with modernist artists to her considerations of the uses of commercial culture and finally of representativeness and lists, with her growing uneasiness about the distribution of cultural capital and the fetishization of culture, I have come to think that one cannot easily use Moore's name or her work as representative of what it means to include women poets in literary history. At the same time, although literary traditions are always contingent, imagined totalities, their absence also can only be imagined. To learn how to read from Moore, I would conclude, is to be given "some way of working" within these contradictory recognitions.

Notes

1. T. S. Eliot, "Tradition and the Individual Talent," in *The Sacred Wood* (1920; repr. London: Methuen, 1960), 50.

2. Raymond Williams, *Problems in Materialism and Culture* (London: Verso, 1991), 39; John Guillory, "Canon, Syllabus, List: A Note on the Pedagogic Imaginary," *Transition: An International Review* 51 (1991): 170.

3. Jeanne Heuving, *Omissions Are Not Accidents: Gender in the Art of Marianne Moore* (Detroit: Wayne State University Press, 1992), 11–13.

4. John M. Slatin, *The Savage's Romance: The Poetry of Marianne Moore* (University Park: Pennsylvania State University Press, 1986), 120–27.

5. Marianne Moore, *The Complete Poems of Marianne Moore* (1967; repr. New York: Macmillan, 1981), 267. Hereafter cited as *CP*.

6. William Wordsworth, *The Prelude, 1799, 1805, 1850* (New York: Norton, 1979), bk. 12, line 302 (1805).

7. The poem was first published in *The Egoist*, vol. 3 (1 May 1916): 71, and appeared in all Moore's books of collected poetry. See Patricia C. Willis's comment on the poem in " 'He Wrote the History Book,' " *Marianne Moore Newsletter* 5 (Spring 1981): 19–20, in which she notes the poem stems from Moore's notes about ice-skating with the son of Charles McLean Andrews, one of her Bryn Mawr history professors.

8. William Doreski, "Extra-Literary Voices in Williams and Moore," *William Carlos Williams Review* 14 (Spring 1988): 46.

9. Again in the *Marianne Moore Newsletter*, Patricia Willis notes that Andrews later won a Pulitzer Prize for his four-volume American history, *The Colonial Period of American History* (1934–38); the 1903 college text, *The History of England for Schools and Colleges*, may well have been the book Moore used in the class she took from Andrews. The letter from Moore about her history class is also quoted by Willis, p. 20.

10. 2 July 1975 conversation with Naomi Rosenblum, cited in Paul Strand, *Sixty Years of Photographs* (Millertown, N.Y.: Aperture, 1976), 143–44, and Karen Tsujimoto, *Images of America: Precisionist Painting and Modern Photography* (Seattle: University of Washington Press for the San Francisco Museum of Modern Art, 1982), 92.

11. William Carlos Williams, *Autobiography* (1948; repr. New York: New Directions, 1967), 134–42.

12. 9 January 1919 letter to Ezra Pound, reprinted in *Marianne Moore: A Collection of Critical Essays*, ed. Charles Tomlinson (Englewood Cliffs, N.J.: Prentice-Hall, Inc., 1969), 18. Indeed, the paragraph from which the quotation is drawn is specifically a response to Pound's claim to have "had a hand in the publishing of T. S. Eliot." See also Bonnie Costello, *Marianne Moore: Imaginary Possessions* (Cambridge, Mass.: Harvard University Press, 1981), 187–89, 203–10, and Linda Leavell, "Marianne Moore and Georgia O'Keeffe: 'The Feelings of a Mother—A Woman or a Cat'," in *Marianne Moore: Woman and Poet*, ed. Patricia C. Willis (Orono, Maine: National Poetry Foundation at University of Maine, 1990) especially pp. 300–304, which discuss how Georgianna Goddard King, Moore's English teacher at Bryn Mawr, was a friend of Gertrude Stein's and used to circulate copies of *Camera Work* in class; it is in Moore's notebook containing her notes for this class that the reference to Stieglitz is found. Although Moore did not get to see 291 until 1915, did not manage to move to the New York area until 1916 (when she moved to Chatham, New Jersey), and did not have an actual New York address until 1918, her earliest scrapbooks and reading diaries are full of clippings and quotations on the arts, and especially those involving responses to the 1913 Armory Show from journals like *Letters and Arts* and *Current Opinion*.

13. *America & Alfred Stieglitz: A Collective Portrait,* ed. Waldo Frank et al. (New York: Literary Guild, 1934), 236–38.

14. The following discussion of "Bowls" draws on Lisa Steinman, "The Precisionists and the Poets," in *Precisionism in America 1915–1941: Reordering Reality* (New York: Abrams, in assoc. with Montclair Art Museum, 1994). Moore admired the art of Hartley, O'Keeffe, Stieglitz, Strand, Arthur Dove, Charles Demuth, and John Marin. See Marianne Moore, *The Complete Prose of Marianne Moore,* ed. Patricia C. Willis (New York: Viking, 1986), 150–51. Hereafter cited as *CPr.* As Charles Molesworth notes in *Marianne Moore: A Literary Life* (New York: Atheneum, 1990), 191, 325, she also met many of the artists through the New York salons and galleries, and in 1923 accompanied Williams on a visit to Demuth, who was in a sanitarium being treated for diabetes; by the thirties, if not before, she was clearly interested in Charles Sheeler's work.

15. Reprinted in Jacqueline Vaught Brogan, *Part of the Climate: American Cubist Poetry* (Berkeley: University of California Press, 1991), 286. Williams also often mentions Stein's modernity (see, for example, *Selected Essays* [1954, repr. New York: New Directions, 1969], 113–20; 104).

16. I quote from Marianne Moore, *Observations* (New York: Dial Press, 1924), 70. Moore revised "Bowls," which first appeared in *Secession* 5 (July 1923): 12, and was reprinted in the 1924 *Observations* and the 1935 *Selected Poems,* for her 1951 *Collected Poems.*

17. Moore's first gesture precedes Paul Rosenfeld's 1924 *Port of New York* description of O'Keeffe's work having "the precision of the most finely machine-cut products," which Tsujimoto points to as one of the earliest uses of "precision" to describe the precisionists' work (*Images of America,* 23). In fact, Lewis Mumford was using the word "precision" to describe a modern style at least as early as 1922 in "The City," in Harold E. Stearns's *Civilization in the United States: An Inquiry by Thirty Americans* (New York: Harcourt, Brace, and Co., 1922), 12, so the association between being precise and American modernist art—although not the precisionist label per se—was in circulation before "Bowls" was written. Stearns's book was reviewed in *The Dial,* vol. 72 (June 1922): 555, where Moore would have read of it.

18. Stein's piece is reprinted in Brogan, *Part of the Climate,* 33–34.

19. Marius de Zayas (founder of the Modern Gallery) and Francis Picabia (whose 1915 trip to New York involved him with Stieglitz and 291) both experimented with "object portraits." By 1915, Picabia's portrait of Stieglitz appeared in *291,* and his January 1916 exhibit at the Modern Gallery included the machine work *Fille née sans mère [Girl Born without Mother],* also published in *291* in June 1915 and then purchased by Stieglitz. See Patrick L. Stewart, "The European Art Invasion: American Art and the Arensberg Circle, 1914–1918," *Arts Magazine* 51 (May 1977): 110.

20. Marjorie Perloff, " 'To Give A Design': Williams and the Visualization of Poetry," in *William Carlos Williams: Man and Poet,* ed. Carroll F. Terrell (Orono: National Poetry Foundation at the University of Maine, 1983), 174–75. See also William Innes Homer, *Alfred Stieglitz and the American Avant-Garde* (Boston: New York Graphic Society, 1977), 190–93, for an alternate reading of the portrait.

21. See Susan Fillin-Yeh, *Charles Sheeler: American Interiors* (New Haven, Conn.: Yale University Art Gallery, 1987), 12, on Stieglitz and Sheeler's interiors. Fillin-Yeh also notes Sheeler's interest in the lines of vernacular architecture between 1915 and 1917.

22. See Rosalind Krauss, "In the Name of Picasso," *October* 16 (Spring 1981): 20–22.

23. The poem was first published as "A Graveyard" in *The Dial*, vol. 71 (July 1921): 34; Moore reprinted it in her 1924 volume *Observations*.

24. Finally, Picabia invites multiple readings, including erotic overtones, with his play between visual and verbal elements, for instance, his use of words like "foi," "amour," and "ideal" (see Perloff, "'To Give a Design,'" 174).

25. As early as 1925, Moore singled out Stieglitz's "Equivalents" for praise (*CPr*, 151). Stieglitz himself did not provide the metaphor of "equivalence" until the 1920s; see Rosalind Krauss, "Stieglitz/Equivalents," *October* 11 (Winter 1979): 129–40.

26. Strand, "Photography and the New God," *Broom* 3 (November 1922): 255–56. Most later critics second Strand's view; thus, for Wanda Corn, Demuth's "motion" is "futurist," not part of an aesthetic shared with precisionism (Wanda Corn, *In the American Grain: The Billboard Poetics of Charles Demuth* [Poughkeepsie, N.Y.: Vassar College, Agnes Rindge Claflin Endowment Series, 1991], 8), while for Hilton Kramer, "Nothing *moves* in this [precisionist] style. Everything is . . . *still*" (Hilton Kramer, "The American Precisionists," *Arts Magazine* 35 [March 1961]: 37).

27. The United States was often negatively associated with speed, as in Karel Čapek's comment that "America's predilection for . . . speed and success, is corrupting the world." (The comment, from the 16 May 1926 *New York Times*, was picked up and refuted by Moore [see *CPr*, 174].) For more on the association between American culture and speed, see Cecelia Tichi, "William Carlos Williams and the Efficient Movement," in *Prospects* ed. Jack Salzman (New York: Burt Franklin, 1982), 267–79, and "Twentieth Century Limited: William Carlos Williams' Poetics of High-Speed America," in *The William Carlos Williams Review* 9 (Fall 1983): 49–72.

28. Williams, *Selected Essays*, 123.

29. 10 January 1938 letter to Constance Rourke; cited in Mike Weaver, *William Carlos Williams: The American Background* (Cambridge: Cambridge University Press, 1971), 62.

30. Williams's judgment is also a product of his reaction to the Depression, as well as of his growing interest in (and experiments with a style for) motion; see Lisa M. Steinman, *Made in America: Science, Technology, and American Modernist Poets* (New Haven, Conn.: Yale University Press, 1987), 97–112. The exchange was an active one, which is to say that Sheeler was well aware of what his work omitted: "We are all confronted with social comment, but for myself I am keeping clear of all that. I am interested in intrinsic qualities in art. . . . I don't believe I could ever indulge in social comment" (cited in Carol Troyen and Erica E. Hirshler, *Charles Sheeler: Paintings and Drawings* [Boston: Boston Museum of Fine Arts, 1987], 142).

31. See *A Marianne Moore Reader* (New York: Viking, 1965), 215–24.

32. The piece on Moore is entitled "Life Goes on a Zoo Tour with a Famous Poet," *Life*, 21 September 1953, 202–7; the piece on Sheeler was entitled "Sheeler Finds Beauty in the Commonplace," *Life*, 8 August 1938, 42–45. For a discussion of how *Life* came to write about Sheeler, see Joan Shelley Rubin, "A Convergence of Vision: Constance Rourke, Charles Sheeler, and American Art," *American Quarterly* 42 (June 1990): 215.

33. Eliot, "Tradition and the Individual Talent," 59.

34. The poem under its original title appeared in *Others*, vol. 1, no. 6 (December 1915): 106, six months before the publication of "'He Wrote the History Book.'" The latter alone was reprinted in *Poems*, but in the first volume Moore put together (*Observations*), the poem is placed with "'He Wrote the History Book,'" and retitled with the Eliotic "The Past Is the Present."

35. Margaret Holley, *The Poetry of Marianne Moore: A Study in Voice and Value* (Cambridge: Cambridge University Press, 1987), 42; Holley quotes the passage from "So far as the future is concerned."

36. See Lisa M. Steinman, "Moore, Emerson and Kreymborg: The Use of Lists in 'The Monkeys,'" *Marianne Moore Newsletter* 4 (Spring 1980): 7–10.

37. As historians like Richard Pells have pointed out, related issues were under discussion in the late thirties, especially in magazines such as *Common Sense, The New Republic,* and *The Nation;* see Richard H. Pells, *Radical Visions and American Dreams: Culture and Social Thought in the Depression Years* (New York: Harper and Row, 1973), esp. 292–368.

38. See John M. Slatin, "'Something Inescapably Typical': Questions about Gender in the Late Work of William Carlos Williams and Marianne Moore," *William Carlos Williams Review* 4 (Spring 1988): 98–99.

39. Guillory, "Canon, Syllabus, List," 176–77.

40. I quote from "The Student," the middle section of "Part of a Novel, Part of a Poem, Part of a Play," *Poetry* 40 (June 1932): 122–26.

41. Heuving, *Omissions Are Not Accidents,* 30–35, discusses Moore's reaction to modernist portraits of ladies, and especially to Eliot's poem, which Moore's review of *Prufrock and Other Observations* singled out as "cruel."

Chapter 6
"The Frigate Pelican"'s Progress: Marianne Moore's Multiple Versions and Modernist Practice

Robin Gail Schulze

In 1987, *Poetry* magazine celebrated the centenary of Marianne Moore's birth with a two-day symposium at the Newberry Library in Chicago devoted to reappraisals of Moore's contribution to modernist verse. Hosted by Joseph Parisi, the gala event featured papers by poet-critics David Bromwich, Sandra Gilbert, John Hollander, Alicia Ostriker, and Robert Pinsky. At the end of the symposium, Parisi gathered his illustrious participants together for a panel discussion, which he moderated. One would think that a poet well-known enough to draw such distinguished literary company together could claim a secure and significant position in literary history. Yet, when a member of the audience asked the assembled panel to "speculate about Moore's place in literary history," the responses that ensued were both tentative and pensive. Although the panel came to a vague agreement about Moore's "influence" as a poet, the members also seemed to feel that Moore's poetry had yet to be truly esteemed or, at the very least, comprehended. John Hollander cautiously remarked, "I think Moore, despite attempts to claim her for all sorts of sectarianisms, is simply like a number of other major poets in not being understood or appreciated except by other major poets, and being gotten systematically wrong by literary journalism in all sorts of ways for a long time, until finally the point begins to emerge." [1]

Whether or not "the point" of Moore's modernism has yet begun to emerge remains a matter of debate even among those critics most devoted to her verse. In his preface to the published Newberry conference proceedings, Parisi himself observes that "compared with the industrial-sized scholarship that Eliot, Pound, Stevens, Williams, and others among her contemporaries have been accorded, including most recently her friend H. D., Moore has suffered relative neglect." [2] Unlike Pound, Eliot, Stevens, and Williams, all of whom recognized Moore's talent and importance, Moore currently has no scholarly journal dedicated to the ongoing study of her poems. Despite the scope of her work and the voluminous richness of her archival record, the number of book-length studies devoted to Moore's verse remains surprisingly small. As Andrew Kappel lamented during a conversation we had at the Modern Language Association convention a few years ago, critics of Moore's verse cannot yet claim to have generated competing readings for more than a mere handful of her poems.

The question of why Moore's work remains so undervalued in relation to her peers is complex, but Kappel's comment points to a problem central to Moore's reception. In part, Moore's role in the development of modernist practice and her position in literary history generally have been difficult to assess because of the slippery and unstable nature of her texts. Just what constitutes the text of a given Moore poem is not an easy question to answer. Throughout her lifetime, Moore remained an avid editor of her own verse. The bulk of Moore's poems appear in numerous, at times vastly different, published versions that occur over a period of some fifty years. Indeed, in the realm of textual scholarship, Moore has become a key example of a writer whose works baffle the established postwar editorial principle of an "author's final intention." In the traditional Anglo-American school of editing as formulated by W. W. Greg and extended by Fredson Bowers, it is the job of the critic or editor to discover and then to enact an author's "final intention" in regard to the reading of his or her text.[3] Examining the different versions of a text, the editor selects among the variant readings and assembles an eclectic "ideal" text out of disparate elements—the text that, in G. Thomas Tanselle's words, the author "wished the public to have."[4] As George Bornstein and Jerome McGann have pointed out, however, Moore's poems express a large number of seemingly "final" published intentions—arrays of changing designs and desires that, in terms of the chronology of her career, end only with her death.[5] Before critics can even begin to develop competing readings of particular Moore poems, they must first wrestle with the knotty questions of which version or versions they wish to address and why—questions that presently lie at the heart of theories of textual editing.

The problem of Moore's textual instability is further complicated by the present availability of her poems. Those who teach Moore on a regular basis know that the current standard edition of Moore's verse— *The Complete Poems of Marianne Moore* (Viking/Macmillan, 1981)—offers little by way of a satisfactory resolution to the vexed question of Moore's textual presentation. A reprint of the 1967 *Complete Poems* that Moore compiled five years before her death, the current edition proclaims loudly on its cover: "Definitive Edition, with the Author's final revisions."

Adopting the *Complete Poems* as the canon of Moore's verse certainly solves a number of problems involved in teaching and studying her poetry, but to consider Moore's "final revisions" as in any way "definitive," in essence to privilege the latest versions of her poems over all others, obscures the dynamic course of an entire literary career.

  The problems posed by the (in)*Complete Poems* have cast a long shadow over the study of Moore's poetry and prompted critics to a number of uncomfortable and incongruous accommodations. In her book *The Poetry of Marianne Moore: Study in Voice and Value*, Margaret Holley conducts a chronological "study of the development of Marianne Moore's poetic voice."[6] Yet, rather than trace the "development" of Moore's poems from version to version throughout her career, Holley selects the 1981 edition of the *Complete Poems* as the basis of her analysis—a stabilizing choice of Moore's "final intentions" directly in conflict with Holley's historical approach. Laurence Stapleton attempts to solve the problem of Moore's multiple texts in *Marianne Moore: The Poet's Advance* by basing her study of Moore's poetic development on the "first finished text" of each of Moore's poems—that is, the first version Moore approved in her various volumes beginning with *Observations* (1924).[7] Such an approach proves more historically satisfying, but it both ignores pre–volume versions of Moore's poems and persists in presenting each of Moore's texts as a single "finished" entity. Stapleton also fudges here and there with regard to her announced editorial principle. Abandoning the "first finished text" of a given poem as inferior, she often simply chooses to address a different version on purely aesthetic grounds. For example, Stapleton declares Moore's abridged 1951 version of "Nine Nectarines" "a distinct improvement" over Moore's detailed 1935 version, "Nine Nectarines and Other Porcelain" (the first finished text by Stapleton's definition), and devotes her interpretive energy to the shorter, later poem.[8] Predisposed to read Moore as a poet of contractility and compression, Stapleton at times selects that version of a poem that best reflects her notion of Moore's poetic. Such choices result in ahistorical inconsistencies that violate Stapleton's chronological narrative. Still other critics throw up their hands and plead practicality when faced with the editorial problems that attend Moore's poems. In *Marianne Moore: The Poetry of Engagement*, Grace Schulman argues against attempts to stabilize Moore's texts. "As for the major revisions," she states in her introduction, "they present a difficulty we should be grateful for. They are the lifeblood of the poems, and are fundamental to an understanding of what the body of work consists of."[9] Yet, despite this assertion, Schulman ultimately bows to the necessity of availability when deciding which versions of Moore's poems to address. Since no other volumes of Moore's work are readily available without access to a good research library,

Schulman, like Holley, chooses reluctantly to base her study on Moore's *Complete Poems.*[10]

Given the difficult nature of Moore's textual history, it is easy to see why so few critics confront her revisions in any depth.[11] Yet, where some scholars might envision Moore's multiple texts as a "notorious" problem, to use McGann's words, I tend to see her various versions as an opportunity to essentially rethink the nature of modernist poetry. As Moore's currently better known and more frequently studied contemporaries, Wallace Stevens, William Carlos Williams, Ezra Pound, T. S. Eliot, and H. D., all acknowledged, Moore played a central role in the shaping of modernist poetic practice. Restoring Moore and her poetics of radical instability to a place of primacy in the study of modernist poetry does much to undercut the concept, dear to many critics, of a closed, totalized, ahistorical, authoritarian modernist aesthetic. Changing her texts over the course of her career, Moore consistently denied the ahistorical authority of her own literary events and inevitably situated both herself and her variant texts in time. In each act of versioning, Moore altered her verse to suit a different sense of both self and context. By way of exploring how the fact of Moore's multiple versions might influence perceptions of modernist poetry, this essay offers a case study of one of Moore's most unstable texts—her poem "The Frigate Pelican." Moore first published "The Frigate Pelican" in 1934 in T. S. Eliot's journal, *The Criterion.* One year later, she made a few minor changes to the 1934 text and printed the poem again in her 1935 *Selected Poems.* When planning her *Collected Poems* in 1951, however, Moore returned to her Depression-era poem and severely abridged her 1935 version. Moore ultimately included the greatly shortened 1951 "Frigate Pelican" in her *Complete Poems.* Moore's revisions resulted in a radically different "Frigate Pelican" and her versions highlight the historical and social contingency of her modernist practice—a practice, in Moore's view, of dynamic process.

I

In the early 1930s, as America slipped into the desperation and want of the Depression, Moore became increasingly concerned with the question of the artist's debt to society at large. Faced with the growing weight of American misery and the strident demands of leftist poets for more socially conscious verse, Moore began to wonder if the poet could ever balance the pull of worldly obligations with the potentially escapist call to spiritual heights. In a 1932 letter to her former *Dial* magazine colleague Kenneth Burke, Moore complained that many of her fellow modernists seemed determined to avoid civic duties even while they professed their concern for the state of the world. Ezra Pound, she charged, "disapproves so strongly of Washington that he writes it a pamphlet of instructions but he has not been voting and does not expect to vote." Glenway Wescott, in turn, "asks the world to give him the necessary hours in which to write a book about its troubles and when we have the book, it is about him and not about the world." American artists, Moore conceded, had the nasty habit of asking parents "to eat their third baby, for to see so many hungry mouths about us is agitating and a menace to art." Turning a critical eye on her own behavior, Moore continued:

I am not prepossessed by patriotism in abstentia, but hypocrisy is equally abhorrent and at the risk of making myself look worse than I am, I confess to buying butter and potatoes at the A & P though my small grocer whom I occasionally patronize, goes out of business; and to writing a poem on a persimmon, let us say, instead of joining with our capitalist friends in handing out the local dole; and I should hate to see you interrupt your remarkable writing, for it is that, to make speeches for Norman Thomas or organize such emergency unemployment for labor as you yourself approve.[12]

While chiding herself for taking an easy road around social problems, Moore equally regretted the sacrifice involved when artists abandoned their work to pursue social causes. Should Burke neglect his "remarkable writing" and devote himself to stumping for the Socialists, the world, Moore implied, might ultimately be a poorer place for his choice. "We, most of us," Moore admitted to Burke with a sigh at the end of her letter, "abhor public service."

Choosing to forgo more concrete forms of "public service," Moore continued to write verse in a time of national upheaval that prompted her to pose disturbing questions about the potentially isolationist nature of poetic activity. As the world around Moore grew increasingly fractious, she turned her attention to the poet whose artistic prowess and imaginative power she found the most striking and, potentially, the most escapist—Wallace Stevens. Throughout the 1920s Moore penned several comments about Stevens that indicated both her appreciation of his aggressive imagination and her fear that his violent poetic mind sometimes went too far in its attempts to escape the mundane. In her well-known 1924 review of *Harmonium*, "Well Moused, Lion," Moore admired Stevens's "sharp, solemn, rhapsodic, elegant pieces of eloquence" and likened him to Crispin whose "mind was free / And more than free, elate, intent, profound."[13] She also noted, however, that Stevens had a poetic tendency to behave like a "wild jungle animal." "One resents the temper of certain of these poems," she complained in her review of *Harmonium*. "Mr Stevens is never inadvertently crude; one is conscious, however, of a deliberate bearishness—a shadow of acrimonious, unprovoked contumely." Certain of Stevens's verses indicated "a pride in unservice-

ableness," which made them, in Moore's view, "microcosm[s] of cannibalism." Disdaining propriety and utility, Stevens's verse at times violated
the deepest of social codes.

In the worst years of the Depression, Moore returned to her earlier
critique of Stevens's sometimes offensive and unserviceable evasions to
consider the proper role of the poet in times of national distress. Should
the poet be, like Stevens, an impolite, uncooperative creature, uncon-
cerned with the plight of the people and committed to the production
of private beauty at the cost of all social connection? Or, should the poet
be a creature committed to public service, a working member of a community focused on social matters of common interest? Moore posed the
question of the poet's role directly in terms of Wallace Stevens in her
1934 poem, "The Frigate Pelican." Moore's manuscript notes for her
poem clearly identify the frigate pelican as Wallace Stevens—his name
appears directly underneath a prominent mention of the bird in her
drafts and her manuscripts are filled with comments about Stevens's poetry borrowed from the pages of her earlier review of *Harmonium*, "Well
Moused, Lion." [14] In her finished poem of 1934, Moore casts the Stevensian frigate pelican as a strong and skillful imaginative voyager, the
"fleetest extreme fairy / among birds," a "marvel of grace" who soars
"full of feints" and keeps "a height so great the feathers look black and
the beak does not / show." [15] Named for a war ship, the Stevensian frigate
is well protected by his potentially violent art and supremely secure in
his individuality. Yet, like Stevens, the frigate poet lives by escaping into
a private lofty realm of the imagination that inevitably separates him
from his fellows. Reiterating her sense of Stevens's "pride in unserviceableness" from her review of *Harmonium*, Moore writes between draft
lines of her frigate poem that Stevens's "Pride in unserviceableness is not
synonymous with the beauty of aloofness." [16] Next to this damning comment in her worksheets Moore creates an image of the frigate pelican's
evasions that directly ties the bird to her vision of Stevens's aesthetic:

> This is how the mind works
> It is made to swell your body out
>   so that the others must fall back. [17]

The picture Moore paints is one of poetic power and potential arrogance. Rising above the others, the frigate's imagination puffs up the
bird in a beautiful display inevitably tied, as the word "swell" implies, to
pride—the top of Moore's list of artistic sins.

Yet, where Moore in earlier days would have chastised Stevens for his
seemingly antisocial artistic violence, in "The Frigate Pelican" of 1934

the issue of the poet's serviceableness becomes both difficult and debatable. Indeed, Moore constructs her poem in a way that specifically questions the desirability and feasibility of the frigate's attachment to the ground of worldly events. Moore devotes the first five and one half stanzas of the 1934 "Frigate Pelican" to a grounded viewer's description of the bird's astonishing artistic skill. Playing on the image suggested by the frigate pelican's name, Moore invokes the bird's boatlike qualities and offers a series of comparisons that, in the opening movement of the poem (the first six stanzas), subtly argue the necessity of the frigate's high-flying detachment:

> And, steering beak to windward always,
>   the fleetest extreme fairy
>   among birds, outflies the
>
> aeroplane which cannot flap its wings nor alter any quill-
>   tip. For him, the feeling in a hand, in fins, is
>   in his upbent downbent crafty oar. With him
>   other pelicans aimlessly soar
> as he does; separating until—
>   not flapping—they rise once more,
> closing in without looking, and move
>   outward again to the top
>   of the circle, and stop
>
> and blow back, allowing the wind to reverse their direction.
>   This is not the stalwart swan that can ferry the
>   woodcutter's two children home; no. Make hay; keep
>   the shop; I have one sheep, were a less
> limber animal's mottoes. This one
>   finds sticks for the swan's-down dress
> of his child to rest upon and would
>   not know Gretel from Hänsel.
>
>   (*Criterion*, 557–58)

Set against the vision of the frigate's lofty, facile, and potentially prideful artistic flight, Moore's image of the society that the Stevensian bird leaves below seems, in part, to warrant his escape. Strangled by what Coleridge termed the lethargy of custom, obsessed with practical commercial industry and everyday economies, those creatures trapped on the social surface in Moore's poem remain mentally rigid and blind to matters of the spirit. "Make hay; keep / the shop; I have one sheep, were a less limber animal's mottoes," writes Moore of the stiff imaginationless American animals of the thirties. Content to measure their lives with clichés, such grounded thinkers systematically seek to contain wild or free flying artists like the frigate and put such creatures to practical social use. Constructing a verbal/visual pun Moore states that the materialistic populace of the 1930s prefers the Grimm brothers' storybook stalwart swan to the agile frigate pelican, the practical domesticated bird/boat to the aggressive bird/warship, the industrious "ferry" of established social ideals to the fleetest extreme "fairy" poet who ignores the common run of acceptable maxims. Rather than serve the social needs of less limber minds, the male frigate ignores restrictive gender roles and compassionately cares for its own offspring. Utterly removed from familiar social symbols, the frigate, Moore states, "would not know Gretel from Hänsel."

The image of the Grimm brothers' dutiful swan leads Moore to consider the fate of another artist (German-born) who struggled against the imposed values of a domestic and domesticating culture, George Frideric Handel—a musician Moore associated with Stevens and his art throughout her career. As Moore notes of Stevens's artistry in her 1937 review of *Owl's Clover*, "Conjuries That Endure":

He [Stevens] has naturally in some quarters been rebuked for his skill; writers cannot excel at their work without being, like the dogs in *Coriolanus*, "as often beat for their barking / As therefore he kept to do so." But like Handel in the patterned correspondences of the Sonata No. 1, he has not been rivaled.[18]

Moore's 1937 connection between Stevens and Handel provides a telling gloss on her Stevensian frigate. Echoing her concerns in the 1934 "Frigate Pelican," Moore constructs an image of Stevens as a genius with a troubled relationship to the public sphere in which he writes. Moore's reference to the curs in *Coriolanus* implies that artists like Stevens actively warn society against impending harm, but, like watchdogs, they are often punished for their efforts to sound the alarm. The notion of great skill coupled with Shakespeare's play, however, also invokes the image of Coriolanus himself. Like Moore's Stevensian frigate pelican, Coriolanus embodies genius, nobility, and an open disdain for deadening custom. Shakespeare's senator, however, also remains the soul of destructive pride, the very sin that Moore fears most in the frigate's art—a "pride in unserviceableness not synonymous with the beauty of aloofness."

Moore's link between Stevens and Coriolanus in her review, however, gives way to her comparison of Stevens and Handel—a shift that signals her move away from a critique of creative solipsism toward a condemnation of a rigid public that cannot appreciate the artist's gifts. Like Coriolanus, Handel pursued his genius only to find himself banished from the domestic culture he called home—an image of unwilling artistic exile that Moore applies to her 1934 Stevensian frigate. "It is not retreat but exclusion from / which he looks down," she writes in the 1934 "Frigate Pelican." The issue of the artist's "pride" fades before the apparent painful necessity of the poet's withdrawal. Comparing Handel's experience to that of her Stevensian bird, Moore states that

> As impassioned Händel—
>
> meant for a lawyer and a masculine German domestic
>   career—clandestinely studied the harpsichord
>   and never was known to have fallen in love,
>   the unconfiding frigate-bird hides
>   in the height and in the majestic
>   display of his art.
>
> (*Criterion,* 558)

In an image that recalls Stevens's dual role as poet and lawyer/insurance man, Moore implies that Stevens, like Handel, remains free from the sin of pride by virtue of his spiritual calling. Moore's adjective "impassioned" marks not only Handel's creative fervor, but his predilection for sacred musical subjects like Christ's passion. The originator of the oratorio, Handel spent his career writing choral works based on Christian scriptures—musical acts of devotion that contradict the notion of the artist's prideful genius. Moore further suggests that, in refusing to merely fulfill his "masculine" role as worldly professional, Handel, like the Stevensian frigate, resists socially inscribed notions of gender and romantic love. Moore is careful to write that Handel "never was known" to have fallen in love, separating herself in the space of a passive construction from those who make such a judgment. The frigate is clearly "impassioned," but he directs his passion in ways that those blinded by custom cannot understand or appreciate. Moore ends the opening movement of "The Frigate Pelican" with an image of the bird's agility that doubles as a warning against such a narrow-minded public's potential intolerance:

> He glides
> a hundred feet or quivers about
>   as charred paper behaves—full
>   of feints; and an eagle

of vigilance, earns the term aquiline; keeping at a height
    so great the feathers look black and the beak does not
    show.
                                                (*Criterion*, 558)

Moore's description of the frigate in the first six stanzas of the poem culminates in an eerie equation between the bird and the remnants of a burned book—one hundred poetic feet reduced to ash by public demand. Moore implies that the domestic, practical populace expels such free spirits with violence, driving the bird/poet into a solitary position as an alien, all but invisible speck that those rooted to the surface can never see properly.

Thus, throughout the first six stanzas of her 1934 "Frigate Pelican," Moore fashions a description of the Stevensian bird that interrogates the poet's relationship to social convention and argues against the idea of the imaginative artist as arrogant solipsist. Indeed, in the middle section of her poem, stanzas seven through nine, Moore herself leaves the conformity of the domestic surface behind and follows the frigate into the air in order to see the world through his eyes. Freed from the lethargy and implied brutality of custom, the frigate's vision is by no means "domesticated." Drawing directly on Crispin's voyage to the "Caribbean amphitheater" in Stevens's "Comedian as the Letter C," Moore presents the frigate's poetry as a jungle aesthetic—"tough, diverse, untamed, / Incredible to prudes," to use Stevens's phrase—of violent and dangerous elements. From his vantage point, the frigate sees, not stalwart swans, but wild animals—"A jaguar / and a crocodile are fighting." Crispin's tropics "thick with sides and jagged lops of green, / So intertwined with serpent-kin encoiled / Among the purple tufts" appears through the eyes of Moore's frigate as a clinging union of the "spattered blood," a deadly orchid, and the fer-de-lance, a poisonous snake.[19] "Centaur- / like," Moore remarks of enjoined plant and serpent-kin, "this harmful couple's amity / is apropos."

Painting a tropical scene of color and violence in her 1934 poem, Moore presents and participates in the frigate's vision in a way that revises her earlier sense of Stevens's verse. In her 1924 review of *Harmonium*, Moore criticized Stevens for the "deliberate bearishness" and "pride in unserviceableness" that at times made his poems "microcosms of cannibalism." As much as she loved his "ferocity," Moore, in 1924, felt that Stevens's poems had a tendency to "go native," often wandering too far into the jungle and too far away from socially accepted notions of civilized poetic decorum. In her 1934 frigate poem, however, rather than critique the bird's jungle vision, Moore again works through a point of comparison and offers an image of socially decorous verse—the more "popular" art of the time—that frankly endorses the frigate's flight from custom:

> And here,
>   unlikely animals learning to
>   dance, crouch on two steeds that rear
>   behind a leopard with a frantic
>   face, tamed by an Artemis
>   who wears a dress like his,
>
> and a hampering haymaker's hat.
>   (*Criterion*, 559)

Moore presents an image of an artist who panders to the crowd, one who, clad in a "hampering haymaker's hat," caters directly to the social customs of those who "make hay," "keep the shop," and "have one sheep." Such a poet, Moore implies, simply gives the crowd what it wants—wildness domesticated, animals, like the stalwart swan, twisted into human service. The public prefers the familiar poetry of a bad circus to anything new or creative and the mock-Artemis poet—a sad sideshow version of the wild Greek moon goddess of the imagination—gladly complies, obscuring her own original vision beneath the constraints of the customs she adopts. Such an image of grounded artistry makes the frigate's wild, expansive poetic seem particularly attractive.

Moore's contrast between the hampered poetry of the circus Artemis and the frigate's successful escape from constraining customs ultimately leads her to the poem's central question of social responsibility. Having seen the ground through the frigate's eyes, Moore returns to the surface and wonders aloud if a poet of the spirit can, or should, serve the polis. "*Festina lente*," she admonishes the frigate, only to question her own grudging command: "Be gay / civilly, How so?" As John Slatin rightly notes, Moore's translation of "festina lente" (literally "make haste slowly") as "be gay civilly" points to her reckoning of the artist's debt to society at large.[20] Moore's response to her self-posed question of artistic decorum and civic duty marks a further revision of her earlier critique of Stevens's unserviceable verse:

> 'If I do well I am blessed
>   whether any bless me or not, and if I do
>   ill I am cursed.' We watch the moon rise

on the Susquehanna. In his way
   this most romantic bird flies
  to a more mundane place, the mangrove
     swamp, to sleep. He wastes the moon.
    But he, and others, soon

rise from the bough, and though flying, are able to foil the tired
   moment of danger, that lays on heart and lungs the
  weight of the python that crushes to powder.
    The tune's illiterate footsteps fail;
the steam hacks are not to be admired.
    These, unturbulent, avail
  themselves of turbulence to fly—pleased
    with the faint wind's varyings,
    on which to spread fixed wings.

The reticent lugubrious ragged immense minuet
   descending to leeward, ascending to windward
  again without flapping, in what seems to be
    a way of resting, are now nearer,
but as seemingly bodiless yet
    as they were. Theirs are sombre
  quills for so wide and lightboned a bird
    as the frigate pelican
    of the Caribbean.

                        (*Criterion*, 559–60)

Quoting a Hindu saying that she associated with Gandhi—"If I do well . . ."—Moore dismisses her admonition to socially acceptable gaiety as essentially flawed. The determination of poetic value, she insists, cannot rest with those whose minds have been hindered by convention or clouded by merely material concerns—the social python that crushes to powder. Those poets whom society damns and excludes may be blessed in their pursuit of spiritual imperatives higher than the condition of the state or the entertainment of the public.

As critics have noted, Moore ultimately pulls back from the frigate's aerial perspective and situates herself with a social group—a grounded "we" who remain rooted. But, as the final stanzas of the poem reflect, the frigate's vision has granted Moore a new and sorrowful sense of the planted position she claims. Watching the "moon rise on the Susquehanna," Moore returns to the landlocked Pennsylvania countryside where she spent much of her girlhood and leagues herself with those still fixated by old romantic tropes—a position that seems perilously allied to that of the domesticated poet moon goddess, the circus Artemis, of the previous stanza. "The tune's illiterate footsteps fail; / the steam hacks are not to be admired" writes Moore of the wheezing circus calliope— the popular debasement of the Greek muse of epic poetry—that haunts her grounded moon gazing. The frigate, by contrast, "wastes" such tired, reflected images of beauty and creates a violent Caribbean romantic that escapes the social python in ways that the landlocked romantic simply cannot. Confronting worldly concerns (the "more mundane place") "in his way," the frigate, Moore implies, serves a vital social function given the present domestic circumstances. Rising from the branch at the end of the poem, the frigate takes "others" with him, a sign that his verse plays a role in actively releasing those oppressed by deadening thoughts. Unrestrained by the blinders of custom, the bird has the power to lift others out of habitual blindness to a point of expansive spiritual vision. The frigate pursues a higher calling and rightly leaves the ground and the crippling steam hacks of "serviceable verse" behind.

At the end of "The Frigate Pelican," Moore suggests that her "unserviceable" Stevensian bird is, in fact, a socially responsible artist.[21] Rather than mere frivolous acts of prideful pleasure, the frigate's verses, she concludes, constitute serious and painful tests of spiritual devotion. The bird/poet who seemed so playfully ecstatic at the start of the poem appears "sombre" at the lyric's end—an adjective that reflects Moore's deepened sense of both the lonely cost of the frigate's vigilance and the serious dangers posed by a rigid domestic culture that crushes all but serviceable art and serviceable people. Indeed, Moore confirms the grave necessity of the frigate's lofty and liberating vision in the larger structure of her poem. Written in three distinct sections—Moore's description of the frigate, her participation in his vision, and her reassessment of his role—Moore's 1934 "Frigate Pelican" constitutes a variation of the kind of poem, common to Coleridge and Wordsworth, that M. H. Abrams terms the "greater Romantic lyric." As Abrams defines the genre:

The speaker begins with a description of the landscape; an aspect or change of aspect in the landscape evokes a varied but integral process of memory, thought, anticipation, and feeling which remains closely intervolved with the outer scene. In the course of this meditation the lyric speaker achieves an insight, faces up to a tragic loss, comes to a moral decision, or resolves an emotional problem. Often the problem rounds out upon itself to end where it began, at the outer scene, but with an altered mood and deepened understanding which is the result of the intervening meditation.[22]

George Bornstein modifies Abrams's "out-in-out" scenario by noting that, in modernist poems in particular, the "in" portion of the poem is more imaginative vision than meditation.[23] Moore's 1934 "Frigate Pelican" proves a variant of the description-vision-evaluation poem—a vicarious greater Romantic lyric in which the vision the speaker presents as the "in" portion of the poem is an imaginative conception of what another mind sees. Moore thus structures her 1934 poem in a way that demonstrates the frigate's vital social role. In the interior stanzas of the poem, the frigate pulls the speaker up from the crushing surface and grants her a moment of expanded vision—a new perspective on her condition that, while it sobers and saddens her, also saves her from the abuses of the sideshow Artemis. Like the "others" who rise from the bough at the lyric's end, the speaker flies for a time under the frigate's power and refreshes her own potentially habitual vision.

Moore thus concludes that the Romantic impulse that she feared as escapist in the twenties can and should prove a socially responsible and politically radical "foil" to the suffocating power of habit and custom in the thirties. The frigate becomes a Jeffersonian hero—an "eagle of vigilance" who proves that "Eternal vigilance is the price of liberty." Only the watchful who question custom and rise with imaginative power beyond oppressive thoughts remain free.

II

Moore's 1934 "Frigate Pelican," then, is very much a poem of its time—Moore's response, through her reading of the work of Wallace Stevens, to pressing questions of aesthetic responsibility and the social role of the romantic imagination inspired by both the Great Depression and the rise of totalitarian governments around the globe. In the case of the 1934 "Frigate Pelican," as with most of her poems, however, Moore took the matter of the frigate's endless agile vigilance to heart in her own work. Rather than conceive of her poem as a fixed entity, complete and rigidly dogmatic, she saw "The Frigate Pelican" as a work in progress—a statement to be reexamined and changed in response to changing conditions. In 1951, Moore returned to the text of "The Frigate Pelican" during the preparation of her *Collected Poems* and altered her lyric in dramatic fashion. In a flurry of excision, Moore cut her original twelve-stanza poem (one hundred and eight lines) to a skeleton of five and one half stanzas (forty-seven lines). Moore included the 1951 version again in her 1967 *Complete Poems* and the shortened form remains by far the better known of Moore's versions.

For those who have studied the intricacies of the 1934 poem, however, the 1951 version presents only a bare outline of Moore's original lyric—a testimony, in part, to Moore's altered circumstances. The world of 1951 in which Moore edited her poem was certainly much changed—transformed irreparably by the horrors of the Second World War and the death of Moore's beloved mother, Mary Warner Moore, with whom Moore had lived since birth. Throughout her life, Mrs. Moore was her daughter's closest friend, editor, and critic, and Moore greatly valued her mother's contributions to her work. In 1945, Mrs. Moore's health began to fail and Moore's own strength and spirit suffered under the strain of her mother's need for constant care. When her mother died in 1947, Moore entered a long period of deep depression during which she often found literary work a painful reminder of her personal loss. Moore's preparation of her *Collected Poems* occurred at an important point in her professional recovery, just as Moore, after many years, returned in earnest to the task of writing original verse.

Moore also returned to the text of "The Frigate Pelican" at a very different point in her relationship with Wallace Stevens. By the time of her excisions, Moore counted Stevens, whom she had not yet met in 1934, among her personal friends. In 1950, Stevens introduced Moore to the widowed wife (Barbara) of his longtime friend and colleague, Henry Church. Barbara Church and Moore quickly became devoted companions and Moore and Stevens, through the aegis of their mutual friend, met socially with increasing frequency in the early fifties. Also in 1950, Moore visited Stevens at his place of business, the Hartford Accident and Indemnity Company in Hartford, Connecticut, and published a subsequent poem of thanks to him for his years of public and poetic service. Entitled "Pretiolae" (little pretzels) after the treat made in Stevens's home town of Reading, Pennsylvania, Moore's lyric compares the classical facade of the Hartford building to "A temple of Apollo on a velvet sward." [24] Moore's image of the Hartford melds Stevens's office with a poetic shrine, his place of business with a place of artistic inspiration, and Stevens the insurance man with Stevens the poet. The Hartford building becomes a comfortable symbol of Stevens's ability to combine artistic pursuits with more practical obligations. Moore's sense of the spiritual poet's inevitable exile from domestic affairs that inspired her poem to Stevens in 1934 fades in the wake of a synthetic image of Stevens as a man of both artistic and worldly activity.

Given the remarkably different personal and political context in which Moore reshaped her poem, it is not surprising that the "Frigate Pelican" of 1951 bears little relation to the original. Yet, critics rarely consider the content or significance of her self-editing. One of the few scholars to analyze the scope of Moore's 1951 revisions in any depth, Andrew Kappel claims that the material Moore cuts from her poems when assembling them for her *Collected Poems* is "always material of the same sort." "Again and again," he writes, "she cuts passages given over to the . . . presentation of particularities." [25] Kappel argues that Moore's conscious pruning of descriptive details in 1951 shifts the balance of her verse "away from particularity and toward generalization," away from the presentation of rich empirical data and toward the consideration of abstract or philosophical questions. Moore's 1951 version of "The Frigate Pelican" provides Kappel with a key example of the type of material he claims that Moore was most likely to remove. "Her [Moore's] cuts from "The Frigate Pelican," he contends,

> are of passages given over largely to description of the admired bird of the title. These lines from the dropped original third stanza are typical: "The toe / with slight web, air-boned body, and very long wings / with the spread of a swan's— duplicating a. / bow string as he floats overhead—feel / the changing V-shaped scissor swallow- / tail direct the rigid keel." [26]

Kappel ultimately locates the impetus for Moore's revisions in her mother's dislike of poetic excess. Returning to her verse after her mother's death, Moore, Kappel suggests, excised large chunks of descriptive material because they seemed to violate her mother's artistic ideal of Presbyterian austerity.

While I agree, in part, with Kappel's assessment of Moore's cuts of 1951—certainly the death of Moore's mother and the deep depression Moore suffered as a result haunt her *Collected Poems*—I find Kappel's comments on Moore's revision of "The Frigate Pelican" in particular misleading. To cast the lines Moore removes from "The Frigate Pelican" as "given over largely to description" blurs the issue of the significant structural and tonal differences between the 1934 and the 1951 versions of the poem. Indeed, the very lines that Kappel claims as "descriptive" and "typical" of Moore's excisions—the approximately seventeen lines (part of stanza two, all of stanza three, and part of stanza four) that Moore cut from the opening movement of the 1934 "Frigate Pelican"— constitute more than a running account of the frigate's particulars. In the original version of the poem, Moore's attempt to picture the frigate throughout the lyric's opening four stanzas develops into an extended metaphor between the frigate pelican and the boat that shares its name. Moore's 1934 poem portrays the bird as a pirate ship. He is a "dishonest" frigate with a "rigid keel" and "crafty oar" that "steers" to "windward always." In her 1951 version, Moore elides her comparison and distinctly pulls back from the poetic act of making the bird into a water vessel. Moore's excised lines also contain heavy doses of alliteration meant to imitate the frigate's own technical artistic expertise. The consciously poetic phrases "superlative / swallow," "v-shaped scissor swallow-tail," and "fleetest . . . fairy," disappear along with Moore's punning side by side contrast of bird boats, frigate "fairy" and swan "ferry."

Thus, while it is true that the lines Moore excises from the start of the poem do describe the frigate's particulars, they also mimic the playful facility of his music. In the opening movement of her 1951 version, Moore suppresses her attempts to imitate the frigate's exuberant poetic repertoire and her first cut speaks directly to the more profound changes that she makes to later parts of the lyric. Moore's deepest cut to her 1934 "Frigate Pelican" occurs at the center of the poem and the heart of her greater Romantic lyric. In her 1951 version, Moore removes all of stanzas seven, eight, and nine of the original, roughly twenty-eight lines, the whole of Moore's view of the world through the frigate's liberating eyes. As Kappel suggests, the interior lines are indeed "descriptive," but they describe not the bird's particulars but what the Stevensian frigate himself observes—the dense jungle of violent elements that ties the poem to Crispin's introspective visionary voyage to the Caribbean amphitheater. Excising her stanzas devoted to the frigate's lofty imaginative perspective, Moore erases, in a neat package, the "in" or vision section of her greater Romantic lyric. In her 1951 version, she no longer rises under the frigate's power.

Just as Moore elides the vision portion of her vicarious greater Romantic lyric, so too she alters her subsequent consideration of the frigate's flight. In her 1951 version, Moore pares all but the first three lines of stanza eleven and all of stanza twelve from the final "out" or evaluation section of her 1934 greater Romantic lyric. Having removed the frigate's vision of the circus Artemis from the middle of the poem, Moore also excises her own comprehending evaluation of the debased nature of the Artemis poet's creations. Moore's emphatic damnation of serviceable verse—"the tune's illiterate footsteps fail; / the steam hacks are not to be admired"—disappears from the poem along with the sense that the speaker learns from the frigate to see beyond the customary abuses of circus poetry. At the end of the 1934 "Frigate Pelican," Moore, having shared the frigate's vision, claims a newfound understanding of the "sombre" social necessity of the frigate's flight from custom. Moore ends the 1951 version of the poem, however, not with the speaker's comprehension and appreciation of the frigate's lesson, but with the frigate's abrupt departure:

> —full
> of feints; and an eagle

> of vigilance. . . . *Festina lente.* Be gay
>   civilly? How so? 'If I do well I am blessed
>   whether any bless me or not, and if I do
>   ill I am cursed.' We watch the moon rise

on the Susquehanna. In his way,
    this most romantic bird flies
to a more mundane place, the mangrove
    swamp, to sleep. He wastes the moon.
    But he, and others, soon

rise from the bough and though flying, are able to foil the tired
    moment of danger that lays on heart and lungs the
    weight of the python that crushes to powder.[27]

At the end of her 1951 poem, Moore simply juxtaposes two different types of "romantic" vision: the frigate's vision that "wastes the moon" and resists the suffocating weight of the python, and the speaker's grounded civil vision that leaves her "crushed to powder." The frigate escapes, the speaker does not, and Moore concludes the poem with an image of the desperate "moment of danger" that the speaker's moon gazing cannot "foil." Any implication that the speaker can learn from or follow the frigate's example collapses in a pile of ground powder.

Looking closely at Moore's cuts to the 1934 "Frigate Pelican," it seems that, read together, they reflect far more than Moore's desire to weed out extraneous particulars. Indeed, each of Moore's excisions to the 1934 poem increases the creative gap between the grounded speaker and the imaginative frigate. In the opening of the 1951 poem, Moore suppresses her impulse to mimic the frigate's technical artistic facility. Metaphor, alliteration, and puns disappear. At the center of the 1951 poem, Moore excises the whole of her shared vision with the frigate and denies herself participation in his liberating flight. The freeing vision of the greater Romantic lyric disappears. At the end of the 1951 poem, Moore, unable to claim the frigate's sight as her own, leaves the reader with an image of the social python's pulverizing force. All three cuts of 1951, then, reflect Moore's doubts about her ability to share in the frigate's imaginative freedom. Suppressing the figurative and visionary points of her 1934 poem, Moore implies that she can no longer fly, even with the frigate's help. Any "view from the top," any imaginative counterpressure, becomes impossible in her 1951 poem and Moore remains painfully rooted, trapped beneath the crushing pressures of a sadder world.

In 1951, then, Moore returns to "The Frigate Pelican" and cuts it into a much darker poem—one that questions not only the notion of civil gaiety, but, in the speaker's case, the possibility of gaiety itself. As Kappel suggests, the grim message behind Moore's excisions is primarily one of the personal loss of her mother. Yet, where Kappel sees Moore's removal of "particulars" as an homage to her beloved mother's Presbyterian plainness, I see Moore's cuts to "The Frigate Pelican" as a statement of her own imaginative incapacity—a crisis of imaginative faith in a sad and diminished world. Moore excises not details, but the imagination itself from her 1951 poem and her collapse of the greater Romantic lyric seems to question whether the mind can ever adequately protect the self from the weight of worldly tragedy. In 1951, Moore cannot join the Stevensian frigate who seems calmly complete and guarded by a majestic display of art that she can no longer share or duplicate. Indeed, in 1951 the image Moore creates of Stevens—insurance man and Apollo in one—is a wishful image of a man utterly impregnable. Both Stevens's worldly pursuits, the marketing of insurance, and his artistic endeavors, the making of spiritual verse, provide protection against the random hazards of the actual world. In the 1951 "Frigate Pelican," Moore longed for, but could not claim, such safety and pictured herself crushed by the dangerous python of everyday existence.

Moore thus makes two different poems for two different times—one a greater Romantic lyric that, through the work of Wallace Stevens, argues the social necessity of the poet's lofty vision in an age of spiritless materialistic ignorance, the other a visionless skeleton that denies the speaker's ability to imaginatively rise above the ground. The first portrays Moore's 1934 hope that poets like Stevens and herself might somehow serve as saving keepers of the good in socially dangerous and oppressive times. The second betrays Moore's disappointment and acknowledgment that, after a long season of both national and personal tragedy (the war poets could not prevent and the death of her mother that Moore could not avert), even she cannot muster or trust in the imagination's defensive balm.

The question remains then, which do we consider to be the definitive text of Moore's poem? Each version reflects the context in which it was created; each is the product, as the above case study reveals, of a different poet responding to a different set of personal and political circumstances. Indeed, the issue of Moore's "final authorial intention" in the text of "The Frigate Pelican" becomes even more complicated in light of the particular way in which Moore removes the frigate's vision from her 1951 poem. As Kappel notes, Moore roughly papers over her first point of excision from the opening movement of the poem. She combines the second and fourth stanzas of the original in a manner that disrupts the syllable count of her established template and shortens the stanza by one line, but maintains the off-rhyme at the end of the first and fifth lines of the stanza as well as the full rhyme of the stanza's closing couplet. The resulting stanza in the 1951 poem bumps a bit, but sustains the pattern of contraction (the move from an opening line of fifteen syllables to a closing line of six) common to the stanzas of the original poem. At her second point of excision—the frigate's vision—however, Moore engineers her cut much differently. Keeping the phrase "of vigilance" from the seventh stanza of the original version, Moore inserts an ellipsis that takes the place of the whole of the frigate's vision and cuts directly to the phrase "*Festina lente*" in the first line of the tenth stanza:

> —full
> of feints; and an eagle
>
> of vigilance. . . . *Festina lente.* Be gay
> civilly? How so? 'If I do well I am blessed
> (*Collected Poems*, 32)

Kappel claims that Moore's ellipsis gives the impression of "continuous discourse," that the poet observes the bird and then pauses to consider the spectacle in terms of the foreign phrase that haunts her consciousness. In Kappel's view, Moore's ellipsis hides, rather than announces, the fact of her excision and "bears witness to her lingering commitment to hiding omissions."[28] While I agree with Kappel that Moore's approach to the gaping hole in the middle of her poem constitutes a "crucial moment" in the history of her revisions, I read the event differently. Moore precedes her ellipsis with a period at the end of the phrase "of vigilance," a construction that, in itself, indicates omission as much as a reflective pause. Also, given the cut-and-paste reduction that Moore makes of stanzas two and four of the original poem, it seems reasonable to assume that, if Moore had truly wished to hide her omission completely, she would have found a similar solution in her combination of stanzas seven and ten. Moore ultimately leaves her new composite first line noticeably lacking in syllables, eleven rather than fifteen. As Kappel himself notes, other poems Moore cut for *Collected Poems* in 1951 also contain full line ellipses—"The Buffalo" and "Nine Nectarines" to name two—that frankly emphasize, rather than obscure, the fact of missing material.

My point here is that it is possible to read the 1951 "Frigate Pelican," and several other 1951 versions of Moore's texts, as poems in which Moore advertises her omissions—a strategy that has profound implications for the study of both Moore's verse and modernist poetry generally. Rather than simply remove the interior lines that she no longer finds suitable from "The Frigate Pelican," Moore leaves behind a small marker, an ellipsis that reminds the reader that something once part of the poem is now missing. Moore, in essence, refers the reader of the 1951 "Frigate Pelican" to the earlier 1934 version of her poem. Moore's ellipsis in the 1951 "Frigate Pelican" keeps both versions of the poem in play at once and foregrounds the fact that her poetry constitutes a continuous process rather than a fixed product. "Omissions are not accidents," Moore proclaims in the flyleaf to her *Complete Poems* in 1967, but neither are Moore's omissions textual acts meant to supersede all previously existing versions of a particular poem. Moore's ellipses challenge the reader to consider what has been left out, to think back to the previous versions of a poem and examine what the act of omission itself contributes to the meaning of the most recent version. In the context of the 1951 "Frigate Pelican," Moore's ellipsis sends the reader back to the 1934 poem and the lines that portray the frigate's lofty vision. The ellipsis marks an absence of the visionary romantic imagination and only in reading back to the liberating release depicted in the previous version does the social python in the 1951 poem reveal its horrible crushing power. The ellipsis stands for the flight the poet can no longer achieve— a flight Moore wishes her readers to remember and to miss.

"The Frigate Pelican" remains only one of the many poems that Moore radically revised later in her career, but the differences between Moore's versions of her frigate poem show just how much a sole reliance on the many excised texts of the 1981 *Complete Poems* alters the shape of Moore's career. Inclined to cite Moore's phrase "Omissions are not accidents" as a clear statement of her final (and singular) authorial intentions, critics who rely on the late versions of Moore's poems have a tendency to read her as primarily a poet of compression and contractility—a poet at all times obsessed with plain effect and "neatness of finish" who spent her life in a self-defeating revisionary quest for ideally neat poems. Yet, as Moore emphatically proclaims in her tour de force 1924 poem "An Octopus," "neatness of finish" is not the goal of the thinking artist, but rather "relentless accuracy." The Moore of 1924 declares that art can never be "neat" or "finished," that intellectual discovery is always, by nature, changing, messy, and incomplete. Certainly the Moore of *Complete Poems* compresses her texts, but to read compression as her always and only aesthetic robs her career of all complexity and endows the *Complete Poems* with a teleological rightness that Moore's late texts themselves dispute. Moore's later radical excisions and abridgments, her glaring disruptions of meticulous syllabic patterns, her obvious open gaps and fissures marked with ellipses (yes, she says, something is missing here) all signal that her late versions of poems have, for lack of a better phrase, a collective memory of changes made over the course of time. Moore implies, in her 1951 version of "The Frigate Pelican" and elsewhere, that the meaning of a particular poem rests not in a single version, but in the unstable and messy distances and differences between versions—distances that critics must recognize if Moore's contribution to a modernist aesthetic of textual instability and historical contingency is to be properly acknowledged.

Notes

This article is dedicated to the late Andrew J. Kappel, with whom I miss arguing.

1. For a printed record of this discussion see "Marianne Moore: The Art of a Modernist Master—A Symposium" in *Marianne Moore: The Art of a Modernist*, ed. Joseph Parisi, (Ann Arbor: University Microfilms Press, 1990): 105–24. Hollander's comment appears on page 121.

2. Ibid., xi.

3. For the development of the traditional theoretical notion of an "author's final intention" in scholarly editing, see W. W. Greg, "The Rationale of Copy-Text," *Studies in Bibliography* 3 (1950–51): 19–36, and Fredson Bowers, "Some Principles for Scholarly Editions of Nineteenth-Century American Authors," *Studies in Bibliography* 17 (1976): 223–28. For a general summary and critique of the concept of authorial "final intention," see Jerome McGann's important rethinking of the issue in *A Critique of Modern Textual Criticism* (Charlottesville: University Press of Virginia, 1983).

4. G. Thomas Tanselle, "The Editorial Problem of Final Authorial Intention," *Studies in Bibliography* 29 (1976): 167–211.

5. See Bornstein's introduction "Why Editing Matters" in George Bornstein, ed., *Representing Modernist Texts* (Ann Arbor: University of Michigan Press, 1991): 1–16, and McGann's chapter "The Problem of Literary Authority" in *A Critique of Modern Textual Criticism*, 81–94.

6. Margaret Holley, *The Poetry of Marianne Moore: A Study in Voice and Value* (Cambridge: Cambridge University Press, 1987), xi.

7. Laurence Stapleton, *Marianne Moore: The Poet's Advance* (Princeton: Princeton University Press, 1978), xvi.

8. Ibid., 78–79.

9. Grace Schulman, *Marianne Moore: The Poetry of Engagement* (Urbana: University of Illinois Press, 1986), 5.

10. Ibid., 6.

11. A notable exception is Andrew J. Kappel, whose work I will address later in this essay.

12. Marianne Moore to Kenneth Burke, 30 November 1932, Marianne Moore Collection, Rosenbach Museum and Library, Philadelphia, Pa.

13. Marianne Moore, "Well Moused, Lion," *The Dial* 76 (January 1924): 84–91. Reprinted in Marianne Moore, *The Complete Prose of Marianne Moore*, ed. Patricia Willis (New York: Viking, 1986), 91–98.

14. Marianne Moore, unpublished poetry notebook, Marianne Moore Collection, Rosenbach Museum and Library, 1251/12. The pages in this notebook are loose and unnumbered.

15. Marianne Moore, "The Frigate Pelican," *The Criterion* 12 (July 1934): 557–60. In her slightly revised 1935 version of the poem, Moore changes the phrase "fleetest extreme fairy" to "fleetest foremost fairy." Her small alteration speaks to her growing admiration for Stevens's artistry. Where the word "extreme" may still imply a movement beyond acceptable boundaries of poetic decorum, the

word "foremost" completes the alliterative sweep of the phrase with a word of praise. All subsequent references are to Moore's 1934 *Criterion* version of "The Frigate Pelican" unless otherwise noted.

16. Marianne Moore, unpublished poetry notebook, Marianne Moore Collection, Rosenbach Museum and Library, 1251/12.

17. Ibid.

18. Marianne Moore, "Conjuries That Endure," *Poetry* 49 (February 1937): 268–72. Reprinted in *The Complete Prose of Marianne Moore*, 347–49.

19. Wallace Stevens, "The Comedian as the Letter C," in *The Collected Poems of Wallace Stevens* (New York: Knopf, 1954), 35.

20. John Slatin, *The Savage's Romance: The Poetry of Marianne Moore* (University Park: Pennsylvania State University Press, 1986), 206.

21. In John Slatin's interpretation of "The Frigate Pelican," the community that the frigate generates is not endorsed by the speaker as a possible alternative to the crush of present conditions. In Slatin's view, the birds remain condescending—they look down on the earth in a way that Moore does not deem civil. See *The Savage's Romance*, 207–8. Yet, Moore's harsh picture of the human cost of civility in the present political climate makes the flight of the frigate, in my reading of the poem, seem an indispensable model.

22. M. H. Abrams, "Structure and Style in the Greater Romantic Lyric," in *The Correspondent Breeze: Essays on English Romanticism* (New York: W. W. Norton and Co., 1984), 77.

23. George Bornstein, *Transformations of Romanticism in Yeats, Eliot, and Stevens* (Chicago: Chicago University Press, 1976), 9.

24. Marianne Moore, "Pretiolae," *Wake* (1950): 4. Reprinted in Patricia Willis, *Vision into Verse* (Philadelphia: Rosenbach Museum and Library, 1987), 66.

25. Andrew J. Kappel, "Complete with Omissions: The Text of Marianne Moore's *Complete Poems*," in Bornstein, *Representing Modernist Texts*, 125–56.

26. Ibid., 142.

27. Marianne Moore, "The Frigate Pelican," in *The Collected Poems of Marianne Moore* (New York: Macmillan, 1951), 31–32.

28. Kappel conducts a detailed discussion of Moore's ellipsis. See "Complete with Omissions," 148–49.

Part IV
Edna St. Vincent Millay
(1892–1950)

Chapter 7
Jouissance and the Sentimental Daughter: Edna St. Vincent Millay

Suzanne Clark

> The effect was at first, to embarrass me: it was a little as if a Shake-spearean actor were suddenly, off the stage, to begin expressing pri-vate emotions with the intonations of the play.
> —Edmund Wilson, *I Thought of Daisy*[1]

> Long ago, when I was mooning and dreaming through the pigtail period, I used to think how fine it would be to be the greatest woman poet since Sappho. The audacity of youth—the near-childhood—would have scorned any lower goal.
> —Harriet Monroe, "Comment: Edna St. Vincent Millay"[2]

I

In the age of Eliot, defined by the failure of relationship and the anti-heroics of the poetic loner, Edna St. Vincent Millay was writing most of all about love, and her sentimental subject was only the beginning of her crime: more than that, she was writing in a way that is easily understood, that invites the reader in, that makes community with the reader and tries to heal alienation. Millay was of course flagrantly engaged during the twenties in the bohemian leftish life-style of Greenwich Village, with its tenets of free love and support for the working masses. She worked on behalf of Sacco-Vanzetti and chaired the committee to raise funds for Emma Goldman's autobiography. But her radical life-style never put off her readers the way a radical poetics might have. She did not practice the modernist anarchy of style: Millay's poetics were founded on com-monality. She might shock her readers, but she did not separate herself from them. The accessibility of her work seemed from the beginning of her career more important to her audience than her bohemian attitudes. In Millay, we see that the gestures of social revolt don't always sever ties. She could write "My candle burns at both ends" and take a flippant attitude about her lovers, but the fact that she did it in sonnet form kept her credentials as the poetess of the American middle-class consensus in order. The epithet "bourgeois" or "middle-class" in the mouth of a modernist critic was meant to be as devastating as the charge of sentimentality. But some continuity with the middle class was for Millay as for many other women writers a prerequisite for maintaining a woman's tradition and for creating a community with women readers.

This context helps us to understand the antagonistic critical reception given Edna St. Vincent Millay as she grew in popularity during the thirties and forties. John Crowe Ransom criticized Millay for her sensibility: "Miss Millay is rarely and barely very intellectual, and I think everybody knows it."[3] Allen Tate said, "Miss Millay's success with stock symbolism is precariously won; I have said that she is not an intellect but a sensibility: if she were capable of a profound analysis of her imagery, she might not use it."[4] And Cleanth Brooks simply picked up Ransom's theme to conclude that Millay was "immature." She failed to be a major poet because she lacked irony: "Miss Millay has not grown up."[5]

In spite of the continuing influence of modernism and its elevation of intellect over sensibility, let us not forget the small numbers of its audience. Millay had a popular and sweeping success as a "poetess." Her sentimental readers were in the majority, and they recognized her immediately. I found an early piece on Millay appearing in a 1922 volume called *Flames of Faith*, written by a New York evangelist popularly known as "Wild Bill" Stidger. Remembering the long-term connections between revivalism and feminine rhetoric, I was not so completely surprised, even though Millay's reputation as a "new woman" would seem contrary to attracting such readers. Stidger was responding to Millay's sentimental rhetoric, which he read as an expression of feeling: "Whose heart will not be won by these lines" he asked by way of introduction to Millay's little poem, "Tavern."[6] A poem about a tavern may not seem a likely topic for the sentimental reader. But Stidger went on to say, after quoting as well from "God's World" ("O World, I cannot hold thee close enough!") and "Renascence" ("The soul can split the sky in two, / And let the face of God shine through!"), that "her first message was one of a great, groping sense of suffering. So men and women sing who have lost some loved one."[7]

The loss, one might argue, is a loss of female community itself, although the community of suffering and of loss is not simply female. By Millay's time, the codes of pathetic appeals, together with the literary inheritance from sentimental narratives that had been associated with female writing, were under attack by literary modernists. What we have in Millay is in part at least a writing that unites rhetoric and poetics, appeals to conventional ideas, and appeals to feeling. Speaking from a place of authority that is female, Millay refused the separation of the subject from social convention. Her work is at once personal and conventional. It's easy enough to call it sentimental.

Modernism has given us an ideal of an impersonal, serious art, a poetics severely separated from rhetoric. This modernist poetics is indeed at odds with Millay's poetic practices, as with any text that fails to separate itself sufficiently from the personal or from the drama of its performance. Modernism assumes an estrangement between the poem and the reader—difference, not familiarity. Exile, not community.

The marginal subject has difficulty participating in the modernist revolution of poetic language. As we see with Millay, the marginal speaker must do something familiar. Difference is different if you're in danger of never being listened to in the first place. Millay's poetry may be read rhetorically, as an argument that she is to be considered a real poet. However, the very fact that this persuasive appeal is going on keeps the poetry from being read as poetry, as modernist text. Because she is accessible to readers, she is "marginal" only in a special sense, though it is a sense that she cared about very much. Millay is marginal as her readers have been—all the readers of *Vanity Fair* and *Ladies Home Journal,* and all the high school students who have put her poems to memory, and the former students who can recite them still, generations later. Because this powerful community, influenced by women as readers (and teachers), was invisible to literary criticism, it did indeed inflict on Millay a literary marginality. To this day she may seem not quite interesting, not really subversive, her passion perhaps even a little nauseating to the ironic reader.

In spite of the reputation for rebellious marginality she acquired by her penchant for dramatic gesture, then, Millay wrote poetry that appears to do the opposite of demonstrating female difference. Far from subverting the masculine tradition by using poetic conventions in new ways, in the very age of "make it new," Millay was writing sonnets. She subverts male modernism by appropriating conventional male poetics from a more classic past, speaking a colonized discourse.

More popular and more widely read to this day than Pound or Williams (but not, of course, by readers who can be classed as "literary"), Millay disappears into the crowd. She writes within conventions so much a part of the dominant culture that she is easily assimilated by it. Millay's poetry celebrates the failure of independence even in its defiance, seeming to advocate a return to the domain of the natural, the simple, the pastoral order—to the myth that joins Christian sacrifice to nature in the figure of the mother. Thus Millay uses the rhetoric of sentiment on be-half of aspirations admittedly bourgeois, to a kind of power women were already used to claiming in the early years of this century—a power over human feelings and community that, in fact, modernist male writers re-jected as they rejected all rhetorical and political ambitions for poetry. Readers could recognize immediately that she speaks as a poet in favor of interests long supported by the middle class—interests of importance to women because they had been established through the whole of the nineteenth century by female writers as the best means for women to exercise power, as Jane Tompkins's work on *Uncle Tom's Cabin* has dem-onstrated.[8] The alienation of affection and the personal that was mod-ernism was bound to reject Millay, as it rejected in a larger sense the claims of women and sentimentalism to power and value.

II

Though the differences between Julia Kristeva and other French femi-nists like Hélène Cixous and Luce Irigaray are significant, they reflect a similar hope of joining feminism and the avant-garde in a literary prac-tice that would rupture the phallogocentricity of language from within the discourse of the Western tradition. However, the kinds of rupture and renewal effected by women's writing depend upon the historical reading it might receive. In the twenties, the question of whether to "make it new" by writing in free verse and abandoning traditional forms did not simply involve women writers in a debate about new and old *forms*. The choice of form, convention, and style had consequences that were ideological and that propelled women writers into professional im-passes at all levels of their work.

Freud limited the wishes of women to erotic longings. John Crowe Ransom allowed us "sensibility." Women should be interested only in feelings or love, not the intellect. But, as Roland Barthes said, "love falls outside of *interesting* time; no historical, polemical meaning can be given to it; it is in this that it is obscene."[9] Making herself a poetess of love, Millay took up a position that would not be interesting and, indeed, would take on a certain obscenity.

As Barthes signaled, the figures that make up the lover's discourse are not connected by plot—"interesting" or historical time defines the love story from outside it, so that the lover's discourse is made up of figures that must be recuperated by the master narrative. These figures of love—these lyric moments—appear then as episodes of the imaginary, some-thing to be gotten over, grown out of. They are the figures of a discourse without warrant:

the lover's discourse is today *of an extreme solitude.* This discourse is spoken, perhaps, by thousands of subjects (who knows?), but warranted by no one; it is completely forsaken by the surrounding languages: ignored, disparaged, or derided by them, severed not only from authority but also from the mechanisms of authority (sciences, techniques, arts). Once a discourse is thus driven by its own momentum into the backwater of the "unreal," exiled from all gregarity, it has no recourse but to become the site, however exiguous, of an *affirmation.*[10]

The figures of love in Barthes have some qualities of the Lacanian "imaginary," articulated by the master codes of history, a symbolic order, but they partake as well of the Kristevan "semiotic," that motility that is before meaning. Sensibility inhabits the figure. Jane Gallop has already looked at some of the difficulties presented by the differences between the Kristevan semiotic and the Lacanian imaginary, and by our rejecting stance toward the imaginary: "The symbolic is politically healthy; the imaginary is regressive. . . . Since the imaginary embodies, fleshes out the skeletal symbolic, it is possible to see the Lacanian devaluation of the imaginary as related to a hatred of the flesh, of woman and of pleasure." [11] This devaluation of the imaginary in the name of history may also imply a refusal to recognize the conventional power of the feminine, love, the psyche, the sentimental. It is a refusal to recognize that these very categories are not timeless but the creations of the time-bound. Barthes, like Ransom, inhabits modernity, and so to him the relentless renewal of intellectual novelty appeared as the master narrative of historical time.

A modern woman poet could not be a woman poet without speaking a discourse that would violate the unconventionality of modernism and seem politically regressive. Karl Shapiro's review of Millay's poetry shows us the critical refusal:

> The poems have an intimacy which makes the reader recoil, even if he is susceptible to this flirtation. What is worse, it is the intimacy of the actress and (off-stage) the *femme fatale.* All this has been said before, and it is said best in the poems. The center of her experience is love, but it is the most desperately middleclass love poetry one can imagine, with neither rough-and-tumble nor courtliness nor high sacrifice. But it rings so true—that makes it worse—and it is so well said, with all its horrid mannerisms; it is such a parody of the great love poets that one is dissolved in tears.[12]

Like the rebellious Jo in *Little Women,* Millay does not escape the sentimental plot.[13] Millay's boyish posturing as "Vincent" scarcely disguises her girlish allegiances to a world governed by women, especially the mother, and her mastery of traditional male literary forms at the historical moment of modernism serves only to put her into a tradition that has lost its cultural endorsement, now become the genteel codes of women writing for women. Ransom says Millay is "the best of the poets who are 'popular' and loved by Circles, Leagues, Lyceums, and Round Tables," and Delmore Schwartz echoes the horror of such fame: "The late John Wheelwright remarked that Miss Millay had sold free love to the women's clubs." [14]

But visibility with the women's clubs was precisely what Millay, "greatest woman poet since Sappho," needed to accomplish. Harriet Monroe's unusually gushy accolade only underscores the great gap between Sappho and any modern poetic tradition for women. As Susan Gubar has suggested, the influence of Sappho on modernist women shows their need for precursors, some kind of literary ancestry, a "fantastic collaboration" with a missing past. [15]

III

How does one grow up to be a woman and a poet? What kind of transformation or conversion is required? What is the female version of the plot? The famous poem that won Millay a place as "poet" with her first publication (perhaps too soon) is a liminal narrative of rebirth, "Renascence." It is a poem of adolescence, but it is also a narrative that announces the major issues of Millay's future poetry, the issues of separation and identity. Recognition for the female poet required her to ask how she could write like a man.

In "Renascence," the speaker, in what begins as a Romantic experience of nature, is soon overwhelmed by the natural intimacy. The encounter makes the speaker recoil, leads to burial in a womb/tomb, and the rebirth of the subject involves an escape from an engulfing, undefined female body, as from the immersion (underground) in nature. The speaker's anxiety about maternal influence does not quite fit the Oedipal plot; it is related to the ambivalence of being a mother's daughter. We may read such a plot again and again in Millay's poetry, for it involves her historical encounter with the difficulty of the woman as poet. The particularity of the poem's speaker is overwhelmed by the scene of poetry. The imaginary figure of the cultural feminine (mother, nature, sympathy) looms threateningly over the girlish hyperbole, transforming the childish excesses, the imitations and the mimes, into the oracular musings of a goddess, lover of art, poetess. [16]

What appears in this poem as a private encounter with the transcendental turns out to represent public events, for the poem tells the story of the same capture by an ideology that equated woman, other, nature, poetry, and sometimes God, which was Millay's fate from the moment of that poem's publication in the 1912 *Lyric Year*, with its attendant "discovery" of her, and the publicity's ensuing creation of her image as *the* American poetess. Millay's great success with this poem, making the rest of her career seem an anticlimax, came in part because the poem fit the hopes of middle-class readers. But a woman poet cannot afford to reject precursors when her struggle is all toward entering the lineage of poets. And, notoriously, the woman's plot does not sever maternal connections.

Nevertheless something remains from "Renascence" once we have acknowledged the familiar (frequently anthologized) comforts of what appears to be a feminized version of transcendental resurrections. There is, perhaps, a *difference*, something besides the threats and reassurances of inspiring verse. The Oedipal struggle of child and parent is translated into several registers—the self and mother nature, the sinner and God, the poet and romantic precursors—and at every level the seductions of identification contend against successful separation. The *difference* of "Renascence" as it enters literary history is a failure to become fully "different" or reborn.

The plot of "Renascence" engages the speaker of the poem in a death and rebirth that may be read in Freudian terms as a crisis in the relationship of a child to a maternal principle. However, the daughter/poet of "Renascence" cannot simply solve the problem of identity by separating from the other. From the beginning of the poem, the reciprocity of speaker and world is both threatening and necessary, an enclosure of the senses. The circular boundary of the horizon is also a temporal return "Back to where I'd started from," to a womb-like enclosure. Distance between self and the world collapses—"things seemed so small," even the distance to the sky, "I see the top" and "reaching up my hand to try, / I screamed, to feel it touch the sky." [17]

Critical to Millay's struggle in "Renascence" is an ambiguity about the gender of the "other." She undergoes what seems at first to be a Leda-like rape by the infinite: "I screamed, and—lo!—Infinity / Came down and settled over me" (4). But in the middle, the overwhelming is an imaginary identification with an "other" that, rather than violently establishing difference, enforces sameness, a joining to the other (a mother?), which at once defines her and forces her knowledge of a universal poisonous (or poisoned?) wound. The encounter suggests the mirror stage in its visual mode of identification:

And, pressing of the Undefined
The definition on my mind,
Held up before my eyes a glass
Through which my shrinking sight did pass
(4)

The universe is "cleft to the core," not phallic, and the "Undefined" is like a great female body of the mother. The self's return is not to the breast, however, but to a "great wound" she must suck (the place of the female "castration"?):

> The Universe, cleft to the core
> Lay open to my probing sense
> That, sickening, I would fain pluck thence
> But could not,—nay! but needs must suck
> At the great wound, and could not pluck
> My lips away till I had drawn
> All venom out.—Ah fearful pawn
>
> (5)

The sucking at the wound is an identifying with pain—self as suffering and compassion, a universal sympathy: "All sin was of my sinning, all / Atoning mine, and mine the gall / Of all regret" (6). The other side of the sentimental promise appears here—the reminder that the pleasures of the ecstatic and the abject are akin, perhaps even incestuous. The speaker's omniscience is the opposite of a differentiated and mediated selfhood. It is an "Atoning" or "At-one-ing" that makes castration the universal principal. There is no "masculine," or "symbolic" order, no limit, no finite, no mediation.

The look of the other constructs a self with a wound, a lack: it is the recognition scene of the sentimental.

> A man was starving in Capri;
> He moved his eyes and looked at me;
> I felt his gaze, I heard his moan,
> And knew his hunger as my own.
>
> (6)

This scene of sympathetic identification has a long literary history and, in particular, a strong connection with women's literature because it is the very type of the sentimental moment. It has the chief characteristics described, for example, by R. F. Brissenden in his work on the sentimental novel.[18] The encounter resembles the sympathetic pause of the sentimental traveler to be found even in Wordsworth, but it is an emotional witnessing that the modernists rejected. The site of recognition, where lack appears, is also the site of what Ransom calls "the limitation of Miss Millay . . . her lack of intellectual interest, or masculinity." This lack is not just "feminine" for him, but connected to the sentimental: "I used a conventional symbol, which I hope was not objectionable, when I phrased this lack of hers: deficiency in masculinity. It is true that some male poets are about as deficient; not necessarily that they are undeveloped intellectually, but that they conceive poetry as a sentimental or feminine exercise." [19]

But in "Renascence," the speaker rejects the encounter with suffering and lack (Millay thought she was rebelling against the sentimental with her entire career). However, her efforts to escape the confinement of the feminine all seem to entail her abject return. The maternal moment of omniscience brings contact with the horrible, the abject, the wounded, the suffering. Why would anyone want to have anything to do with the infinite (or any other other) after such an experience? Indeed, in Millay's story, the weight of it at last crushes the speaker down into the grave, exactly where she longed to be. However, this "death" (like her rebirth) does not involve rejecting the earth, passivity, or mother. It is only then (her soul having fled), that she receives the kinds of motherly attention a child might wish for:

Deep in the earth I rested now.
Cool is its hand upon the brow
And soft its breast beneath the head
Of one who is so gladly dead.

(8)

This retreat to the womb/tomb is what makes sound and life desirable again. "A grave is such a quiet place" (9)—and, as the calling up of Marvell's line reminds us, also a place where none embrace. It is a retreat from desire itself, a withdrawal into *aphanisis*, which might be associated with the feminine.[20] Again, the plot is from one angle familiar enough— death reminds us how good it is to be alive (and when it is too late we will desire): "I would I were alive again / To kiss the fingers of the rain" (9). The "solution" to the death of desire here appears to be a kind of nostalgia, like the plot of *Our Town* or *It's a Wonderful Life* in miniature. The speaker turns from a horror of being touched to embracing the world, from an identification with all suffering and all lack to—what? An acceptance of suffering? Or the recognition of what is missing, the wounding—to an assumption of lack? The conventional resolution of the plot is not available to this speaker. The turn and rebirth of Millay's poem may dramatize a questionable *difference*. The abject and the ecstatic seem here to be close, two versions of the same marginal relationship to the world, to the other. The poem excludes figuration as it allegorizes the process of birth/rebirth on the analogy of mother/nature. The earth does not provide the poet with a text of objects, but rather remains the intimate other, and separation from this other remains the unresolved issue.

For it is the regret, the sense of loss—a desire to return to the past that we might call *sentimental* (or "love")—that motivates the rebirth of this poem, a rebirth as return.

> O, multi-colored, multi-form,
> Beloved beauty over me,
> That I shall never, never see
> Again! Spring-silver, autumn-gold,
> That I shall never more behold!
>   (10)

The reader must become as a child to return to this ecstasy, the pleasures of this text—they come from loss of the familiar and not from the indefinite teasing of desire. At the moment of absence comes the subject's movement—not to control absence by the "fort-da" of symbolicity, but to return to the "beloved beauty" of the past, of childhood. The "reborn" subject avoids death by submitting to a "God" who is the earth. It is acquiescence to sublimity, a decisive abjection—schizo-salvation ("like one gone mad"):

> Ah! Up then from the ground sprang I
> And hailed the earth with such a cry
> As is not heard save from a man
> Who has been dead, and lives again.
> About the trees my arms I wound;
> Like one gone mad I hugged the ground;
> I raised my quivering arms on high;
> I laughed and laughed into the sky;
> Till at my throat a strangling sob
> Caught fiercely, and a great heart-throb
> Sent instant tears into my eyes:
> O God, I cried, no dark disguise
> Can e'er hereafter hide from me
> Thy radiant identity!
>   (12)

The language belongs to the representation of *jouissance.* However, if Jacques Lacan had read the poem, it would not seem sexual, like the statue of Saint Teresa, it would not seem that she was "coming." [21] Lacan finds no female ecstasy in language. Apparently, it is impossible for the poetess to act as the statue of herself, portraying for us the event of her own female ecstasy. What remains unclear from the Lacanian perspective is how to read this representation. On the one hand, one can read it as conventional religious sentiment attributed to a subject now fixed in the male position, any "man / Who has been dead, and lives again." But then the sublimity vanishes, belonging to no one, because it is not material, not in the *writing* (or reading). On the other hand, to the extent that poetic language ruptures the convention, the sublime experience belongs to every reader, because, as Julia Kristeva argues in *Powers of Horror*, literature *is* the signifier of the abject.[22] And this poem would make its subject the signifier of literature (a poet).

Kristeva argues that there is an intimate relationship of *jouissance* to the abject, that "jouissance alone causes the abject to exist as such." But in "Renascence," ecstasy follows upon a release from the "compassion" that identifies the poet with all sin and suffering, that is, upon a release from the abject, as "all." Kristeva defines the abject as "a frontier, a repulsive gift that Other, having becoming *alter ego*, drops so that 'I' does not disappear in it but finds, in that sublime alienation, a forfeited existence." [23] What seems to be abjected here, however, is not only the maternal but the female difference of the speaker.

In contemporary literature, the sinning word itself lures us into the *jouissance* of abjection, its sublimation, as the sacred once did. But in Millay's poem, the abjection from without, not within, points to a structure more archaic than the resurrection of the word. The body of Millay's poem is not a sort of "carnal reminder." In "Renascence," the remainder is a reminder, an excess, the round, not flat soul. Her word, that is, refuses to sin, re-presents the speaker as the one who repeats dramatically within bounds, within the codes, the one who masters—and is mastered by—the identity of the conventional.

Edmund Wilson, in his "Epilogue, 1952: Edna St. Vincent Millay," says that "Renascence" sets forth the terms of Millay's life, portraying the experience of "claustrophobia" from which she frequently suffered.[24] This eternal return of the sensation of enclosure that appears as the opening of the poem may also be connected to her fame as a "poetess," as a member of the tradition, ably reciting and repeating the forms of literature. If Millay appears to be torn between a loss of self to an archaic maternal principle and a loss of self to an identification with the literary fathers and a male tradition, it is perhaps because she maintains herself on the borders of literature, in the position of the extra one, the child, the girl, at the limits of inside/outside where she is that which exceeds the experience, that which is more than the (circular and repetitive) plot.

Associated with the turn and return of the poet's rebirth is a transformation both of poet and God to masculine positions. As she comes to life again, she sounds a cry like a man, "a man / Who has been dead, and lives again." And the final lines of the poem may almost be read to declare that a masculine soul is required to keep from further scenes of obliteration—distance and difference and the pronouns "he" and "him" must be maintained:

> But East and West will pinch the heart
> That can not keep them pushed apart;
> And he whose soul is flat—the sky
> Will cave in on him by and by.
>
> (13)

With this hardness, "The soul can split the sky in two / And let the face of God shine through."

The issue of her gender as poet defines the staging of Millay's work from this beginning. The speaker of "Renascence" is reborn into the likeness of a poet's soul, one who is not flat—but it is a likeness only. The reader remembers her past. She remains a border character, a girl who writes like a man.

IV

Perhaps as a joke, Arthur Davison Ficke wrote in his letter to Ferdinande Earle praising the poem: "No sweet young thing of twenty ever ended a poem precisely where this one ends: it takes a brawny male of forty-five to do that." [25] Millay wrote Ficke:

Mr. Earle has acquainted me with your wild surmises. Gentlemen I must convince you of your error; my reputation is at stake. I simply will not be a "brawny male." Not that I have an aversion to brawny males; *au contraire, au contraire.* But I cling to my femininity!

Is it that you consider brain and brawn so inseparable?—I have thought otherwise. Still, that is all a matter of personal opinion. But, gentlemen: when a woman insists that she is twenty, you must not, must not call her forty-five. That is more than wicked; it is indiscreet.

Mr. Ficke, you are a lawyer. I am very much afraid of lawyers. Spare me, kind sir! Take into consideration my youth—for I am indeed but twenty—and my fragility—for "I do protest I am a maid"—and—sleuth me no sleuths!

Seriously: I thank you also for the compliment you have unwittingly given me. For tho I do not yet aspire to be forty-five and brawny, if my verse so represent me, I am more gratified than I can say.[26]

Like the poem, the letter shows a doubleness about the gender of the poet. There are the pleasures of girlish cleverness and wit—a real mastery of a certain coquettish use of language, which nevertheless might also be called a clinging to femininity. This cleverness, this mastery, this clinging characterizes Millay in all of the letters she writes in her life; one could argue, as Elizabeth Frank has in "A Doll's Heart," that she never ceases to be this "Girl" in her poetry as well.[27] There is also the desire to be in the position of mastery with respect to poetry—that is, to be male. The "compliment" for which she thanks Ficke, for which she is "more gratified than I can say," is not that her verse represents her as forty-five and brawny, of course; we must make the substitution of the omitted term and read: "For tho I do not yet aspire to be male . . ."[28]

In this question of gender and identification, then, let us hesitate, withdraw, and look around again at the rebirth at issue here. On the one hand, Ficke says, as a compliment, that Millay writes like a man. On the other hand, her critics—notably John Crowe Ransom—say she is not intellectual because she writes like a woman. One way of reading "Renascence" and the traditional poetics adopted by Millay would be to say she has tried to deny the place of the woman, or escape it, and to write from the place of the man, of the male subject. If so, according to Ransom and the other modernist critics, she failed to be sufficiently masculine. The omniscient (motherly) infinite in Millay's poem generates several complexities of gender. Jane Gallop offers a convenient summary of the differing positions of male and female implied by the Lacanian view of the subject's relationship to language:

Woman is . . . the figuration of phallic "lack"; she is a hole. By these mean and extreme phallic proportions, the whole is to man as man is to the hole.
. . . The "whole" in relation to which man is lacking has its basis in what in Freudian terms is called the "phallic mother." The "whole" is the pre-Oedipal mother, apparently Omnipotent and omniscient, until the discovery of her castration, the discovery that she is not a "whole," but a "hole." So the woman (phallic mother) is to the man what the man is to the (castrated) woman. It is not that men and women are simply unequal, but they occupy the same position in different harmonic ratios, at different moments. The effect is a staggering of position.[29]

That is to say, the "phallic mother" or figure of omniscience and the castrated woman or figure of lack represent the opposite poles of male positioning.

The representation of "Infinity: the Undefined" in "Renascence" as an overwhelming experience of closeness, a loss of differentiation, a merging, suggests the figure of the "phallic mother." But in this poem the trauma arises from the self's identification—as if she encounters the mother at the moment of realizing her castration, her wound—rather

than narcissistic plenitude; the self as whole is also the self experienced
as the universe "cleft to the core."

If the way out is the death of the self, or the ego, the way out for the
subject of this poem nevertheless is not simply escaping from identification with the mother. In the conclusion of the poem, the speaker seems
to enter safely into the literary codes of the symbolic, taking the place of
the male subject. It does not matter that we think of the imagery of nature as God in connection with the yearning for the phallic mother; the
subject no longer has a relationship with the transcendental of identification or merging, but now occupies the male position with respect to
the "whole," which is now *whole,* a "radiant identity." The rebirth of the
subject rescues her, not from the threat of castration or wounding, but
from boundless abjection. Kristeva has argued that women cannot escape or refuse the symbolic, even though women's writing thereby is
made subject to a phallocentric culture, precisely because women are
otherwise (in their writing as in their psyches) made vulnerable to such
an identification with the mother.[30]

But the stance described in the concluding lines of "Renascence" has
some rather curious features if we are going to read it as an accession to
the symbolic, to successful (and male identified) poethood. In it, Millay
returns to the opening difficulty—the relationship between subject (now
"soul") and a world that presses in on it.

> The world stands out on either side
> No wider than the heart is wide;
> Above the world is stretched the sky,—
> No higher than the soul is high.
> The heart can push the sea and land
> Farther away on either hand;
> The soul can split the sky in two,
> And let the face of God shine through.
> But East and West will pinch the heart
> That can not keep them pushed apart;
> And he whose soul is flat—the sky
> Will cave in on him by and by.
>
> (13)

This precarious ending can be read from different positions. From the
point of view of the male subject of the symbolic, who desires (but can
never fully have) a return to the plenitude of the phallic mother, soul
contact with the "other" is a longed-for goal. The closing offers an "inspiring" version of the liberal reassurance that the "free" individual (as

soul) has control over its relationship with the world—that it is up to the individual soul to get what it desires. Thus it seems to promise imaginary fulfillment in rather predictable ways that, moreover, would be pleasing to the ideology of the moment. But we know that the particular subject of this poem is interested in gaining differentiation or distance from a mother world that always threatens to again press in and become overwhelming.

The poem closes with the warning to "he whose soul is flat" that he will suffer the same fate that the subject of the poem has just recounted—"the sky / Will cave in on him by and by." A "flat" soul could describe a state of *aphanisis*—that is, a soul not satisfactorily desiring, not phallic.[31] Of course, there is an identification for a girl that is not the mother. It is the imaginary identification with the nonflat soul, the phallic soul, subject of the symbolic, which is, of course, male. There is a contradiction in the story. The subject of this poem undergoes a double narrative. The feminine rebirth reverses the direction of the Oedipal progression, beginning with the wounded woman (the hole), and proceeding toward a phallic relationship with the whole (that is, desiring it). But the power relations move in the usual Oedipal order—from the "infinite" to the individual "soul," from the powers of the other to the desiring subject.

The poem does not encourage us to notice heterogeneity and contradiction. It is possible to read "Renascence" as a vision of the overwhelming horrors of a total identification with the other, and a resolution that the principle of differentiation must be maintained, resisting a collapse, even though with great difficulty. But this would be a partisan translation of an earlier code, of "Renascence" as the transcendentalist reassertion of faith after an encounter with evil, its message the credo of liberal individualism. Nevertheless, in any event, what we are recording is a formal and thematic turn toward insertion of the subject (and poem) into a conventional social order. The pleasures of the text then are the pleasures of security, of being disturbed in our reading, having our expectations upset, but feeling that everything has turned out all right in the end—what the poem seems to say fits in with what would be expected. These are the pleasures of ideological confirmation.

We can still argue that Millay's poem is far too identified with the dominant ideology to be more than repetition of the same, imitative, the submission of the daughter to the father in order to get out of being overwhelmed by her mother. We can note the kinds of pleasures that seem to be offered here and disdain them. It is perhaps easy for us, in fact, to refuse to be the subject whom the poem thus addresses, because there are no longer the kinds of ploys that might seduce us. Readers of Millay in 1912 could still hear masculine resonance to the Emersonian or Whitmanian "I" constructed by certain key phrases and moments of "Renascence." The daughter puts on the fathers' garb, their vocabulary, their form—she dresses for success in a version of American transcendentalism that connects the codes of rebirth from Christianity to a Romantic idealizing of nature and the optimistic assertions of a liberal individualism:

> Ah! Up then from the ground sprang I
> And hailed the earth with such a cry
> As is not heard save from a man
> Who has been dead, and lives again.
>   (12)

The climactic reencounter of poet/subject with nature is rewritten in terms that equate nature with both Christian God and with the more archaic (and motherly) "heart": "God, I can push the grass apart / And lay my finger on Thy heart!" (13). Conventional reading protects the reader from the implications of the poet's place, the uncertainty of the ending.

If the reader, however, takes the final section of the poem as asserting the potency of the individual soul, the rebirth of the speaker is threatened by the natural, outside world. The poem has an ending, with a paean to a familiar optimism, but only as long as it is decoded according to a Romantic faith in the powers of the individual soul:

> The soul can split the sky in two,
> And let the face of God shine through.
> But East and West will pinch the heart
> That can not keep them pushed apart;
> And he whose soul is flat—the sky
> Will cave in on him by and by.
>   (13)

In a gesture of daughterly obedience, the poet takes on the codes of the fathers (or the Father): it is the responsibility of the individual heart and soul to keep the world at its proper distance. In this final section, the "I" of the poem disappears and the code speaks (it is the place of the moral lesson). But the terms in which the code is presented suggest a reading besides the inspirational optimism that the poem allows. We can see the daughterly dilemma: an obedient and duplicitous "rebirth" into the manhood of the free subject, the strong soul, the "individual," defends the poet against a collapse of boundaries but also makes impossible the very inventiveness the role demands. The poetess acts the part of the free subject, but the narrative line of the poem suggests the drama of a different plot.

In "Renascence," then, it is the plot itself that is bound. There is a split between a free subject and a narrative enslaved to return. As the warning of the final two lines intimates, the rebirth of the speaker has not changed the position of the subject—that is, surrounded by a world, an outside, that threatens to "cave in" on "he whose soul is flat." The split is not within the subject, but between inside and outside, at the boundary of self and "sky." The borders of internal and external do not reliably maintain difference, but are permeable, penetrable. The incestuous moment of recognition leads the poet not to separate from the maternal infinite, but to take on the abject ("All sin was of my sinning . . ."). Thus the "Renascence" of this poem involves a ritual of return, finally, to the same boundedness.

The writing appears to be male not only because it exploits the formal traditions of English lyric poetry, but also because the drama of the self with which it is invested reinforces the myth of male superiority at two levels, seeming to inscribe the figure of the rebellious female into her "proper" place. She would rather die than identify with the suffering of the powerful martyr-mother (to recapitulate the plot as it appears in "Renascence"), but her rebirth as a free self requires that she masquerade as a man in the old lyric forms of "individual" selfhood: she cannot take an active, inventive part in the speaking, for the terms of her entry into the subject of lyric poetry require a daughterly submission to the role.

The lyric role directs the reader to certain expected responses. The feelings of a lyric poet in the Romantic tradition are read as "originally" private; they are reported in (expressed by) her poem. Lyric emotion, in this convention, is personal, and the private becomes public as the reader "shares" the experience of the poet, looking over her shoulder as it were, identifying with the speaker's drama, enacting as readers the gesture of the sentimental traveler who pauses to sympathize. The pleasures are vicarious; we feel someone else's feelings, frequently the painful ones of loss or failed love. Only the assumption of original privacy keeps the poet and the reader safely contained in separate categories, as individuals, and allows Ransom to hold Millay guilty of causing his distress in the role of sentimental reader.

Perhaps one reason sentimental literature quickly seemed so very unacceptable has to do with the threat it poses to this reader-writer relationship. In the sentimental tradition, the "personal" quickly became a clear

matter of convention—the tears, the joys, the sacrifices, and reconcilia-
tions all as predictable as they continue to be in the "soaps" and the
Harlequin romances. This overt conventionality erodes the carefully
maintained barriers between public and private emotions as between
high and mass culture. But when Edna St. Vincent Millay wrote, modernism was getting desperate to make those barriers work—excluding "feelings" and "the private" (or autobiographical) and "intentionality" from
a poetry that could only be "original," could only "make it new," by
strictly delimiting the constituting *difference* of the poetic text. The New
Critics had a considerable amount of interest in devaluing Millay, fixing
her position as a minor poet, in the good company of the male Romantics. Thus Allen Tate asserts: "Neither Byron nor Miss Millay is of the first
order of poets. They are distinguished examples of the second order." [32]

A number of theorists—importantly Stanley Aronowitz and Fredric
Jameson—have argued that the valuing of the intellect, of theory, and of
"high" art overlooks the extent to which even the avant-garde participates in the commodification of art, and that the repeated demands for
intellectual originality create a kind of consumerism that is like any other
fashion.[33] And furthermore, Aronowitz argues, even the practices of mass
culture contain the possibility for critique of dominant ideology as well
as conventionally reproducing it. Tania Modleski called our attention to
the importance of this critique for women's cultural productions in her
Loving with a Vengeance: Mass-Produced Fantasies for Women.[34] The critique
of the modernist ideal of "serious" art is also important for a poet like
Millay who has been abandoned to the *other* order of poetry—that of
"sensibility" rather than the intellect, as Tate would have it.

When a woman writes poetry, her failure to escape the order of "sensibility" may make us uncomfortable to the extent that it seems she
should be writing more masculine forms—that is, to the extent that the
poetry seems to aspire to the first, powerful order of language. But the
passive female position in narrative will be defined by the Oedipal plot
wherever it occurs within a cultural situation that articulates meaning
according to such a mythology. If the Freudian Oedipal myth can be
taken as a version of the cultural sense of value and purpose—with the
woman as object of desire—the same story will appear repeated everywhere. The open narrative is closed by the figure of a woman. Teresa de
Lauretis writes of desire in the narrative of films, arguing that "woman
properly represents the fulfillment of the narrative promise (made as we
know, to the little boy), and that representation works to support the
male status of the mythical subject." [35]

The figure of the woman—Millay, poetess—stands behind her poems,
provoking a doubleness, a kind of oscillation between an ostensibly male

speaker and the image of the female poet, like the doubleness of her nickname, "Vincent," and the very feminine—girlish—figure she presented. There is a gap between sign and meaning, form and (female) content, that theatricalizes lyric poetry and turns conventional intimacy into indeterminacy. The parodic element persists to the end of "Renascence," without, however, undermining conventional pleasures of the text. The reason for the poem's resistance to closure has little to do with modernist versions of irony. The plot is asserted at the same time that it is undone, not as a function of textuality alone, but of *context*, the extra-literary fact: the poet is a woman. At the same time that Millay's spectator is made perhaps all too comfortable by the predictable directions of the drama, the poem has managed to suggest that contradictory elements coexist in the way the subject may be heard, that the female author may identify both with male and female positions, that female readers might do the same. Behind the pleasures of submitting to mastery—mastery of form as of ideology—Millay's spectators might discover a reminder of other pleasures as well, the supplementary pleasure masquerading as mere cleverness or wit, the pleasure of the other, which shows itself in rebellious duplicities, the pleasure of the masquerade.

Pleasure for this poet seems to lie in cross-dressing. But how long can one sustain the boyishness of adolescent girlhood as an acceptable persona? Frank's detailed characterization of Millay's "Girl," the "unflappable flapper whose sophistication has taken her beyond libertinage and rebellion toward an epicurean balance of urbanity and lyricism," leads her to conclude that the poetry is not serious enough: "Capable of moving readers and hearers, the skillful, charming verse through which the Girl had life was even so too dependent on implied gesture to be taken seriously as meant speech." Millay has, that is, developed a poetry of persona, which is simply too theatrical: "It is all so staged, so visible, so temporary." [36] What we can already see, however, in the story outlined by "Renascence" is the maternal shape of the maturity Millay must keep on avoiding. [37]

As the place of the subject is made problematic, so is the structure of desire and the nature of *jouissance*. The question of feminine sexuality, the phallic function, and *jouissance* has notoriously been taken up by Lacan in *Encore*, where he argues that the subject of desire is masculine. The woman is "excluded by the nature of things which is the nature of words." The side of the woman is *not all.* That is, "There is no such thing as *The* woman, where the definite article stands for the universal.

There is no such thing as *The* woman since of her essence . . . she is not all." [38] Millay's girl does not represent herself as "*The* woman." However, even though she seems to wish to escape the feminine, she does not, by her mimicry, assume the phallic function either. She seems at times, in the interest of maintaining girlhood, to resist adult sexuality altogether: "The sky, I thought, is not so grand; / I 'most could touch it with my hand!" (4). This regression, this cuteness approaching baby talk—can we even give Millay credit for a mastering of mimicry when she allows herself this "most"?

We might ask, taking these words up again, where this absence, this elision of "all," could lead us. Instead of showing her adolescent, "almost"—that is, close, near to the edge of a boundary (or maturity)—this elision gives us "I" as the excess, "most," that which is, if childish, nonetheless *over all.* A few lines earlier there appears a rather superfluous "after all." This is the time "after all"—the post-all experience. The plot may be summarized: "After all *I* becomes the excess of *all.*" It is a belatedness, but a narcissistic version.

The earlier moment of the abject in Millay's poem is not written; rather, it is narrated in a totalizing style that achieves a paranoid reversal of the abject—it is the *all* that is repugnant, not the "I," whose separateness has been lost to the engulfing "All":

> All sin was of my sinning, all
> Atoning mine, and mine the gall
> Of all regret. Mine was the weight
> Of every brooded wrong, the hate
> That stood behind each envious thrust,
> Mine every greed, mine every lust.
>
> (6)

It is the *all* that causes her fall, reversal of religious and literary versions of abjection. The important question of the subject's relationship to "all" is thus revealed with "all" as an absence, disguised or hidden, before the masquerade of abjection, when "All sin was of my sinning, all / Atoning mine, and mine the gall / Of all regret." What remains after all, most of all, is the girl who must speak, a "most" whose place at the borders of dependency, of master-slave or parent-child relations, depends on keeping the "all" elided and asserting the one (child, woman) who remains.

Since Millay practices no subversions against the linguistic forms of the fathers, she offers no challenge against the phallocentrism embedded in those forms, except by the small incongruity of her girlish figure, whose person says the same thing with a difference. In *Woman and the Demon,* Nina Auerbach argues that the potent female figure of the nineteenth century loses power in the hands of twentieth-century modernism in part because it depends on a valuing of *character,* which modernism rejected.[39] But Millay's poetry is the play of a character, the girl become poet-prodigy, loving daughter, little woman. Millay in her person, that is, represents and reenacts the drama of female selfhood with each presentation of each poem—her signature sets the stage for a reprise of the plot never to grow up, to escape the confines of the old images, the models of maternal sacrifice. Carolyn Heilbrun has argued for the pervasive influence of Alcott's Jo who "may have been the single female model continuously available after 1868 to girls dreaming beyond the confines of a constructed family destiny to the possibility of autonomy and experience initiated by one's self." [40] Like Heilbrun's, Millay's plot sees freedom in terms of trying to separate herself from the mother's self-sacrifice without rejecting the mother, either in the person like Jo's "Marmie," or the myth, like Millay's world. If the great theme of Millay's poetry— love—marks her as a female poet, her great ambivalence about the dependency relationships created by love marks her daughterly character, marks her as the daughter of a strong mother.

Millay's own family history is like a rewriting of *Little Women*—the absent father, the supportive and hard-working sisters, the loving and much-loved mother who exacted loyalty and high aspirations from her daughters. A letter to her mother shows Millay conscious of how loving (or sentimental) her correspondence with her family sounds:

Dearest Mother,—
You do write the sweetest and the most wonderful letters! They are so lovely that very often I read parts of them aloud to people, just as literature. It was delicious what you told me about the turtle. . . .
P.S.—Do you suppose, when you & I are dead, dear, they will publish the *Love Letters of Edna St. Vincent Millay & her Mother?*
P.P. I am sending you a poem I just wrote.—Show it to the girls too, darling.
xx—V.[41]

More importantly, perhaps, this letter to her mother shows how thoroughly interwoven were the literary and family relationships for Millay. Elizabeth Hardwick, in her review of Millay's *Letters,* exclaims that they sound like something out of *Little Women,* even the letters to other poets, to publishers (grown-up occasions, that is).[42]

"Vincent" grows up, writes, loves, and lives as a character invented by Edna St. Vincent Millay to fit the circumstances, a character soon legendary, soon providing a model herself for the young flappers of the twenties who eagerly followed her bohemian life-style and repeated the defiant lines from *A Few Figs from Thistles.* Griffin Barry of *The New Yorker* reported in 1927:

her public cohered quickly in 1919 when the boys got back from France. Crowds of them came—boys fresh from the wars, hungrily fierce about love and as trivial as you please and the young women of the day became fierce and trivial, too. It is not an easy way of life for women—not always. The young women needed a poet. Edna Millay became that one, hardly aware of it herself, at first.

Not until 1925 did the author of the love sonnets decide to print them all. But in 1921 I stumbled on a tableful of American strangers in Paris who knew the lot, producing them in scrawled versions from pocketbooks or from memory. Millay couplets had floated by word of mouth for years through colleges.[43]

This is the era when poetry—serious poetry—divorced itself from character to become impersonal, when all serious writing was also seriously objectified, alienated, aloof in its literariness from context. Millay, more than any other poet, male or female, represented the opposite extreme, a merging of public and private identities, of self, subject, and persona, a failure to establish by irony or invention any distance between her writing and the ritualized declamations of mass ceremony, mass selfhood. Millay's poetess was, as Elizabeth Frank puts it, "plucking an ancient lyre." Her achievement was a "hybridized diction we must ruefully call 'poetic' ": "That is, starting with her earliest verses, Millay's style was a resplendent pastiche of Sapphic simplicity, Catullan urbanity, homeless Chaucerian idiom, uprooted Shakespearean grammar, Cavalier sparkle, Wordsworthian magnanimity, Keatsian sensuousness, and Housemanian melancholy."[44]

Indeed, the slavishly "poetic" reminiscence called up by Millay's style has had a similar effect on many of her readers, prompting them to feel obligated as part of a Millay reading to call out the resemblances and possible influences they recognize. It is as if the figure of the girl prompts her audience to join in the game, as if something about her attention to the sounds of the lyric code theatricalized the lyric tradition—the convention, that is, of identifying "poetry" with the canonical inheritance exemplified by the rhymed forms of elegy, sonnet, or even ballad. Millay's lifelong habit of committing great poetry to memory and declaiming it for her friends hints of the recitation and the actress; this was frequently her way of composing her own work as well, having it in her memory before she ever committed any of it to paper.

Millay, then—Vincent—however heterogeneous her text, however multiple the sounds of the voices she conjures from the (masculine) lyric past, gives us repeatedly only the singleness of Millay, girl poet, figure of the female "individual," character, chief protagonist in a drama of relationship, female voice marking the imposture of her boyish speakers and male pronouns, speaking in the female body that is the subject of her work. The reader of Millay is not likely to find writerly pleasures in her text, called so frequently from play back to the spectacle of personality.

Millay's work addresses the reader, instead, as spectator—as a male or female subject who may be called upon to identify with her, to take a role in her drama, to enjoy the parody and the masquerade.

That is, the pleasures of Millay's poetry may have much to do with the processes of identification, theatricality, and the cultural construction of the gendered subject—pleasures we are growing used to talking about in studies of the cinema, but that (thus attached to "mass culture" and its political unconscious) may not appear as a "proper" reaction to poetry. The reader of modern poetry does not want to be soothed or persuaded into unconscious gender identification; modern poetry and the avant-garde writing that encourages an active reader also, precisely, disrupt the unknowing assumption we hold about the subject, especially the assumption of "character" that there is a single individual with whom we can identify, a single plot that will give us happy or unhappy endings. That is, a single Oedipal plot. But this discomfort about the subject's identifications, this playing double with the singleness of plot, takes another—supplementary—form in Millay.

One of the pleasures of Millay's poetry, then, is a pleasure we could call "unpoetic," a pleasure that seduces the otherwise serious reader. It comes out of her repetition of conventions, beloved but old-fashioned and "sentimental" (the maternal matrix). And it comes out of the way the dramatic story incarnates a female other, a feminine voice of lyric poetry, the muse. Since the codes whereby Millay's work accomplishes this process are not inscribed within the boundaries of the poetic text but in the context in which her poetry appeared (that is, they are not all "poetic"), the spectator of her work is seduced by her extrapoetic "'most," by that dramatic supplement that gives us the Romantic spectacle: the mere-slip-of-a-girl-poet heroically playing those weighty antique lyres. It is this figure who protests charmingly: "I simply will not be a 'brawny male.' Not that I have an aversion to brawny males; *au contraire, au contraire.* But I cling to my femininity!" The spectator is seduced by the difference: the writing appears to be competently masculine, but not all—the writer is someone's daughter at the same time, *'most* a woman.

Edna St. Vincent Millay does not seem a likely candidate to be called a feminist writer. She does not, at first glance, offer any of the elements Teresa de Lauretis lists as essential to feminism: "a critical reading of culture, a political interpretation of the social text and of the social subject, and a rewriting of our culture's 'master narratives.'"[45] Unlike modernist critics, however, we can take seriously her real power during the 1920s and 1930s. Millay made women's writing a part of literary history, and her cross-dressing and gender-bending troubled heterosexual ideals of womanhood. Her struggle provokes our awareness of the contradictory status of the woman author, whose authority, as de Lauretis emphasizes, comes from a masculine literary language. Her status, then, depends not on any absolute literary value, but on a criticism that extends its interest to the difference that gender makes in literature.

Notes

The critique of modernism and the recuperation of plural modernisms has now become widely successful in the work of feminist critics and scholars, as the present collection demonstrates. This essay—a shorter version of a chapter appearing in my book, *Sentimental Modernism: Women Writers and the Revolution of the Word* (Bloomington: Indiana University Press, 1991)—reflects an earlier stage of inquiry, so that it fails to acknowledge much important work that has gone on since it was written.

1. Edmund Wilson, *I Thought of Daisy* (New York: Charles Scribner's Sons, 1929), 64. This description is of Rita, Wilson's version of Millay in the novel.

2. Harriet Monroe, "Comment: Edna St. Vincent Millay," *Poetry* 24 (August 1924): 266. Harriet Monroe's uncritical endorsement suggests the power of Millay's work to generate the fantasy of becoming a poet. Later Monroe retreats in the face of criticism, still defending Millay's ability, but confessing "a certain sense of frustration, of disappointment" in her review of the love sonnets in *Fatal Interview*, finding there "an emotional reservation as seductive and remote as a cloister." "Advance or Retreat," *Poetry* 38 (July 1931): 216–21.

3. John Crowe Ransom, "The Poet as Woman," *Southern Review* 2 (Spring 1937): 784.

4. Allen Tate, "Miss Millay's Sonnets: A Review of *Fatal Interview*." *New Republic* 6 May 1931, 335–36.

5. Cleanth Brooks, "Edna Millay's Maturity," Book Review Section, *Southwest Review* 20 (January 1935): 2.

6. William Stidger, *Flames of Faith* (New York: Abingdon Press, 1922), 48.

7. Ibid., 49.

8. Jane Tompkins, *Sensational Designs: The Cultural Work of American Fiction, 1790–1860* (New York: Oxford University Press, 1985).

9. Roland Barthes, *The Lover's Discourse*, trans. Richard Howard (New York: Hill and Wang, 1978), 175.

10. Ibid., 1. Emphasis in original.

11. Jane Gallop, *The Daughter's Seduction* (Ithaca, N.Y.: Cornell University Press, 1982), 149.

12. Karl Shapiro, "Review: Edna St. Vincent Millay, *Collected Poems*," *Prairie Schooner* 31 (Spring 1957): 13.

13. And Judith Fetterley has written about a story by Louisa May Alcott that suggests the possibility of a radicalism behind the masks of the Little Women, and the theatricality of the roles: "Impersonating 'Little Women': The Radicalism of Alcott's *Behind a Mask*," *Women's Studies* 10 (1983): 1–14.

14. Ransom, "The Poet as Woman," 783; Delmore Schwartz, "The Poetry of Millay," *The Nation* 157 (16 December 1943): 735–36. Recently scholars have begun to seriously question the assumptions behind such snide judgments against the women's clubs and the "genteel codes" associated with them. Sheryl O'Donnell is responsible for persuading me that an analysis of such materials uncovers multiple, complex, and unexamined aspects of women's writing. See her "Letters

from Nice Girls: Genteel Codes in Women's Writings," Proceedings of GITAP, University of North Dakota, 1983; "Professing Culture: A History of North Dakota Clubwomen," *Day In, Day Out: Women's Lives in North Dakota* (Grand Forks: University of North Dakota, 1988), 31–55.

15. Susan Gubar, "Sapphistries," *Signs: Journal of Women in Culture and Society* 10, no. 1 (Autumn 1984): 47.

16. The figure of the muse generated by female poets is as wonderful and terrible, as helpful and threatening—as ambivalent—as the figure of the mother. See, for example, Mary Kirk Deshazer's study, *Inspiring Women: Re-Imagining the Muse* (New York: Pergamon, 1986).

17. Edna St. Vincent Millay, "Renascence," in *Collected Poems of Edna St. Vincent Millay*, ed. Norma Millay (New York: Harper and Row, 1981), 4. All subsequent references are to this edition.

18. R. F. Brissenden, *Virtue in Distress* (New York: Macmillan, 1974).

19. Ransom, "The Poet as Woman," 797.

20. See Teresa de Lauretis, *Alice Doesn't: Feminism, Semiotics, Cinema* (Bloomington: Indiana University Press, 1987), re femininity: "Desire itself, then, is in question. If desire is the question which generates both narrative and narrativity as Oedipal drama, the question is an open one, seeking a closure that is only promised, not guaranteed. For Oedipal desire requires in its object—or in its subject when female, as in Freud's little girl—an identification with the feminine position" (133–34).

21. See his reflection on "God and the *Jouissance* of the Woman," in *Feminine Sexuality*, ed. Juliet Mitchell and Jacqueline Rose (New York: W. W. Norton/Pantheon, 1982), 147.

22. Julia Kristeva, *Powers of Horror* (New York: Columbia University Press, 1982), 5.

23. Ibid., 9.

24. Edmund Wilson, *The Shores of Light* (New York: Vintage, 1952), 744–93.

25. In *The Letters of Edna St. Vincent Millay*, ed. Allan Ross Macdougall. (New York: Grosset and Dunlap, 1952), 18.

26. Ibid., 20.

27. Elizabeth (Perlmutter) Frank, "A Doll's Heart: The Girl in the Poetry of Edna St. Vincent Millay and Louise Bogan," *Twentieth Century Literature* 23, no. 2 (May 1977): 157–79.

28. Later, when she has a brief but intense affair with Ficke, she writes a sonnet, which "was written both about you & about myself—we were both like that":

I only know that every hour with you
Is torture to me, and that I would be
From your too poignant lovelinesses free!
Rainbows, green flame, sharp diamonds, the fierce blue
Of shimmering ice-bergs, and to be shot through
With lightning or a sword incessantly—
Such things have beauty, doubtless; but to me
Mist, shadow, silence—there are lovely too.
There is no shelter in you anywhere;
Rhythmic, intolerable, your burning rays
Trample upon me, withering my breath;
I will be gone, and rid of you, I swear:
To stand upon the peaks of Love always
Proves but that part of Love whose name is Death.

Neither male nor female, Ficke nor Millay is clearly the speaker. From Norman A. Brittin, *Edna St. Vincent Millay* (New York: Twayne Publishers, 1967), 40.

29. Gallop, *The Daughter's Seduction*, 22.

30. The omniscience that threatens Millay's speaker does not allow her separation, difference, or distance—but that does not equate it with the Kristevan "semiotic." The difference that precedes the paternal order of language is at issue. As Jane Gallop helps us see, the Lacanian and Kristevan versions of the maternal "imaginary" or "semiotic" are in conflict: "the incompatibility of Lacanian and Kristevan theories, the difficulty in thinking a relation between the 'imaginary' and the 'semiotic,' ought to be attended to as a locus of conflict between two maternals—one conservative, the other dissident—as a way of keeping the position of the mother 'both double and foreign'" (ibid., 125). "Renascence" seems a poem of the "imaginary" in the sense of presenting an image that resists disruption. But that's not all.

31. We would expect a description of a "soul" that is in an "imaginary" or narcissistic illusion of identification with the other to be described as "full" or "total." Could a "flat" soul be one without desire, but also the one that does not enter into the kind of identification that we have just seen as so very traumatic? Then isn't a "flat" or even an escaped soul precisely what women want? But in this poem, the underground woman is out of touch with reality.

32. Tate, "A Review of *Fatal Interview*," 335–36.

33. See Stanley Aronowitz, *The Crisis in Historical Materialism* (South Hadley, Mass.: J. F. Bergin, 1981), and Fredric Jameson, "Reification and Utopia in Mass Culture," *Social Text* 1 (1979): 130–48.

34. Tania Modleski, *Loving with a Vengeance: Mass-Produced Fantasies for Women*, (New York and London: Methuen, 1982). See also the collection edited by Modleski: *Studies in Entertainment: Critical Approaches to Mass Culture.* (Bloomington and Indianapolis: Indiana University Press, 1986).

35. De Lauretis, *Alice Doesn't*, 140.

36. Frank, "A Doll's Heart," 162, 164.

37. This is not to say that Millay does not write about a mother figure; she most assuredly does. For example, in "The Harp Weaver" the magic gifts of the mother are used to clothe her child and she sacrifices for him, weaving all through the frozen night. "Sonnets from an Ungrafted Tree" gives us an unyielding and grim portrayal of the woman's sacrificial part. Walter Minot ("Millay's 'Ungrafted Tree': The Problem of the Artist as Woman," *New England Quarterly* 48 [June 1975]: 260–69) argues that these sonnets demonstrate the "psychic price that she, as a woman, had to pay" and that it was "too high a penalty." Millay's domestic imagery and its part in the tradition of women's poetry are discussed by Jeanine Dobbs, "Edna St. Vincent Millay and the Tradition of Domestic Poetry," *Journal of Women's Studies in Literature* 1 (Spring 1979): 89–106.

38. Lacan, "God and the *Jouissance*," 144.

39. Nina Auerbach, *Woman and the Demon: The Life of a Victorian Myth* (Cambridge, Mass., and London: Harvard University Press, 1982).

40. Carolyn Heilbrun, "Louisa May Alcott: the Influence of Little Women," in *Women, the Arts, and the 1920's in Paris and New York*, ed. Kenneth W. Wheeler and Virginia Lee Lussier. (New Brunswick and London: Transaction Books, 1982), 21.

41. Millay, *Letters* (23 July 1921), 120. Also, "I was telling somebody yesterday that the reason I am a poet is entirely because you wanted me to be, even from the very first. You brought me up in the tradition of poetry, and everything I did you encouraged" ([15 June 1921] 118).

42. Elizabeth Hardwick, "Anderson, Millay, and Crane in their Letters," *Partisan Review* 20 (November–December 1953): 690–96.

43. Griffin Barry, "Vincent," *New Yorker* 12 February, 1927, 26.

44. Frank, "A Doll's Heart," 159.

45. See Teresa de Lauretis, *Technologies of Gender* (Bloomington: Indiana University Press, 1987), 113.

Chapter 8
Antimodern, Modern, and Postmodern Millay: Contexts of Revaluation

Cheryl Walker

A recent catalog of the J. Peterman Company advertises a "storm blue" pleated skirt with "smoked-pearl buttons" called simply *Millay*. The introductory narrative about this skirt is typically Petermanesque—that is, romanticized, hyperbolic, imperial, full of pirouettes and winks—but it is also suggestive of something real: a turn back toward this early twentieth-century poet that remembers her in ways both old and new: "Did you forget how beautiful Edna St. Vincent Millay was?" it begins. "I didn't. She lived in The Village in a house only 9 1/2 ft. wide. Then on an island off Maine. Often seen in a skirt like this. Looking wonderful. So will you. Wearing old riding boots, a heavy sweater, or the thinnest crepe blouse." [1] The idea that Edna St. Vincent Millay can be used to sell clothes in the 1990s—that is, that she is still (or once again) a resonant figure in an age of postmodernism—is more than a sign that *fin-de-siècle* culture is afflicted with nostalgia. Somehow it is fitting that the first American woman poet to become a full-fledged media figure should re-emerge in an era given to the overlapping presences of antimodernism, modernism, and postmodernism. In fact, Edna St. Vincent Millay was always a complex figure—part vaudevillian, part Latinist—both in and out of the tidal pools of literary history. Now her protean persona seems appropriate again in a world where Hillary Rodham Clinton and Madonna share the cultural stage and where literary values seem in perpetual motion.

In this volatile atmosphere, there are numerous signs that a rehabilitated Millay is poised to resume a position in the canon she was forced to vacate in the late thirties and forties. For example, a recently released college textbook—*The Heath Introduction to Poetry* (1992)—chooses only two poets for its section on "The Sonnet": William Shakespeare (who is represented by twenty-seven sonnets) and Edna St. Vincent Millay (represented by twenty). In this college textbook—and such books, we must remember, constitute an important site of canonization—Millay assumes the "representative" role that canonical figures are so frequently asked to play, as when, in the English literature survey course for instance, a selection of Wordsworth's lyrical ballads stands in for Romanticism and T. S. Eliot's *The Waste Land* sums up certain modernist principles. Here Shakespeare speaks for the English Renaissance (male) and Millay for American modernity (female), a point to which I will return later.

For the *Heath* volume editor, Joseph DeRoche, Millay's work "shows how the form evolves as well as coils back to its Petrarchan origins."[2] She pays homage to the past while heralding a world undreamt of by Shakespeare, a world of "subways and cigarettes." This, too, suggests a positioning of her work within the rubrics of the canon, for those who enter the canon must always be seen as continuous with "the great tradition" and yet disruptive of some aspects of its legacy. Though DeRoche argues that her sonnets evoke "Petrarchan origins," he also claims: "Millay's sonnets display the obvious changes in language, syntax, metaphor, image [that have occurred over time]; they are clearly modern, closer to us in temper and testament, in scheme and skepticism. The scenes and imagery of Millay are obviously closer to us, heralding the ending of the 20th century and anticipating the beginning of the 21st."[3] Now this is very interesting, it seems to me, because in a few sentences we go from the Italian Renaissance and Petrarch to a "clearly modern" Millay (who might be seen as firmly situated in the twenties and thirties) and then on to a transitional (postmodern?) presence who heralds the end of the twentieth century and anticipates the beginning of the twenty-first.

This sweep of time certainly accords the poet a different directional velocity from the one allowed her in even so recent a text as Jan Montefiore's *Feminism and Poetry* (1987), where Millay is said to follow "appropriately from Shakespeare in that her poetic approach is traditional in a straightforward sense. The experiments of Modernism passed her by; despite the freedom and colloquialism of her later work, she uses mainly Romantic conventions."[4] Montefiore sees Millay as living out Wordsworth's (and Edmund Wilson's) belief that "poetry is the articulation of a straightforward subjectivity";[5] thus, she is hardly modern at all, let alone postmodern. For Montefiore, Millay makes few demands upon the reader and thus can provide "pleasure" but no real challenge.

However, change is in the air. New readings of Millay's work from a variety of critical perspectives—formalist, new historicist, biographical, psychoanalytic, feminist—are calling into question the notion that Millay is simply transparently pleasurable. At the Skidmore Conference in

1992 ("Millay at 100"), which celebrated the centennial of the poet's birth, we heard a number of papers arguing for a different—more difficult, less "straightforwardly subjective"—Millay. Furthermore, when Nancy Milford's monumental biography of Millay is released (a section of which we heard read at the Skidmore Conference), readers will be asked to struggle with conflicting stories and contradictory evidence, making the biographical subject (Millay) one with the epistemological quandaries of the late twentieth century.

New volumes of the poetry have been published recently, in particular, Colin Falck's *Selected Poems* (1991) about which more will be said later. In 1986 Harper and Row brought out a stunning compilation of poems with black and white photographs by Ivan Massar called *Take Up the Song*. And a further sign of Millay's resurrection is that Films for the Humanities and Sciences has recently added to their Twentieth-Century American Literature Series an hour-long video called "Edna St. Vincent Millay: Renascence," the only *new* video not to focus on a contemporary writer. (The others concern Toni Morrison, Alice Walker, Gloria Naylor, Susan Sontag, August Wilson, John Wideman, and Charles Johnson.)

Does all of this renewed interest in Millay require us to rethink the principles upon which the canon has been traditionally based? Does Millay's reentry force us to "reconfigure the contexts and history of modern or postmodern poetry," as an early proposal for this volume of essays phrased it? Or, alternatively, have new contexts of evaluation, new readings, made possible a return of Edna St. Vincent Millay that leaves the principles upon which the canon is based essentially unchanged? In other words, which comes first: the poetry itself—its nature and contexts implicit in the texts—or the critical apparatus that allows us to situate the poetry in the literary present (or not, as the case may be)? To put it *most* succinctly: Does the poet change literary fashions or do literary fashions change the poet?

As you may have already surmised, my answer to this question is not in doubt. I think that literary fashions change the poet, and in what follows I will argue that we are no longer reading the same Edna St. Vincent Millay once read by Edmund Wilson. But how did this happen? In subsequent sections of this essay I will briefly examine the trajectory of Millay's reception up to the present period, then investigate the three different Millays—antimodernist, modernist, and postmodernist—who are presently receiving attention, and finally look (again briefly) at Millay's representation in college anthologies, which are often guideposts to the way a poet is being read and taught. Ultimately I want to argue that whether a poet becomes central to literary study has less to do with the "quality" of the poetry, that elusive essence, than with complex cultural factors that allow us to situate the poems in familiar and reusable contexts.

If Gertrude Stein, H. D., Marianne Moore, Laura Riding, Elizabeth Bishop, and Muriel Rukeyser seem central to us today, they did not seem so in the memorable past, though critics were not unaware of their work. Gwendolyn Brooks and Edna St. Vincent Millay are the great exceptions in this volume because they have always been widely read but their readers have not always been academics. Having won the Pulitzer Prize for poetry in 1950, Gwendolyn Brooks established her reputation early and never lost it, but her readership was largely African American and white populist up to 1975; she was not much taught in modern (or contemporary) poetry courses and in fact does not even appear in the *Pelican* guide to American literature (1988), which is an index to the kind of elite cultural perspectives that govern the canon.[6]

Then again, Edna St. Vincent Millay does not appear in the Pelican guide either (though Gertrude Stein, H. D., Marianne Moore, Elizabeth Bishop, and Muriel Rukeyser do). Since the Second World War, Millay's reputation has been under a cloud. In 1944 Winfield Townley Scott wrote that "the greatest insult you can offer any young woman poet in this country is to warn her that she be the Edna Millay of her generation; which, being interpreted, means that she is in danger of glibness and of popularity."[7] What happened to this poet who was once so firmly established that Thomas Hardy could say America had made only two great contributions to the culture of the twenties: its architecture and Edna St. Vincent Millay?

There is no question that Millay was considered the most important woman poet in America for many years. Her reputation grew from the early moment when "Renascence" was *not* chosen as the best poem submitted to *The Lyric Year*, an anthology that ran a competition for poets in 1912. Though Millay, who was only twenty at the time, did not win first or second prize, her poem was published in the anthology and became an overnight sensation. *Renascence and Other Poems* appeared in 1917 and the poet's career was launched. As she continued to publish book after book throughout the twenties and thirties, she was widely reviewed and generally highly praised. Hailed as the greatest woman poet since Sappho, her work was read by both men and women—A. E. Housman claimed he got more pleasure from her poetry than from that of either Edwin Arlington Robinson or Robert Frost—and many tried to imitate her lyric gift.

However, the strength of her critical reputation was destined to wane in the late thirties as academic criticism, heavily influenced by T. S. Eliot, came to dominate the literary scene. In an excellent study of Millay's reception called "Poet as Persona: Edna St. Vincent Millay and the Problems of Representation," Jo Ellen Green Kaiser describes the change in critical weather that began the process of raining on Millay's parade:

> By the late 1930s, however, the world-view which "Renascence" offered was no longer understood to be representative. Instead, the strengths of "Renascence" become reinscribed as Millay's weaknesses, as in a review from 1939 by critic Seldon Rodman, who laments that Millay is "still rearing towers to Beauty, still uneasily celebrating the 'honesty' of her 'anguish,' the incandescence of her thought." Rather than being representative, Millay's attempts to describe the "limits of experience" are now understood as being personal, a *presentation*, to paraphrase T. S. Eliot, of Millay the person "who suffers," rather than a representation by Millay of the "mind which creates." [8]

The disciplining of English studies and their incarceration within the walls of academe led to an even greater marginalizing of poets like Millay who had once had mass appeal. (For an extended discussion of this, see Cary Nelson's *Repression and Recovery*.) [9] Critics increasingly defined their project as one of uncovering buried meanings rather than judging transhistorical value, which to previous generations seemed the crucial task. As every Millay scholar knows, John Crowe Ransom wrote a scathing attack upon the poet of *Fatal Interview* in an essay entitled "The Poet as Woman," published in 1937.[10] Here he identified the quality most important for a woman of talent—intellectuality—and found Millay (like most women, in his judgment) wanting. Ransom and Allen Tate, both associated with universities rather than with the New York world of publishing that had dominated criticism in the twenties, were part of the new nerve center of the literary world located on campuses and in elite journals rather than in urban public spaces—bars and offices—or in pamphlets and "little magazines." Both were influential in downgrading Millay's reputation.

Kaiser asks: "Why did [later] critics continue to read Millay as a sentimental, feminine personality of the twenties who could not adapt to the political, masculine, public emphasis of the thirties, when we have seen that Millay did in fact refashion herself to become representative of her age? The answer may lie in part in the notable divergence between elite and popular evaluations of Millay's later career. Millay clearly lost her high culture currency by the forties." [11] The final nails in Millay's critical coffin were hammered in with her radio broadcasts in support of America's entry into the war and her publication of the propaganda poems in *Murder of Lidice* and *Make Bright the Arrows*. Though Susan Schweik has recently turned a much more sympathetic eye on these poems in her book *A Gulf So Deeply Cut: American Women Poets and the Second World War*,[12] the critical reception of them at the time was mostly chilly. Millay was seen as, once again, sounding off about her feelings rather than analyzing the structural components of the political impasse. She died in 1950 and, again according to Kaiser, "After a spate of essays summarizing her career, Millay is mentioned only intermittently [in the *MLA Bibliography*] through the fifties, sixties, and seventies; most of the essays published on her appear in the *Colby Library Quarterly*, then a modest journal primarily devoted to Maine writers." [13]

New writers were coming into prominence in this period, writers who offered more to graduate students in search of intellectual nuts to crack. Bette Richart published an essay called "Poet of Our Youth" in *Commonweal* in 1957 reflecting this change of fashion.[14] Though Richart had loved Millay as she was developing her own talents as a writer, she now saw her as primarily an adolescent enthusiasm, preferring the far more restrained and obviously challenging poems of Marianne Moore. Elizabeth Bishop and Marianne Moore were both beginning to move to the center in this period. As Daniel Hoffman describes this shift: "From the time her first booklet, *Poems*, appeared in 1920, Miss Moore had been a poet whose idiosyncrasies secured her only the most discriminating of audiences. Eliot had introduced her *Selected Poems* in 1935, but it was her *Collected Poems* (1951), published when she was sixty-four, that brought fame and, for the first time, a wide public." [15]

It is worth noting in Kaiser's and Hoffman's respective descriptions of Millay's fall from grace and Moore's rise to prominence that these shifts in popularity were not governed by what we might call, hypothetically, "the poetry itself." Millay *had* changed, but critics continued to see her as the same poet she was in the twenties. Conversely, Moore had *not* substantially changed, indeed had a full corpus of work behind her, but the *Collected Poems* of 1951 suddenly gave her a readership that many of the individual poems contained in that collection had not done at an earlier period.

Perhaps to notice this does nothing more than add support to Stanley Fish's old point that texts are the product of "communities of readers" rather than fixed entities in themselves. However, this point can seem benign, even delightful, when it is thought to refer only to the endless possibilities for reinterpretation implicit in each poem. When we turn instead to the exclusionary effects of literary fashions on a poet, say, as talented as Edna St. Vincent Millay, the instability of the text as it is buffeted by the winds of change has its darker side. The last decade of Millay's life was certainly plagued by her sense of this slippage. According to Edmund Wilson, when he visited her at Steepletop (her country house near Austerlitz, New York), Millay seemed desperate to reinforce her belief in the power and substantiality of the text to withstand the destructive force of time. Though clearly in very bad psychological shape (and probably relying upon both alcohol and drugs), she read "The Poet and His Book"—a work about the transfiguration of the poet's body as the poem—in a highly emotional voice: "Read me, margin me with scrawling,/Do not let me die!"[16] For many years this plea seemed to fall upon deaf ears as Millay's work went out of fashion and Millay herself was remembered mainly as a cultural phenomenon rather than as a poet.

Now, however, there are signs of a return of the repressed. The reasons for Millay's reemergence are no doubt extremely complicated and one cannot do much more here than suggest a range of factors that may be part of this overdetermined change of perspective. Not to be ignored, it seems to me, is the presence of women faculty influenced by feminism in the graduate English programs, which have always included a good many female students but which have only recently been receptive to projects on women writers such as Millay. As we saw at the Skidmore Conference, there are quite a number of talented young faculty and graduate students currently working on Edna St. Vincent Millay at such places as Brown, Cornell, the University of Pennsylvania, the University of Washington, and the University of California, Berkeley. It hardly needs restating that when graduate students work on a writer, a market for material about that writer develops. Articles and books may be published by them down the line; courses begin to appear, creating a ripple effect and, again, a market for new texts. Since poetry is read mainly within the academy, academic attention is the key to critical recognition. Graduate students become professors and teach undergraduates and eventually it is no longer necessary to argue for the value of a writer's work. She has, for all intents and purposes, entered the canon.

These are merely instrumental factors, however. Culturally, too, we are at a point at which Millay might once again appear relevant. This is not due to the uniformity of cultural configurations, however, but to their diversity. For instance, many in the academy feel resentful about the way critical theory and cultural studies (feminism, multiculturalism, and gay and lesbian studies in particular) have taken over what used to be the department where universal values and the techniques of prosody were taught. Though Millay offers rich opportunities for those interested in early twentieth-century American culture, she is also a poet who took form very seriously. Her poems advocate "universal values"—which she herself believed in—and they are models of formal elegance (as the *Heath Introduction to Poetry* recognizes in choosing her sonnets to juxtapose to Shakespeare's). One reading of Edna St. Vincent Millay casts her, in her use of traditional forms, as a kind of antimodernist (a bulwark to those who find Cultural Studies arid) but one who may still appeal to students due to the modern settings and themes of her poems.

Feminism, however, is undoubtedly the single most important cultural factor in the return of Edna St. Vincent Millay. Sandra Gilbert and Susan Gubar, probably the most broadly influential of American feminist critics, began the Millay revival by including an essay on her work in their 1979 anthology *Shakespeare's Sisters,* and they have continued to keep the poet before the eye of the feminist reading public by drawing attention to her in all three volumes of *No Man's Land,* their magisterial reassessment of literary modernism.[17] (The third volume includes an entire essay on Millay.) Earlier Gilbert published a piece on her as a "female female impersonator," available in the new *Critical Essays on Edna St. Vincent Millay* edited by William Thesing.[18] In their *Norton Anthology of Literature by Women* (1985), which is in the process of being revised, they wrote: "despite the obscurity into which her work fell in the fifties and sixties— decades when former acolytes like [Sylvia] Plath and [Anne] Sexton felt it necessary to repudiate her as an old-fashioned 'poetess'—Millay's art has endured and seems, sometimes, surprisingly fresh: indeed, not too long ago one prominent editor remarked that her *Childhood Is the Kingdom* reads like 'a twenty-first century poem.' " [19] Note again the projection of Millay's work into the twenty-first century, signaling a momentum propelling her toward the future.

As a modern (as opposed to an antimodern) poet, Millay can be reconstructed along many lines, not just those of feminism. For New Historicists and cultural critics, her life-text is a gold mine. She lived through two world wars, supporting conscientious objectors in the first and advocating military engagement in the second. She picketed in favor of Sacco and Vanzetti and was accused of being a Communist sympathizer. She advocated free love. Many of the cultural currents of the early twentieth century ran through her life. Perhaps this is why her book-length dramatic poem *Conversation at Midnight,* which is rich with discussions of politics, consumerism, art, and advertising, is now being reappraised as a fascinating document of the 1930s. Her antiwar poetry and her propaganda poems have also found new readers among people preoccupied with the political conflicts presently erupting around the world.

In contrast to the comparatively well-established interest in Millay as a modernist, her postmodern potential has only recently begun to appear. Yet with even a superficial knowledge of the poet one can see where she might fit in to contemporary schools of postmodernism. Performance and spectacle were her calling cards. She wrote for the theater and acted in a number of productions herself. Furthermore, rumor has it that we will soon know quite a bit more about her relations with various lesbian communities in New York and Paris. Indeed she never denied that she had bisexual tendencies, for all that her love life seemed to be made up of one male lover after another. Flirting with cross-dressing and possessed of a male name ("Vincent"), she became famous for the butch suits in which she was photographed. In fact, her bodily image—multiply constructed as ultrafeminine and androgynous—was an important component of her public persona. (Note, for instance, the first sentence of Paul Engle's 1956 essay called "A Summing-Up of Her Work": "What is untrue of most poets was beautifully true of Edna St. Vincent Millay— her poems were as well-turned as her own slim ankle."[20] Though this association may strike us in the nineties as more than a bit demeaning, Millay herself exploited the possibilities of using her physical presence as a form of art. She was always "on"—except, that is, when she was visibly "off" and out of control. In many ways Edna St. Vincent Millay might be seen as the Judy Garland of American women poets: passionate, vulnerable, and campy. Even in her fifties she could seem, like Garland, childlike and jaded at the same time.

In contrast to other women poets of her day, such as Louise Bogan, Marianne Moore, and H. D., Millay's persona never really gelled, and it has thus been hard to locate the poet and her work definitively. This, of course, makes her a prime candidate for the decentered subject of postmodernism. It also opens her work to psychoanalytic investigations by readers who apply the ideas of Jacques Lacan, Julia Kristeva, and Luce Irigaray, central figures in literary psychoanalysis of a postmodern kind. In some ways the very fact that Millay herself resisted the influence of psychoanalysis makes her work *more* accessible to such readings rather than less. By comparison, Louise Bogan's direct address of psychoanalytic issues in poems such as "The Sleeping Fury" and "Psychiatrist's Song" impresses one as modern rather than postmodern.

In each of these contemporary approaches to Edna St. Vincent Millay—the formalist (antimodern), the modern, and the postmodern— certain poems emerge as significant that were not frequently addressed before. Or, in the case of "Renascence," for instance, new readings transform the text so completely that it seems an entirely new work.

Let us take these three Millays one at a time, beginning with the formalist. Perhaps it is not strictly accurate to connect contemporary formalist accounts of the poet with antimodernism per se. Two critics who come to mind as centrally concerned with Millay's use of form are Colin Falck (the editor of the new Harper's centenary edition of the *Selected Poems*) and Debra Fried. Both insist that Millay did more than simply reuse traditional forms—both see her as modern in a sense—but both acknowledge that part of the pull of her poetry is against the tide of facile modernity. Falck insists:

Her use of traditional forms, for example, is often deceptive: for all the poems where she seems to fall into pastiche (as in some of her sonnets, or some of her Housmanish early quatrains), there are others where she is engaged in something rather more subtle. The interplay between the grand manner and the artless-conversational is essential to much of her work (it first shows itself in "Renascence"), and it enables her, as it also did later poets like Auden or Philip Larkin, to give the traditional forms a new lease of credibility.[21]

Like many a critic steeped in the "great tradition," Falck respects Millay as a lyric and philosophical poet whose flashes of insight and control of form mark her as one of the preeminent poets of the age. After quoting the closing lines of "New England Spring, 1942," Falck concludes: "Nothing like this exists anywhere else in English poetry, unless it be in others of Millay's later poems" (*SP*, xxviii). Let me also acknowledge here that Falck first drew my attention to "Winter Night"—a poem otherwise neglected—with its mysterious and musical final lines:

> The day has gone in hewing and felling,
> Sawing and drawing wood to the dwelling
> For the night of talk and story-telling.
>
> .   .   .   .
> Here are question and reply,
> And the fire reflected in the thinking eye.
> So peace, and let the bob-cat cry.
>   (*SP*, 81)

Falck enjoys these lines, as do I, because of the sheer pleasure of hearing their sound patterns; the sudden shift from cosy fire to wildcat outside is also pleasurably uncanny. In sum, the delights of Millay's work to which Colin Falck draws attention are those of the traditional English poem, and he is scathing about "academically-inclined critics who have interested themselves only in poetry which presents verbal and intellectual complexities that can be discussed in professional articles or in the seminar room" (*SP*, xxix). Thus, he can be seen as arguing for an antimodernism of sorts, though he calls his essay "The Modern Lyricism of Edna Millay." In keeping with his fundamentally formalist view, a feminist criticism that focuses on oppositional politics also makes him uncomfortable, as we can see by the criticism he levels at Sandra Gilbert in his introduction.

In contrast, Debra Fried's concern with Millay's use of form makes a feminist point. In her "Andromeda Unbound: Gender and Genre in Millay's Sonnets" (which won the 1986 *Twentieth-Century Literature* prize in literary criticism), Fried argues that Millay's use of the sonnet was a bold stroke in the pursuit of freedom rather than a capitulation to male tradition or a necessary checkrein for overwrought emotions. Not surprisingly, Fried has a lot to say about Millay's late sonnet "I Will Put Chaos into Fourteen Lines," in which, she claims, "Millay makes enjambment positively sexy."[22] Carefully comparing sonnets by Keats and Wordsworth with others by Millay, she argues that Millay's use of form makes a point different from theirs. Whereas Wordsworth turned to the sonnet to get away from too much freedom, Millay saw women as threatened with various forms of entrapment, including those hidden in modern clichés about sexual freedom. "By identifying the sonnet's scanty plot of ground with an erotic grove of excess, turning the chastity belt of poetic form into a token of sexual indulgence, Millay invades the sanctuary of male poetic control with her unsettling formalism in the service of freedom, a freedom that can, as the lovers learn in 'Not with Libations,' turn into another kind of entrapment" (Fried, 243). Thus, Fried sees Millay turning the tables on male tradition and asserting a countermeaning instead.

But even Debra Fried concedes that Millay "was called upon to uphold the tradition of binding lyric forms against the onslaught of what her supporters saw as a dangerously shapeless modernism" (235). Thus, in many ways the Edna St. Vincent Millay who emerges from Debra Fried's analysis is an antimodernist because the particular strategy Millay is said to have employed to make her modern feminist points was a response to the past and a reinvigoration of traditional forms. Her analysis of "I Will Put Chaos into Fourteen Lines" focuses particularly on the sonnet's final lines:

> Past are the hours, the years, of our duress,
> His arrogance, our awful servitude:
> I have him. He is nothing more nor less
> Than something simple not yet understood;
> I shall not even force him to confess;
> Or answer. I will only make him good.
>
> (*SP*, 153)

Though elsewhere Fried finds Millay deploying the sonnet form in order to assert her mastery of it, here Fried equivocates: "The tug of line against syntax figures the poet's constant struggle with 'Chaos,' not the assurance of Miltonic authority, or the comforting sense of respite and accomplishment Wordsworth claims to derive from the sweet order of sonnet constraints" (239). Millay chooses to confront tradition directly rather than seek (vainly, according to Fried) to elude its force. Fried concludes: "Her sonnets reshape those [patriarchal] myths with the revisionary force of a woman poet who, *however rearguard in the phalanx of modernism*, recognizes that she has inherited a genre laden with figurations exclusive to a male poetic authority, and who knows that her adaptations of that genre must engage those very myths and figurations that would bar her from the ranks of legitimate practitioners of the sonnet" (243, emphasis added).

Yet, even these formalist critics give us a somewhat different Edna Millay to consider from the one beloved by readers in the twenties, whom John Hyde Preston in 1927 called "a sensitive spirit on a romantic pilgrimage through an over-sophisticated civilization." [23] The formalist must argue craftsmanship, intentionality, and control whereas Millay got more credit in an earlier period for spontaneity and an ardent temperament, as if her finely crafted lyrics were simply the effusions of a highly tuned sensibility.

It is worth noting, therefore, that in contrast to the craftswoman we see in formalist criticism, the "modern" Millay tends once again to be less an example of intentionality and control than a figure through whom certain cultural scripts were memorably articulated. Here we find the feminist, the political activist, and, simply, the "woman writer." In Suzanne Clark's study of the divorce between modernism and the "sentimental," entitled *Sentimental Modernism: Women Writers and the Revolution of the Word*, Millay's unhappy case represents the consequences of disciplining modernism away from authorial biography and personal feeling, a disciplining that Clark sees as resulting in Millay's loss of prestige. In arguing for the present importance of Millay, Clark does not insist upon her craftsmanship or her ability to realize her intentions in verse but instead upon the "difference" of her attempt to replay the old conventions and thus conjure back into view the exiled maternal. Deeply influenced by French theory, Clark deemphasizes the importance of Millay's conscious feminism here, preferring instead to locate her value *for feminism* as intertextual. "Her struggle provokes our awareness of the contradictory status of the woman author, whose authority, as [Teresa] de Lauretis emphasizes, comes from a masculine literary language. Her status, then, depends not on any absolute literary value but on a criticism which extends its interest to the difference that gender makes in literature." [24]

Clark does provide new readings of texts, however, and most notably of "Renascence," which under her scrutiny does not offer the heartwarming affirmation of universal values it suggested to earlier readers. Nor does it represent Edmund Wilson's apotheosis of heterosexual love. Instead, Clark sees "Renascence" as articulating the problems of the woman poet forced to renounce the maternal matrix of woman-identified pre-Oedipal feeling in favor of the patriarchal symbolic. She says: "In 'Renascence,' the speaker, in what begins as a kind of romantic experience with nature, is soon overwhelmed by the natural intimacy.

The encounter makes the speaker recoil, leads to burial in a womb/ tomb, and the rebirth of the subject involves an escape from an engulfing, undefined female body, as from the immersion (underground) in nature. The anxiety of influence is not Oedipal but is related to the ambivalence of being a mother's daughter." [25]

In my own treatment of "Renascence" in *Masks Outrageous and Austere*, I also see it as a drama about the predicament of the woman writer, also invoke French psychoanalytic theory with its discussion of the Imaginary and see the speaker at the end as forced to submit to the Law of the Father. However, I see the Imaginary in the poem less as the domain of the maternal matrix than as the realm of the sorceress. "In the first place, though the speaker is herself a victim of violence, she also seems to cross a dangerous boundary where aggression and seduction constantly change places. This is the realm of the sorceress." [26] Like Suzanne Clark, whose work I did not know at the time I wrote this chapter, I too felt that Millay's example was compelling less because she was able fully to realize her intentions than because her work allowed unconscious material to filter through.

Other critics who wish to reclaim Millay for modernism do credit her with deliberation and control, however. In "Female Female Impersonator: Millay and the Theatre of Personality" Sandra Gilbert emphasizes Millay's conscious manipulation of the roles of femme fatale and embodied woman poet. Discussing the arch and ironic poems in *A Few Figs from Thistles*, Gilbert comments: "These early verses, which made the poet notorious, function as wittily feminine manifestations of the New Woman's new determination to be free. Celebrating sexual liberation, they reveal this self-assertively sexy and consciously feminist young female author's determination to revel in 'modern' woman's unprecedented erotic autonomy." [27] Similarly, in discussing "Sonnets from an Ungrafted Tree"— possibly the work by Millay most widely admired by critics today—Gilbert sees the poet brilliantly exposing a woman's view of problems in marriage: "Besides dramatizing the tedium of this woman's life . . . Millay explores the origins of wifely bitterness, recounting how youthful eroticism had forced the young woman into a bad marriage. Significantly, indeed, it is only when the husband dies that he becomes a figure of tragic dignity and, indeed, an icon of new life for his widow." [28]

Contemporary readings of the modernist Millay's political poetry may equally focus on her skill in creating indictments of her time or on her imprisonment within the disempowering frames of culture. Susan Gilmore's essay "'Poesies of Sophistry': Impersonation and Authority in Edna St. Vincent Millay's *Conversation at Midnight*" takes the former route, claiming for Millay the intention to destabilize male notions of femininity as represented in the dialogue of the various male characters at this evening's homosocial entertainment.[29] Exemplifying the latter position, Susan Schweik's readings of Millay's World War II poetry, though they are often complimentary to the poet, are situated within a cultural context that emphasizes the connections between work dismissed as "propaganda" and notions of femininity. Thus they contribute to the view of Millay as an effect of modernism more than a creative force within it.

This brings us to the last of our three versions of the resurrected Edna St. Vincent Millay: Millay as postmodernist. At the Skidmore Conference of 1992, we heard a number of fascinating papers that employed postmodern perspectives in their treatment of this early twentieth-century poet. Among the papers delivered by panelists—many of them still at that time graduate students—I think particularly of Marilyn May Lombardi's "Vampirism and Translation: Millay, Baudelaire, and the Erotics of Poetic Transfusion," Camille Roman's "Millay's Dialogism: Negotiating Cultural and Assimilative Feminisms," Kerry Maguire's "Through the Looking Glass, or *Sonnets from an Ungrafted Tree* and the Gaze of the Domestic Mirror," and Lisa Myers's "Her Mother's Voice: Feminism, Poetry, Psychoanalysis." (Myers also delivered this paper at the Modern Language Association Convention in December 1992 where it drew appreciate laughter for its creative reading of what has been, for me, one of the most difficult of Millay's poems to like, "The Ballad of the Harp-Weaver.")

Another sign of the times at Skidmore in 1992 was that both Suzanne Clark and I, who were giving plenary speeches, had chosen (independently) to depart from what had been the thrust of our published work on Millay—seeing her as a kind of modernist—and to discuss her as a postmodern instance instead. These papers now appear in Diane P. Freedman's anthology *Edna St. Vincent Millay at 100: A Critical Reappraisal* so I will not dwell upon them in detail. However, it is worth noting here that Clark's paper—entitled "Uncanny Millay"—emphasizes the decentered subject forced upon the reader's awareness in Millay's poetry and argues: "We can see that the question of the imaginary identity is a matter for public and political struggle. The double sense of strangeness and familiarity which marks the uncanny should alert us to the struggle over the terrain of the subject taking place in Millay's poetry." No longer does Millay's interest (or her feminism) belong to a realm outside the poetry as it often did in *Sentimental Modernism.* Instead, Clark writes, "In her words, poetry speaks again, with an uncanny resonance precisely because it was a male tradition that would exclude it. Such speech is a kind of activism, a feminism on her part." [30]

In this paper Suzanne Clark drew our attention to a wonderful Millay poem I had overlooked before called "The Pond." Its narrator seems to be telling us about a farmer's daughter who long ago drowned herself after being jilted by her beau. But in her fantasy of this girl, the narrator changes the love plot into an uncanny performance where even at the moment of death the urge to "camp it up" overcomes what might be read as authenticity.

> Can you not conceive the sly way,—
>   Hearing wheels or seeing men
>
> Passing on the road above,—
>   With a gesture feigned and silly
> Ere she drowned herself for love,
>   She would reach to pluck a lily?[31]

What interests Clark is the way this uncanny gesture dissimulates the girl's extremity, calling into question the whole romantic narrative of a jilted woman drowning herself for love; in its histrionics, Clark suggests, this fantasy plays havoc with notions of art as based upon a woman's dead body, the body of the sublime male text.

My own paper, "The Female Body as Icon: Edna Millay Wears a Plaid Dress," focused on two poems—"The Fitting" and "The Plaid Dress"— where I too found a decentered and antifoundational subjectivity, though it seemed to me in this paper (as in Susan Bordo's discussion of Madonna, which I quoted) a cause less for celebration than for lament.[32] In one of the many startling moments of uncanniness at the conference, Sandra Gilbert had also chosen to discuss these same poems.

Clearly we are witnessing a rejuvenation of interest in Edna St. Vincent Millay, and that interest is beginning to crystallize around some previously underanalyzed texts. I'm not sure, however, that we can say that Millay has fully reentered the canon since it is hard to know to what extent her work is being taught in survey courses across the country. The new Films for the Humanities video suggests broader attention to her work but in itself does not provide the data we need. (I can say, however, that I was struck recently by the fact that Charles Altieri, whom I would classify as a philosophical critic interested in aesthetics, and who is certainly an advocate of canonical modernism, was rereading and enjoying Millay in preparation for teaching her.) One way of assessing how a poet's reputation is changing is by looking at teaching anthologies, and therefore I will conclude this assessment of Millay's current status by making a few brief comments about her presence (or lack of presence) there. To take an example at random from something I can quickly pull off my shelf, in Lionel Trilling's 1967 anthology, *The Experience of Literature*,[33] dozens of male modern poets are represented but the only woman included is Marianne Moore, allowed two poems: "Poetry" and "Elephants."[33] The Prentice-Hall *American Literature* anthology, revised in 1991, is a much more contemporary work and shows some influence of feminism and multiculturalism on the literary establishment, but its choices among modern poets are, in fact, only marginally more thoughtful. Under "Early 20th-Century Poetry" one finds Robinson, Frost, Sandburg, Stevens, Williams, Pound, Eliot, Cummings, Crane, and then some less obvious choices: Ivor Winters, Allen Tate, Langston Hughes, and Stanley Kunitz. The women poets in this section are H. D. (who has definitely entered the canon now), Marianne Moore, and Louise Bogan. There is no mention of Edna St. Vincent Millay, even in the introductory essay providing cultural context for early twentieth-century poetry. In the introduction to Louise Bogan, who was deeply influenced by Millay as well as by other women poets such as Sara Teasdale, Bogan herself is linked only to male friends: Edmund Wilson, Malcolm Cowley, and Rolfe Humphries. Léonie Adams is mentioned but merely as someone with whom Bogan shared the Bollingen Prize, not as the friend and influence she was.[34]

The anthology that has done most to shake up previous orthodoxies about who deserves inclusion is *The Heath Anthology of American Literature*, first published in 1990 and recently revised. The *Heath Anthology* does indeed include Millay (as well as Gertrude Stein, Lola Ridge, Gwendolyn Bennett, H. D., Marianne Moore, and Louise Bogan) among the moderns. The introductory essay is written by John J. Patton, long an admirer of Millay's work. He notes in his conclusion that the "last twenty years have witnessed a resurgence of interest in Millay,"[35] yet his selections of her work—if indeed they are his—are curiously conservative. None of the poems that stimulated so much interest at the Skidmore Conference is included here.

What about other mass-market anthologies? Here is a quick survey. The Macmillan anthology (1989), edited by George McMichael, has no Millay. *The Norton Anthology of American Literature*—volume 2—long a favorite of mine, has not only Millay but Bogan, Moore, Lowell, H. D., Rukeyser, Angelina Weld Grimké, and Genevieve Taggard. (Sadly, they have now removed Elinor Wylie.) The 1994 fourth edition has also changed the Millay offerings, reducing the love poems from the 1989 sample and expanding the political poems; it also now includes "I Will Put Chaos into Fourteen Lines."[36] One could, of course, suggest other poems. *The American Tradition in Literature* (published by McGraw-Hill and most recently updated in 1990) gives an unusually long three-page introduction to the poet and includes several of the passionate sonnets as well as "Justice Denied in Massachusetts" (on the Sacco and Vanzetti trial) and "Passer Mortuus Est."[37]

However, among the anthologies I have mentioned, only the new revised *Heath Anthology* provides any recent bibliographical references. What this suggests to me is that the anthologies have not yet caught up with what has happened to Millay scholarship in the last five years and this is hardly surprising. I suspect that in the coming decade we will see a very different positioning of Millay's work and probably different selections from the poetry. *The Heath Introduction to Poetry*—soon to appear in a new edition—will be a place to look for evidence of change in Millay's reputation and critical construction.

In many ways the whole direction of literary studies has changed in recent years and what used to be a highly male-dominated and British-oriented discipline has become increasingly American and female. The *Heath Anthology* reflected these changes earlier than others with its far broader representation of women and minorities. Edna Millay is somehow peculiarly appropriate to this reconstructed discipline, not only because of her stress on issues of interest to young women, such as love, identity, and politics, but also because she interrogated the theme of nation, which is so prominent in literary studies today. (See, for example, her "Not for a Nation.")

But what about the canon? Does the presence or absence of Edna St. Vincent Millay signal major differences in our understanding of who can be part of the canon? Some years ago, let us say in Lionel Trilling's time, no modern women poets except for Marianne Moore were recognized as among the greats. Now a lot more women are taken seriously. Even more than Edna Millay, Gertrude Stein has come to seem an important literary (instead of simply cultural) figure. I would suggest, however, that Stein could not occupy this position were it not for critical and cultural postmodernism and the popularity of gay and lesbian studies. It is not that we have suddenly come to see what was always valuable about her work. It is rather that, given our present literary values, we can make Stein into a representative figure. She lends herself to it.

The same can be said for Edna St. Vincent Millay who, because she combines elements we now associate with past and future, seems again to have "the right stuff." The canon, indeed the whole idea of canonicity, is founded upon a conception of change and continuity. No matter how strange a writer may at first appear, she must ultimately be seen as readdressing the past as well as forging ahead into the future. This principle has not changed and will not change with the introduction of a few women writers; they too must have friends in high places and some of these friends must belong to the old order.[38] That is, they must be men.

What *has* changed, perhaps, is the construction of the usable past. But this is always changing. We are always refocusing the lens and, as we do, it is only to be expected that some figures will lose definition while others, who once hovered in the background, will suddenly gain a clarity of image and an expansiveness of presence we fool ourselves into thinking was always there to be seen.

Notes

1. *The J. Peterman Company Owner's Manual No. 25b* (Fall 1993): 11.
2. Joseph DeRoche, ed. *The Heath Introduction to Poetry*, 4th ed. (Lexington, Mass.: Heath, 1992), 442.
3. Ibid., 442–43.
4. Jan Montefiore, *Feminism and Poetry: Language, Experience, Identity, in Women's Writing* (London: Pandora, 1987), 115.
5. Ibid., 124.
6. Boris Ford, ed. *American Literature: The New Pelican Guide to English Literature*, vol. 9, (London: Penguin Books, 1988).
7. Winfield Townley Scott, "Millay Collected," *Poetry* 63 (March 1944): 335.
8. Jo Ellen Green Kaiser, "Poet as Persona: Edna St. Vincent Millay and the Problems of Representation" (unpublished manuscript), 1–28.
9. Cary Nelson, *Repression and Recovery: Modern American Poetry and the Politics of Cultural Memory, 1910–1945* (Madison: University of Wisconsin Press, 1989).
10. John Crowe Ransom, "The Poet as Woman," *Southern Review*, 2 (Spring 1937): 783–806.
11. Kaiser, "Poet as Persona," 17.
12. Susan Schweik, *A Gulf So Deeply Cut: American Women Poets and the Second World War* (Madison: University of Wisconsin Press, 1991).
13. Kaiser, "Poet as Persona," 20–21.
14. Bette Richart, "Poet of Our Youth," *Commonweal*, 10 May 1957, 150–51.
15. Daniel Hoffman, ed. *Harvard Guide to Contemporary Writing* (Cambridge, Mass.: Harvard University Press, 1979), 456.
16. See Edmund Wilson, "Epilogue, 1952: Edna St. Vincent Millay," in *The Shores of Light: A Literary Chronicle of the Twenties and Thirties* (New York: Farrar, Straus, 1952), 787; and Joan Dash, *A Life of One's Own* (New York: Harper and Row, 1973), 215. For "The Poet and His Book," see Edna St. Vincent Millay, *Collected Poems*, ed. Norma Millay (New York: Harper and Row, 1956), 87.
17. Sandra Gilbert and Susan Gubar, eds., *Shakespeare's Sisters: Feminist Essays on Women Poets* (Bloomington: Indiana University Press, 1979), and *No Man's Land*, 3 vols. (New Haven, Conn.: Yale University Press, 1988, 1989, and 1994).
18. Sandra Gilbert, "Female Female Impersonator: Millay and the Theatre of Personality" in *Critical Essays on Edna St. Vincent Millay*, ed. William B. Thesing (1985; New York: G. K. Hall, 1993), 293–312.
19. Sandra Gilbert and Susan Gubar, eds. *The Norton Anthology of Literature by Women* (New York: W. W. Norton and Co., 1985), 1554.
20. Paul Engle, "Edna Millay: A Summing Up of Her Work" in Thesing, *Critical Essays*, 97.
21. Colin Falck, "Introduction: The Modern Lyricism of Edna Millay" in Edna St. Vincent Millay, *Selected Poems* (New York: HarperCollins, 1991), xxix. Hereafter cited parenthetically as *SP*.

22. Debra Fried, "Andromeda Unbound: Gender and Genre in Millay's Sonnets" in Thesing, *Critical Essays*, 238. Subsequent references to this work are given parenthetically in the text.

23. John Hyde Preston, "Edna St. Vincent Millay," *Virginia Quarterly Review* 3 (1927): 343.

24. Suzanne Clark, *Sentimental Modernism: Women Writers and the Revolution of the Word* (Bloomington: Indiana University Press, 1991), 96. A version of that essay appears in this volume.

25. Clark, *Sentimental Modernism,* 78.

26. Cheryl Walker, *Masks Outrageous and Austere: Culture, Psyche, and Persona in Modern Women Poets* (Bloomington: Indiana University Press, 1992), 148.

27. Gilbert, "Female Female Impersonator," 300.

28. Ibid., 302.

29. Susan Gilmore, " 'Poesies of Sophistry': Impersonation and Authority in Edna St. Vincent Millay's *Conversation at Midnight* " in *Edna St. Vincent Millay at 100: A Critical Reappraisal,* ed. Diane P. Freedman (Carbondale: Southern Illinois University Press, 1995).

30. Suzanne Clark, "Uncanny Millay," in Freedman, *Millay at 100,* 24–25.

31. Millay, *Collected Poems,* 176. This poem does not appear in Falck.

32. Cheryl Walker, "The Female Body as Icon: Edna Millay Wears a Plaid Dress," in Freedman, *Millay at 100,* 85–99.

33. Lionel Trilling, *The Experience of Literature* (New York: Holt Rinehart, 1967).

34. *American Literature: A Prentice-Hall Anthology,* vol. 2, ed. Emory Elliott et al. (Englewood Cliffs, N.J.: Prentice-Hall, 1991).

35. John J. Patton, "Edna St. Vincent Millay 1892–1950," in *The Heath Anthology of American Literature,* ed. Paul Lauter et al. (Lexington, Mass.: Heath, 1990, 1994), 1247.

36. *The Norton Anthology of American Literature,* vol. 2, ed. Nina Baym et al. (4th ed.; New York: Norton, 1994).

37. *The American Tradition in Literature,* vol. 2, ed. George Perkins et al. (7th ed.; New York: McGraw-Hill, 1990).

38. For an interesting argument in favor of attempting to understand the canon as a counterpoise to contemporary fads and pressures, see Charles Altieri's *Canons and Consequences: Reflections on the Ethical Force of Imaginative Ideals* (Evanston, Ill.: Northwestern University Press, 1990).

Part V
Laura (Riding) Jackson
(1901–1991)

Chapter 9
Laura (Riding) Jackson's "Really New" Poem

Jeanne Heuving

Although Laura (Riding) Jackson's work has been highly acclaimed by many prominent twentieth-century poets and intellectuals, she has not received the concerted critical attention she deserves.[1] While the reasons for this disregard are complex, (Riding) Jackson has decisively contributed to her own neglect.[2] Objecting to the ways that anthologies misrepresent poets' larger works, (Riding) Jackson routinely refused to have her work anthologized. Further, until her death in 1991, she publicly attacked even her most sympathetic critics, meticulously correcting their mistakes in lengthy critical commentary. For (Riding) Jackson, any frame of reference falsified the precise language and thought that each of her poems brought into existence, leading her to enjoin against interpretation itself.[3] Yet, by her very vigilance she discouraged the development of a fuller critical response, important for her far-reaching and difficult work.

In the limited critical attention she has received, (Riding) Jackson has been labeled alternately a modernist, a New Critical, and a postmodernist poet. The multiplicity of terms suggests the problems critics have had in locating (Riding) Jackson's poetry within literary history. Yet, (Riding) Jackson's career offers one of the most singular and willful efforts of our time: to arrive at a "true" human universality through a complex intervention in signifying practices themselves. Although (Riding) Jackson is utopian, she ever seeks to realize her vision through a reworking of the very languages of her existence.[4]

Crucial to (Riding) Jackson's utopian vision of a new human universality is her gender critique. In the 1920s and 1930s at the same time that (Riding) Jackson was formulating her poetics, she arrived at a perspective on gender that bears remarkable similarities to poststructuralist critiques of the suppression of the feminine in discourse.[5] Indeed, (Riding)

Jackson came to the understanding that what went by the name of universality was actually a form of masculine domination. As she saw it, men in projecting their needs for self-importance onto women make women's difference into a mirror that reflects themselves. As the sole standard of the universal, "man" only "creates arbitrarily comprehensive notions of himself; by negating the sense of difference, by denying that which is different." But (Riding) Jackson did not conclude from her gender critique that she should write a women's poetry. Rather, she wished to alter the entire set of gender and linguistic relations that maintained this masculine domination. If a new human universality were to be achieved, it would only come about "through the ordering of all the implications of difference" (*WW*, 41, 43, 87).[6] As such, (Riding) Jackson worked to develop a poetics of "thought in its final condition of truth," countering those holistic and mirroring relations that she saw as critical to an art of the "patriarchal leer" (*P*, 267).[7]

In her antiholistic and antimirroring poetics, (Riding) Jackson bears important affinities with Gertrude Stein and early Marianne Moore.[8] Although in the twentieth century, clearly holistic and mirroring relationships have been important to both men's and women's poetry (albeit more problematically to women's poetry, I contend), these three women poets engaged in important forms of poetic innovation, which put these relations into question.[9] Certainly a number of twentieth-century male poets have been committed to an antiholistic (or anti-illusionistic) poetry, yet, for the most part, their work remains tied in important ways to the linguistically formative use of women and additional designated "others" as mirrors.[10] As such, the poetry, say, of William Carlos Williams or Wallace Stevens, or even Robert Creeley or John Ashbery, retains a psychological *vérité* that has enabled these male writers to escape the blanketing pejorative judgments historically visited upon (Riding) Jackson, Moore, and Stein for their obscure and coy language play.[11] But it is precisely these women poets' refusal of this technique of othering which makes their work so innovative.

In my conclusion, I will return to the larger question of (Riding) Jackson's place in literary history. First, I wish to establish the specificity of (Riding) Jackson's own poetic practice, concentrating on the relationship between her poetics and her gender critique.[12] While (Riding) Jackson is best known for her poetry, she also produced a prodigious body of prose works, including several brilliant, if uneven, treatises on gender and on poetics.[13] Indeed, her books on poetics address many of the most prominent poetical issues of her time and provide an important alternative perspective to entrenched discussions of twentieth-century poetics. Responding negatively to T. S. Eliot's "zeitgeist" poetics, she nonetheless establishes a poetics that shares a number of tenets with New Critical poetry, but for different reasons and ends. In fact, (Riding) Jackson may well have been instrumental in the establishment of the New Criticism itself.[14] Although (Riding) Jackson did not consistently link her poetics to her gender critique, they reinforce each other. Developing a poetics of the "individual-unreal" and "analysis," in opposition to a poetics of the "individual-real" and "synthesis," (Riding) Jackson counters those holistic and mirroring relations on which an art of the "patriarchal leer" depends (*A*, 41–132).

The "Really New" Poem

(Riding) Jackson established her innovative poetry and poetics at the confluence of modernist and New Critical poetics. Her poetry first appearing in small magazines in the early 1920s, (Riding) Jackson was a "discovery" of the Fugitive poets (later the New Critical poets), publishing in their journal *The Fugitive* and winning in 1924 the magazine's annual prize for "the most promising poet of the year."[15] Encouraged to join the Fugitives in Louisville, (Riding) Jackson's bold and emotional presence made a poor fit with Louisville patrician society, and she lived there for only a short time. In 1926, (Riding) Jackson moved to England at the invitation of Robert Graves, who, having admired (Riding) Jackson's poetry in *The Fugitive*, proposed a collaborative venture.[16] In England, (Riding) Jackson met, among others, T. S. Eliot, Ezra Pound, Gertrude Stein, and Virginia Woolf.[17] With Graves, (Riding) Jackson wrote her first of several book-length treatises on poetics, *A Survey of Modernist Poetry* (1927), followed by *A Pamphlet Against Anthologies* (1928).[18] At the same time, she also published two critical works of her own, *Contemporaries and Snobs* (1928) and *Anarchism Is Not Enough* (1928).

But even before meeting Graves, (Riding) Jackson had published her essay "A Prophecy and a Plea" (1925), establishing poetical principles that would serve as a defining basis for her entire career.[19] In fact, several critics have speculated that (Riding) Jackson's influence was far greater on Graves than his on her during the more than a decade they lived and worked together and that she provided Graves with the psychological and ideological framework he needed to wrest his work from a genteel Georgianism.[20] The occasion for (Riding) Jackson's writing of "A Prophecy and a Plea" was as a rejoinder to John Crowe Ransom and Allen Tate, both of whom had addressed the "future of poetry" in separate editorial essays in *The Fugitive*.[21] Despite differences between them, both Ransom and Tate assume a distinction between life and aesthetics, to which (Riding) Jackson objects: "For art is the way we live, while aesthetics in divorcing art from life, sets the seal of approval upon the philosophy of escape" ("PP," 275). Further, neither Ransom nor Tate envision the poet as the powerful maker that (Riding) Jackson conceives. For (Riding) Jackson, the poet is importantly a creative maker who must not try "to force meaning out of [life]," but rather "press meaning upon it" ("PP," 278). Indeed, (Riding) Jackson dismisses most poetry as producing a "vitiation of life in art," since the poet has failed to "envisage life not as an influence upon the soul but the soul as an influence upon life" ("PP," 276). One of the few poets to get a nod of approval in the essay is Shelley, who, like (Riding) Jackson, stresses how the poet is foremost a creative maker who in reordering language vitalizes human existence. But even Shelley is not sufficiently of the here and now. Moreover, in opposition to Shelley, (Riding) Jackson upholds the act of analysis over synthesis. (Riding) Jackson remarks to those who maintain that "the way of analysis is the way of destruction, I can only answer that if one is faithful enough, constant enough, the analysis will induce the synthesis. . . . By taking the universe apart [the poet] will have reintegrated it with his own vitality" ("PP," 280).

In establishing ideas in "A Prophecy and a Plea" that would direct her entire career, (Riding) Jackson importantly formulates principles that counter those commitments to aesthetic wholes so important to twentieth-century poetics. By allying her poetics with "life" and not "aesthetics," (Riding) Jackson sided with what she came to call "total actuality" rather than with an "ideal order" of literary "monuments" or other idealized wholes (*WW*, 12).[22] (In fact, [Riding] Jackson eventually came to renounce poetry because she believed its aesthetic demands got in the way of "truth": there was a conflict between its "creed . . . and its craft tying the hope [of truth] to verbal rituals" and between actual "underlying problem[s]" and its "*effect* of completeness" [*SP*, 12; "WI," 3, 6].) Her emphasis on analysis led her to devise a decreative poetics that countered a dominant poetics in which the poem was foremost to synthesize heterogeneous materials.

One of the poets singled out in "A Prophecy and a Plea" for being insufficiently imbued with life was T. S. Eliot: "T. S. Eliot and his imitators endeavor to show how their chastity and ennui remain intact through all their orgies of intellectual debauchery" ("PP," 279). In subsequent writings, Eliot becomes (Riding) Jackson's central target for attack. His belief in "a communal poetic mind" and in a "world-tradition of poetry" goes against (Riding) Jackson's emphasis on the singular nature of the "really new work of art."[23] In insightful and vituperative commentary, (Riding) Jackson repeatedly takes Eliot and his generation to task: "[This generation] invents a communal poetic mind which sits over the individual poet whenever he writes; it binds him with the necessity of writing correctly in extension of the tradition, the world-tradition of poetry; and so makes poetry internally an even narrower period activity than it is forced to be by outside influences. . . . Already, its most 'correct' writers, such as T. S. Eliot, have become classics" (*SM,* 264). Acknowledging poetry's reduced significance during her time, (Riding) Jackson judges Eliot's reliance on the communal mind and world-tradition as merely a compensatory re-action—a form of restriction that makes poetry even narrower than it need be. Eliot's emphasis on history is similarly problematic, leading to a "zeitgeist poetry" rather than to a poetry of "truth" and "goodness." [24]

(Riding) Jackson disparages Eliot for his elevation of criticism to the same level as creation. By doing so, he separates out the " 'literary' sense" of the poem, validating it over the poet's fresh activity: "The 'lit-erary' sense comes to be the authority to write which the poet is supposed to receive, through criticism, from the age that he lives in. . . . More and more the poet has been made to conform to literature instead of litera-ture to the poet—literature being the name given by criticism to works inspired by or obedient to criticism." Indeed, "Creation and critical judgment being made one act, a work has no future history with readers; it is ended when it is ended" (*CS,* 10, 132). From (Riding) Jackson's per-spective, Eliot is attempting to exercise a kind of monopoly over the work of art, thereby depriving not only the writer, but the reader, of her own activity. Thus, Eliot's poems are "ended" when they are "ended," having no separate life apart from his own safekeeping of them. But for (Riding) Jackson, the poet must be more than a "servant and interpreter of civili-zation" (*CS,* 134). Rather, poetry should be seen as "an ever immediate reality confirmed afresh and independently in each new work rather than as a continuously sustained tradition, confirmed personally rather than professionally" (*CS,* 134). (Riding) Jackson enjoins: "It is . . . always important to distinguish between what is historically new in poetry be-cause the poet is contemporary with a civilization of a certain kind, and what is intrinsically new in poetry because the poet is a new and original individual" (*SM,* 163).

But if (Riding) Jackson viewed T. S. Eliot's emphasis on tradition and criticism in a highly negative light, she, despite her remarks about his lack of personalism, develops her own ethos of impersonalism. (Riding) Jackson condemned what she called Eliot's "shame of the person," com-menting that Eliot was too interested in the "abstract nature of poetry" and not enough in "the immediate personal workings of poetry in him" (*CS,* 10, 133). But (Riding) Jackson herself hardly advanced a concept of self that is anything like the social or psychological self that is usually meant by the term. Rather, for (Riding) Jackson the self was importantly an "unreal self" or an "individual-unreal." [25] (Riding) Jackson, who felt that existing social orders in their normative assumptions belied the self, postulated through her concept of an "unreal self" an entity apart from these orders. Indeed, the "unreal self" is perhaps best described as the ensuing, creative willfulness of a self deliberately estranged from social orders. (Riding) Jackson writes: "In every person there is the possibility of a small, pure, new, unreal portion which is, without reference to personality, in the popular, social sense, self. I use 'self' in no romantic connotation if only because it is the most vivid word, I can use for this particular purification." As (Riding) Jackson put it, the "unreal self is to me poetry" (*A*, 96, 99).

In establishing her ideas, (Riding) Jackson compares the "individual-unreal" to a despised, "individual-real." For (Riding) Jackson, in a literature of the "individual-real," self "authenticates" itself in relationship to existing social orders. The writer uses "the material of the collective-real to insinuate dogmatically the individual-real" (*A*, 48). As (Riding) Jackson saw it, most of the literature of her time was a literature of the "individual-real." Castigating numerous contemporaries, (Riding) Jackson singles out Virginia Woolf's *To the Lighthouse* as "a perfect example of the individual-real":

it is individual: not in the sense that it is personal, warm, alive to itself, indifferent to effect or appreciation, vividly unreal, but in the sense that it individualizes. . . . To do this, language must be strained, supersensitized, loaded with comparisons, suggestive images, emotional analogies; used, that is, in a poetic way to write something that is not poetry. . . . In works like this neither the author who is obsessed by the necessity of emphasizing the individual-real, nor the reader, who is forced to follow the author painfully (word for word) in this obsession may do as he pleases. (*A*, 46–47)

In authenticating self through the "collective real," Woolf endlessly finessed language without addressing the self's "unreality." Eliot proved "how individually realistic the childish, mass-magicked real stuff can be if sufficiently documented" (*A*, 70). Indeed, an art of the "individual real" despite its emphasis on "particulars" was compelled by "the nostalgic desire to reconstitute an illusory whole that has no integrity but the integrity of accident" (*A*, 104). Such an art was hopelessly "synthetic": "imitative, communicative, provocative of association." In contrast a poetry of the "individual-unreal" was "analytic": "original, dissociative, and provocative of dissociation" (*A*, 115).

The problem with Woolf, Eliot, and others like them were that they took existing social orders seriously. The best way to deal with society was to take it impersonally, not as a means to self-discovery:

To attempt to discover and form personality in the social pattern is to make social life dull, vulgar, and aggressive, and life with self, dull, morbid, and trivial. To treat social life as an impersonal pattern is to give it the theatrical vitality of humor and to make life with self strong and serious. The social problem is for each individual how to read the proper degree of humorous formality in his communicative language, his clothes, his home; not how to acquire a vicarious personal life which has no content but a gross synthetic personality-desire. (*A*, 119)

Alienated both from a genteel, bourgeois way of life as well as from socialistic politics, (Riding) Jackson urged that social orders themselves be seen as arbitrary. Language, clothes, and home thus could become a means for humorous commentary.

Indeed, for (Riding) Jackson, the poem itself as the product of an "unreal self" is the "result of an ability to create a vacuum in experience." Correspondingly a poem consists of "generalizations that mean something without instances, that are unreal since they mean something by themselves" (*A*, 17, 83). In one of her most provocative descriptions of poetry, (Riding) Jackson comments: "There is a sense of life so real that it becomes the sense of something more real than life. . . . It introduces a principle of selection into the undifferentiating quantitative appetite and thus changes accidental emotional forms into deliberate intellectual forms. . . . It is the meaning at work in what has no meaning; it is, at its clearest, poetry" (*CS*, 9). For (Riding) Jackson, poetry is intensely motivated—by "a sense of life . . . more real than life." (Here "real" is used in an entirely positive way.) Importantly, this "sense of life" intuited by an "unreal self" cannot be questioned by any frame of reference outside herself. Through the "unreal self's" selectivity, "accidental emotional forms" tied to "the undifferentiating quantitative appetite" can be transformed into "deliberate intellectual forms."

Indeed, what makes a poem a poem is the new linguistic relationships it brings into being through its self-referential relations: "the way [a poem] corresponds in every respect with its own governing meaning . . . [is] the necessity of the poem to be written" (*SM*, 133). In such an autonomous and unparaphrasable poem, the poet is saying exactly what she means: "its final form is identical in terms with its preliminary form in the poet's mind" (*SM*, 142). To paraphrase a poem is to fail to attend to the specificity of its thought: its necessity to be written. Such poems might be condemned by inadequate readers as both "didactic" and "obscure" (as many of [Riding] Jackson's poems have), but there is no help for it (*SM*, 138–39). The poem only exists in its exact wording, not in its paraphrase.

The emphasis on the autonomy and the unparaphrasableness of the poem are, of course, hallmarks of the New Criticism. Although Eliot himself asserted the autonomy of the poem and the unparaphrasableness of his own "objective correlative," these tenets were not for him the raison d'être they became for the New Critics, or for (Riding) Jackson.[26] Yet, in (Riding) Jackson's case, the principles of the poem's autonomy and unparaphrasableness are in service of a very different kind of poetry than for the New Critics. For (Riding) Jackson, a poem is autonomous and unparaphrasable because as a product of an "unreal self" it brings new linguistic relations into existence. While the "unreal self" must be situated in "entirety"—"to be not merely somewhere but precisely somewhere in precisely everywhere"—the "unreal self" importantly brings her "new, unreal portion" to the making of the poem, dislocating preexisting meanings (*P*, 409), (Riding) Jackson describes this process:

> The end of poetry is to leave everything as pure and bare as possible after its operation. It is therefore important that its tools of destruction should be as frugal, economical as possible. When the destruction or analysis is accomplished they shall have to account for their necessity; they are the survivors, the result as well as the means of elimination. . . . The greater the clutter attacked and the smaller, the purer, the residue to which it is reduced (the more destructive the tools), the better the poem. (*A*, 117)

For (Riding) Jackson, a poem is successful to the extent that its decreative practices establish a language voided of unwanted connotations, such that the writer could mean what she wished to mean.

In contrast, for the New Critics, the autonomy of the poem was linked to preexisting wholes: to larger literary, mythical, and ontological orders of which the poem was exemplary. Indeed, the New Critics frequently resorted to a rhetoric of organicism, emphasizing the poem's holistic relationship to holistic entities. Moreover, a poem was unparaphrasable not because of the spareness of its denoted thought but because of the complexity of its connotative meanings. For the New Critics the poem was importantly a synthetic entity that brought heterogeneous elements into harmonious relationships; but for (Riding) Jackson it was a set of analytic relations that altered existing meanings through decreative techniques. As (Riding) Jackson saw it, a false autonomy, or absoluteness, was often claimed for poems that did not in fact possess it. In fact, there was no such thing as absolute autonomy; different poems possessed autonomy in varying degrees depending on the rigorousness of their decreative operations. (Riding) Jackson noted that many poets asserted an "authority" for their poems that "the poet is unable to find in life." Only those poems that established their "irrefutability" on the basis of their new linguistic relations could claim to be unparaphrasable and autonomous (*CS*, 38).

For both the New Critics and (Riding) Jackson, paradoxes constitute an important poetic relation. But for the New Critics, their paradoxes were to achieve a balanced equilibrium through the ultimately harmonious relations poems brought into being. For (Riding) Jackson, paradoxes were often irresolvable contradictions, attesting to the irreducible disparities between diverse entities (*SM*, 154). Meaning itself was highly problematical, best intimated through definitions based on negations and through sense eclipsed by the materiality of signification.

In (Riding) Jackson's "The World and I," the speaker meditates on how she is unable to state "exactly" what she means.[27] While the poem bears a likeness to the "metaphysical poems" Eliot and the New Critics admired, if not always to their poems themselves, its paradoxes work to demarcate disparate and unreconcilable relationships. The poem begins:

> This is not exactly what I mean
> Any more than the sun is the sun.
> But how to mean more closely
> If the sun shines but approximately?
> What a world of awkwardness!
> What hostile implements of sense!
>   (*P*, 187)

By beginning with an entirely open and vague, "This is not exactly what I mean," (Riding) Jackson calls attention to her desire and frustration to make meaning. Contrasting this statement with the seeming least problematical kind of meaning statement, "the sun is the sun," (Riding) Jackson discloses the vast spaces between the kinds of meanings she can make. Further, the "sun shines but approximately," since an unbridgable chasm separates language and physical phenomena and since not even the gaseous ball we call the sun is coincidental with itself from moment to moment. Having explored the dimensions of the meanings she cannot command, the speaker then questions her own demand for exact meanings:

> Perhaps this is as close a meaning
> As perhaps becomes such knowing.
> Else I think the world and I
> Must live together as strangers and die—
> A sour love, each doubtful whether
> Was ever a thing to love the other.
> No, better for both to be nearly sure
> Each of each—exactly where
> Exactly I and exactly the world
> Fail to meet by a moment, and a word.
>   (*P*, 187)

The deliberately vague "this is as close a meaning" suggests that the conditions of knowing may themselves be inexact; and, therefore, a demand for exact meaning can only lead to inexact meanings. In fact, this demand can only result in a "sour love," that belies the need for love between the "world and I." Better, then, to acknowledge how "where / Exactly I and exactly the world / Fail to meet by a moment, and a word." Rather than lose the world or herself, the speaker considers their very lack of correlation best bespeaks such disparate entities as "I," "world," "a moment," and "a word." So exact is the inexactness between these entities as explored by the poem that it can only be intimated, not stated. The difference between (Riding) Jackson's poetic predilections and Ransom's "miraculism" could not be more pronounced. For Ransom, "miraculism arises when the poet discovers by analogy an identity between objects which is partial, though it should be considerable, and proceeds to an identification which it is complete." [28]

In her "Disclaimer of the Person," (Riding) Jackson explores the irresolvable contradiction between the immaterial and material makeup of meanings. The speaker meditates on herself at once as constituting and constituted by her meanings and as apart from and caught up in her writing as a material production. The poem concludes:

> If I my words am,
> If the footed head with frowns them
> And the handed heart which smiles them
> Are the very writing, table, chair,
> The paper, pen, self, taut community
> Wherein enigma's orb is word-constrained.
> Does myself upon the page meet,
> Does the thronging firm a name
> To nod my own—witnessing
> I write or am this, it is written?
> What thinks the world?
> Has here the time-eclipsed occasion
> Grown language-present?
> Or does the world demand,
> And what think I?
> The world in me which fleet to disavow
> Ordains perpetual reiteration?
> And these the words ensuing.
>
> (*P*, 235–36)

By turning her statements into questions, the speaker establishes herself as both implicated in and outside of the complex relations set into play by the questions themselves. Thus, while the opposites posed in the questions strongly suggest the ways that the speaker is constituted through her act of material signification, the voice works as a kind of an "unreal self" questioning this constitution. The speaker by her "footed head" and her "handed heart" calls up not only her physical body, but the look of letters on the page. These serifed and linked letters have the look of truncated bodies, as the speaker's own body is foreshortened by the words of her poem. But the speaker is not only caught up by the materiality of her words, but by her very means of production: "the very writing, table, chair / The paper, pen, self, taut community." In this "thronging" on the page, the speaker senses herself as either "I write or am this, it is written." Writer and written are merely flip sides of the same poem, as are "What thinks the world" and "What think I." The world has "Grown language-present" and the "The world in me . . . / Ordains perpetual reiteration." Yet, while the poem seems almost a demonstration of the materiality of signification, the questioning voice provides a separate reality: asking if this "thronging" "firms" "a name / To nod my own."

In an age of science and specialization, (Riding) Jackson shared with Eliot and the New Critics the attempt to formulate a poetry that would have legitimacy as an important form of knowledge. But whereas Eliot and the New Critics sought to secure poetry's importance by asserting a separate realm for it, (Riding) Jackson eschewed what she saw as a professionalization and aestheticization of art. She thought that in an age devoted to specialization, poetry, like any other sphere of human activity, should feel compelled to examine itself, ironically commenting: "A professional conscience dawns on the poet; as when the prestige of any organization is curtailed—of the army, or the navy, for example—a greater internal discipline, a stricter morality and a more careful evaluation of tactics result" (*CS*, 128). From (Riding) Jackson's point of view, Eliot and the New Critics were trying to bolster poetry rather than to examine it. While they asserted poetry's autonomy, they contradictorily attempted to make poetry more relevant to its time by increasing its range, cluttering up their poems with "contemporary data," learned allusions, and connotations run awry. (Riding) Jackson thought that what the age needed was for poetry to become more itself: "thought in its final condition of truth," urging a poetry in which an "unreal self" "by taking the universe apart will have reintegrated it" with her own "vitality."

Strangers in the Country of Men

At the same time that (Riding) Jackson was establishing her poetics, she was also forming her gender critique. (Riding) Jackson came to see the uses to which women had been put in civilized society as critical to the social orders she despised. Concentrating on the word "woman" as a linguistic function, she arrived at a perspective on gender that possesses remarkable similarities to poststructuralist critiques of the suppression of the feminine in discourse. But while (Riding) Jackson developed this feminist perspective, she was not interested in writing a specifically women's poetry. Rather, she wished to alter the entire set of gender relations in order to arrive at a new human universality. Formulating in her critique the ways that women have served as a central prop for the "solemn masculine machine," she in her poetry elects to alter the machine itself (*A*, 196). That is, in rejecting those holistic and synthetic relationships that define Eliot's and the New Critics' poetics and in insisting on her own decreative and analytic techniques, (Riding) Jackson works against existing linguistic orders. Further, she disengages from those mirroring relationships that directly underwrite an art of the "patriarchal leer."

As early as her essay "Jocasta" in *Anarchism Is Not Enough*, (Riding) Jackson evinces her poetics as a corrective to prevailing sexual economies. Formulating in this essay her important distinction between a literature of "an individual-unreal" and of "an individual-real," she dismisses a literature of the hated "individual-real" as a "nostalgic, lascivious, masculine, Oedipean embrace of the real mother-body by the unreal-son mind" (*A*, 70). The "unreal" son's mind, rather than inquiring into itself, uses the mother's body to produce a lascivious and nostalgic literature. By entitling the lengthy essay "Jocasta," (Riding) Jackson signals that this incestuous state is pervasive—and that, at least in this essay, Jocasta herself is its avenging subject.

In a more extensive critique of gender in the same volume, in "The Damned Thing," (Riding) Jackson analyzes the production of sexuality within civilization, dismissing literary sensibilities as deeply implicated in such a production. As she saw it, men's "phallus-proud-works-of-art" amount to little more than men's "private play with [women] in public" (*A*, 205, 208). Indeed, sexuality itself has been vastly overwritten by a civilization uncomfortable with it. The kingpin of this system is women's "impersonal sexuality" that "if not philosophized would wreck the solemn masculine machine" (*A*, 196). In its civilized version, sexuality is produced as a kind of rare brew of bodily impulses, scientific phrases and literary sentiments, which all conspire to keep women in a passive state. (Riding) Jackson discloses just what "this diffusion which modern society calls love" consists of by revealing what a man's "I love you" speech means:

"My sexual glands by the growing enlargement of my sex instinct since childhood and its insidious, civilized traffic with each part of my mental and physical being, are unfortunately in a state of continual excitement. I have very good control of myself, but my awareness of your sexual physique and its radiations was so acute that I could not resist the temptation to desire to lie with you. Please do not think this ignoble of me, for I shall perform this act, if you permit it, with the greatest respect and tenderness and attempt to make up for the indignity it of course fundamentally will be to you (however pleasurable) by serving you in every possible way and by sexually flattering manifestations of your personality which are not strictly sexual." (*A*, 189)

(Riding) Jackson well reveals the unsavoriness of a speech that pretends to nobility when it is so perversely construed. Importantly her ultimate target of attack is neither men nor sexuality, but the ways sexual desire has been produced through an "insidious, civilized traffic": "The social mechanism for disposing of sex makes sex as large and complicated as itself, intensifies its masculinity. Its femininity reduces merely to an abstract passive principle of motion in the great moving masculine machine" (*A*, 195). As (Riding) Jackson saw it, feminine passivity was actively maintained by masculine domination.

But by far Riding's most sustained and trenchant gender critique is *The Word "Woman,"* written in 1933 to 1935, but only recently published. In a recent introduction (Riding) Jackson directly links this critique to a corrective vision of literature: "I believe that a close reading of the text of *The Word "Woman"* may strip literature of its mythologies of ludicrous pieties." As one example of such "ludicrous pieties," (Riding) Jackson singles out "the hypocrisies of the Graves order of upper-notch Anglo-Saxon romanticism" (*WW*, 13). Throughout their relationship, (Riding) Jackson served as a harsh critic of Graves's work, but after her break with Graves she took to denouncing his work in often scathing public attacks. Appalled by Randall Jarrell's suggestion, among others, that she herself was the model for Graves's *The White Goddess*, she denounced Graves's text as a "spectacular show of poet-piety," of "nothingish spiritualistics," written by a "self-crowned genius of poetic masculinity" (*WW*, 208, 211).[29] (Riding) Jackson found Graves's text repugnant because of what she perceived as a misuse of her own ideas and person. Graves's "white goddess" upheld the old masculine orders; her new woman was to decisively alter them.

In *The Word "Woman,"* (Riding) Jackson arrives at a perspective on women that is uncannily similar to the poststructuralist critique of the suppression of the feminine in discourse, as theorized by Luce Irigaray. As Luce Irigaray most succinctly describes this "specular discourse": women are "the projective map" that "guarantees the system."[30] While (Riding) Jackson and Irigaray's theories can be criticized for their totalizing aspects, they have direct and relevant application to lyric poetry. One of the pervasive conventions of twentieth-century poetry is that the speaker constitutes his authority through the mirroring others of his poem. Yet, for women, as the "projective map" that "guarantees the system," such mirroring relations are problematical. Indeed, women simply cannot use men in the same way as men use women to establish their authoritative stances. Further, (Riding) Jackson and Irigaray urge that women's "self"-expression is troubled by the uses to which women have been put.

(Riding) Jackson begins *The Word "Woman"* by analyzing the ways the word "woman" has been used in multiple cultures and times, concluding that "women are strangers in the country of men" (*WW*, 19). The reason for this state of affairs is that man, in projecting his need for his own self-importance onto women, has made women's difference into a mirror by which to reflect himself: "Man, in his growing self-importance, reads differences as negativeness—namely the absence of, or deficiency in, male characteristics. Women become more and more a foil to male positiveness" (*WW*, 87). Since men have denied women their own reality, (Riding) Jackson dismisses their concepts of the universal as reflective only of men: "We cannot avail ourselves of man's universalizations because when he uses himself as the standard . . . he only creates arbitrarily comprehensive notions of himself; by negating the sense of difference, by denying that which is different" (*WW*, 41). For (Riding) Jackson as for Irigaray, women's position as other, as foil, can't be easily turned around because most of language, most of history, reflects this male appropriation. In (Riding) Jackson's terms, women are sleepwalkers in an order that does not reflect them; indeed, they are only just awakening.

So total is the stronghold of this masculine appropriation that women must engage in subversive forms of behavior, if they are to break the sexist culture's codes. As Irigaray encourages women to mimic femininity—to reveal their difference from its projections—(Riding) Jackson encourages women to meddle with their mask, their makeup: "The mask is woman's trade mark. And at this stage [of history] she does well to brand her actions as womanly until man sees the necessitous relation between her action and her physical difference from him: until the impression 'different action' is identical with the impression 'different appearance'" (*WW*, 120). By emphasizing the activity they put into making themselves up, women can disrupt men's equation of their appearance with passivity, establishing themselves as different than they are projected to be within a masculine economy (*WW*, 119–22).

However, for (Riding) Jackson, unlike Irigaray, the establishment of women's difference is only the means to a greater end: the realization of a new human universality not based on women's exclusion. Positioned outside existing social orders, women have an important historical role to perform as agents of change. Women, unlike men, do not need to establish their identity through their sexual difference—and therefore do not need to make it the be-all and end-all of their existence. They can help bring about a new human universality precisely because they are able to acknowledge that life is a "composite." Indeed, if a new unity is to be realized, it will only be "through the ordering of all the implications of difference" (*WW*, 42–43).

Throughout her poetry (Riding) Jackson struggles to realize a new human universality, based on changed gender relationships. In one of (Riding) Jackson's relatively early poems "Life-Size Is Too Large," the speaker contemplates how she can't see herself in a life-size mirror. But rather than concluding, as does Irigaray, that she should inscribe a fluid and contradictory writing, (Riding) Jackson opts (at least in her poetry) for an incremental, if also contradictory, thought. The poem begins with the seeming paradox that if the speaker is to see herself, she can only see herself in "microscopy," if she is "To have room to think at all." For when she commands the " 'Cramped mirror, faithful constriction, / Break, be as large as I,' " she loses herself to desolation:

> Then I heard little leaves in my ears rustling
> And a little wind like a leaf blowing
> My mind into a corner of my mind,
> Where wind over empty ground went blowing
> And a large dwarf picked and picked up nothing.
> (*P*, 86)

Through the "microscopy" that the "cramped mirror" provides her, the speaker can think with a sense of repleteness, but as soon as the compass expands into a large, life-size mirror, she is wracked with absence—with abjection.

In "The Biography of a Myth," (Riding) Jackson traces the evolution of a myth—of a woman who begins by "delivering beauty / like a three hour entertainment" (*P*, 179). As an "other" that is leered at, she can bring no good to others or herself:

> Then they went home, grinning at otherness,
> And she to lour in shame, out of which night
> She rose unseen, absent in counted presence. . . .
> (*P*, 179)

Importantly only as an absence can this woman begin to realize herself. Suffering from exposure, she turns inward, whispering to herself:

> "She whom they did not see though saw
> Myself now am, hidden all away in her
> Inward from her confiding mouth and face
> To deep discretion, this other-person mind."
>
> (*P*, 179)

Away from her "confiding mouth," she can only turn to "deep discretion" and to "this other-person mind." And although "In this pale state she had prediction of self," there can be no beyond, since the world does not yet exist, "Where she the world, and he inhabiting / Like peace unto himself" (*P*, 179, 180). The woman exists as a kind of truth onto herself, "So long she is no measured, proven seeming" (*P*, 180). But present to the world, she can only produce the conditions of false belief:

> [She] gave them back
> Their faith, a legal gospel like false oaths
> Adhered to with the loyalty of words
> That do not pledge the mind to believe itself.
>
> (*P*, 180)

The female figure as source is most efficacious as an absent, inward-turning "unreal self," existing apart from the compromised orders of the world.

In "The Need to Confide" the speaker tells of her need to relate to an "other:"

> My need to confide,
> My friend man,
> Is not my mouth's way of stealth
> Nor my heart's need of nakedness.
>
> It is my need for myself, man,
> To be talking with it—
>
> (*P*, 265)

(Riding) Jackson deliberately abstracts the word "confidence" from its connotations of secretive self-revelation. Her use of the word "man" is both deliberately gender-specific and universal: for her need to confide can only happen through existing languages. And while she is compelled by the ideal of universality that the word "man" can suggest, she also realizes its limited, gender bias. Rather than blurring these two senses of "man," (Riding) Jackson's poem articulates them through her disjunctive address: "It is my need for myself, man." The kind of unavailable confidence she is attempting to experience is expressed jarringly as an "it"—so much does she need "it" and so little does "it" resemble what is typically meant by the word "confidence." While "man's" words remain with "love-meant" not with "love could," her desire to be "day-same," a "flushed double dark," can only "join to itself" (*P*, 266).

While these poems address the problematics of meaning within meaning systems in which woman as an "other" is compromised and muted, they also directly counter existing poetic modes. That is, by refusing those forms by which poetic meaning and closure are achieved—holistic and mirroring relationships—they eloquently bespeak women's dilemmas. While this eloquence necessarily brings with it the indirection and silence that characterize (Riding) Jackson's poetry, for (Riding) Jackson women can most mean when they are obliquely "talking with it." And only when women are "talking with it," actualizing their "unreal selves" within the existing problematics of language, can a new human universality emerge.

In conclusion, I wish to consider the larger question of (Riding) Jackson's place in literary history. Within existing periodizing concepts, (Riding) Jackson's poetry can only be seen as a strange kind of amalgam of modernist, New Critical, and postmodernist poetics. Indeed, (Riding) Jackson has been labeled alternately and in combination by each of these terms. Yet, given the willful singularity of her work, such confusion seems highly inadequate. Further, (Riding) Jackson's work points to limitations of each of these poetics. That is, (Riding) Jackson's understanding of language as the very subject of her poetry compels notice of how many modernist poets use language in far more naturalized ways. Her emphasis on such New Critical tenets as the autonomy and unparaphrasableness of the text to write a poetry that discloses irresolvable contradictions and the materiality of signification reveals how these tenets can be put to very different ends. And, (Riding) Jackson's willful agency, her concept of the "unreal self," points to the inadequacy of much postmodernist poetics to formulate any sense of human agency or will. Indeed, her poetry underlines the ways that such periodizing concepts as modernism, New Criticism, and postmodernism do not articulate a culminating aesthetic, but are highly reified, highlighting the poetics of some poets over others.

Moreover (Riding) Jackson's example should well demonstrate how gender must be made prominent in any history of poetic innovation.

The persistence of the use of periodizing concepts, especially in discussions of poetics apart from considerations of race, class, and gender, ultimately validates those very selected texts on which their definitions are based. While it might seem that these days poets are only poorly served by the term New Critical, the category makes recognizable, and therefore legitimates, a certain body of poets and poetry, making way for their reiteration and comeback.[31] Indeed, not to consider (Riding) Jackson's poetics of an "individual-unreal" and "analysis" with respect to gender is to fail to establish a sense of sufficient motivation for her difficult poetry. Further, it is to disregard the kind of innovation she needed to engage in order to write her "universal" poetry.

As I commented at the beginning of this chapter, a more suggestive context for (Riding) Jackson's poetry than existing periodizing concepts is the poetics of early Moore and of Stein. Stein, in fact, was one of the few poets (Riding) Jackson publicly praised during her lifetime. All three women poets in disengaging from those holistic and mirroring relations crucial to an art of the "patriarchal leer" engage in important forms of poetic innovation that subvert existing gender relations. In their rejection of holistic and mirroring relations, these poets explore meanings apart from a far more simply communicative poetics of the "individual real" and its recognizable psychology. Yet literary history provides no convenient term that legitimates their antiholistic *and* antimirroring poetics. That Moore and Stein as well as (Riding) Jackson are frequently labeled modernist-postmodernists provides only further evidence of the ways that literary history has been unable to articulate their important poetic projects.[32] Ironically, while all three writers at times take on stances of universality problematical to a postmodernist ethos, it may be their very presumption of universality that leads them to the kind of deconstructive or decreative poetics that has caused critics to add the term postmodernism to their modernism.

Surely (Riding) Jackson's poetry is not entirely outside of those mirroring and holistic relations she works against, as ultimately even deconstructed or decreated meanings are at least partially dependent on these relations. In fact, (Riding) Jackson's eventual renunciation of poetry carries through the logic of her poetics, as she came to reject all poetry for the ways its "*effect* of completeness" obscured actual "underlying problems."[33] (Riding) Jackson is an important twentieth-century poet because her far-reaching commitment to change those holistic and mirroring relations on which a poetry of the "patriarchal leer" depends. The range and depth of her inquiry into meaning, including the meaning of poetic form itself, constitutes a major contribution to poetic history.

Notes

1. I have followed the example of the poet in referring to her as Laura (Riding) Jackson. In her later years, (Riding) Jackson elected to use her married name, even in republication of work written under the name of Laura Riding.

2. W. H. Auden, John Ashbery, and Robert Graves accorded (Riding) Jackson's writing major significance. W. H. Auden, declaring (Riding) Jackson "our only living philosophical poet," paid (Riding) Jackson the tribute of copying her diction. (Riding) Jackson, who saw philosophy as a far more limited practice than poetry, failed to appreciate Auden's compliment, and she and Graves accused Auden of poetic theft. See Joyce Piell Wexler, *Laura Riding's Pursuit of Truth* (Athens: Ohio University Press, 1979), 48, and Deborah Baker, *In Extremis: The Life of Laura Riding* (New York: Grove Press, 1993), 187, 323, 349–50. John Ashbery recently gave his Norton Lecture at Harvard on (Riding) Jackson. As late as 1966, an estranged Robert Graves yet fully credited (Riding) Jackson's poetic endeavors, commenting that she "can be seen now as the most original poet of the Twenties and Thirties." Wexler, *Pursuit of Truth*, 143, is citing Graves's "Comments on James Jensen's 'The Construction of Seven Types of Ambiguity,'" *Modern Language Quarterly* (September 1966): 256. More recently the critic Jerome McGann has summarized (Riding) Jackson's career: "Her writing executes a standard of self-examination so deep and resolute that it cannot be decently evaded. Later writers who have not at least attempted to meet its challenge risk being seen—not least of all by themselves—as trivial, attendant lords and ladies" (*Black Riders: The Visible Language of Modernism* [Princeton, N.J.: Princeton University Press, 1993], 134). McGann may have taken his lead from the poet Charles Bernstein who refers to (Riding) Jackson in several instances in his *Content's Dream: Essays 1975–1984* (Los Angeles: Sun and Moon Press, 1984). See especially, pp. 340–42. Jane Marcus comments that "Riding ought to be restored to the ranks of writers like Hart Crane and Gertrude Stein, where she belongs as a shaper of our speech, a poet of powerful and original irony." See her "Laura Riding Roughshod," *Iowa Review* 12 (1981): 298. Yet despite this high acclaim only two book-length critical studies of (Riding) Jackson's work exist: Wexler, *Laura Riding's Pursuit of Truth* and Barbara Adams, *The Enemy Self: Poetry and Criticism of Laura Riding* (Ann Arbor, Mich.: UMI Research Press, 1990).

3. For provocative essays on (Riding) Jackson's decanonization of herself that address many of these issues, see Jo-Ann Wallace, "Laura Riding and the Politics of Decanonization," *American Literature* 64, no. 1 (March 1992): 111–26, and K. K. Ruthven, "How to Avoid Being Canonized: Laura Riding," *Textual Practice* 5, no. 2 (Summer 1991): 242–60. As Wallace points out, (Riding) Jackson rejected both feminist and deconstructivist interpretive frameworks. (Riding) Jackson's negative remarks about feminism need to be considered in context. (Riding) Jackson dismissed virtually all twentieth-century political and intellectual movements as falling short of her own vision. Further, (Riding) Jackson issued several negative comments on feminism in the 1960s and 1970s because of what she perceived as its exclusive focus on a social realm defined by men. Dismissing a feminism that she perceived as too much preoccupied with women's rights in a social realm that ill suits them, she called for a redefinition of "woman," for a new order based on "an adequate idea" of woman (*WW*, 197).

4. Wexler, *Pursuit of Truth*, stresses (Riding) Jackson's "insistence on the value of the universal and immutable" (4). By pairing the "universal" and the "im-

mutable," Wexler fails to convey how (Riding) Jackson's belief in "truth" and "goodness" was as a utopian possibility. Jerome McGann stresses the ways that (Riding) Jackson was a poet of interactive language: "The poem is not allowed to point toward any truth beyond its own interactive features, its own textuality." While McGann brings an important corrective perspective to (Riding) Jackson, his failure to address her simultaneous commitment to a universal "truth" and "goodness" dehistoricizes her effort. See his *Black Riders*, 133. Recent criticism, of course, has noted the ways that universalizing stances have been instrumental in silencing diversity. Yet, universality has been a value of many twentieth-century writers, including many writers who address oppression. Rather than ignoring or repressing this problematic commitment, it would seem that contemporary criticism would have much to gain by exploring how the ideal of "universality" functions in diverse writers and texts. (Riding) Jackson may use the term "human unity" more frequently than "human universality," perhaps in order to avoid the false claims of a masculinized universal and also to emphasize the composite nature of unity. I use the term "universal" to link her poetics with Enlightenment ideals of which it surely partakes.

5. This critique is crucial to the many books written by Luce Irigaray and by Hélène Cixous, among other French feminists. For a discussion of this critique in men's poststructuralist writing, see Alice Jardine, *Gynesis: Configurations of Woman and Modernity* (Ithaca, N.Y.: Cornell University Press, 1985).

6. Quotations from (Riding) Jackson's works are cited in the text with the abbreviations listed below.

A:	*Anarchism Is Not Enough* (Garden City, N.Y.: Doubleday, Doran and Co., 1928).
CS:	*Contemporaries and Snobs* (Garden City, N.Y.: Doubleday, Doran and Co., 1928).
P:	*The Poems of Laura Riding: A New Edition of the 1938 Collection* (New York: Persea, 1980).
"PP":	"A Prophecy and a Plea," *First Awakenings: The Early Poems of Laura Riding* (New York: Persea, 1992).
SM:	*A Survey of Modernist Poetry*, with Robert Graves (Garden City, N.Y.: Doubleday, Doran and Co., 1928).
SP:	*Selected Poems: In Five Sets* (New York: Persea, 1993).
"WI":	"What, If Not a Poem, Poems?" *Denver Quarterly* 9, no. 2 (1974): 1–13.
WW:	*The Word "Woman" and Other Related Writings*, ed. Elizabeth Friedmann and Alan J. Clark (New York: Persea, 1993).

7. Gary Lenhart quotes, but does not cite, (Riding) Jackson's useful phrase "thought in its final condition of truth." See his "Combat and the Erotic," *American Book Review* 15, no. 4 (October–November 1993): 1.

8. In *Omissions Are Not Accidents: Gender in the Art of Marianne Moore* (Detroit: Wayne State University Press, 1992), I argue that Moore's early poetry is feminist precisely because of her rejection of the use of others as mirrors. See especially chapter 1, "An Artist in Refusing," 17–29. Several critics discuss the antipatriarchal commitments of Stein's writing, although not exactly in these terms. See, for example, Marianne DeKoven, *A Different Language: Gertrude Stein's Experimental Writing* (Madison: University of Wisconsin Press, 1983), and Ellen Berry, *Curved Thought and Textual Wandering: Gertrude Stein's Postmodernism* (Ann Arbor: University of Michigan Press, 1992).

9. Romantic and post-Romantic poetry are particularly dependent on mirroring relations between an "I" and a "you" or an "I" and an "other." Indeed, I would suggest that an informing convention in the production and reception of poetry up to and including our time, when it is not overtly symbolic, is a mirroring aesthetic—a sense that the speaker is reflected in some unique ways by the poem's representation of that which is outside of or other than the speaker. While certainly most women poets practice some version of this convention, it is a convention made problematical for a woman by her own prominent figuring as the other. I develop this argument at greater length in conjunction with a discussion of Luce Irigaray's theories in *Omissions Are Not Accidents*, 21–27.

10. For a discussion of this dynamic, see Rachel DuPlessis, "Pater-Daughter: Male Modernists and Female Readers," in *The Pink Guitar: Writing as Feminist Practice* (New York: Routledge, 1990), 41–67; Nancy J. Vickers, "Diana Described: Scattered Woman and Scattered Rhyme, in *Writing and Sexual Difference*, ed. Elizabeth Abel (Chicago: University of Chicago Press, 1982): 95–110; and Heuving, *Omissions Are Not Accidents*, 30–48.

11. I am assuming that the reader will be aware of how women and other "others" serve as projective foils in Williams, Stevens, and Creeley's poems. Although this representational convention is far less evident in Ashbery, he utilizes its dynamics and psychology in many of his poems, including his important "Self-Portrait in a Convex Mirror."

12. Although (Riding) Jackson's feminist orientations have been noted by several critics, very little feminist criticism has been written. Only two articles, to my knowledge, discuss (Riding) Jackson's poetry at any length with respect to her gender: Susan Schultz, "Laura Riding's Essentialism and the Absent Muse," *Arizona Quarterly* 48, no. 1 (April 1992): 1–24, and Peter Temes, "Code of Silence: Laura (Riding) Jackson and the Refusal to Speak," *PMLA* 109, no. 1 (January 1994): 87–99. Although Schultz's article raises provocative questions, she wrongly dismisses (Riding) Jackson as essentialist. Temes explores how in order "to escape from the role of object, of the seen and the judged," (Riding) Jackson elected silence, within her poetry and in her renunciation of poetry (87). Temes stresses (Riding) Jackson's need for self-protection and control within an androcentric culture that will only misread and misuse her words. While I find many of his observations compatible with my own, I emphasize (Riding) Jackson's utopianism, rather than her defensiveness.

13. The prodigiousness, scope, and diversity of (Riding) Jackson's prose writings are little known. In the first part of her life, she published an impressive number of fictional, critical, and cross-genre works. For a description of (Riding) Jackson's many unknown works, see Joyce Piell Wexler's excellent bibliography: *Laura Riding: A Bibliography* (New York: Garland Publishing, 1981), 39. (Riding) Jackson published only one book after 1940 until her death in 1991, her prose work *The Telling* (New York: Harper and Row, 1972).

14. (Riding) Jackson's instrumentality in the formation of the New Criticism may have occurred in two ways. (Riding) Jackson claims to have influenced the Fugitive poets' practice of close reading in the 1920s. While there is debate around who influenced whom, (Riding) Jackson was trained in close reading at an early age, urged on by her Marxist father to read newspapers with an eye for the capitalist subtext (Baker, *In Extremis*, 28). If (Riding) Jackson is right, a curious footnote to literary history would be the leftist derivation of a practice of reading that enabled the politically conservative New Criticism. Secondly, William Empsom credited Robert Graves's and (Riding) Jackson's ideas in *A Survey*

of Modernist Poetry (Garden City, N.Y.: Doubleday, Doran and Co., 1928) for inspiring his *Seven Types of Ambiguity* (London: London, Chatto, and Windus, 1947), which, in turn, has been seen as a catalyst to the New Criticism. See Wexler, *Pursuit of Truth,* 14–16; James Jensen, "The Construction of *Seven Types of Ambiguity,*" *Modern Language Quarterly* 27, no. 3 (September 1966): 243–59 and (Riding) Jackson, "Some Autobiographical Corrections of Literary History," *Denver Quarterly* 8, no. 4 (Winter 1974): 1–33.

15. Adams, *The Enemy Self,* 7.

16. Baker, *In Extremis,* 14–16; 86.

17. Adams, *The Enemy Self,* 12. (Riding) Jackson's first book of poems, *The Close Chaplet,* was published in 1926 by Virginia Woolf and Leonard Woolf's Hogarth Press.

18. *A Survey of Modernist Poetry* was published first in Britain in 1927 by William Heinemann publishers and later in America in 1928 by Doubleday, Doran and Company.

19. "A Prophecy and a Plea" first appeared in *The Reviewer* 5, no. 2 (April 1925): 1–7.

20. Adams, *The Enemy Self,* 12, 15. Wexler, *Pursuit of Truth,* 142.

21. John Crowe Ransom, "The Future of Poetry," *The Fugitive* 3, no. 1 (March 1922): 2, 3. Allen Tate, "One Escape from the Dilemma," *The Fugitive* 3, no. 2 (April 1924): 34–36.

22. T. S. Eliot comments how in literature "existing monuments form an ideal order among themselves." See *Selected Prose of T. S. Eliot,* ed. Frank Kermode (New York: Harcourt Brace Jovanovich and Farrar, Strauss, and Giroux, 1975), 38.

23. The "really new work of art" is T. S. Eliot's phrase, *Selected Prose of T. S. Eliot,* 38.

24. (Riding) Jackson uses the word "zeitgeist" throughout her writings to disparage Eliot's poetry. (Riding) Jackson frequently criticizes the modern division between aesthetics and morality. See, for instance, *Contemporaries and Snobs,* 91.

25. Many critics note (Riding) Jackson's concentration on the self, but overpsychologize it. Barbara Adams stresses (Riding) Jackson's "enemy self," establishing a dichotomy between (Riding) Jackson's presumably "real" and "ideal" selves (*The Enemy Self*). M. L. Rosenthal alludes to (Riding) Jackson's "egocentric stress on identity." See his "Laura Riding's Poetry: A Nice Problem," *The Southern Review* 21, no. 1 (Winter 1985): 92.

26. (Riding) Jackson, of course, saw Eliot's "zeitgeist" poetry as very different from her own self-referential poetry. Patricia Waugh emphasizes Eliot's "expressive" and "situated" poetics in contrast to the New Critics. See her *Practicing Postmodernism/Reading Modernism* (London: Edward Arnold, 1992): 138–47. John Guillory, *Cultural Capital: The Problem of Literary Canon Formation* (Chicago: University of Chicago Press, 1993), analyzes the differences between Eliot and the New Critics: Eliot attempted "to refind in literary tradition the ground of a *total* culture, inclusive of belief . . . in the case of the New Critics, the social inhibition that disallows literary culture from making doctrinal claims of the 'orthodox' sort drives these claims back into the refuge of literary form" (154–55).

27. By failing to consider (Riding) Jackson's manifold questions about meaning itself, Adams and Wexler emphasize (Riding) Jackson's dualism in "The World and I." For Adams, the poem "explores the relationship between language and objective reality" (*The Enemy Self,* 110), and for Wexler, "the gap between [(Riding) Jackson's] consciousness and her ability to articulate it is widened by the 'hostile implements of sense'" (*Pursuit of Truth,* 64).

28. John Crowe Ransom, "Poetry: A Note in Ontology," *The World's Body* (New York: Charles Scribner's Sons, 1938), 139.

29. Randall Jarrell, "Graves and the White Goddess," *Yale Review* 45 (1956): 467–78.

30. Luce Irigaray, *This Sex Which Is Not One*, trans. Catherine Porter (Ithaca, N.Y.: Cornell University Press, 1985), 108. Irigaray uses and plays with the concept of "specularity" in many of her writings. See especially her chapter "The Power of Discourse and the Subordination of the Feminine" in *This Sex Which Is Not One*, 68–85, for the ways she relates this concept to discourse formation.

31. I only need to refer the reader to the well attended and interesting session at the 1994 MLA Conference in San Diego, "The New Criticism and Contemporary Literary Theory: Multicultural Perspectives," and the recently published, *The New Criticism and Contemporary Literary Theory: Connections and Continuities*, ed. William J. Spurlin and Michael Fischer (Hamden, Conn.: Garland Publishing, 1995). Part of my fascination with (Riding) Jackson herself was my recognition of certain New Critical tenets in a poetics very much at odds with the New Criticism. (Or as Jane Marcus puts it in far more dramatic terms, "Will we be forced to acknowledge that it was a woman who invented Chinese footbinding of the critical imagination?" ["Laura Riding Roughshod," 296].) As my own early literary training was influenced by New Critical practices, study of (Riding) Jackson enabled me a careful unhinging rather than a full-scale rejection of certain New Critical precepts: a detailing of difference within the realm of the same.

32. For example, Taffy Martin sees Marianne Moore as defined by both modernist and postmodernist poetics, *Marianne Moore: Subversive Modernist* (Austin: University of Texas Press, 1986), x–xi. Ellen Berry, *Curved Thought*, focuses much of her discussion on considerations of Stein's modernism and postmodernism.

33. In (Riding) Jackson's late prose work *The Telling*, many of her previous ideals for poetry are now translated into a prose work in which she seeks to inspire a multiplicity of voices all trying to tell the "One Story." (Riding) Jackson extols, "we bear . . . each singly the burden of the single sense of manifold totality . . . as a speaking self of it, owing its words that will put the seal of the Whole upon it" (6). And while each self's telling will necessarily differ from the next, despite their mutual concerns with the whole, the unison of their telling will enable a self-correcting practice that will result in a more certain and enhanced truth: "when we have corrected ourselves with ourselves . . . we shall know that we have begun to speak true by an increased hunger for true-speaking" (16). Now the medium for truth-telling is no longer poetry, but rather this communal activity of self-correcting, "unreal selves" who in addressing "totality" in unison can establish a human universality in the very actuality of their unfolding conversation. Throughout her existence (Riding) Jackson refused to give up either her belief in the value of a corrected language or of human universality. Indeed, she initially sought to rescue the ideal of human universality from an exclusively aesthetic realm, urging the ways that poetry as *the* medium for truth was independent of aesthetic wholes, and then rejected poetry itself.

Part VI
Elizabeth Bishop
(1911–1979)

Chapter 10
The Elizabeth Bishop Phenomenon

Thomas Travisano

In a 1955 review of "The Year in Poetry" for *Harper's*, Randall Jarrell composed a notice of Elizabeth Bishop's latest book that would prove prophetic in more ways than one. He began:

> Sometimes when I can't go to sleep at night I see the family of the future. Dressed in three-toned shorts-and-shirt sets of disposable Papersilk, they sit before the television wall of their apartment, only their eyes moving. After I've looked a while I always see—otherwise I'd die—a pigheaded soul over in the corner with a book; only his eyes are moving, but in them there is a different look.
>
> Usually it's Homer he's holding—this week it's Elizabeth Bishop. Her *Poems* seems to me one of the best books an American poet has ever written: the people of the future (the ones in the corner) will read her just as they will read Dickinson or Whitman or Stevens, or the other classical American poets still alive among us.[1]

Despite breathless predictions, Papersilk never really went anywhere, but the universal television-wall has nearly made it, awaiting only the high-resolution digital TV signal to begin its inevitable march into the American home. However, Jarrell's most prophetic vision was to foresee that "pigheaded soul over in the corner" holding Elizabeth Bishop. Just as Jarrell anticipated, many of those pigheaded children of the television age who are still holding onto Homer or Dickinson or Whitman or Stevens have come to value, and with like intensity, that most understated and mysteriously inward of midcentury American poets, Elizabeth Bishop.

When Jarrell composed his review forty years ago, the prediction he made seemed bold indeed, for Elizabeth Bishop, though her poems were already valued for their brilliant surfaces, keen observation, and formal perfection, was then commonly placed on the fringes of literary history. Her reputation remained somewhere near the fringes thirty years ago, or twenty, or perhaps even ten. As late as 1977, John Ashbery, one of her keenest admirers, alluded to the select nature of her audience in his now-famous description of Bishop as a "writer's writer's writer." [2] For while her work had been passionately admired by successive generations of poets, as well as by a small but impassioned circle of readers and critics, the scale of her reputation remained modest (a word also frequently used to describe Bishop as both a person and a writer), and the people writing the surveys and histories of modern and postmodern poetry still had trouble placing her, perhaps even seeing her. David Kalstone's 1977 essay in his book *Five Temperaments*, for many years the best single critical treatment of Bishop, suggested that "there was something about her work for which elegantly standard literary analysis was not prepared." Hence Bishop remained, in a phrase of Kalstone's that surely exaggerates her position in 1977, "the most honored yet most elusive of poets." [3] Honored by her fellow poets but elusive to critics and historians Bishop certainly had proven to be. When Bishop died two years later in 1979, her profile within the academy perfectly mirrored the working definition of a "minor" poet: a single outdated critical book in the Twayne series, [4] two or three unpublished dissertations, a handful of extended critical articles by academics (most of the commentary to date had taken the form of brief reviews or appreciations, the best of these mostly by poets), and a few dismissive footnotes by the literary historians. As recently as 1984, it was possible for a historical survey like James E. B. Breslin's *From Modern to Contemporary* to dismiss Bishop in a sentence or two. Breslin portrays Bishop as suffering the "apparent defeat" of "the middle generation of poets," a poet who "worked steadily and independently, but the cost was isolation and critical neglect." [5] Breslin's vision of Bishop, of course, has proved less prophetic than Jarrell's, for in her case the defeat really was only "apparent." Today, Bishop's career seems far from defeated, and her work is certainly not suffering from either isolation or critical neglect.

The dramatic reversal in Bishop's fortunes with readers and critics, achieved so quickly after her death in 1979, and, as Breslin's remarks make clear, still quietly gathering momentum in the mid-1980s and thus still invisible to many, is by no means the standard fate of a literary reputation. The poet John Malcolm Brinnin has noted that after the death of most poets their reputation descends for a time "into a trough of indifference." "But," Brinnin continues, "in the case of Elizabeth Bishop we have seen just the obverse of that phenomenon. From the moment of her death, it seems that her reputation has continually ascended." [6] The consequence, states Langdon Hammer in a recent review-article entitled "The New Elizabeth Bishop" is that "We are witnessing that most interesting and mysterious of literary events: the making of a major poet, by something like consensus."[7] Bishop's influence on younger poets, dismissed by Breslin in 1984, is now pervasive, perhaps to the point of excess. Hammer, in fact, claims that, "No poet has more widely or powerfully influenced current poetic practice than Bishop" (137). And Bishop seems just as highly regarded within the academy, if one measures this regard in terms of the volume and intensity of critical study currently being directed at her work. As recently as 1988, in an introduction to only the second critical monograph ever published on Bishop, and the first in twenty-two years, I had occasion to say that "we are still in an early stage of Bishop studies."[8] Less than a decade later, the once-tiny universe of Bishop studies has undergone the literary equivalent of a Big Bang: it is rapidly expanding in all directions, at what appears to be an ever-accelerating rate. Bishop's "steady" and "independent" work has won through, after all, to her present eminence in American letters. And the process of reconsidering—and restating—her position in literary history seems to have only begun.

Bishop's dramatic emergence, which might aptly be termed "The Elizabeth Bishop Phenomenon," is taking place at the very moment when the making and remaking of literary history, understood as a political as well as a critical and historical activity, provides the focus for intense theoretical and practical debate, with special attention to the processes by which canons are formed and reformed. The Bishop phenomenon, an event with a long history and a significant paper trail, offers a valuable case study in the process whereby a writer moves from the margins of literary history into the spotlight. One can learn a great deal about the present requirements and mechanisms of our literary culture by studying this phenomenon. But to embark on this study, it appears one must construct one's own model of the mechanisms that have combined to create it.

For example, despite his useful recognition of the evolutionary nature of the canon and literary history, the process of "repression and recovery" described in a recent book by Cary Nelson does not appear to answer Bishop's case.[9] Bishop's image was never truly "repressed," in Nelson's sense of being completely effaced from the record of American literary culture; it was merely miniaturized. Nor have literary historians played, in Bishop's case, the heroic role, outlined by Nelson, of "recovering" a body of work by reconstructing its lost cultural moment in contemporary terms. As I will detail in the course of this chapter, the phenomenon has depended, instead, on the widespread recognition, across a range of constituencies, of the way Bishop's life and work respond to an extraordinary variety of contemporary perceptions and concerns. The Bishop phenomenon has taken place for the most part outside the history books, surging ahead of any attempt by literary historians to describe it, let alone to shape it. Historians must now struggle to catch up with the new cultural reality.

What has driven the Bishop phenomenon so vigorously? Bishop's emergence strongly indicates the significance of five principles, working together amid a complex matrix of shifting pressures and influences, that have propelled her rise in literary status. The shift in a single one of these factors might not suffice to bring about a dramatic rise or fall in a writer's reputation. On the other hand, when several factors work together, as they have done in Bishop's case, they can combine to achieve powerful synergistic effects, repositioning the writer in a dramatic way.

Five principles have combined to set the Bishop phenomenon in motion. They are:

1. A shift in the cultural perspective of the readership.
2. A shift in the critical paradigm.
3. The emergence of new evidence about the author.
4. The clamor of influential advocates.
5. Assimilation of the intrinsic qualities of the work.

Critics who attempt to account for Bishop's shift in status by attaching causality to only one or two of these principles run the risk of denying or ignoring principles at odds with their stated or implicit assumptions. Hammer, noncommittal on the fifth principle, insists on the significance of the first, which I call "a shift in the cultural perspective of the readership." As he put it: "The new view [of Bishop] is in fact unthinkable without feminism: the growing interest in Bishop's life and work participates in the general effort to recover and interpret women writers." [10] On the other hand, J. D. McClatchy, a longtime Bishop observer and advocate, pointedly dismisses the significance of the first two principles, and in particular the influence of feminism, while insisting on the primacy of the fifth, which I call "assimilation of the intrinsic qualities of the work": "Neither the tides of literary fashion nor the sort of feminist boosterism she herself deplored accounts for this phenomenon. It's simply that more and more readers have discovered the enduring power of her work—quicksilver poems lined with dark moral clouds." [11] Hammer and McClatchy contradict one another because neither seems prepared to acknowledge or explain the complexities of the process. Hammer does not explain, for example, *why* Bishop has been accorded a posthumous acclaim not enjoyed by other women poets far more vocally "feminist" than Bishop herself, while McClatchy does not explain how or why "more and more readers have discovered" Bishop's work, which had long remained the more or less private preserve of neoformalist poets such as himself.

The "Bishop Phenomenon" can best be explained if one recognizes *each* of the factors cited so far by Hammer and McClatchy, along with other factors considered causal by neither. For in Bishop's case each of the five principles mentioned above was until recently working against her. At present, due to profound changes in commonly held cultural and critical perspectives, allied with profound changes in common perceptions of Bishop's life and work, all five of these factors have reversed themselves. All five are now working in Bishop's favor. Dramatic shifts in the values and norms of Bishop's potential readership, combined with significant changes in readers' perceptions of Bishop and her work, account for the otherwise "mysterious" force and suddenness of Bishop's recent emergence. Her work has built a consensus not by any mysterious process, but in the way a consensus commonly is built: representatives of differing points of view have recognized and united around a common interest, while in other respects holding on to their differences.

It is now time to take a closer look at the five principles as they have operated in Bishop's case, propelling her to her current status as a valuable cultural commodity. Let me add a cautionary note. I am not attempting to outline here the process as it *ought* to work. Rather, I am attempting to analyze how—in at least one extremely dramatic and suggestive case—the process of making a major poet actually *does* appear to work. Nor am I trying to speak for the continuing presence of distinctions like "major" and "minor." As a long-standing advocate for Bishop, I remain acutely aware that Bishop's case placed her, at different times, at opposite ends of the literary spectrum. Her early experience suggests how often distinctions may be claimed on the basis of impulses that are arbitrary, capricious, poorly informed, or prejudicial. But the Bishop phenomenon nonetheless confirms that such distinctions still exist in the minds of literary people, male and female, and that these distinctions continue to influence perception and behavior.

1. A Shift in the Cultural Perspective of the Readership

Shifts in cultural perspective, of course, very frequently precede the rediscovery of a neglected writer or the projection of a neglected work into literary prominence. One obvious case in point is Kate Chopin's *The Awakening*. Chopin's brief, poignant novel was widely praised for its artistry by reviewers upon its publication in 1899, but it was nonetheless largely rejected by them—on moral grounds. The views of a commentator for the *Chicago Times-Herald* were echoed widely: "That the book is strong and that Miss Chopin has a keen knowledge of certain phases of feminine character will not be denied. But it was not necessary for a writer of so great refinement and poetic grace to enter the overworked field of sex fiction." [12] *The Awakening* soon passed into the oblivion of an "unread book," but it has since been recovered and elevated to a secure place in the canon: in large part, of course, though by no means exclusively, as the consequence of a dramatic shift in the cultural perspective of its readership.

Twenty years back, Bishop's work just didn't give off the aura that most readers expected of a great poet. Her friend and fellow poet James Merrill has spoken of Bishop's "instinctive, modest, life-long impersonations of an ordinary woman." [13] But while these impersonations protected Bishop from various forms of scrutiny—her lesbian sexuality, her lonely and often painful emotional life, her struggles with alcoholism and asthma, and the intensity and scope of her artistic ambitions were all aspects of herself that she chose to keep private—in some respects the act succeeded almost too well. The fact that her tone was that of a quiet-spoken woman rather than that of a prophetic male, or—failing that—a prophetic female defining her independence against the domination of males, left earlier critics, both male and female, grasping for a handle. And Bishop's work further embodied an almost complete refusal to generalize and an absence of obvious literary, historical, or political reference points, offering few handles, likewise, to either critic or historian. Hence, while Bishop received few really negative reviews over a career spanning four decades, she received many in which praise was undercut by condescension. Male critics might compare Bishop's voice, in so many words, to that of "a much prized, plain-spoken, pleasantly idiosyncratic maiden aunt," as one did in a 1969 review significantly titled "Minor Poet with a Major Fund of Love," a title the reviewer apparently intended as a compliment.[14] At the same time, early feminists were troubled by the quietness and apparent impersonality of Bishop's tone and by her refusal to appear in female-only anthologies. Alicia Ostriker, for example, in the influential 1986 feminist history of women's poetry *Stealing the Language,* types Bishop as an "apolitical poet" and reads a poem like "Roosters" as "a capsule representation of the restraints inhibiting poets who would be ladies." [15] As Betsy Erkkila has observed, "feminist critics tended to dismiss Bishop's work in favor of more explicitly personal and confessional women poets." [16] Bishop herself explained in a 1979 letter that when she was described as looking " 'like anybody's grandmother' " or " 'like somebody's great aunt' " her anger "has brought my feminist facet uppermost." [17] But although this privately observed resentment provided the subtext for many poems and stories by a poet who described herself in a *Paris Review* interview as a "strong feminist," [18] Bishop's ultimate acceptance by feminist readers, themselves growing gradually more influential as they slowly worked their way into positions of cultural authority, was far from automatic.

Hence, when Hammer asserts that the new Bishop is "unthinkable without feminism," his analysis glides a little too smoothly over a roadblock that the Bishop legacy had, in fact, to confront: before feminism could contribute its momentum to the Bishop phenomenon, feminism had first to recognize and claim Elizabeth Bishop.

Marilyn May Lombardi alludes to this rapidly evolving historical process in her prologue to the recently published *Elizabeth Bishop: Geography of Gender*, the first collection of essays to explore Bishop's work from a feminist perspective:

The reasons for Bishop's belated and somewhat uneasy assimilation into the feminist critical canon are multiple and germane to any discussion of feminism's role in mapping such a tradition. Bishop's poetry emerges from this reconsideration as more amenable to feminist interpretation than previously imagined. At the same time, her art expands our narrow definitions of the "woman poet" or "woman's poetry" and so poses a greater challenge to feminist orthodoxies than earlier readers may have been willing to admit.[19]

Lombardi notes that a landmark in this reclamation process came with Adrienne Rich's 1983 review of Bishop's *Complete Poems, 1927–1979*, which predates every essay in Lombardi's collection and is arguably the first successful feminist reading of Bishop's life and work. Rich asserts in that review, "In particular I am concerned with her experience of outsiderhood, closely—though not exclusively—linked with the essential outsiderhood of a lesbian identity; and with how the outsider's eye enables Bishop to perceive other kinds of outsiders to identify, or try to identify, with them."[20] As the eighties have moved into the nineties, critics have become ever more practiced and adept at reading the many texts by women that meet Rich's criteria, understated texts observed "with an outsider's eye" and encoded with the perceptions, identifications, and quiet protests of outsiderhood. Rich is particularly acute in directing attention toward Bishop's subtle rendering of acts of attempted identification, attempts that often remain imperfect and incomplete in Bishop's poems but, that, in the process, achieve subtle miracles of authenticity, surprise, and humor. Rich was perhaps the first to read Bishop as a poet "who was critically and consciously trying to explore marginality, power and powerlessness, often in poetry of great beauty."[21]

Recent feminist readings of Bishop have generally taken Rich's review as a point of departure, then branched out in all directions, defining the significance of Bishop's legacy variously across a spectrum of opinion that represents the diversity of present-day feminism. Lombardi herself reads Bishop's refusal to appear in female-only anthologies as a valid act because it was "consistent with her lifelong aversion to systems of polarization, exclusion, and subordination."[22] And Joanne Feit Diehl argues in an essay reprinted in the Lombardi collection that "Bishop's poem reveal the complex tensions between women poets and the Romantic tradition she identified as her own." [23] Diehl reads Bishop as extending the Romantic tradition by subverting patriarchal habits of perception. "With an Emersonian audacity tempered by a tact requisite to her radical vision, Bishop's poems aim at nothing short of freedom from the inherently dualistic tradition that lies not only at the foundations of the American Sublime but at the very heart of the Western Literary tradition" (34). For Diehl, then, Bishop's "sexual poetics carries us . . . to an experimental sublime that assumes a form freed of the ascriptions of gender" (42).

Lorrie Goldensohn reads Bishop less in terms of external nature than in terms of the female body, locating in the body an eroticized, yet erotically and emotionally troubled Bishop who is not so much "freed of the ascriptions of gender" as determined by gender, a figure struggling with internalized longings and constraints linked to or imposed by both her sex and the marks of early childhood losses. Reflecting on "those awful hanging breasts" in "In the Waiting Room," Goldensohn comments, "the fascination with the female seems as closely linked to the theme of the abandoning mother as it does to the seductive, eroticized female body, whether powerless or not. We could as easily associate the fear of breasts with a suppressed longing for them and for the monstrous and disturbing power to evoke longing that they retain; negatively colored feeling could be said to stem from early deprivation." [24] Jeredith Merrin, by contrast, though she acknowledges "the recurrent psychological and philosophical dilemmas in her work," chooses to emphasize "the playful rather than the troubled Bishop, because it provides a way to address the pleasure and quiet excitement of reading a poem by her." Hence, for Merrin, "the pleasurable qualities or the gaiety of her poetry . . . may be seen as related to her sexuality, her lesbianism or gayness." [25]

A 1994 review of the Lombardi collection by Adrian Oktenberg for *The Women's Review of Books* goes further in its demand for a more radically feminist reading of Bishop. Oktenberg dismisses Diehl for reading Bishop "against a background mostly of men," attacks Goldensohn for remaining "mired in whiteness, in bafflement and fear," and Merrin for failing to read Bishop in terms of Rich's "pointedly political tradition of outsiderhood to heterosexual culture." Oktenberg cites instead the collection's title essay by Lee Edelman to validate reading Bishop as "a deeply subversive writer, one who challenged imperatives of gender and sexuality, who 'wages war against the reduction of women to the status of literal figure,' who 'makes a war cry to unleash the textuality that rips the fabric of the cultural text.' " And, summarizing Jacqueline Vaught Brogan's essay, "Elizabeth Bishop: *Perversity* as Voice," the review urges further that we consider Bishop as "a conscious resister of things as they are, and as a conscious maker of oppositional texts."[26]

Despite their differences, each of the readings cited so far agrees that Bishop should be read as an "outsider," a writer whose viewpoint was fixed by her gender and her lesbian sexuality. But if one looks at Bishop's life from an alternate perspective, it is clear that she also enjoyed many privileges of an "insider." She attended fine schools; she was supported for most of her life by a modest inheritance; she shared a beautiful house and estate in Brazil with Lota de Macedo Soares, a member of the intellectual and cultural elite; she won prestigious fellowships and awards; and she closed her career by teaching at Harvard. Indeed, Charles Tomlinson once dismissed Bishop's portraits of the disadvantaged with the remark, "The better-off have always preferred their poor processed by style."[27] Victoria Harrison, in her 1993 study *Elizabeth Bishop's Poetics of Intimacy*, responds by reading Bishop as a contemporary pragmatist whose work reflects a "double point of view." "Bishop's poetry," asserts Harrison, "particularly her late poetry, defies such distinctions of inside and outside; or rather, it enacts a slippage, locating the 'significant, illustrative, American, etc.' precisely in the voices of the traditionally marginalized—children, tourists, an island recluse, a stray dog, the clutter of a poet's desk."[28] Returning to the Lombardi collection, one finds Barbara Page reading Bishop in a way that overlaps Harrison, while emphasizing Bishop's potential links with a postmodern indeterminacy: "Against the finality of closure, Bishop asserted her preference for unofficial and unstable positionings." Borrowing a phrase from Bishop's Key West notebooks, Page concludes: "By the time she moved on from Key West, she had herself become a poet of 'interstitial situations,' truant from the rules governing the lives of women, in but not altogether of the club of male poets, the artist of oblique realities."[29]

The spectrum of opinion represented here reveals, perhaps, as much about the range of currently available feminist readings as it does about the poet being read. The range of overlapping but significantly differing perspectives that are already forming around Bishop displays her emerging role as a leading representative of a feminist poetics. When readers look into Bishop's incisively faceted work, they seem to find themselves mirrored there. The very absence of determining normative statements in her poems, combined with the highly charged, emblematic images that so strongly suggest meaning, apparently encourages this extraordinary spectrum of reading. In any case, her readers seem to agree that the considerable latent emotional and intellectual power of her work grows in significant part out of Bishop's subtle but trenchant exploitation of her viewpoint as a woman. That Bishop can be and has been incorporated within the feminist canon is no longer in doubt—a startling fact, given Ostriker's vigorous dismissal as recently as 1986. Nor does any doubt remain that a diversity of feminist readings of Bishop's work can be sustained. That contending branches of feminism show an emergent determination to read Bishop according to their own lights underscores the power and suggestion of the texts she left behind, even as it confirms Bishop's present importance as a cultural commodity.

Of course, renewed attention to the perspective of the outsider is not the sole domain of gender studies. This new attention has emerged as one phase of a larger cultural critique that is also reexamining the conditioning assumptions of imperialism, capitalism, social class, race, and ethnicity. Contemporary literary culture's recent attention to and appreciation of cultural variety and difference cast many of Bishop's poems in a new light. Rich's reading of Bishop as "outsider," Edelman's reading of a poet who "rips the fabric of the cultural text," Brogan's and Oktenberg's reading of Bishop as "conscious resister," Harrison's reading of a "double point of view," and Page's reading of her "unofficial and unstable positionings," might each function in the context of a broader examination of Bishop as a poet of history, culture, and politics. Bishop's travel writings were once widely dismissed as trivial: in part because of where she chose to travel, in part because of why she chose to go there. Tomlinson complained that Bishop "travels because she likes it, not because she is homeless as Lawrence or Schoenberg were." [30] Two years after Bishop's death in 1979, a Pulitzer Prize–winning literary biographer asked me, in apparent bewilderment, what had motivated Bishop to spend all those years living in and writing from Brazil. If Bishop had chosen to reside in and write about Paris, London, or Rome, the question might not have arisen or might have been couched in a different tone. An "expatriate" departing from or moving toward a European capital then garnered a respect of which a "tourist" seemed unworthy— to use the word reviewers commonly applied to Bishop-as-traveler. That Bishop had been living all those years in Brazil with her friend and lover Lota de Macedo Soares, a choice based in part on a yearning for privacy and independence from predominant sexual and romantic mores, was a biographical fact still more or less unavailable, in 1981, to all but the most closely informed of the literati.

In any case, Bishop's long sojourns along subtropical coastlines and in the villages of North American backwaters, her residencies in Florida, Key West, Mexico, Maine, Morocco, Nova Scotia, and Brazil, once seemed to place her on the geographical and cultural margins. Readers newly drawn to Bishop's work might well be impressed by the authenticity of her interest. [31] Fifty, forty, or thirty years ago, when Bishop was writing all of those poems and stories and long letters studying and appreciating the individuality and integrity of indigenous peoples—or examining the "history" (to use her word) embodied in postcolonial artifacts—in ways that dramatize and hold up for contemplation the gaps between Western and non-Western modes of conditioning, perception, and social behavior, she was simply following her own proclivities in a way that placed her characteristically ahead of the curve.[32] Bishop is being revalued, then, because she can be read as a poet whose apparently small-scale poems open outward into explorations of large and complex problems, including the problems of gender, love, sexuality, nature, poverty, and culture outlined above, as well as a related set of problems that I am about to touch upon: experiences of grief and loss, and of moral, emotional, and perceptual uncertainty and insecurity.

2. A Shift in the Critical Paradigm

The emergence in the 1920s and 1930s of a critical paradigm that valued and knew how to explicate the ambiguity, irony, and narrative disjunctions of modernism led directly to the revaluation of a good deal of earlier writing, including metaphysical poetry, Jacobean tragedy, Dickinson's poetry, Sterne's *Tristram Shandy*, and Melville's *Moby-Dick*, that had previously been dismissed as contrived, confused, or obscure. It also led to the apparently permanent exile of Longfellow and Whittier from the major canon of American poetry and to the far more partial and temporary demotion of Milton from the English canon. Shakespeare, throughout the latter half of the seventeenth century considered by most readers— Dryden and Milton were the exceptions—as the rough-hewn inferior of that polished and learned courtier Ben Jonson, was elevated to his current place as England's chief cultural icon in the mid-eighteenth century, due in large part to shifts in cultural perspective and to a new critical paradigm that revalued nature and sensibility and encouraged greater formal freedom in the arts. Critical paradigms come and go, and as they do, the reputations of selected writers rise and fall.

From the 1960s through at least the 1970s, a prevailing critical paradigm for recent verse was the model of confessional poetry. M. L. Rosenthal explained in 1967 that "The term 'confessional poetry' came naturally to my mind when I reviewed Robert Lowell's *Life Studies* in 1959, and perhaps it came to the minds of others just as naturally. Whoever invented it, it was a term both helpful and too limited, and very possibly the conception of a confessional school has by now done a certain amount of damage."[33] Indeed, this invention of the critics was far from universally popular with the poets. When an interviewer asked John Berryman, a longtime admirer of Bishop's work and himself the recipient of a verse tribute from Bishop, how he reacted to the label "confessional poet," he replied: "With rage and contempt! Next question!"[34] Berryman rejected the confessional label and insisted that the Henry of the *Dream Songs* is "essentially about an imaginary character (not the poet, not me)," because, while there are clearly parallels between himself and Henry, he could not accept reductive readings of the relation between an author and that author's fictive things.[35] Still, Rosenthal felt that "because of the way Lowell brought his private humiliations, sufferings, and psychological problems into the poems of *Life Studies*, the word 'confessional' seemed appropriate enough."[36] Rosenthal's model was particularly influential with academic critics and literary historians, including, as we have seen, some early feminists like Ostriker, since it offered a humanly compelling and rather clear-cut way of evaluating poetry. Poems involving daring self-revelation could be assumed to be bold and sincere. Bishop's own poetry, widely viewed as "reticent," failed to conform to this reigning critical paradigm and was thus often dismissed as artificial and too polite. Women poets like Sylvia Plath and Anne Sexton, both former disciples of Lowell, seemed to mark out a bolder style, as did the poetics of feminist protest forged by Adrienne Rich and others, and the poetics of political protest that then centered on the war in Vietnam. Bishop's understated poetry (which never explicitly mentioned Vietnam) seemed peculiarly remote in the face of these demands for relevance. In *The Modern Poets* (1960), Rosenthal paired Bishop with Richard Wilbur, asserting that while these poets have "done exquisite and richly suggestive work" they have "touched the imagination of their generation very little. The reason seems to be that they remind us only of what we have already been taught to value: elegance, grace, precision, quiet intensity of phrasing."[37]

Significantly, the putative inventor of confessional poetry, Robert Lowell, did not share Rosenthal's view of Bishop's work. Lowell's own frequent public acknowledgment that his style, especially in *Life Studies*, derived to a significant degree from Bishop's example was generally ignored by contemporary critics and historians, as was Bishop's declaration of the grounds of her own affinity with Lowell in a blurb on the jacket of *Life Studies* itself.[38] She found his poems "as big as life . . . alive, and rainbow-edged," and she read the poems, perceptively, I think, for their underlying strokes of Jamesian art, appreciating their subtlety and gentleness, their social insight, their graces of refinement and structure, in concert with their more visceral effects: "In these poems, heart-breaking, shocking, grotesque and gentle, the unhesitant attack, the imagery and construction, are as brilliant as ever, but the mood is nostalgic and the meter is refined. A poem like 'My Last Afternoon with Uncle Devereux Winslow,' or 'Skunk Hour,' can tell us as much about the state of society as a volume of Henry James at his best."[39] Readers in the sixties and early seventies may have had trouble making a connection that seemed natural enough to Bishop and Lowell themselves because they failed to recognize both Lowell's own subtle manipulation of his artistic materials and the quiet yet profound unease at the heart of Bishop's poems. Bishop's published work might disguise the pressures that produced it, but her life was full of "private humiliations, sufferings, and psychological problems," and in her work the personal intensity simmers just below the surface. Bishop's work might *appear* not to conform to the reigning critical paradigm, but in the long run she would both encompass and subvert it.

Today, of course, confessional poetry no longer seems new and the urgencies and meat-cleaver clarities of sixties' political poetry and early feminist poetry can seem embarrassing. References to contemporary events that once seemed so urgent now require scholarly footnotes. Indeed, many poems of the sixties may soon be candidates for the recovery process described by Cary Nelson. On the other hand, the very absence of personal and contemporary reference in Bishop's writing, which worked against her at one time, now works in her favor. Bishop's poetry, with its "enormous power of reticence" noted by Octavio Paz,[40] offers an antidote to the confessional school, while in another sense her work quietly continues and reinforces many of the more artistically compelling features and traditions of an autobiographically grounded aesthetic. Berryman's *Dream Songs*, for example, confesses only to incidental and symptomatic experiences of suffering and humiliation. Berryman's crucial relationship with his father, who took his own life when Berryman was a boy of twelve, is merely hinted at in a few "Songs," poems more conspicuous for elisions and emotional blockage than for revelations. And Berryman barely mentions his still more haunted and trouble relationship with his mother, a still-living woman whom he hated, feared, and loved. The most compelling emotional issues of the *Dream Songs*, then, are *not* confessed and exist only as subtext. Bishop admitted to Lowell in 1962 that she found Berryman difficult, but she continued, "One has the feeling 100 years from now *he* may be all the rage—or a 'discovery'—hasn't one?"[41] Bishop's estimate is beginning to look plausible, for at this writing Berryman has been read far less successfully than has Bishop herself.

Bishop has emerged as perhaps the key figure in a contemporary neoformalist canon, here advertised by the poets themselves, that continues to look back to figures such as Berryman and Lowell while forging a language of its own. Quiet inwardness, controlled self-exploration and self-revelation, conversational poise in a context of emotional impediment, verbal invention within visible reach of the formal conventions, and an environment of brooding moral uncertainty are some of the qualities valued by neoformalist poets and celebrated in surveys by poet-critics like Robert Pinksy, J. D. McClatchy, and Dana Gioia—surveys that look to Elizabeth Bishop as, in Gioia's words, "a crucial figure in our development as poets." [42] McClatchy appreciates "the way her line and her tone transfigured each of the forms she worked in—none more so, as Merrill notes, than the villanelle," and he goes on to confess that: "I remain fascinated by those few poems—uncharacteristic, one might say, except that they are as central to an understanding of her work as anything else—that are private (or seem so), that defy decoding, are mysterious in their references and effect." [43]

James McCorkle's survey *The Still Performance*, on the other hand, places Bishop in a line of postmodern poets including John Ashbery, W. S. Merwin, Adrienne Rich, and Charles Wright. Referring back to Edelman, McCorkle delineates a postmodern reading of Bishop as an explorer of "the provisionality of interconnectedness" in poems that represent "ambiguity, the play of observations and probing, and *ekphrasis*, rather than the authority of the observed and the observer's place," qualities she shares, according to McCorkle with "seventeenth century Dutch painters." [44] As one can see, Bishop's artistic legacy is being claimed simultaneously by representatives of both a neoformalist and a postmodern canon, along lines that recall the contention of rival feminists over her cultural legacy. Ashbery, a poet who has himself been claimed by both the neoformalists and the postmodernists, comments: "It shouldn't be a criticism leveled at Miss Bishop that her mind is capable of inspiring and delighting minds of so many different formations." [45] And Ashbery offers a possible resolution of the contention over how to read Bishop when he notes the way her work projects the "strange divided singleness of our experience." [46] Could it be that both the neoformalist and the postmodern readings are valid? For Ashbery, in any case, "it is this continually renewed sense of discovering the strangeness, the unreality of our reality at the very moment of becoming conscious of it *as* reality, that is the great subject of Elizabeth Bishop." [47]

3. The Emergence of New Evidence

Emily Dickinson, Gerard Manley Hopkins, and Franz Kafka offer examples of the possible effect that a new body of evidence can have on that author's reputation. In each of these cases, of course, the posthumous publication of an entire body of work in manuscript transformed a brilliant but obscure figure who had insisted upon lifelong anonymity into an author of world-class renown. Bishop had significant affinities for each of these writers and courted a lesser degree of anonymity in her own life. She was not rescued from real obscurity by her late and posthumous work, by any means, but the new evidence contained in an on-going series of posthumous publications and in a recent series of critical and biographical studies has made a decisive contribution to the Bishop phenomenon. The figure she cuts in the literary world has been more or less completely transformed.

Bishop published relatively little during her lifetime; her four books were slim, and they appeared a decade apart. Some of the strongest evidence for Bishop's importance and scope emerged late in her career, with the publication of her last, most personal, and most arresting book, *Geography III* in 1976. The impact of this published legacy may be measured in a remark of Denis Donoghue. He used the expanding Bishop canon to explain why he was adding a chapter on Bishop in 1984 to a new edition of *Connoisseurs of Chaos,* a survey of modern poetry based on his Elliston Lectures at the University of Cincinnati in 1965. Donoghue explains, "When I was writing the book, only *North & South* (1946) and *A Cold Spring* (1955) were published: there was no sign of *Questions of Travel* (1965). *Geography III* was many years to come. The achievement of *North & South* was remarkable, but it was impossible to predict how the complete work would appear, and the scale of the last two books." [48] Read all together, Bishop's work makes a stronger impression.

For a long time, little was publicly known of Bishop's life, and the intensely introspective quality of her poetry, its elusive depth, was easily overlooked. It took some years for this condition to alter, even after Bishop's death. Indeed, when Ian Hamilton needed to refer to Bishop's homosexuality in his 1982 biography of Lowell, a fact that he had to establish because it naturally impinged on Lowell's recurring impulse to propose marriage to Bishop, he was forced to cite an interview, recorded in that same year, with a "friend who wishes to remain anonymous." This unnamed friend explained: "I mustn't be the source of this, but I'm sure Elizabeth Bishop told me these things because she wanted them to be on the record to some extent." [49] It would have been difficult to inaugurate a reading of Bishop's work in terms of the "essential outsiderhood of a lesbian identity" earlier than Rich did in 1983 because of the tacit ban on public discussion of her sexuality that Bishop imposed during her own lifetime, a ban still respected by her friends in the years just after her death in 1979. This friendly conspiracy of silence was only beginning to relax, as one can see, in 1982.

The introspective nature of Bishop's work could thus be overlooked even by acute critics. Alan Williamson justified the exclusion of Bishop from his 1984 book *Introspection and Contemporary Poetry* with the remark: "This turning inward has, of course, not been universal; good poets (Bishop and Wilbur, to name two) have ignored or resisted it." [50] It is hard to imagine anyone offering a similar judgment today. Indeed

Williamson appears to retract it in an essay on Bishop subtitled "The Poet of Feeling": "It is increasingly evident that the force of Elizabeth Bishop's poetry is not altogether accounted for by that image of her so often put forward, in praise or blame: the heiress-apparent of Marianne Moore; the crowning glory of a canon of taste that emphasized surface exactitude, the elimination of the personal, and an arch, slightly inhibiting, self-consciousness about how the imagination works."[51]

Bishop, who published so little during the course of her life, has remained a publishing phenomenon after her death. A steady flow of major collections has been issued under the supervision of her loyal publisher, Robert Giroux, including *The Complete Poems* in 1983, which contained a number of important, previously uncollected lyrics and *The Collected Prose* in 1984, which published for the first time a revealing cluster of autobiographical stories and memoirs, and collected others that had been buried in the back issues of literary journals for decades and had been known previously only to a handful of Bishop scholars.

Giroux also saw to the completion and publication of David Kalstone's *Becoming a Poet: Elizabeth Bishop with Marianne Moore and Robert Lowell,* a critical work, left unfinished at the author's death and arranged for the press at Giroux's request by Robert Hemenway. Kalstone's groundbreaking study appeared in 1989, enriching the reading public's critical, biographical, and historical understanding of Bishop while indirectly extending the published Bishop canon through many extracts from Bishop's workbooks and a detailed and nuanced reading of Bishop's extensive correspondence with two key correspondents, Moore and Lowell. Kalstone's book made it impossible to dismiss Bishop as an isolated or a marginal figure by showing how deep, intimate, and complex was her relationship with two of the leading poets of the century.

One Art: Letters, selected and edited by Giroux, constitutes yet another significant expansion of the Bishop canon. It further documents Bishop's extended relations with important writers and cultural figures while taking us deeper into Bishop's complex emotional world. Moreover, it makes available, at a stroke, more than six hundred pages of frequently wonderful writing. Adrian Oktenberg comments wryly on Giroux's "deliberate presentation of Bishop as A Great Poet (which she *was*, to be sure); one can almost see Bishop being elevated in the canon by it."[52] In the *Times Literary Supplement* Tom Paulin lets out all the stops, proclaiming: "The publication of Elizabeth Bishop's Selected Letters is a historic event, a bit like discovering a new planet or watching a bustling continent emerge, glossy and triumphant, from a blank ocean. Here is an immense cultural treasure being suddenly unveiled—and this hefty selection is only the beginning. Before the millennium is out, Bishop will be seen as one of this century's epistolary geniuses, like that modernist Victorian Gerard Manley Hopkins, whom she lovingly admired and learnt from."[53] Significantly, despite the length of the selection, many reviewers lamented specific omissions of important letters (I have noted dozens myself), omissions that were perhaps inevitable in a book selecting 541 letters from the more than 3,000 available. And the reviewers have generally concurred with Giroux's own comment that Bishop "deserves a multivolume edition of all her letters." "If," writes Paulin, "that work is still waiting to be commissioned, let it begin soon. Let it start tomorrow."[54]

Moreover, many more of Bishop's writings have come to light outside the official Farrar Straus editions. These newly available writings, in some cases published in journals, in some cases cited in critical works, include a diverse range of juvenile prose and verse, erotic, "confessional," and political poems, stories, essays, letters, and other writings. Besides bringing a lot of good writing into print and confirming Bishop's excellence in previously undocumented genres, these publications have provided new and revealing evidence that has enriched and complicated our image of Bishop as a writer and a person. Lorrie Goldensohn based a distinguished book on a previously unpublished poem of lesbian eroticism that she uncovered in Brazil. The biographical revelations in Kalstone's *Becoming a Poet* added nuance and contour to the Bishop profile. Brett Millier's 1993 critical biography makes comprehensive use of the rich documentary material to be found in the manuscript archive at the Vassar College Library, while Gary Fountain and Peter Brazeau's 1994 oral biography draws on the perspectives of friends ready, at last, to place their views of Bishop on record. Recent monographs by Bonnie Costello, Victoria Harrison, Carole Doreski, Joanne Feit Diehl, Susan McCabe, and Marilyn May Lombardi have continued an exploration-in-depth of the letters and unpublished poems and stories in the Vassar archive, in the process further mapping Bishop's interior world.[55] The fussy early image of the ladylike poetess has simply been exploded by all this new material, and Bishop emerges as a far more complex and compelling figure than she once seemed.

Bishop herself had a repressive effect on Bishop studies during her lifetime, limiting access to whatever letters were already in libraries and disapproving of all but the most conservative readings of her work. More than one Bishop critic and editor has confessed to fearing the poet's posthumous wrath. On the other hand, Bishop went to great lengths to preserve her manuscript legacy, spending weeks on the packing and shipping of her materials from Brazil after Lota de Macedo Soares's death, at a time when it was no longer pleasant or comfortable to live there. Perhaps events have turned out more or less as Bishop wanted them to. Her privacy was preserved while she lived and her fascinating inner world revealed after her death. The three-dimensional figure of Bishop visible to today's readers and critics—a figure who is vulnerable, fallible, bohemian, lonely, alcoholic, tenacious, ambitious, libidinous, and humorous—may not be, as yet, the "real" or "complete" Elizabeth Bishop, but it is a far more human, extensive, detailed, complex, and downright interesting persona than that two-dimensional figure of the acolyte-of-pure-art-posing-as-ordinary-woman that Bishop and her friends conspired to present before her death. At last, the reading public has an image capable of sustaining the impression of a major writer.

As we have seen, the Bishop canon is still expanding, at a rate that often seems to exceed her rate of production while she lived. And plenty of material remains in manuscript, enough to keep scholars busy for a long time, enough, indeed, to sustain a high-profile Elizabeth Bishop industry. An author who leaves behind a complex and extensive body of work that promises to keep generations of scholars in business has, of course, found one way to help insure a place in the canon and in literary history. Paulin insists, "There is an urgent need for a complete edition of the prose writings which includes her reviews and the work she published while an undergraduate at Vassar (the reissue of her *Collected Prose* is welcome, but it is not sufficient). A book which reproduces her paintings and discusses her very considerable knowledge of the visual arts would also be welcome."[56] Let me add an interim request for the complete correspondence of Bishop and Moore, and the complete correspondence of Bishop and Lowell. We also obviously need a far more complete *Complete Poems* than the two previously offered. The emergence of all of this new evidence, and the promise of more, has clearly played a crucial role in the Bishop phenomenon.

4. The Clamor of Influential Advocates

It was partly through the advocacy of Johannes Brahms that an obscure Bohemian musician named Antonín Dvořák came to worldwide recognition. The advocacy of performing musicians has also had a measurable impact on the history of the art. In the 1920s and 1930s the Austrian pianist Artur Schnabel brought the poignantly introspective sonatas of Schubert, neglected for a century, to the attention of the musical public. At the same time, the Polish harpsichordist Wanda Landowska was bringing fresh attention to a forgotten instrument and to the enormous and neglected canon of baroque keyboard music that could be played on it. In the 1950s, Greek-American soprano Maria Callas revived forgotten bel canto operas by Bellini, Rossini, and Donizetti. Gertrude Stein's advocacy was crucial to the emergence of Cézanne, Picasso, Matisse, and other modernist painters, particularly in the English-speaking world, while

Ezra Pound's advocacy was crucial to the emergence of T. S. Eliot, James Joyce, and other Anglo-American literary modernists. Advocacy by a new generation of feminist critics helped to bring *The Awakening*, mentioned earlier, to the renewed attention of the literary world. And feminist musicologists have helped to recover the compositions of Clara Schumann, Fanny Mendelssohn Hensel, Amy Beach, Lili Boulanger, and other neglected female composers. The importance of advocacy by fellow artists and by contemporary critical arbiters must not be overlooked when we assess the rise or fall of a writer's reputation. These advocates are by no means all-powerful, particularly in a negative role—Eduard Hanslick, the most influential music critic in the German-speaking world, could not block Wagner's ascendancy in the field of music drama—but they can play a vital role in the emergence of neglected or forgotten work, work that often serves as a vehicle for the artist's or critic's own personal and cultural agenda.

Bishop, from the start, had what might seem an enviable array of advocates. How could one improve on Marianne Moore, Louise Bogan, Robert Lowell, and Randall Jarrell, or later, James Merrill and John Ashbery? But advocates like these had not been able to assure Bishop's place in literary history during her lifetime, nor at the moment of her death. Why should this be so? In part, at least, because, until very late in her life, Bishop had very few advocates within the academy, the arena wherein canons have been formed and reformed in the second half of the twentieth century and the arena wherein literary history itself is generally written. Bishop's early advocates were fellow poets who stressed both her modesty and the superb nature of her artistry. As I have already suggested, however, the image of a modest artist is demonstrably insufficient to project a writer beyond the level of a minor figure. A writer must also stand for something, and Bishop's early advocates had difficulty expressing what she stood for, beyond the refinements and discipline of art itself. Indeed, Marianne Moore's review of Bishop's first book labeled her a "Modest Expert," and the first essay collection devoted to Bishop was titled *Elizabeth Bishop and Her Art*. This 1983 volume includes, among its many brief appreciations, pieces on Bishop by all of the poets mentioned above, and others by the likes of Richard Wilbur, Richard Howard, William Meredith, Mark Strand, John Hollander, Lloyd Schwartz, Frank Bidart, and Robert Pinsky: a virtual catalog of leading neoformalist poets of two generations—and, for that matter, a group conspicuously dominated by males. These advocates and others of similar stamp helped Bishop to win the prizes and fellowships Kalstone alluded to in 1977, since poets often have a majority vote on award committees. But Bishop still seemed, in Kalstone's phrase, "hard to place." [57] Senior professors were not producing the books or articles that would have given Bishop's work an aura of academic legitimacy, let alone urgency, nor were these scholars directing doctoral theses on Bishop in any quantity. Research was further blocked by the absence of scholarly reference tools or manuscript materials, so copious today. The conditions essential to the academic field of Bishop studies had yet to come into being.

However, at about the time Kalstone was publishing his observations, Bishop was beginning to pick up advocates who represented significant constituencies within the academy. For example, in 1977 Helen Vendler contributed a strong essay to a special Bishop issue of *World Literature Today*, the first special issue in any journal devoted to Bishop's work. The other essays and appreciations were notably the work of poets or of quite junior scholars. Combining with Kalstone's own essay on Bishop in *Five Temperaments*, Vendler's piece lent a seal of approval to Bishop in the arena of academic formalism. Also in 1977, Harold Bloom wrote a pointed review of *Geography III* for *The New Republic*, placing Bishop in a tradition of American nature poetry stretching back to Emerson and Whitman and extending through Stevens and Crane. Adrienne Rich's 1983 review of the *Complete Poems* may not have been the work of an academic, but it proved similarly influential within the academy, empowering a new generation of feminist critics.

Perhaps most important of all to Bishop's growing profile within the academy was the fact that, in her mid-fifties, Bishop had returned to America and was teaching for the first time in her life, at the University of Washington in Seattle, where she temporarily replaced the late Theodore Roethke, and then more permanently at Harvard, where she replaced the departing Robert Lowell. Bishop had always avoided the New York literary scene, had never published reviews, had avoided teaching, and these omissions and avoidances had hurt her recognition not a little. In Boston, more or less against her will, Bishop began to establish for the first time in her career a professional presence in a major cultural and academic center. She made friends with contemporaries like Octavio Paz and with younger poets like Sandra McPherson and Frank Bidart. Moreover, although she was a somewhat reluctant and uncomfortable teacher, she began to educate a core of disciples who emerged with a strong loyalty to her as a person and an artist. These disciples, some of them publishing poets equipped with Ph.D.'s and thus able to enter literature as well as writing programs, have since fanned out into the academy. There they have written about and edited Bishop's work. And, as teachers, they have helped bring that work to the attention of a rising generation of M.F.A. and Ph.D. candidates.[58]

At last, then, starting tentatively in the late 1960s, and gathering momentum through the 1970s, Bishop began to project a new presence within the academy. Her latest book, *Geography III*, had been her most compelling. The leaders of important critical constituencies had begun speaking out in favor of her work, thus granting permission to their disciples and students to explore her work more closely. And, as we've seen, shortly after Bishop's death, the rich and revealing Bishop archive housed in the Vassar College Library would become available to scholars. A more complex and engaging biographical portrait of the artist stood ready to emerge. The elements essential to the launching of the Bishop phenomenon had almost come together.

But Bishop's triumph has extended beyond the academy. Perhaps the single most influential piece of advocacy with a broader public came through the medium Jarrell had most feared: television. The *Voices and Visions* series, created by the New York Center for Visual History under the supervision of Bishop stalwart Helen Vendler, was aired over the Public Broadcasting System in 1988. The series placed Bishop in a thirteen-poet pantheon that included all of the most imposing and familiar names in American poetry. Bishop was one of only four poets born in the twentieth century to appear in the series, the others being Langston Hughes, Robert Lowell, and Sylvia Plath. In a single stroke, this series vastly increased the readership for Bishop and gave her work a new aura of glamour and legitimacy. It also made available to newly interested readers a taste of the human background and visual environment out of which her work emerged.

Bishop was at last ready to move from the coterie status of "writer's writer's writer" to the altogether new status of "hot poet."

5. Assimilation of the Intrinsic Qualities of the Work

The work of individual artists is assimilated by its potential audience at widely differing rates. The intrinsic qualities of the work of some really superb artists—the composer Franz Joseph Haydn is one example—so mirror the requirements of the culture in which they live that these qualities are assimilated immediately by the artist's potential audience. Haydn, greeted by nearly universal comprehension and approbation throughout Europe while he lived, suffered thereafter from nearly a century of relative condescension and neglect—the "Papa Haydn" syndrome—as the critical paradigms and cultural perspectives of Romanticism replaced those of classicism. The scope of Haydn's achievement would only be recognized again in recent decades, when the cultural and critical climate had again become propitious.[59] The intrinsic characteristics of other brilliant creative figures may not achieve assimilation until many years after the creator's death. In such cases, eventual assimilation may not be possible except as the result of strenuous advocacy under more favorable critical and cultural conditions.

Until the mid-1970s, the intrinsic qualities of Bishop's work were very largely unassimilated by the academy or by all but a very narrow segment of the literary world. Except among a familiar circle of active writers who displayed an "extraordinary intense loyalty," [60] Bishop's work was commonly greeted by a bemused and condescending style of commentary, as when, in a 1956 review, the academic critic Edwin Honig referred to Bishop's *Poems* as a "limited performance," and complained that while "the poems arrest by their brilliant surfaces and transparency . . . underneath is a curious rigidity, a disturbing lack of movement and affective life, betraying a sprained and uneasy patience." [61] In the early years, many readings of Bishop seemed blinded by her "brilliant surfaces," vexed by a "transparency" apparently too absolute to allow the reader to see the life beneath. Hence the tone of dismissal mixed with irritation in so many early notices of her work. When, in a 1957 review titled "Imagism and Poetesses," A. Alvarez wrote, "Miss Bishop's poetic imagination does not, so far as I can see, deal directly with her feelings; instead it provides her with scenes, and she feels about them," or when in a 1969 piece Jerome Mazzaro wrote that "the separate observations of her poems do not gain from appearing in concert with one another. An unconscious element which might . . . serve as the link by way of recurrent, unresolved patterns is minimal," or when, in a 1974 piece, Peggy Rizza wrote that Bishop "possesses what might be called an 'objective imagination,' . . . her . . . poems are absent of the pathetic fallacy," these and similar readings had so far failed to assimilate the leading characteristics intrinsic to Bishop's verse.[62] Until that assimilation had become more general, the Bishop phenomenon could not take place. Thanks, in part, to the determined efforts of many poets, critics, editors, and biographers, Bishop's readers have learned to glimpse beneath those dazzling surfaces to witness the movement, the affective life, the keen dynamics of feeling, the unconscious elements, the recurrent, unresolved patterns, and the engaging play of subjective and objective imagination that animate and complicate Bishop's written world. Readers will continue to disagree about how Bishop should be read and to dispute the meaning of her legacy, but "surface" readings like those just outlined are unlikely to ever regain the ascendancy they once enjoyed.

For as the other principles I've described above began to work in Bishop's favor, as cultural perspectives began to shift in ways that valued the marginal, the silenced, the "queer," and the female, as critics began to search for alternatives to the dominance of the "confessional" model, as a compelling range of new evidence, beginning with Bishop's own late poetry, began to alter dramatically the reading public's view of Bishop as a person and an artist, and as Bishop began to enjoy the advocacy of critics within the academy who represented a broad range of competing academic constituencies, the moment was ripe for the assimilation of a body of work whose artistic qualities were as unique as they were compelling. When readers began to look closely at the stunning range of verse and prose that Bishop had produced, they stood poised to enter her extraordinary, powerful, disquieting, and strangely appealing artistic world.

I began this essay by citing Jarrell's forecast that Bishop would be read with Homer, Dickinson, Stevens, and "the other classical American poets still alive among us." Robert Lowell, perhaps Bishop's most frequent correspondent, made a similar, and equally spot on, prediction regarding the success of her letters: "When Elizabeth Bishop's letters are published (as they will be), she will be recognized as not only one of the best, but one of the most prolific writers of our century." [63] James Merrill spoke of her as an "extraordinary, fresh genius," and Mark Strand, echoing another remark of Merrill's, introduced Bishop at a 1977 reading as "our greatest national treasure." [64] Two years later Robert Pinsky would wistfully observe, in a memorial tribute: "The obituaries for Elizabeth Bishop were not loud or hyperbolic; they were immensely respectful, and perhaps slightly uncomprehending, just like the 'local museum' that she drily invented to accept for vague public use the loner Crusoe's chattels. The year 1979 may be remembered for her loss, long after many of the clowns, heroes, and villains of our headlines fade from memory." [65]

How did readers like Moore, Jarrell, Lowell, Merrill, Strand, and Pinsky anticipate a phenomenon that has taken others by storm so much later? Why, to cite Pinsky's remarks again, did these readers "find the emotional force and penetration of her work simply amazing"? Why did they see her as "profoundly ambitious"? Why did they discover in her work a "geography of survival"? Why did they notice the way, in a Bishop line, "the wit is made to bear up triumphantly under the pressure of a large intellectual construct—the way wit operates in Shakespeare"?—when, all the while, other readers were finding only the "charming little stained-glass bits here and there." [66] They found these qualities, I think, because they looked for them. They read Bishop's poetry with a care, an authority, and a sympathy not widely in evidence until much later: a sympathy that grew out of a shared respect for the rigors and rewards of serious art, an authority that grew of their own mastery of a demanding craft, and a care that grew out of an intuition for quality that remains genuinely rare even in the literary portion of our present culture. As a result, these readers assimilated many of the complex array of qualities intrinsic to Bishop's work well in advance of the general reading public. These readers may not have been able to predict the sequence of factors that would create a cultural climate ready to accord Bishop a sympathetic and an informed reading. As McClatchy's dismissal of the "tides of literary fashion" and "feminist boosterism" appears to indicate, certain "writer's writers" might even refuse to acknowledge the role such factors have unquestionably played in creating the Bishop phenomenon. But it is surely significant that three generations of finely tuned literary intelligences, of writers and readers with tested ears for words and a keenly honed command of their craft, knew for a certainty that Bishop's time would come. Shifts in the cultural perspective, alterations in the critical paradigm, the impact of emerging evidence, and the din of even the most clamorous advocates cannot by themselves create a major writer. The goods really have to be there.

Donald Sheehan, in the process of an early attempt to place Bishop in a pastoral tradition reaching back to Virgil, lamented in 1971 that Bishop's poems "give off no allusive resonance whatsoever." [67] Critics have now overcome this early difficulty and have learned to read Bishop in the context of many important lines of poetic and intellectual development that had been more or less unavailable to earlier generations of readers. Bishop has been read as extending the line of metaphysical poetry running in this century through Eliot. She has likewise been read as extending the line of baroque prose running in this century through Hopkins. She has been placed as an American nature poet by various readers who see her as extending or subverting its traditions. She has been read as a disciple of and a rebel against the Wordsworthian nature lyric. She has been read as an erotic poet, a political poet, a travel poet, a poet of childhood. She has been read across the spectrum of a feminist poetics. She has been placed in the tradition of a postcolonial, multicultural critique. She has been read as a neopragmatist, a neoformalist, and a postmodernist. And this array of readings, each of which makes plausible claims to validity, seems merely to scratch the surface. Other avenues have been barely explored at this writing but are ripe for future attention.

As I have suggested, literary historians did not initiate this process of rereading. They have in fact been lagging behind a process so far dominated by poets, editors, biographers, and author-centered critics. Together, these have made a compelling case for Bishop's deep involvement in most of the main currents of midcentury American poetry. Bishop's recognized achievement and her place in the canon now pose a problem to literary historians that must be addressed. Just as that peculiar poet Emily Dickinson, who seemed to come from nowhere and to speak a unique language, had somehow to be placed, Bishop's prominence now demands a reshaping of outmoded constructs once intended to take us "from modern to contemporary," and this reshaping promises to help us understand that process in a new way.

Let me conclude by alluding to a single aspect of this question that currently engages my attention. What if one were to recognize Bishop's demonstrable importance to a circle once perceived as the sole domain of such male poets as Robert Lowell, Randall Jarrell, and John Berryman? And what if one were to apply many of the approaches to reading Bishop outlined above to the work of this expanded and more complexly gendered circle? One might find that the entire dynamic of their relations undergoes a startling change and not just because of the addition of a woman. Bishop's example might suggest the need to think again about the way we approach the relation between autobiography and fictive art in midcentury American poetry, the need to think again about how these poets use childhood as an artistic material, about how they construct a grammar of dreams, how they implicate pictures and other visual objects in a verbal space, how they incorporate prose rhythms and speech patterns into their verse, and how they deal with problems of knowledge, history, culture, grief, and loss in an environment of epistemological uncertainty. Such a study might help to show how each of these artists escaped the limitations of documentary realism and the excesses of confessionalism. One wants to ask, as well, if each of these poets, male *or* female, might have had occasion to view the world through the "eye of the outsider"? Could the affinity between Bishop and a poet like Lowell, who spent significant portions of his life under confinement in prison or in mental institutions, and who suffered from a major neurological disorder that remained undiagnosed until well into adulthood, be partly explained by a shared experience of outsiderhood? United by a commitment to a demanding art, what anxieties, animosities, and affinities did each of these poets feel as they eyed one another across lines partly defined by gender? Such cross-gender studies offer a potentially significant new direction to the historian who proposes to examine a more fully gendered postmodernism. In any case, Bishop's presence as an artistic touchstone was strong in the minds of these poetic contemporaries, and it has emerged as a phenomenon to be reckoned with today.

Notes

1. Randall Jarrell, "The Year in Poetry," in *Kipling, Auden & Co.* (New York: Farrar, Straus and Giroux, 1980), 244–45.

2. John Ashbery, "Second Presentation to the Jury," *World Literature Today*, 1 (Winter 1977): 8.

3. David Kalstone, *Five Temperaments* (New York: Oxford University Press, 1977), 12.

4. Anne Stevenson, *Elizabeth Bishop* (New Haven, Conn.: Twayne Publishers: 1966).

5. James E. B. Breslin, *From Modern to Contemporary* (Chicago: University of Chicago Press, 1984), 3–4.

6. John Malcolm Brinnin, *The Elizabeth Bishop Bulletin*, 2 (Summer 1993): 2.

7. Langdon Hammer, "The New Elizabeth Bishop," *Yale Review* (Winter 1993): 134.

8. Thomas Travisano, *Elizabeth Bishop: Her Artistic Development* (Charlottesville: University Press of Virginia, 1988), 3. Two weeks after this book appeared, the second book on Elizabeth Bishop in twenty-two years reached the public, Robert Dale Parker's *The Unbeliever: The Poetry of Elizabeth Bishop* (Urbana: University of Illinois Press, 1988).

9. Cary Nelson, *Repression and Recovery: Modern American Poetry and the Politics of Cultural Memory, 1910–1945* (Madison: University of Wisconsin Press, 1989), 3–19.

10. Hammer, "The New Elizabeth Bishop," 138.

11. McClatchy, review of *One Art, Letters*, by Elizabeth Bishop, *New York Times Book Review*, 17 April 1994, 1.

12. "Books of the Day," *Chicago Times-Herald*, 1 June 1899, 9, in Kate Chopin, *The Awakening*, 2d ed., ed. Margo Culley (New York: W. W. Norton, 1994), 166.

13. James Merrill, "Elizabeth Bishop, 1911–1979," in *Elizabeth Bishop and Her Art*, ed. by Lloyd Schwartz and Sybil P. Estess (Ann Arbor: University of Michigan Press, 1983), 259. First published in *New York Review of Books*, 6 December 1979, 6.

14. Charles P. Elliot, "Minor Poet with a Major Fund of Love," *Life*, 4 July 1969, 13.

15. Alicia Suskin Ostriker, *Stealing the Language: The Emergence of Women's Poetry in America* (Boston: Beacon Press, 1986), 7, 54. Ostriker comments more positively on the more autobiographical poems of *Geography III*, Bishop's last book.

16. Betsy Erkkila, *The Wicked Sisters: Women Poets, Literary History, and Discord* (New York: Oxford University Press, 1992), 150.

17. Letter to U. T. and Joseph Summers, 1 March 1979. Quoted from *Elizabeth Bishop: The Geography of Gender*, ed. Marilyn May Lombardi (Charlottesville: University Press of Virginia, 1993), 113.

18. Mutlu Konuk Blasing calls attention to this phrase, quoted from Elizabeth Spires, "The Art of Poetry XXVII" *Paris Review* 80 (1981): 80, in the lead sentence of a recent article, "From Gender to Genre and Back: Elizabeth Bishop and 'The Moose,'" *American Literary History* (Summer 1994): 285.

19. Lombardi, prologue, *Geography*, 5.

20. Adrienne Rich, "The Eye of the Outsider: The Poetry of Elizabeth Bishop," *Boston Review* 8 (April 1983): 16. Cited in Lombardi, *Geography*, 5.

21. Rich, "Eye of the Outsider," 17.

22. Lombardi, *Geography*, 6.

23. Joanne Feit Diehl, "Bishop's Sexual Poetics," in Lombardi, *Geography*, 17.

24. Lorrie Goldensohn, "The Body's Roses: Race, Sex, and Gender in Elizabeth Bishop's Representations of the Self," in Lombardi, *Geography*, 73.

25. Jeredith Merrin, "Elizabeth Bishop: Gaiety, Gayness and Change," in Lombardi, *Geography*, 160, 163.

26. Adrian Oktenberg, review of Lombardi, *Geography* in *The Women's Review of Books*, 11 (July 1994): 28–29.

27. Charles Tomlinson, "Elizabeth Bishop's New Book," review of *Questions of Travel* in *Shenandoah* 17 (Winter 1966): 89.

28. Victoria Harrison, *Elizabeth Bishop's Poetics of Intimacy* (New York: Cambridge University Press, 1993), 142.

29. Barbara Page, "Off-Beat Claves, Oblique Realities: The Key West Notebooks of Elizabeth Bishop," in Lombardi, *Geography*, 210.

30. Tomlinson, "Bishop's New Book," 89.

31. A session titled "Elizabeth Bishop's Translation," organized and chaired by Josef Raab, was devoted to readings of Bishop along these lines at the December 1994 MLA conference.

32. One field likely to emerge in the near future that will also find Bishop ahead of the curve is the field of childhood studies. For an early treatment of Bishop, see Mary Kinzie, *The Cure of Poetry in an Age of Prose* (Chicago: University of Chicago Press, 1993), 88–100. Richard Flynn's *Randall Jarrell and the Lost World of Childhood* (Athens: University of Georgia Press, 1990) offers a superb reading of one of Bishop's friends and contemporaries.

33. M. L. Rosenthal, *The New Modern Poetry: British and American Poetry Since World War II* (New York: Oxford University Press, 1967), 25.

34. Peter Stitt, "The Art of Poetry: An Interview with John Berryman," *Paris Review* 53 (Winter 1972). Cited in *Berryman's Understanding: Reflections on the Poetry of John Berryman*, ed. Harry Thomas (Boston: Northeastern University Press, 1988), 21.

35. John Berryman, *The Dream Songs* (New York: Farrar, Straus, and Giroux, 1969), vi.

36. Rosenthal, *New Modern Poetry*, 26.

37. M. L. Rosenthal, *The Modern Poets* (New York: Oxford University Press, 1960), 253–55.

38. See my *Elizabeth Bishop*, 151–56, and David Kalstone, *Becoming a Poet: Elizabeth Bishop with Marianne Moore and Robert Lowell*, ed. Robert Hemenway (New York: Farrar, Straus and Giroux, 1989), 166–71. Kalstone stresses emerging differences, while I stress Lowell's debt to Bishop, but both readings agree on how intimately entwined Bishop and Lowell were, artistically and psychologically.

39. Elizabeth Bishop, jacket blurb for Robert Lowell's *Life Studies* (New York: Farrar, Straus and Cudahy, 1959).

40. Octavio Paz, "Elizabeth Bishop, or The Power of Reticence," in Schwartz and Estess, *Elizabeth Bishop and Her Art*, 213.

41. Bishop to Lowell, quoted from Charles Thornbury's introduction to John Berryman, *Collected Poems, 1937–1971* (New York: Farrar, Straus and Giroux, 1959), xvii.

42. Dana Gioia, "The Example of Elizabeth Bishop," in *Can Poetry Matter?: Essays on Poetry and American Culture* (St. Paul, Minn.: Graywolf Press, 1992), 237.

43. J. D. McClatchy, "Some Notes on 'One Art,'" in *White Paper on Contemporary Poetry* (New York: Columbia University Press, 1989), 140–41.

44. James McCorkle, *The Still Performance: Writing, Self, and Interconnection in Five Postmodern American Poets* (Charlottesville: University Press of Virginia, 1989), 11, 9.

45. Ashbery, "Second Presentation to the Jury," 8.

46. John Ashbery, review of *The Complete Poems*, by Elizabeth Bishop, in *New York Times Book Review* (1 June 1969): 8.

47. Ashbery, "Second Presentation to the Jury," 10.

48. Denis Donoghue, *Connoisseurs of Chaos* (New York: Columbia University Press, 1984), xxi.

49. Ian Hamilton, *Robert Lowell: A Biography* (New York: Random House, 1982), n. 484.

50. Alan Williamson, *Introspection and Contemporary Poetry* (Cambridge: Harvard University Press, 1984), 2.

51. Alan Williamson, "A Cold Spring: The Poet of Feeling," Schwartz and Estess, *Elizabeth Bishop and Her Art*, 96.

52. Oktenberg, review of Lombardi, *Geography*, 28.

53. Tom Paulin, "Newness and Nowness: The Extraordinary Brilliance of Elizabeth Bishop's Letters," *Times Literary Supplement*, 29 April 1994, 3.

54. Robert Giroux, ed., *One Art: Letters*, of Elizabeth Bishop (New York: Farrar, Straus and Giroux, 1994), 643, 5.

55. For a review of these and other recent publications, see my "Surveying Bishop Scholarship: Publications since 1990," *Elizabeth Bishop Bulletin* 2 (Summer 1993): 4–5.

56. Paulin, "Newness and Nowness," 5.

57. Kalstone, *Five Temperaments*, 12.

58. My own rather early start in Bishop studies benefited both from Bishop's extended later contact with the academic and literary world and from some of her more sporadic early contacts with those worlds. I was introduced to Bishop's work in my first year of graduate study at the University of Virginia in 1975 in an introductory-level class taught by Alan Williamson, a poet-Ph.D. from Harvard who knew Bishop's work from that milieu, where he had chiefly studied with and written on Robert Lowell. Williamson soon departed for another post, but my own work on Bishop was able to continue in a 1977 seminar on contemporary poetry directed by visiting poet Mark Strand, a longtime devotee of Bishop who had known her during a Fulbright-sponsored visit to Brazil. My dissertation on Bishop began that same year, under the direction of J. C. Levenson, a scholar recognized primarily for his work on Henry Adams and his contemporaries. Levenson had developed an enthusiasm for Bishop under the encouragement of one of her few early friends in the academic world, Joseph Summers, a specialist in metaphysical poetry and Levenson's classmate from an earlier era at Harvard. This fortuitous sequence of academic mentors positioned me to begin a thesis on Bishop just after the publication of *Geography III*. Other budding enthusiasts for Bishop's work may not have been so fortunately placed.

59. Indeed, the present vogue for Haydn and Mozart must bear some relation to the present vogue for Bishop: Mozart and Bishop in particular might be said to create quicksilver works lined with dark moral clouds.

60. Ashbery, "Second Presentation to the Jury," 8.

61. Edwin Honig, "Poetry Chronicle," *Partisan Review* (Winter 1956): 115.

62. A. Alvarez, "Imagism and Poetesses," *Kenyon Review* (Spring 1957): 325; Jerome Mazzaro, "Elizabeth Bishop's Poems," *Shenandoah* (Summer 1969): 100; Peggy Rizza, "Another Side of This Life: Women as Poets," in *American Poetry since 1960: Some Critical Perspectives*, ed. Robert B. Shaw (Chester Springs, Pa.: Duforer Editions, 1974), 170.

63. Lowell, book jacket of Giroux, *One Art*.

64. James Merrill from *Voices and Visions: Elizabeth Bishop* television series. Mark Strand, "Elizabeth Bishop Introduction," Schwartz and Estess, *Elizabeth Bishop and Her Art*, 243.

65. Robert Pinsky, "Elizabeth Bishop, 1911–1979," in Schwartz and Estess, 257.

66. Ibid., 256, and Oscar Williams, "New Verse: *North & South*," *New Republic*, 21 October 1946, 525, quoted from Schwartz and Estess, *Elizabeth Bishop and Her Art*, 185.

67. Donald Sheehan, "The Silver Sensibility," *Contemporary Literature* 12 (Winter 1971): 99–120.

Part VII
Muriel Rukeyser
(1913–1980)

Chapter 11

Muriel Rukeyser and Her Literary Critics

Kate Daniels

It is worth remarking when the work of a poet of the achievement of Muriel Rukeyser (1913–1980) has not occasioned a prominent body of critical comment. This chapter is intended to make something of an extended remark along those lines and to document the criticism that has been undertaken. What an overview of the critical response to Rukeyser's work reveals to us is the situation—uncomfortable and in-between—of that individualistic poet whose work fails to entirely conform during his or her lifetime to the critics' prevailing notions of what good work is— who fails to fit completely and neatly into a category that has been critically recognized, defined, and canonized. Such was the case for Rukeyser's work, which, from the beginning, positioned itself squarely in no identifiable poetry camp. Although critics were often quick to label her work according to one or another of current literary fashions, her poetry abjured the kinds of definitions they sought to impose on it. During the 1930s, for example, her technique was often described as "social realist," "revolutionist," or "proletarian," but such words provided only a partial description.[1] Her early poems were as much nourished by the antipolitical highly aesthetic strains of Romantic and modern poetry as they were by the politicized and didactic impulses of social realism—each of which was regarded by its critical proponents as mutually exclusive of the other. Four decades later, during the 1970s, when critics were swept up in another social movement, they rushed to label her "feminist." But Rukeyser herself protested (in both prose and poetry) what she considered the essentially reductive nature of such a description of her work.[2]

Her refusal to choose one way or the other and her stubborn insistence on creating new ways of forming and patterning her poems to serve her idiosyncratic imagination provoked some rather extraordinary responses from literary critics. An examination of these in conjunction with Rukeyser's own critical writings brings to light a fascinating dialogue between poet and critic as they squared off over the aesthetic issues that arose from her work. The more critics objected to the unorthodox nature of her formal practices and her "impure" subject matter, the more committed Rukeyser became to the personal expression of her poetry and to creating a critical atmosphere more hospitable to it. Popular readership was hers from the beginning (her first book went into several printings during its first year of publication alone), but she longed for critical acceptance by her peers. In pursuit of this—even before her first collection appeared in print—she began publishing in her own reviews and essays an explanation and defense of her approach to poetry that argued for a larger perspective on literature, the abandonment of European, elitist intellectual models that sharply differentiated between "high" and "low" art, and fewer enervating turf battles between artists and critics.

Her work, which from the beginning was highly anachronistic, identifiably "female," often self-consciously political, and formally experimental, was initially well-received by the critics. Throughout the 1930s, she was regarded as an important, if not a major, poet among the writers of her generation, which included Delmore Schwartz, John Berryman, and Elizabeth Bishop; and it was Rukeyser who was regularly proclaimed the best woman writer of her generation, the best of recent Yale Younger Poets, the best of the young, "revolutionist" poets by critics such as Malcolm Cowley and Louis Untermeyer.[3] Although her work had always had its detractors, and she had received her share of negative reviews, the critical response to her work underwent a radical change during the 1940s, when she was subjected to a series of highly personal reviews that condemned her entire poetic endeavor and called into question her personal and poetic motives.[4] She was not, of course, the only writer to be subjected to this kind of indignity by the critical establishment: Archibald MacLeish, who, like Rukeyser, was interested in the development of a native American culture, and who, also like her, sought to invigorate it by the standards articulated by Walt Whitman and Ralph Waldo Emerson, was attacked frequently and with similar virulence.[5] What is interesting about the way in which Rukeyser was treated is the *personal* venom that she and her work during the 1940s seemed to arouse in critics and the *permission* that some of them granted themselves to insult her personally under the pretense of reviewing her work.[6] The *Partisan Review*, in particular, found it impossible during this period to review her work with anything approaching the objectivity that criticism had historically claimed for itself. In 1942, its review of *Wake Island*, undertaken by Weldon Kees, read as follows: "There's one thing you can say about Muriel: she's not lazy." *In toto.* A year later, *Partisan* launched a full-fledged attack on Rukeyser entitled, "Grandeur and Misery of a Poster Girl," which dragged on for three issues and which read in part:

If the lines of her verse often seemed to resemble a bathrobe; if Kenneth Patchen was her only equal in the mastery of the inexact adjective and the dangling participle; if she shifted back and forth between the orgiastic diction of D. H. Lawrence at his worst and a style suggesting that of *Time* magazine and a persistent effort to send many telegrams at small cost to oneself—if all this was the case, what of it? A dangling participle is no crime. Everything has its good side; the befuddlement of Miss Rukeyser's syntax rendered her lines less and less meaningful—a keen relief! One thing was clear: this young poetess was intent on being friends with everyone, though in citing Waldo Frank as a source of her ideas she exposed her proper affiliations. It is true that indiscriminate friendship makes for promiscuity. But why carp when so many human beings hate each other?[7]

Louise Bogan, the powerful poetry critic for *The New Yorker*, from 1931 to 1968, was another critic who lost no opportunity to attack— *attack* is not too strong a word—Rukeyser's work, often on grounds so far removed from the actual poetry under examination that the reviews ultimately revealed more about Bogan's psychology than about Rukeyser's poetry. Bogan was, of course, well-known for her ambivalence about women and for her disinclination to review prominently the work of other women poets. Although she devoted a fair amount of space to a very negative review of Rukeyser's third volume of poetry, *A Turning Wind* (1939), she never again granted more than a paragraph to any of the ten volumes that Rukeyser published during the remainder of Bogan's tenure at *The New Yorker*. Her usual tactic was to append a brief, sneeringly dismissive sentence or two at the end of a longer review. Rukeyser never commented publicly on Bogan's animosity toward her work, and, characteristically, she did not let it color her evaluation of Bogan's own poetry. In 1955, when Rukeyser served as a judge for the Bollingen Poetry Prize (along with Marianne Moore, Wallace Stevens, Randall Jarrell, and Allen Tate), the committee awarded the prize to Bogan and Léonie Adams as cowinners. Others, however, were not as forgiving in their assessment of Bogan's abuse of the great power she wielded at *The New Yorker*. Kenneth Rexroth once accused her of conducting "a malevolent vendetta with Muriel Rukeyser, which can only be accounted for by some unknown motivation."[8]

Lest this sound as if Rukeyser was the innocent victim of a conspiratorial cabal of earlier literary critics, it must be said that she herself was implicated in her problematic relationship with them; and it is what might be called this *complicity* that makes the examination of the critical response to her work both interesting and significant. Finding herself unable to silently accept the critics' negative judgments of her poetry—

which proceeded, she was convinced, from their misunderstanding of the principles that organized her poems—she ultimately created a parallel body of prose work that promoted and explained the conditions under which her poetry would be fully appreciated, fully interpretable. Hence my suggestion that she instituted a virtual *dialogue* with the leading literary critics of her lifetime.

To begin with, she knowingly flung herself headfirst into the literary quarrels of the 1930s by publishing, in her first book, poems that were simultaneously tied to the apolitical and highly aesthetic tradition of high modernism and to a self-conscious left-wing political identity derived from Marxist theory. The contradiction that her stance implied did not bother her at all. Thus it was that Stephen Vincent Benet (editor of *Theory of Flight*), himself an apolitical critic and political conservative, declined to consign the book to "the dreary and unreal discussion about unconscious fascists, conscious proletarians, and other figures of straw which has afflicted recent criticism" even though he recognized that Rukeyser was "a Left Winger and a revolutionary" simply because she spoke her politics "like a poet, not like a slightly worn phonograph record, and she does so in poetic terms." [9] Critics of a different ideological persuasion, however, manipulated the contradictions inherent in *Theory of Flight* in other directions. Kenneth Burke, for example, reviewing the volume in the *New Masses*, congratulated the Communists on having gained Rukeyser as an ally.[10] Because all of the critics of this first book noted her age, perhaps they "allowed" her this contradiction as a kind of youthful gaffe, each side hoping for resolution in its favor by the second book. John Crowe Ransom seemed to think something like that; although he wondered whether she would turn out, finally, to be merely a "proletarian gospeller" or a "real proletarian poet," he suggested that the literary left might provide a good apprenticeship for "the too-sensuous younger poet [like Rukeyser] who otherwise would be always exalting his own feelings." [11]

Both Rukeyser's politics and her poetic imagination, however, were far more complicated—and stubbornly individualistic—than any of her early critics realized. Her disinclination to conform to the dictates of any aesthetic or political program was not, as a number of later critics were to suggest, a carelessness or lack of intellectual rigor on her part. Throughout her life, she found herself astonished at the inability of most literary critics to consider work that departed from the conventions of a particular school or norm, and in her own critical writings she demonstrated her ability to transcend the contemporary and topical contexts of a work in favor of what she considered its more enduring artistic qualities. Even at the height of her interest in proletarian literature in 1934, she would not follow the party line in condemning the work of William

Faulkner for its allegedly "decadent" and "bourgeois" characteristics. In a review of *Dr. Martino and Other Stories*, published that year in the *New Masses* (which was the party's main cultural organ), she presented a beautifully written and noticeably apolitical assessment of the book. Her only complaint addressed Faulkner's lack of "emotional documentation." She wished he would focus more on the "internal motion coming out of the story itself" rather than on "maneuvering the situation." [12]

This attitude of hers was demonstrated most clearly in a review from the same period of John Wheelwright's second book of poetry, *Rock and Shell.* Although Wheelwright's work was considered too obscure and linguistically decorative to qualify him as a dependable proletarian poet, Rukeyser pleaded (again in the pages of the *New Masses*) for the accommodation of his attitudes and techniques within a framework of revolutionist literature that could be considered politically correct. She praised the "eccentricity" of the position he had wrought for himself and was adamant that his work not be dismissed for not following the dictates of proletarian poetry more closely. "Such writers," she wrote, "are laying a base of literary activity and revolutionary creation which must be realized as one of the important fronts of the growing cultural movement." [13] Of course, her plea for the acceptance of Wheelwright's "eccentric" and "confusing" poetry was also an argument for her own developing work and for her very similar artistic consciousness that refused to choose a side in the literary and political wars of the period.

In 1938, in her second collection of poetry, *U.S. 1*, she demonstrated more clearly her willingness to submit her own work to the charge of political eccentricity by combining the attitudes of social realism with the techniques of modernism. The opening poem in the book was composed of highly politicized, documentary material that Rukeyser had gathered at a Union Carbide mining operation in West Virginia. The story line—which focused on the real-life corporate cover-up of lethal working conditions in a West Virginia mining operation—was a proletarian poet's dream. How Rukeyser put her imagination to work on this material, however, was enough to make any good Marxist quail in his or her sturdy boots: she transposed it onto a poetic superstructure formed by the translated texts of the Egyptian Book of the Dead, and, again, offered the majority of critics a book that seemed impossible to interpret within the narrow, critical contexts of the 1930s. Her technique (which was highly indebted to John Dos Passos's collage experiments in *1919*) and her materials arose from the mandates of social realism and proletarian poetry. The consciousness that fused the material into a poem was, however, a clear descendant of the great Romantic and modern poets.

There were other difficulties as well. Rukeyser sought, from her first published work, to create new modes of expression that would more successfully transmit her unusual ideas about poetic form. To the revolutionist critics of the early 1930s, such interests were "bourgeois" and needful of being suppressed in favor of clarity, simplicity, and straightforwardness. Stanley Burnshaw, who was the poetry editor of the *New Masses* when Rukeyser first began to submit her work there, chastised her for her idiosyncratic punctuation by which she strove to more accurately render within the poem her sense of timing and breath: "We think that a revolutionary magazine should not put any blocks in the way of communication, and in the opinion of [Joshua] Kunitz and myself, the punctuation, or rather lack of it in your poem should be changed."[14] But Rukeyser believed that "punctuation is biological. It is the physical indication of the body rhythms which the reader is to acknowledge . . ."— hardly a politically correct statement for a self-professed proletarian poet.[15] To the more aesthetic, apolitical critics and editors of the period, like Harriet Monroe, however, Rukeyser's poetry bore too strong a whiff of the overtly political, for all its formal experimentation and involvement with music. When Rukeyser sent *Poetry* a portion of the long title poem from *Theory of Flight*, Monroe rejected it with the blunt observation that it was propaganda—not poetry.

It was not until the end of the 1930s, and the publication of her third book, *A Turning Wind*, in November of 1939, that Rukeyser began to grow more confident of her unusual ideas about form. Throughout the 1940s, with the publication of *Beast in View* (1944) and *The Green Wave* (1948), she developed these ideas into a metaphor that brought together science and poetry: first, in her experimental biography of the nineteenth-century scientist Willard Gibbs, whom she regarded as a signal figure in the *fin-de-siècle* confluence of cultural ideas in this country, and, later, in a series of essays and lectures that were eventually published in book form as *The Life of Poetry* (1949).[16]

The foundation of her ideas about poetic form rested upon the conviction that poetry was a dynamic process that succeeded or failed according to the relationship between its several parts—the poem, the poet, and the reader. Although she had first begun to formulate a scientific metaphor for the poetic process during her research for the Gibbs biography, she had been obsessed with the physics of movement and stasis as long as she could remember; what the study of Gibbs revealed was the true nature of the fascination: it was the rhythmic movement *within* stasis that captured her poetic imagination and carried emotive connotations that resonated back to her childhood and forward into her sexual life as an adult. Once she began to comprehend some of Gibbs's theorems on physical mechanics, she found herself "borrowing" them to explain exactly what effect she strove for in her poems. Gibbs had convinced her of the necessity of being "dynamically minded," and in poetry, she translated this into her own theorem:

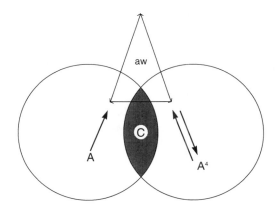

This diagram is false
until all the components are shown in
motion.

Here, she was considering the poem, "like anything separable and existing in time," as a "dynamic system, whose tendencies toward equilibrium, and even toward entropy, are the same as other systems"—more
Gibbs. "Truth is, according to Gibbs," she continued, "not a stream that
flows from a source, but an agreement of components." [17] The nonlinearity of this kind of thought and its relational orientation not only held
strong emotional appeal for Rukeyser but also presented her, intellectually, with possibilities for structuring or patterning her poems.

Much of her fascination with this scientific approach to poetry had its
origins in her personal history. She had exhibited a precocious appreciation of rhythmic textures by the age of three or four; and this led her to
create her own wordless poems and songs before she could write by fitting nonsensical sounds into pleasing musical rhythms. Augmenting this
was a deeply internalized apprehension of New York City (where she
grew up) as an outwardly static, monolithic entity that inwardly teemed
and surged with the rhythmical movements of the people who lived
there. Her father was in the building industry, and this, too, exercised a
strong influence on her developing poetic imagination. What started out
as a kind of romance in which she and her parents were key figures in
the construction of the great city of New York soon acquired, within the
troubled nexus of her family, other significances that she later applied—
or observed—in her poetry. The principle of the expansion joint, for
example, a complex idea that she understood at a very early age, became
incorporated, decades later, into her theories about form and structure
in poetry. As a child, she understood it in a child's simple way:

Concrete must contain expansion joints, the strips of material that allow the forcing heat of these summers, the forcing cold of these violent white winters, to do
their work. The principle of the expansion joint, you learn, runs through all.
(*LP*, 212)

Likewise, she understood that the emotional rigidity and lack of demon-
strativeness in her family belied the wild passions moving beneath her
parents' impassive exteriors. That was somehow analogous to the principle of the expansion joint, wasn't it? The new George Washington
Bridge that she watched being constructed across the Hudson River at
179th Street on her way to and from school each day *looked* static and
still, a constructed object that would not move. But *she*, the daughter of
an engineer, knew that this was not true: without moving, without the
freedom to move, the bridge would become a victim of its own rigidity.
Under the weight of its confinement, it would give way, crack, and collapse into the river. The real truth was the truth of the expansion joint,
not the truth of appearances: the bridge was actually built to move, both
vertically and laterally. No one might ever really perceive this movement
with the human eye, but it existed nevertheless; *it had to*. Without this
movement within stasis, the bridge would fall, relationships would wither
and die, poems would fail.

So, when she spoke, in explaining the formal techniques of one of her
most famous poems ("Ajanta," from *Beast in View*), of constructing an
arch from the aural textures of the words, it was with the understanding
that she took from mechanical engineering: an arch cannot maintain its
form if it cannot move within that form.[18] Thus, a poem needed movement, and not just the artificial, metrical movement that could be produced through a received form. "The form of a poem is much more
organic, closer to organic form, than has been supposed," she wrote,
more than a decade before Robert Creeley made his famous pronouncement on organic form and poetic content. She expounded:

A poem moves through its sounds set in motion and the reaction to these sounds,
their rhymes and repetitions and contrast has a demonstrable physical basis
which can be traced as the wave-length of the sounds themselves can be traced.
The wave-length is measurable; the reaction, if you wish such measurements,
could be traced through heartbeat and breath, although I myself do not place
much value on such measurement. (*LP*, 182–83)

This, of course, was more than enough to confound the critics, particularly in the postwar period when the New Criticism was solidifying its
hold on publishers, academics, and on many writers themselves. The essentially static principles of the New Criticism simply could not be applied to Muriel Rukeyser's work, which, by the poet's self-conscious
design, resisted any kind of formulaic analysis. Throughout the period,

comments by reviewers often revealed their frustration in struggling to fit her work to the test: "a devotee of loose, erratic, and disjunctive rhetoric" (Louise Bogan in *The New Yorker*); "easy reworkings of the automatic images of a rhetorical-emotional trance-state in which everything slides into everything else" (Randall Jarrell in *The Nation*); "exactitude of feeling rather than of form" (Richard Eberhart in the *New York Times Book Review*; "[the poems] have never been learned as ways of feeling and attitudes of control for both feeling and emotion, but operate rather as a vehicle of spontaneity" (R. P. Blackmur in the *Kenyon Review*).[19]

Throughout the 1940s and 1950s, fighting the strong tides of New Criticism whose tenets were not her own—were not, in fact, even remotely compatible with her own—Rukeyser perceived that her work was in a critical decline. Although she stayed faithful to the mandates of her own imagination and interests and would not renege on any of the earlier, more radical expressions of her first volumes of poetry, she soon found that the winds of change had brought more than a new fashion for aesthetic, internationalist verse. The cynicism of postwar American poetry dismayed her deeply, and she deplored "the whole critical circus whose acrobatics are to the effect that poetry is dead. I do not think so," she said (*LP*, 189). While she understood that these attitudes were a product of her generation's dashed hopes and their sense of having been betrayed by their youthful idealism, she herself could not condone a point of view or a poetic theory that pronounced poetry dead and hope irrelevant.

You may see these results in fashionable poetry: in the poetry of the sense of annihilation, of the smallness of things, of aversion, of guilt, and the compulsion toward forgiveness. There is strong magic here: if they want smallness, they will have their smallness; if they want it, they will at last have their forgiveness. But these artists go blaming, blaming . . . [and] emerge with little but self-pity. A characteristic title is The World Has Shrunk in the Wash. (*LP*, 189)

She had, since the 1930s, conducted an ongoing debate in her prose writings (mostly reviews) with the literary critics about aesthetic criteria. Energized after the war by what she considered the spurious attitudes behind the New Criticism, this debate emerged into full view in the lectures and essays that *The Life of Poetry* comprised. In particular, the New Critics' formulaic approach to poetry—their interest in the poem as an *objet d'art* and in formal analysis rather than generative analysis—and their insistence that the system of an individual poem is all that matters conflicted dramatically with her own beliefs. "Poetry is, above all," she said again and again, "an approach to the truth of feeling. . . . One writes in order to feel" (*LP*, 4, 58). She held, as well, a highly unorthodox understanding of the organic nature of the relationship between poets and readers. "[T]he rule of perfection or death does not hold in organic life," she wrote.

> This is not a real choice, between an absolute positive and an absolute negative, with only one moment to choose. In a world of growth, the moment of choice may come as long as there is life. There is process: man can change and go on changing; at any moment he can do the work of re-creation on himself, and purify his consciousness.
>
> The offer of perfection or death is one sign of impoverishment in the artist. (*LP*, 54–55)

Rukeyser saw the New Critics' attempt to remove poetry from any kind of external interpretative context as reactionary, a product of the disillusionments of the decade prior to their emergence. Although she herself was willing to admit the failure of 1930s' experiments in political poetry and the folly of signing over one's poetic allegiance to a central authority, the failures of the decade could not crush her own unassailable belief in the transformative powers of poetry and all art. She was not inclined to reject one formula only to adopt another more politically expedient one that might cultivate a new appreciation for her work in the literary journals.

After she published *The Life of Poetry* in 1949, Rukeyser entered a period of literary inactivity. During the next fifteen years, she—who had been so prolific during her early career—published a mere four books, only one of which was a full volume of new poems, *Body of Waking* (1958). From her earliest years, she had wanted it all—to enjoy complete independence and success in her poetry writing, to make a great career of it, to form a long-term relationship with another person, to achieve a home, domestic serenity, and to have a child. When she gave birth to her son in 1947, it was out of wedlock and she was destitute. But for the generosity of an anonymous patron, it is unclear what might have happened. The gift allowed her to continue her writing and to raise her child without having to end her career as a poet in favor of more financially lucrative work and without entering into either an unsuitable marriage for financial security or humiliating financial dependence on her family. Nevertheless, the demands of motherhood extracted a painful and protracted price from her writing; she saw it reflected in her diminishing output and in lukewarm reviews of the work she did manage to produce.

The very real decline of her literary reputation during the 1950s was partly due to the New Critics' stranglehold on literary opinion and partly due to Rukeyser's own retreat from the scene, occasioned not only by the demands of motherhood, but also by her desire to avoid any publicity that might bring her to the attention of the House Un-American Activities Committee.[20] The selected, reprinted work and the translations that she published during the period drew, for the most part, lackadaisical response from the critics. During her early career, her books had routinely been reviewed by every major newspaper and all the literary journals of note. By 1958, when *Body of Waking* was published, the critical response had dwindled dramatically. Only four reviews of importance appeared. Compared to the fifteen major reviews that *Theory of Flight* had received, twelve for *U.S. 1*, ten for *A Turning Wind*, and eight for *The Green Wave*, this was a significant decline. The situation did not quickly reverse itself. In 1973, when the first edition of the *Norton Anthology of Modern Poetry* appeared, she was not even represented in it.

It was not until the late 1960s that the critics rediscovered Muriel Rukeyser and began, once again, to address her work with the seriousness and depth it had originally occasioned. Her interest in the intersection of private experience and public politics surged into critical favor again as the Vietnam War entered the living rooms of millions of Americans and as fifty thousand vigorous young men were shipped off to lose their lives in a war that most Americans did not understand and many did not support. Buoyed by this new wave of political feeling sweeping the country and by the freedom that her son's college enrollment conferred upon her, Rukeyser enjoyed a burst of poetic energy. She began to write again, in her sixth decade, as she had in her early life—prolifically, but with a new luminance lent by her advancing years and the lessons of the decades through which she had lived.

Her new period of productivity was preceded by a final outburst of critical protest upon the publication of *The Orgy* (1965), which she called, simply, a "book" about the events surrounding Puck Fair, an annual paganistic celebration that takes place each August in West Kerry, Ireland. It was prefaced by a curious disclaimer: "The goat is real; Puck Fair is real; the orgy is real. All the characters and the acts of this book, however, are—of course—a free fantasy on the event." [21] In her private correspondence, she insisted over and over again that the book was neither a novel nor autobiography. What exactly was it, then? The question drove some critics all but wild: "(*The Orgy*) is a book whose ambiguous status makes me very uncertain about how to handle it" (*New York Review of Books*); "The last impression the book leaves is of a richly emotional letter from someone the reader does not know to someone else he has never met" (*Time*); "Indeed, one may perhaps wonder whether so subjective a method is suited to so extrovert an occasion—assuming, of course, that Puck Fair is the actual point of the book" (*The Nation*). [22]

It was the sociologist Helen Lynd, reviewing *The Orgy* for *The American Scholar*, who articulated for the first time the question that lay and lies at the heart of all Rukeyser scholarship: "Why have reviewers had such difficulty with this book?" she asked, and then proceeded to answer:

The impossibility of putting this book into a customary classification is one reason. . . . We cope with the complexity of existence by slogans and labels, and what we cannot classify we tend to brush aside like an Aristotelian accident. We can become aware of the "foul rag and bone shop of the heart," of filth, and sordidness, and depravity if we see them in separate categories as Freud and Genet have taught us to see them. But we still find it hard to come close to them, and even harder to see them close to tenderness and beauty. It is not easy to confront the essential contradictions of existence. But if the world of [Puck Fair, of] the Tinkers, the dung of cattle, the crowning of the goat exist, we must either say that these things have no meaning or try to discover what that meaning is.[23]

However personally gratifying Rukeyser must have found this eloquent interpretation of her aesthetic, she had, by now, grown impervious to the fickle nature and king-making mentality of literary criticism. The reviews of *The Orgy* (a book it had taken her seven years to write), as disappointing as they were, could not discourage her as they once might have. Likewise, the new respect now addressed to her work, the many prizes and honors she began to receive did not carry the meaning that they once would have. Despite the personal pain she had experienced from the earlier attacks on her work, she rarely commented directly on the viciousness and sexism that had often characterized her generation's cadre of literary critics.[24] When she did feel moved to say something that was clearly related to these experiences in her own career, she often phrased it in terms that enlarged the issue beyond her personal experience of it. She was profoundly aware—as well she might be—of the power that critics are capable of wielding over a writer's reputation with the reading public, and she reminded her readers over and over again to trust above all their own responses to the books they read. In a review published in 1967 of D. H. Lawrence's poems (which she had admired since she was a schoolgirl in the 1920s), she observed that "the obstacles which the critics manufactured between these poems and their readers have fallen away, and here they are, lovely in their power."[25] In 1974, she characterized the last poems of Anne Sexton as the product of a poet "who no longer looks at the audience to see how the confession is going."[26] In 1977, she told a class of young women writers at the Cazenovia community in upstate New York that she felt silence was the best and most profound critical response to a poem. The articulated critical analysis was "farther down the line for me," she said.[27] And in 1979, when the academic critic William Pritchard viciously reviewed her life's work, *The Collected Poems of Muriel Rukeyser*, in the *Hudson Review*, she responded in a characteristically private way: by mailing a copy of the piece, without comment, to a young critic who was completing the first book-length critical study of her work.[28]

Of everything that reenergized her flagging critical reputation, it was the feminist movement's discovery of her that brought her once again to the forefront of critical attention. This renewed interest was signaled by the writing of the first critical book on her work, *The Poetic Vision of Muriel Rukeyser,* by Louise Kertesz in 1980; a retrospective account of her entire corpus in the *American Poetry Review,* by Virginia Terris in 1974; and the writing of several Ph.D. dissertations, a number of which considered her in the context of other, younger women writers like Adrienne Rich and Denise Levertov.[29] Although she enjoyed the new attention and was happy to lend her work to various feminist anthologies and enterprises, she declined to formally join any of the rapidly proliferating women's groups and she was wary of the separatism that she discerned within much of the new movement's philosophy. Nevertheless, even while she denied that she was a feminist in any official or organized sense (just as thirty years earlier she had denied being a leftist in any official way), she wrote and published a number of poems that ultimately became visibly and passionately identified with the feminist movement.[30]

Her new critical status was significant enough to find her elected to the National Institute of Arts and Letters in 1967 and to the presidency of the PEN American Center in 1975. There were rumors that she would be or had been considered for the Nobel Prize for literature, and she began to be compared with Pablo Neruda, a poet she had known and admired.[31] The new examination of her work of almost fifty years revealed qualities of her poetry that were similar to those found in the work of Neruda and other writers who had been awarded the world's most prestigious literary prize: her persistent pacifism and her humane consciousness that had focused, from the beginning, on the infinite, positive possibilities of human beings and on the necessity for peace. By the time she died in 1980, the *New York Times* judged her prominent enough to warrant a lengthy obituary that praised the "breadth of a body of work that seemed to mirror United States history from the Depression and the coming of Fascism to World War II and the Vietnam War." [32] Even the *Partisan Review* relinquished its forty year boycott of her work and reviewed her *Collected Poems,* published in 1979, in a brief but friendly piece.[33]

It is likely that she died disappointed: not in her own work, but in her ultimate inability to relay the peculiar, intensely individualistic qualities of her poetic vision and in the intractable nature of an American critical establishment that too often in her lifetime sought not the invigoration of poetry, but the personal elevation of particular poets. She would not have been unaware that the cadre of 1960s and 1970s critics that reevaluated her work and awarded her poetic tenure were, at the same time, disparaging those younger writers who spoke in a more formal and mannered voice during an era when the irrational reigned and traditional form was regarded as politically retrograde. It seems the onus of our critical establishment that critics—like the American society from which they arise—must travel in packs, responding to the latest fads and fashions, and crushing the efforts of those uncategorizable, out-of-sync writers whose ideas are theirs and theirs alone. What is it in our culture that causes such discomfort in the presence of contradiction, that places such a high value on conformity? Muriel Rukeyser pondered this question for the fifty years that she wrote and published her poems. Her entire body of work speaks for the value to be gained from a more generous and accommodating attitude toward our art and our artists. She expressed it most eloquently, perhaps, in this passage from *The Life of Poetry*:

We need a background that will let us find ourselves and our poems, let us move in discovery. The tension between the parts of such a society is health; the tension here between the individual and whole society is health. This state arrives when freedom is a moving goal, when we go beyond the forms to an organic structure which we can in conscience claim and use. Then the multiplicities sing, each in his own voice. Then we understand that there is not meaning, but meanings; not liberty, but liberties. And multiplicity is available to all. Possibility joins the categorical imperative. Suffering and joy are fused in growth; and growth is the universal. (*LP*, 226–27)

Notes

1. See, for example: "Eight Proletarian Poets" in *New Republic*, 28 November 1934, 75–77, and "Portraits of the Artist as a Proletarian" in *Saturday Review*, 31 July 1937, 4.

2. See Rachel Blau DuPlessis, "The Critique of Consciousness and Myth in Levertov, Rich, and Rukeyser," *Feminist Studies* 3 (1975), for a discussion of Rukeyser's "feminist point of view." Rukeyser refuted what she considered reductive feminist readings of her (and others') work in both prose (see an interview with her by Judith McDaniel in *New Women's Times Feminist Review* 10 [11–24 May 1979]) and in some of her later poems like the title poem of *The Speed of Darkness* (1968) and "Despisals," "What Do We See?" and "Searching/Not Searching" from *Breaking Open* (1973).

3. See, for example: Horace Gregory, "A Hope for Poetry," *New Republic*, 5 February 1936, 374; Louis Untermeyer, review of *Theory of Flight* by Muriel Rukeyser, in *American Mercury*, March 1938; P. M. Jack, review of *Theory of Flight* in *New York Times Book Review*, 12 January 1936, 15; Philip Blair Rice, "A New Poet" in *The Nation*, 29 January 1936, 134.

4. Besides those cited below, see Randall Jarrell's review of *The Green Wave* in *The Nation*, 8 May 1948, and later anthologized in his *Poetry and the Age* (New York: Vintage Books, 1953). Critic Jane Elizabeth Curtis, "Muriel Rukeyser: The Woman Writer Confronts the Traditional Mythology and Psychology" (Ph.D. diss., University of Wisconsin, Madison, 1981) suggests that Jarrell's influence during the 1940s and 1950s was powerful enough to permanently damage a poet's reputation if he did not care for the work. In Rukeyser's case, Curtis contends that Jarrell's negative opinion has "impeded Rukeyser's acceptance in traditional literary circles" (29).

5. See, for example, Morton Dauwen Zabel, "The Poet on Capitol Hill," *Partisan Review* 8, no. 1 (January–February 1941), 1–19.

6. For commentary on this, see Curtis, "Muriel Rukeyser," 26–30; and Louise Kertesz, *The Poetic Vision of Muriel Rukeyser* (Baton Rouge: Louisiana State University Press, 1980), 179–81.

7. Weldon Kees, "Miss Rukeyser's Marine Poem," *Partisan Review* 9 (November–December 1942), 540; "Grandeur and Misery of a Poster Girl," *Partisan Review* 10 (September–October 1943), 471–73. In 1985, when I interviewed William Phillips, one of *Partisan*'s founding editors still on staff, he had no recollection of the episode although he agreed with Mary McCarthy's assessment of Rukeyser's Stalinist politics and the animosity that this position necessarily incurred among the anti-Stalinist Marxists at the *Partisan Review* during the 1940s. Reading the piece in my presence, he chuckled delightedly. Later in the same interview, he did say that he remembered an encounter with Rukeyser during 1975 or 1976 when she was president of American PEN. *Partisan Review,* involved in a dispute with Rutgers University concerning the ownership of the journal's archives, sought PEN's assistance as a mediator in the disagreement. Phillips claimed that Rukeyser stated that she was disinclined to lend her assistance to a publication that had made it a policy to attack writers in the manner that *Partisan* had over the years. Phillips also claimed that when Rukeyser's collected poems were published in 1979, just before she died, he published a brief review of the book by her friend Grace Schulman to "make up" to Rukeyser for the way the editors of the journal had treated her—although this was exactly what he claimed not to remember at the beginning of the interview. Phillips also refused several requests to read the correspondence surrounding the Rukeyser "imbroglio," as *Partisan* described the affair in 1942. Since the archives of the journal can only be used with the permission of Mr. Phillips, a full investigation of the incident awaits the efforts of another scholar.

8. For a discussion of Bogan's problem, see Elizabeth Frank, *Louise Bogan: A Portrait* (New York: Alfred A. Knopf, 1985), 77. A typical Bogan review of Rukeyser can be found in the one paragraph Bogan devoted to Rukeyser's *Selected Poems,* which appeared in *The New Yorker* on 3 November 1951, and which begins: "Muriel Rukeyser is the one woman poet of her generation to put on sibyl's robes, nowadays, truly threadbare and unconvincing garments." Kenneth Rexroth's quotation is from the foreword to Kertesz, *The Poetic Vision of Muriel Rukeyser.*

9. Stephen Vincent Benet, foreword to *Theory of Flight* by Muriel Rukeyser (New Haven, Conn.: Yale University Press, 1935).

10. Kenneth Burke, "Return after Flight," *New Masses* 18 (4 February 1936).

11. John Crowe Ransom, "An Autumn of Poetry," *Southern Review* 1 (Winter 1936), 609–23.

12. Muriel Rukeyser (hereafter MR), review of William Faulkner's *Dr. Martino and Other Stories* in *New Masses* 11 (22 May 1934).

13. MR, "With Leftward Glances" (review of John Wheelwright's *Rock and Shell* in *New Masses* 12 (10 July 1934).

14. Stanley Burnshaw, letter to Muriel Rukeyser. A copy of this letter exists in MR's papers, Davis, California.

15. MR, *The Life of Poetry* (New York: Current Books/A. A. Wyn, 1949), 123. Hereafter cited as *LP.*

16. MR, *Willard Gibbs* (Garden City, N.Y.: Doubleday, Doran, and Co., 1942).

17. The quotes and diagram are all from *LP,* 53, 178.

18. Rukeyser's comments regarding this understanding were published in

Talks with Authors, Charles T. Madden, ed. (Carbondale: Southern Illinois University Press, 1968), 134–35, 143.

19. Louise Bogan, review of *The Green Wave, New Yorker,* 5 May 1948; Randall Jarrell, review of *The Green Wave, The Nation,* 8 May 1948, 512–13; Richard Eberhart, review of *Selected Poems, New York Times Book Review,* 23 September 1951, 30; R. P. Blackmur, review of *Beast in View, Kenyon Review* 7 (Spring 1945): 339–52.

20. Rukeyser's most frightening brush with the anti-Communist forces came in 1958 when the Westchester County (New York) American Legion began an investigation of her personal and professional background in connection with her teaching appointment at Sarah Lawrence College in Bronxville, New York.

21. MR, *The Orgy* (N.Y.: Coward–McCann, 1965), 9.

22. Bernard Bergonzi in *New York Review of Books,* 22 April 1965, 15; *Time,* 12 March 1965, 103; Denis Johnston in *The Nation,* 15 March 1965, 282.

23. Helen Lynd, "Three Days Off for Puck Fair," *American Scholar* 34 (Autumn 1965): 668.

24. *Partisan Review*'s 1942 attack on MR, "Grandeur and Misery of a Poster Girl," was almost certainly primarily written by Delmore Schwartz (one of the *Review*'s editors at the time), "with political input from [Philip] Rahv and [William] Phillips [the *Review*'s other editors]," according to a former *Partisan* editor, Dwight Macdonald (cited in Kertesz, *The Poetic Vision of Muriel Rukeyser,* 180). MR responded to this in writing at least twice: In *LP* (49) she described indirectly and without naming names a "pattern" of "accusation" and "lie" utilized by literary critics to censure writers. And in her journals from the fall of 1943, housed in the Library of Congress, she disclosed the private anger that she refused to display in public or in her published writings: "Philip Schwartzmore Phillips, the impotent editor/the sad and pathetic bull wishing he were/the bullfighter . . . first they wished to be persecuted & nobody persecuted them; then they wished they could persecute. they were [illegible] but failed again."

25. MR, Review of D. H. Lawrence and others in *New York Times Book Review* (7 May 1967).

26. MR, "Glitter and Wounds, Several Wildnesses," review of Anne Sexton's *The Book of Folly* in *Parnassus* 2 (Fall–Winter 1973): 215.

27. MR, unpublished audio tape. Private collection of William Rukeyser, Davis, California.

28. William Pritchard's review of MR's *Collected Poems* appeared in *Hudson Review* 32, no. 2 (Summer 1979): 260–61. Exhibiting an attitude that has come to be somewhat typical of him, Pritchard dismissed Rukeyser's work of half a century with comments like these: "I had always presumed her [MR] to be one of the great bores of American poetry" and, after quoting from "The Speed of Darkness," "Had enough? Note the spaces and figure out what to do in them. There is also mention of Auschwitz, always helpful for a poet of profundities to bring in." MR mailed a copy of this review without comment to Louise Kertesz, who was then researching *The Poetic Vision of Muriel Rukeyser.* Kertesz interpreted this as an unspoken comment on MR's sometimes startlingly abusive treatment by certain literary critics and reviewers (cited in letter from Louise Kertesz to Kate Daniels).

29. The dissertations include Curtis, "Muriel Rukeyser"; Bonnie Tymorski August, "The Poetic Use of Womanhood: Five Modern American Poets," (New York University, 1978); Marsha Hudson, "A Woman of Words: A Study of Muriel Rukeyser's Poetry" (University of California at Berkeley, 1978).

30. In particular, MR's long portrait poem, "Kathe Kollwitz," published in *The*

Speed of Darkness (New York: Random House, 1968), became heralded by feminist writers and readers for two remarkable lines: "What would happen if one woman told the truth about her life? / The world would split open." Often quoted, these lines eventually were appropriated for the title of one of the earliest feminist anthologies of poetry by women, *The World Split Open: Four Centuries of Women Poets in England and America*, ed. Louise Bernikow (New York: Random House, 1974).

31. Kenneth Rexroth, for example, affirmed that Rukeyser was "certainly a better poet than Gabriela Mistral [who received the Nobel Prize for literature in 1945] or, in fact, than any other woman who has ever received the prize." Quoted in the foreword to Kertesz, *The Poetic Vision of Muriel Rukeyser*, xv.

32. MR's obituary was published in the *New York Times* on 13 February 1980.

33. Grace Schulman, review of *The Collected Poems of Muriel Rukeyser*, *Partisan Review* 47, no. 4 (1980): 36–38.

Chapter 12
"The Buried Life and the Body of Waking": Muriel Rukeyser and the Politics of Literary History

Richard Flynn

It is not surprising that Muriel Rukeyser's work should have been ignored when New Critical and masculinist conceptions of the poetic held sway. She herself complained about "the old criticism (which at the moment is being called, of course, the New Criticism)" for "thinking in terms of static mechanics":

Their treatment of language gives away their habit of expecting units (words, images, arguments) in which, originating from certain premises, the conclusion is inevitable. The treatment of correspondence (metaphor, analogy) is always that of a two-part equilibrium in which the parts are self-contained.[1]

What *is* surprising, however, is that her leading role in the resurgence of feminist poetry and poetics has been so quickly forgotten. In the mid-1970s, Rukeyser's position as the elder statesperson for women's poetry seemed secure. Two major anthologies of women's poetry drew their titles from her work: Florence Howe and Ellen Bass's *No More Masks* (1973) and Louise Bernikow's *The World Split Open* (1974), to which Rukeyser contributed a preface. By contrast, Rukeyser's work was conspicuously absent from mainstream anthologies such as *The Norton Anthology of Modern Poetry* (1973).[2] The publication of *The Collected Poems of Muriel Rukeyser* in 1978 and Louise Kertesz's *The Poetic Vision of Muriel Rukeyser* in 1980 (the year of Rukeyser's death) along with emerging challenges to the canon promised to correct the critical neglect and condescension Rukeyser's work had suffered for decades—as Kertesz pointed out, "In the major works of literary criticism that deal with American poetry from the thirties to the present, Rukeyser has never been given the good part of a chapter."[3]

But by 1993, this promise remained largely unfulfilled. Writing in the

Kenyon Review, Adrienne Rich describes Rukeyser as "our twentieth-century Coleridge; our Neruda; and more":

> . . . her work as a poet continuously addresses the largest questions of her time—questions of power, technology, gender—in many forms: elegies, odes, lyrics, documentary poems, epigrams, ballads, dramatic monologues, biographical narratives[.] What happens when a woman, drawing on every political and social breakthrough gained by women since Dickinson's death in 1886, assumes the scope of her own living to be at least as large as Whitman's? . . .
> What happens? She fails between the cracks. Her books do not have to be burned.[4]

Rich argues that Rukeyser was the "target of extraordinary hostility and ridicule . . . because she was too complicated and independent" to conform to either political or poetic fashions, particularly to "an idea of what a woman's poetry should look like": "neither asexual nor self-diminutizing, she affirms herself as large in body and desire, ambitious, innovative."[5] In addition, Michele S. Ware argues that "because her poetry defied formal and aesthetic conventions, and was openly political as well, questions of poetic value have plagued her career."[6]

In her last collection of poems, *The Gates* (1976), Muriel Rukeyser published the following bit of subversive black humor:

> Not To Be Printed,
>   Not To Be Said,
>   Not To Be Thought
>
> I'd rather be Muriel
> than be dead and be Ariel.[7]

Though this is more of a joke than a poem, its irony in the 1990s is, perhaps, far richer than Rukeyser intended. Rukeyser has received far more attention as a "literary foremother"—Anne Sexton called her "Muriel, the mother of everyone"—than she has as the brilliant, original poet we are now belatedly beginning to read anew.[8] Working primarily in expansive forms and in the traditionally "nonpoetic" form of biography, Rukeyser is far too risky and unusual a poet to fit neatly into our various master narratives of literary history; neither the conservative (and now largely discredited) New Critical version of modernism, nor a "revisionist mythmaking" too narrowly based on identity politics has treated her work with any seriousness when they have treated it at all.[9]

How do we account for the neglect suffered by Rukeyser's poetry in an age when the feminist, political poetry of Adrienne Rich (work that also defies formal and aesthetic conventions) appears in every major anthology? Why has Rukeyser's work continued to be largely ignored or, at best, sparsely represented even in "progressive" anthologies? Why was the work of such an important poet left out of the first edition of *The Heath Anthology of American Literature* (though, happily, it is present in the 1994 second edition)? The answers lie, I think, in Rukeyser's rejection of foregone conclusions, of "two-part equilibrium," of narrowly defined identity politics and essentialism—her rejection of "any/binary system" (*CP*, 510). Committed to processive and open forms, to the blurring of the generic categories poetry and prose (as in her prose-poem biography of Wendell Willkie, *One Life*), Rukeyser is a poet whose work is hard to anthologize.[10] Despite recognition of her centrality by poets as diverse as Rich, Stanley Kunitz, Kate Daniels (who is writing Rukeyser's biography), Sharon Olds, and others, she still receives little recognition in the academy. In order for her work to be considered "major," as I believe it should be, one must look beyond, as well as into, the politics of canon formation and literary history.

Rich's observation that Rukeyser refused to conform to "an idea of what woman's poetry should look like" was apparent from the first poem included in her very first volume *Theory of Flight* (1935). In "Poem Out of Childhood" the twenty-one-year-old poet declared her independence from a circumscribed version of women's poetry by rejecting a model of victimization and suffering for women's poetry. Refusing "the populated cold of drawing-rooms" in favor of "the affirmative clap of truth," she wishes to combine the "full results" of a "rich past" as a "potent catalyst" to negotiate the complex relationship between youth and maturity: "Dialectically our youth unfolds." Subjectivity and identity are a dynamic "ricochetting from thought to thought," conducted increasingly in opposition to a culture insistent on fixity, in which adult persons become "rigid travellers." A child of "Prinzip's year . . . turning at breast / quietly while the air throbs over Sarajevo / after the mechanic laugh of that bullet," Rukeyser struggles in the poem against both the "horrors [that] have approached the growing child" and the fatalistic expectations imposed on a specifically female child by her distant and silent father:

> We grew older quickly, watching the father shave
> and the splatter of lather hardening on the glass,
> playing in the sandboxes to escape paralysis,
> being victimized by fataller sly things.
> "Oh, and you," he said, scraping his jaw, "what will you be?"
> "Maybe : something : like : Joan : of : Arc. . . ."
> (*CP*, 4)

The child's rebelliousness in this poem is one that resists paralysis, victimization, and reductive notions of appropriate gender roles, while at the same time recognizing the cultural pervasiveness in the equation of child and woman, woman and victim. The poem's most famous line, "Not Sappho, Sacco," is often misread as Rukeyser's rejection of an explicitly feminist, "woman-centered tradition" in favor of a more generalized political activism. But it is not Sappho, per se, that the poem rejects; rather, it is a Sappho that too reductively functions as a trope for women's victimization and passivity:

> Sappho, with her drowned hair trailing across Greek waters,
> weed binding it, a fillet of kelp enclosing
> the temples' ardent fruit   :
>
>   Not Sappho, Sacco.
> Rebellion pioneered among our lives,
> viewing from far-off many-branching deltas,
> innumerable seas.
>
>   (*CP*, 3)

This passage demonstrates not a rejection of "gender-specific female experience," but rather a rejection of what Kate Daniels has called "an inevitable, biologically based femininity."[11] Throughout her career, Rukeyser writes from a female body about female experience, but at the same time refuses to buy into notions of "woman's essential nature" that ultimately threaten to prove more useful to the antifeminist backlash than to the goals of feminism.[12] As poems like "The Conjugation of the Paramecium" (*CP*, 436–37) and "The Speed of Darkness" (*CP*, 484–87) indicate, Rukeyser explicitly rejects a poetics based on gender-separatism or an intractable conception of sexual, racial, or class difference. Sexuality (conjugation) "has nothing / to do with / propagating" (since paramecia reproduce "by fission"), but with the exchange of "some bits / of the nucleus of each" when like organisms "lie down beside" one another. For Rukeyser, as for the subject of her finest poem in the "Lives" series, Kathe Kollwitz:

>   . . . bisexuality
> is almost   a necessary factor
> in artistic production . . .
>   (*CP*, 481)

The body, for Rukeyser, is unmistakably material (she is, as Daniels has noted, a pioneer in writing about pregnancy and childbirth in remarkable poems such as "Nine Poems for the Unborn Child" [1948]), but she cautions against giving in to our "Despisals" based on an unwitting reproduction of difference. In "The Speed of Darkness" (1968) she notes the destructiveness of gendered othering ("Whoever despises the clitoris despises the penis / Whoever despises the penis despises the cunt / Whoever despises the cunt despises the life of the child" [*CP*, 484]), which she denotes more fully and extensively in "Despisals" (1973):

> In the human cities, never again to
> despise the backside of the city, the ghetto,
> or build it again as we build the despised
> backside of houses. Look at your own building.
> You are the city.
>
> Among our secrecies, not to despise our Jews
> (that is, ourselves) or our darkness, our blacks,
> or in our sexuality   wherever it takes us
> and we now know we are productive
> too productive, too reproductive
> for our present invention—never to despise
> the homosexual who goes building another
>
> with touch   with touch   (not to despise any touch)
> each like himself, like herself each.
> You are this.
>   In the body's ghetto
> never to go despising the asshole
> nor the useful shit that is our clean clue
> to what we need.   Never to despise
> the clitoris in her least speech.
>
> Never to despise in myself what I have been taught
> to despise.   Not to despise the other.
> Not to despise the *it*.   To make this relation
> with the it   :   to know that I am it.
>   (*CP*, 491–92)

Rukeyser's strategies in this poem are far more subtle than they at first appear, in that they raise questions about language's relations with the body and of the self with others in ways that New Critical precepts tend to disregard. Indeed, the title itself announces the openly rhetorical nature of the poem, but what seems like a speech soon grounds itself in the specifics of material existence and the materiality of language. Furthermore, the "I" speaking the poem (which "speaks" only in the final verse paragraph) reveals itself to be an "it"—paradoxically rejecting the oratorical stance in which a speaking subject addresses "others." As in "The Speed of Darkness," language ostensibly employed for its shock value ("asshole"; "shit") is reread in order to redefine rather than foreclose signification: what is generally despised as "shit," becomes modified by its usefulness—a "dirty" word offering "clean clues." Likewise, the clitoris silenced for so long in medical discourse about women's bodies, is allowed to "speak." Secrecies, silences, the failure to conceive of the subject as existing in a "system of relations" are implicated in the perpetuation and reproduction of the despised "backsides" in the realm of human relations and material conditions. Moreover, the silences perpetuated by notions of poetic decorum are implicated as well. As much as she emphasizes the materiality of the body in her work, Rukeyser also recognizes the materiality of signifiers and that language has material consequences. Poetic language, the poem argues, that restricts itself to the pristine and the decorous in which certain "poetic" subjects are written about in acceptably "poetic" ways serves to circumscribe the possibilities *and the uses* of poetry. The self in the act of despising the "other" performs for an audience without the exchange that touch (or communication) entails. Rukeyser's dilemma, as she describes it in "Waking This Morning" (1973) is that she is trying "to make my touch poems," "moving among the anti-touch people" (*CP*, 491).

Thus, Rukeyser's poetics specifically resists the objectification of human beings, the human body, and poetic language in favor of what Victoria Harrison has termed "relational subjectivity." [13] Discussing the relationship between poetry and science in *The Life of Poetry* (1949), Rukeyser articulates her faith in a poetic (and scientific) *process* that seeks not the "true nature of things," but rather, "a system of relations" (*LP*, 176). Arguing against "two-part equilibrium" and "static" mechanics, she contrasts the "rigid consequences" of Emerson's idealist theory that "language is fossil poetry" with the relational "truth" she had discovered in writing her controversial biography of Willard Gibbs:

If we can think of language as it is, as we use it—as a process in which motion and relationship is always present—as a river in whose watercourse the old poetry and old science are both continually as countless pebbles and stones and boulders rolled, recognized in their effect on the color and the currents of the stream— we will be closer. To think of language as earth containing fossils immediately sets the mind, directs it to rigid consequences. The critics of the "New" group, going on from there, see poetry itself as fossil poetry. It will simplify the amending of these ideas—which tend with more and more of a list of error toward a wretched and static condition, to which nothing is appropriate but anguish and forgiveness—if we dismiss every static pronouncement and every verdict which treats poetry as static.

Truth is, according to Gibbs, not a stream that flows from a source, but an agreement of components. (*LP*, 178)

"Not to despise the other. / Not to despise the *it*.   To make this relation / with the it" underscores her processive (as opposed to static) poetics, in multiple ways. Rukeyser's identification with the other here is not some colonialist project in which the dominated are subsumed or incorporated by the powerful. Neither is it one in which the female body is subsumed under the rubric of androgyny. While "Despisals" explicitly rejects biological essentialism—by refusing, for instance, to link sexuality and gender to reproduction—it nevertheless insists on the importance of the physical body. Like her hero Whitman, Rukeyser sees her poetic identity as one of possibility rooted in the physical. Making poetry, she argues, is a process in which the poet must "enter that rhythm where the self is lost, / where breathing :   heartbeat :   and the subtle music / of their relation make our dance" (*CP*, 303). But that "lost" self is ultimately saved in the process of creating the body of the poem. Attention to the "subtle music of . . . relation" "hasten[s] / us to the moment when all things become / magic, another possibility" potentially restoring to us "the self as vision":

> at all times perceiving,
> all arts all senses being languages,
> delivered of will, being transformed in truth—
> for life's sake surrendering moment and images,
> writing the poem;   in love-making;   bringing to birth.
> (*CP*, 303)

Writing a poem, lovemaking, and bringing to birth all involve the introduction of a third term (reader, lover, child), thus disrupting dualisms and final pronouncements. Countering the New Critical tendency to view the work of art as an autotelic artifact, Rukeyser posits a relational theory of art in which "both artist and audience create, and both do work on themselves in creating . . . the common ground" of the artwork. A work of art is not a stable object or monument, but rather exists only in the intersection of the work with "the consciousness and imagination of artist and audience" (*LP*, 52). In *The Life of Poetry*, Rukeyser presents this relationship in a diagram, which she notes "is false until all the components are shown in motion" (53; see Figure 1 in Chapter 11 of this volume).

Poetic creation, initiated within the rhythms of the body, is completed only in terms of a "system of relations." This is not to deny the relationship of poetry to the material, nor does it deny the specific conditions of the body and the consciousness where poetic creation finds its rhythms. Rather, poetry is "a way to allow people to feel the meeting of their consciousness and the world, to feel the full value of the meanings of emotions and ideas in their relations with each other, and to understand, in the glimpse of a moment, the freshness of things and their possibilities" (*LP*, unpaginated, untitled preface).

Rukeyser sees her relational poetics as a significant resistance to a tradition of "American poetry . . . [as] part of a culture in conflict" (*LP*, 61). This culture created obstacles for those she saw as "the masters of the nineteenth century," Melville, Whitman, and Gibbs.[14] Though Whitman, in particular, seems a major stylistic influence, Rukeyser hoped to succeed in what she felt was Whitman's failed "attempt to realize himself through the ensemble."[15] In her discussion of Whitman's influence in *The Life of Poetry*, we see that the conflicts and richnesses Rukeyser recognizes in Whitman's work are also her own: that "it was harder for Whitman to identify with himself than with the 'you' of the poems" (*LP*, 75); that "out of his own body, and its relation to itself and the sea, he drew his basic rhythms" (80); that "the rhythms of [Whitman's] sequences is film rhythm, the form is montage" (85); and, foremost, that "he is the poet of possibility" (86).

Whitman and Melville, Rukeyser argues, are our "two master-poets" who "stand at the doors of conflict, offering both courage and possibility, and choosing . . . as they lived toward their forms" (86–87). Living and moving *toward* form, rather than working within the constrictions of received form is the hallmark of Rukeyser's poetics. In an interview with Barbara Page, Rukeyser distinguished her work from Elizabeth Bishop's by noting that Bishop "understands form, and I desire it."[16] If, as Suzanne Gardinier has argued, what is "indispensable" about Rukeyser's work is "its contentious, contradictory presence," her revisionary use of the Whitmanian tradition insists on seeing poetry as cultural work, in which contradictions are not merely embraced, but rather are negotiated by the "full-valued" person intervening actively to produce what Walter Kalaidjian has termed "specific critique."[17] Rukeyser says not only, "Very well then, I contradict myself," but recognizes that "my contradictions set me tasks, errands" (*CP*, 532).

These tasks and errands are informed by Rukeyser's lifelong refusal to separate the personal from the political (years before "the personal is political" was to become a feminist axiom). In terms of specific activism, the poems document Rukeyser's involvement in the Scottsboro Trials (where she was arrested in 1933 for "fraternizing with blacks"),[18] her investigation of the Gauley Bridge Union Carbide disaster, her thwarted attempt to cover the antifascist Olympics in Spain, a disillusioning stint with the Office of War Information during World War II, protests against the Vietnam War (including a trip to Hanoi with Denise Levertov and another arrest in Washington), and a trip to Korea as president of PEN to protest the political imprisonment of poet Kim-Chi Ha. But equally important was her personal tenacity and integrity in refusing to succumb to despair in what she called "the first century of world wars" (*CP*, 450). Confronted with the atrocities of the age and with more than her share of personal difficulties, Rukeyser rejected the "mornings I would be more or less insane" and vowed that by making poems she would try to be one "of those men and women / Brave, setting up signals across vast distances, / Considering a nameless way of living, of almost unimagined values":

> To construct peace, to make love, to reconcile
> Waking with sleeping, ourselves with each other,
> Ourselves with ourselves. We would try by any means
> To reach the limits of ourselves, to reach beyond ourselves,
> To let go the means, to wake.
>
> (*CP*, 451)

The difficulty of this task, as well as the simultaneous power and fragility of human and poetic communication, is her major subject from the early "Effort at Speech Between Two People" (1935) through "The Gates" (1976). And her resolute faith that poetry could send "signals across vast distances" is paradoxically the reason her work has been dismissed in a critical climate in which the "authority" of suffering has earned a more esteemed place in the canon. Rukeyser was really no less an auto-biographical poet than Plath or Sexton, but her insistence on looking at her life as "opening out" opposes, often candidly, the destructive mythology of what she called (in response to Plath's death) "The Power of Suicide" (1963). Her question is not "How can I live in the face of human and personal suffering," but, rather, "How shall we speak . . ." (*CP*, 573) "Through acts, through poems, / through our closenesses— / whatever links us in our variousness[?]" ("The Gates," *CP*, 565).

The undisguised sexism of reviewers' attacks on Rukeyser's work (notably those by Philip Rahv, William Phillips, and Delmore Schwartz in the *Partisan Review* and Randall Jarrell in *The Nation*) led her to joke about herself as a "rare battered old she-poet" (*CP*, 532). In a 1974 interview, she says, "one of the attacks on me for writing that Hariot book [*The Traces of Thomas Hariot* (1972)] spoke of me as a she-poet—that I had no business to be doing this and I was broken for a while and looked out the window for while. And then I thought, yes, I am a she-poet. Anything I bring to this is because I'm a woman." [19] Her "rare" ability to withstand such battering is precisely why she offers women's poetry and American poetry in general an alternative to literary victimhood. Her account of the circumstances surrounding her son's birth downplays her suffering as a "bastard mother" (*CP*, 485)—as well as the physical and emotional suffering from an emergency cesarean and involuntary hysterectomy— in order to affirm survival:

> the father's other son
> born three weeks before my child
> had opened the world
> that other son and his father closed the world—
> in my fierce loneliness and fine well-being
> torn apart but with my amazing child
> I celebrated and grieved.
> And before that baby
> had ever started to begin to run
> then Mary said,
> smiling and looking out of her Irish eyes,
> "Never mind, Muriel.
> Life will come will come again
> knocking and coughing and farting at your door."
>   (*CP*, 570)

Later, in the same poem, she rejects Anne Sexton's characterization of her, "Muriel is serene," by affirming herself as "very dark very large / a silent woman this time given to speech." Hearing of Sexton's suicide, she vows to "Speak for sing for   pray for / everyone living in solitary / every living life" (*CP*, 571).

A poem in Rukeyser's last and best book, *The Gates* (1976), "Double Ode," is emblematic of what is most admirable in her work. In her description of its composition she reveals the ways in which she attempts to fuse the qualities of her "two kinds of poems":

I've always thought of two kinds of poems: the poems of unverifiable facts, based in dreams, in sex, in everything that can be given to other people only through the skill and strength by which it is given; and the other kind being the document, the poem that rests on material evidence. So many parts of life have come into my poems. One recent poem that has formed over several years is called "Double Ode." I didn't know fully what the poem was when I began it. I thought it was a poem in which the figures of father and mother were represented both by remembered parents and also by two small black Mexican statues that are on my windowsill. But as I went on with the poem, pieces came into it from my notebooks, pieces from Spain, from the bells in the towers of Florence, from the exile of my son and daughter-in-law during the Vietnam War. I realized that the doubleness of the ode was the doubleness of looking backwards and forwards, that it was not simply a poem of parents but of generations.[20]

The poem draws on principles long present in her work, such as the concept of "the long body" in "Waterlily Fire"—"an idea from India of one's lifetime body as a ribbon of images, all our changes seen in process." [21] Rukeyser recognizes the need to overcome the binary categories received from her parents, in order to redefine her identity in terms of "the long strip of our many / Shapes, as we range shifting through time" (*CP*, 309).

As Rukeyser notes in "The Education of A Poet" and elsewhere, her early notions of poetic form came from observing the pouring of concrete in her father's "building-business." In "Double Ode" the speaker meditates on the pouring of wine and oil into the two separate Mexican figures, representing "mother" and "father"; "male and female"; "east and west." She seeks to move beyond the divisions between the sexes and between generations, and discover "the music of truth," not through denying her specifically "female powers," but by using them fully to "move toward new form":

> I am the poet of the night of women
> and my two parents are the sun and the moon,
> a strong father of that black double likeness,
> a bell kicking out of the bell-tower,
> and a mother who shines and shines his light.
>
> . . . .
>
> Those two have terrified me, but I live,
> their silvery line of music gave me girlhood
> and fierce male prowess and a woman's grave
> eternal double music male and female,
> inevitable blue, repeated evening
> of the two.   Of the two.
>
>   (*CP*, 541)

Rukeyser's anger about her parents' rejection of her (according to Kertesz her father "disinherited her for her political views and 'disobedience' ") [22] is a source of early poetic power:

The song flies out of all of you the song
starts in my body, the song
it is in my mouth, the song
it is pouring the song
wine and lightning
the rivers coming to confluence
in me entire.

                    (*CP*, 542)

Anticipating the birth of her grandson, Jacob, causes the "rise" of "the old dealings: father, mother," but the poet does not move toward a conventional "forgiveness" but toward the "new form" that will enable her to "carry again / all the old gifts and wars":

Black parental mysteries
groan and mingle in the night.
Something will be born of this.

Pay attention to what they tell you to forget.
                    (*CP*, 542)

The poet says, "Farewell to the madness of the guardians," rejecting self-division because "there is no guardian, it is all built in me" (*CP*, 543). Characteristically, however, she ends the poem not with a pronouncement, but with a question: "Do I move toward form, do I use all my fears?" The form Rukeyser wishes to move toward, then, is not the pouring of new wine (or concrete) into old containers, but a new form operating relationally and intergenerationally, not a "two-part equilibrium," but a "system of relations . . . which will be false until all the components are shown in motion" (*LP*, 176–77; 53).

Though "Double Ode" helps Rukeyser to exorcise the "double ghost" of her personal past, she does not end there, but uses the movement toward new form in "The Gates" where she fuses her insights about her personal difficulties, past and present, with her attempt to free Kim-Chi Ha, "the poet in solitary" (*CP*, 566). Reconstructing her personal identity allows her to construct a political identity as one who tries to "walk[   ] the world" and provide a voice for "everyone in solitary." Visiting Kim-Chi's family, she sees his son, the "child of this moment" and compares Kim-Chi's imprisonment "by tyrannies" with the jailing of "my child's father / by his own fantasies." Such universalizing gestures, however, are deconstructed at the end of the poem after the speaker experiences a momentary hope as the prison gates open. Her hopes are dashed when a friend points out to her that the gates have opened to bring in newly arrived political prisoners: "Fool that I am! I had not seen the ropes, / down at their wrists in the crowded rush-hour bus" (*CP*, 572):

> We go down the prison hill. On our right, sheds
> full of people all leaning forward, blown on some ferry.
> "They are the families of the prisoners. Some can visit.
> "They are waiting for their numbers to be called."
> (*CP*, 573)

The speaker recognizes that although her political identity as a poet (and as a representative of other poets) requires her to intercede on Kim-Chi's behalf, her status as a poet does not, in and of itself, assure political action. The tone of the closing lines combines self-criticism with the conviction that she must continue to assume the role of witness. No longer confident in the efficacy of political poetic speech, she nevertheless maintains the necessity of asking insistent questions:

> How shall we venture home?
> How shall we teach each other of the poet?
> How can we meet the judgment on the poet,
> or his execution? How shall we free him?
>
> How shall we speak to the infant beginning to run?
> All those beginning to run?
> (*CP*, 573)

One way is to insist on the tenacity required to look at oneself as a "rare battered old she-poet." Rukeyser's construction of a political voice in search of what Kertesz calls "images of possibility flowing from the dialectical process" [23] may provide us with an example for reconstructing a history of American poetry that reinscribes neither patriarchal master narratives nor the counternarratives of narrow identity politics. A leftist, an activist, a poet who was unafraid to write about women's experiences, a poet unafraid to write from and about the body, Rukeyser rejects both New Critical aestheticism and essentialist notions of identity. An optimist in a depressing century, relentlessly pursuing her impulse to "move toward form . . . to use all [her] fears," she recognizes the power of our cultural constructions of "eternal double music male and female" but insists as a poet on "the rivers coming to confluence / in me entire"

(*CP*, 541–42). We would do well to remember Rukeyser's insistence in "Double Ode": "Pay attention to what they tell you to forget." Paying renewed attention to Rukeyser's exploration of what she calls "the buried life and the body of waking"[24] may allow us to break open the confines of both "conservative" and "liberal" canons that rest on reified versions of male and female, subject and object.

Notes

1. Muriel Rukeyser, *The Life of Poetry* (New York: Current Books/A. A. Wyn, 1949), 177. (Hereinafter cited parenthetically with the abbreviation *LP*.)

2. Florence Howe and Ellen Bass, eds. *No More Masks* (Garden City, N.Y.: Anchor, 1973); Louise Bernikow, ed. *The World Split Open: Four Centuries of Women Poets in England and America* (New York: Random House, 1974); Richard Ellmann and Robert O'Clair, eds., *The Norton Anthology of Modern Poetry* (New York: W. W. Norton, 1973).

3. Louise Kertesz, *The Poetic Vision of Muriel Rukeyser* (Baton Rouge: Louisiana State University Press, 1980), 4.

4. Adrienne Rich, "Beginners," *Kenyon Review* 15 (1993): 16.

5. Ibid., 16–17.

6. Michele S. Ware, "Opening 'The Gates': Muriel Rukeyser and the Poetry of Witness," *Women's Studies* 22 (1993): 297.

7. Muriel Rukeyser, *The Collected Poems of Muriel Rukeyser* (New York: McGraw-Hill, 1978), 558. Subsequent references to Rukeyser's poetry will be cited parenthetically using the abbreviation *CP*, unless otherwise indicated. It is an unfortunate consequence of the deplorable state of contemporary publishing that this volume is out of print; many of the poems will be found in Kate Daniels's excellent edition of Rukeyser's selected poems *Out of Silence: Selected Poems* (Evanston, Ill.: Triquarterly Books, 1992), which includes Rukeyser's major sequences in their entirety. This volume is the best collection of Rukeyser's poetry currently available, though it omits some important work, notably "Double Ode." Another useful contemporary edition of Rukeyser's work is Jan Heller Levi, ed., *A Muriel Rukeyser Reader* (New York: W. W. Norton, 1994), which includes selections from Rukeyser's prose as well as her poetry; however, Levi's practice of excerpting major poetic sequences, rather than presenting them in their entirety, limits its usefulness.

8. Quoted in Kertesz, *Poetic Vision*, 389. Rukeyser can be said to be the "mother" of poets like Anne Sexton primarily because, throughout her career, she spoke openly of specifically female experience. As I shall discuss later, however, Rukeyser's refusal to depict herself as a victim stands in direct contrast to what she called Sexton's "long approaching / . . . over-riding over-falling / suicide" (*CP*, 571). Kertesz astutely contrasts Rukeyser with Sexton and Plath in light of their poems about motherhood:

Rukeyser's poems about motherhood and children are rare in contemporary poetry. They are as exciting as the actualities they deal with: pregnancy, birth, mothering. The reader of contemporary poetry knows the "motherhood" poems of Sylvia Plath and Anne Sexton. These women in several memorable poems detail the horror of bearing and caring for children when one has effectively lost belief in the value of living. Rukeyser's poems about motherhood, as would be expected, are quite different. (225)

9. The sheer volume of Rukeyser's work (as well as the variety of genres she worked within) appears to have been an impediment to a fair assessment of her achievement. An egregious example is Alberta Turner's biographical sketch, "Muriel Rukeyser, 1913–1980," *Dictionary of Literary Biography* 48 (Detroit: Gale, 1986), 369–75, in which she skips from her assessment of *Theory of Flight* (1935) to *The Gates* (1976), remarking that "no profound or startling changes took place in her choice of subjects, themes, or styles during her forty-one years of publishing poetry" (372). Faced with her voluminous and various output, critics have too often chosen to ignore her genuine poetic development by insisting that it doesn't exist—an elision replicated in the anthologies.

10. The recent "rediscovery" of Rukeyser's work in two 1994 American literature anthologies is a case in point. The revised *Heath Anthology of American Literature*, (ed. Lauter et al., 2d ed. [Lexington, Mass.: Heath, 1994] contains eight poems, two of them short excerpts from major poetic sequences, "The Book of the Dead" (1938) and "Ajanta" (1944). Though Cary Nelson's headnote asserts that "The Book of the Dead" is "one of the major poem sequences of American modernism" (2231), the editors have chosen to include only one poem from the twenty-poem sequence. Though the *Norton Anthology of American Literature*, ed. Nina Baym et al., 4th ed. (New York: W. W. Norton and Co., 1994) reprints thirteen poems, the excerpt from "The Book of the Dead" is both shorter and less representative of its documentary method. The *Norton* furthermore places Rukeyser's work in its "American Literature Between the Wars" section, downplaying Rukeyser's significant production and influence during the postmodern period. And yet, it is not only attempts to add Rukeyser's poetry to a developing canon that misrepresent her poetry. In Sandra Gilbert and Susan Gubar's *Norton Anthology of Literature by Women* (New York: W. W. Norton and Co., 1985), there is no representation whatsoever of Rukeyser's left-activist thirties poetry. Alternative canons also serve to silence some of the more radical and innovative aspects of her work, reinscribing binaries that Rukeyser worked her entire life to dismantle.

11. In her essay, "The Demise of the 'Delicate Prisons': The Women's Movement in Twentieth-Century American Poetry," in *A Profile of Twentieth-Century American Poetry*, ed. Jack Myers and David Wojahn (Carbondale: Southern Illinois University Press, 1991), Daniels makes a provocative case for Rukeyser as the "predecessor—or matriarch—of the women's movement in twentieth-century American poetry" (224). Yet one of the most popular accounts of that movement, Alicia Ostriker's *Stealing the Language: The Emergence of Women's Poetry in America* (Boston: Beacon Press, 1986), participates in a too narrowly essentialist account of that movement, based on an identity politics that uncritically accepts the binary thinking Rukeyser argues against her whole career. Consequently, Ostriker devotes many pages to poets like Anne Sexton, but gives only brief mention to Rukeyser, who does not fit so easily into her account. In contrast to Sexton's poems, which too often emphasize the grotesque body in an act of self-loathing, Rukeyser's poems about her body celebrate its expansiveness. For a cogent critique of the limitations of Ostriker's study, see Bonnie Costello, "Writing Like a Woman," *Contemporary Literature* 29 (1988): 305–10.

12. Rukeyser's resistance to the dominant notions of feminine beauty located in the woman's corpse in this poem is elaborated on in "More of a Corpse than a Woman" (1938), where she vows to "destroy the leaden heart / We've a new race to start!" (*CP*, 115)

13. Victoria Harrison, *Elizabeth Bishop's Poetics of Intimacy* (New York: Cambridge University Press, 1993), 17.

14. Muriel Rukeyser, *Willard Gibbs* (Garden City, N.Y.: Doubleday, 1942), 365.

15. Ibid., 362.

16. Barbara Page, "Muriel Rukeyser: 'Breathe-in experience, breathe-out poetry,'" *Vassar Quarterly* 79 (Winter 1979): 11.

17. Suzanne Gardinier, "'A World That Will Hold All the People': On Muriel Rukeyser," *Kenyon Review* 14 (1992): 90; Walter Kalaidjian, *American Culture between the Wars: Revisionary Modernism and Postmodern Critique* (New York: Columbia University Press, 1993), 160.

18. Kate Daniels, "Searching/Not Searching: Writing the Biography of Muriel Rukeyser," *Poetry East* 16-17 (Spring/Summer 1985): 82.

19. Muriel Rukeyser, "Craft Interview with Muriel Rukeyser," in *The Craft of Poetry: Interviews from The New York Quarterly*, ed. William Packard, (Garden City, N.Y.: Doubleday, 1974), 175–76.

20. Muriel Rukeyser, "The Education of a Poet," in *The Writer on her Work*, ed. Janet Sternburg (New York: W. W. Norton, 1980), 226–27.

21. Muriel Rukeyser, *Waterlily Fire: Poems 1935–1962* (New York: Macmillan, 1963), 200.

22. Kertesz, *Poetic Vision*, 90.

23. Ibid., 348.

24. Rukeyser, *Body of Waking* (New York: Harper, 1958), 106. Rukeyser's decision to include "poems" from *One Life* (her Willkie biography) seems to have taken the place in *The Collected Poems* of the selection (and revision) of these poems as they were included in the volume *Body of Waking*. In any event, I can find nothing resembling the poem titled "Body of Waking" in the *Collected Poems*. Thus, I give the original volume's citation.

Part VIII
Gwendolyn Brooks
(1917–   )

Chapter 13
Whose Canon? Gwendolyn Brooks: Founder at the Center of the "Margins"

Kathryne V. Lindberg

Black Poet, White Critic

A critic advises
not to write on controversial subjects
like freedom or murder
but to treat universal themes
and timeless symbols
like the white unicorn.
A white unicorn?—Dudley Randall,

"You can say anything you want about black women"—

or so said a poet-critic colleague of mine when I mentioned that I was
writing an essay on Gwendolyn Brooks. This could be a green light or a
roadblock. Except for the solipsist or the most *entitled,* either by unexamined literary expertise or a valid license, as it were, to represent *the*
BLACK WOMAN, it is not a simple declaration of fact. Let us not
quibble—but mustn't we profoundly quibble?—over "can" and "may,"
over competence and permission. Depending on the race, gender, and
politics of speaker and auditor, the force and function of the irony of my
colleague's statement cut in rather different directions. Did s/he mean
"go right ahead, *you* can be trusted?"—issuing, as it were, a *carte blanche.*
Did he/she mean that black women poets are fair game, while black
male critics remain untouchable? Did s/he mean that, given the spread
of interest and jaggedness of identity politics, the playing field is level
enough for even a professional (can't one, in these days of overidentification, silently assume the modifiers "white" and "androcentric" if not

"male"?) reader of, say, Ezra Pound to cross gender or color lines?[1] Or did s/he mean, rather as Gwendolyn Brooks might have coached, to finish that half sentence with a resounding, "but *we* don't have to listen!!!"

Putting aside my own double or treble academic (dis-)qualifications, is Gwendolyn Brooks's own license to represent *the* BLACK WOMAN current and negotiable? Some, including most black feminist literary academicians, who, not without evidence, find her critical comrades and male-defined position troubling, would say "no" or "no longer." While such issues will dance around the margins of my text, I do not presume to choose or deny representativeness, acceptable blackness or whiteness, and/or proper feminism. Instead, guided by the later poetry and programmatic statements of Gwendolyn Brooks, I hope to open certain issues that seem confused, yet hardly muted by recent academic appropriations of black women's writing and the legitimation routines that authorize such de- and recanonizations.[2] I *set up* this essay, not assertively to apologize for what may be deduced as/reduced to my whiteness or womanhood, but with the hope that I am a better ironist than those who would mark the limits of (my) authority with the same assurance as they/ we (the old New Critics of poetry and culture) were wont to remark its limitlessness. Instead, I wish to open, in what I hope will be a challenging way, issues of the poetics and reception of Gwendolyn Brooks since her 1967 turn away from white literary mainstream values and publication.

From the beginning of her poetic career, Brooks has shown an acute consciousness of and responsibility regarding issues of representation, audience, and authority. The first black woman to receive a Pulitzer Prize, trumpeted for the longest time by the white liberal establishment as a prodigy for adding just enough political correctness while observing strictures of form, she has always addressed and never easily hierarchized the treble joy/oppression of womanhood, poverty, and blackness.[3] While it should be noted that adoption and emphasis of this last category, "blackness," as against Negro-ness, marks a momentous shift in Brooks's work, it is somewhat inaccurate to rend her corpus in two or three: into a before, during, or after the Black Power and Black Arts moment(s), or, for that matter, a complete shift in focus from the oppression of women to support for what looks to some like the simply misogynist and nationalist Black Arts tradition.[4] Brooks, I contend, did not radically change her poetic themes. Even obvious modulations in her line and other organizing musical techniques are, on the whole, unremarkable. After having cut a figure in several strict verse forms, she took a typically modern and American turn to free verse, and moved closer to the ordinary language of her elected community. Certainly the texture of her poems, her palette of allusions and affiliations, has shifted from the white Anglo-American canon, but *In the Mecca* (1968), which Haki Madhubuti plausibly claims " 'blacked' its way out of the National Book Award" (*RFPO*, 21), is as remarkable for its range of verse forms as for its direct treatment of race and class oppression.[5] Nevertheless, black and/or feminist critics have tended to narrow her politics to one aspect of the struggle, while white mainstream poetry reviewers have dismissed her apparently less artful later style as flat and too political. There is no reason to assume that a particular political commitment must turn one toward or away from artistic experiment or accomplishment; but, perhaps in part because (white, mostly male, academic) critics have been so busy excusing or obscuring (bad) politics in the name of high art, they have not trained themselves or prepared us to hear music in the heteroglossia that assaults the urban eye and ear. Questions about Brooks's abandonment of artistry persist, framed as the opposition between craft and commitment. In a 1969 interview by George Stavros for *Contemporary Literature*, Brooks answers charges about having "abandoned lyric simplicity for an angrier, more polemical voice" with

> Those are the things that people say who have absolutely no understanding of what's going on and no desire to understand. No, I have not abandoned beauty, or lyricism, and I don't consider myself a polemical poet. I'm a black poet, and I write about what I see, what interests me, and I'm seeing new things. (*RFPO*, 151)

Brooks has always questioned, and, in the mid-sixties, she articulately and consistently refused the limits placed on the reputed natural "clowning" or super respectability of "colored people." If only by implication later made explicit, her earliest work also questioned the exceptional "race" and "gender" writers—artists, musicians, sports figures, politicians, or "exception Negroes" in general—when she literalized the politics and epistemology of *representation*. As teacher, critic, and inspirational speaker, Brooks increasingly began to use her position as respected artist to give voice to a solidarity that begins to resolve the double bind of a black woman artist who would be heard as something other than victim of or exile from her race and class. Awareness of divided and divisive loyalties to a conventional (white, European, Aristotelian, or simply "decorous") notion of art and to a constricted notion of her "People" was hardly born with the sixties. It is fitting that Brooks's most significant mentor, Langston Hughes (whom she first heard in the church where she also first heard and met James Weldon Johnson), gave such clear voice to his own dilemma as a Negro artist.[6] In "The Negro Artist and the Racial Mountain" (*The Nation*, 1926), Hughes, whose own metaphors are underwritten by W. E. B. Du Bois's "double consciousness" as well as by the strictures of *The Crisis* against which the poet rebels, sounds a condition that Brooks would almost of necessity turn into a poetic theme:

The road for the serious black artist, then, who would produce a racial art is most certainly rocky and the mountain is high. Until recently he received almost no encouragement for his work from either white or colored people. . . .

The Negro artist works against an undertow of sharp criticism and misunderstanding from his own group and unintentional bribes from the whites. "O, be respectable, write about nice people, show how good we are," say the Negroes. "Be stereotyped, don't go too far, don't shatter our illusions about you, don't amuse us too seriously. We will pay you," say the whites.[7]

With full knowledge that, as a mainstream Negro writer, her representations were going to be (designated) more representative—if not more "equal"—than others, Brooks worried both how blacks (then *Negroes*) should be represented in literature, and how whites misread, cruised, or otherwise misused *the* black experience—which was hardly monolithic. *Annie Allen*, the 1949 collection that secured her the Pulitzer, shows Brooks's manifold concern about how blackness is constructed and perceived from outside.[8] Even if she sometimes too-much-protests a bourgeois respectability she would later dismiss, a poem like "I love those little booths at Benvenuti's" assaults certain images and expectations of "Bronzeville" in the minds of white readers and spectators. Brooks exposes and returns the oppressive (white male) gaze of outsiders, and she does so by temporarily adopting the outsider's or suburbanite's perspective. In this way, she more than slightly confuses subject looking and object seen, "they" and "one." But by the same token, we get a clear sense of "us *versus* them":

> They get to Benvenuti's. There are booths
> To hide in while observing tropical truths
> About this—dusky folk, so clamorous!
> So amorous,
> So flatly brave!
> Boothed-in, one can detect,
> Dissect.
>
> . . . .
> But how shall they tell people they have been
> Out Bronzeville way? For all the nickels I
> Have not bought savagery or defined a "folk."
>
> The colored people will not "clown."
>
> The colored people arrive, sit firmly down.
> Eat their Express Spaghetti, their T-bone steak.
> Handling their steel and crockery with no clatter,
> Laugh punily, rise, go firmly out of the door.
>
> (*WGB*, 110–11)

Maud Martha (1953), Brooks's lyric novel and her only published long fiction, not only focused on what it means to be black Maud (as against golden Helen, her sister), but it also turns the tables on what it means to be reduced—or is it inflated?—to a synecdoche for one's race.[9] By making one white visitor to the black community representative of his race, Brooks again makes the reader look at the spectator who, because he cannot step outside his whiteness, does not recognize himself as an intruder. We don't get inside the head of the visitor, any more than we are exactly in the booth with the "good view" at Benvenuti's, but Maud fixes the visiting white man by fully elaborating the ways she protects her personal space. Long before Black Power declarations of racial self-definition, Brooks more than once subtly makes visible the assumptions that underwrite white control over the figurative power of racial interaction. Maud Martha refuses simply, as Brooks would later say, to worship whiteness or whine about race. If blackness and femaleness can be essentialized, whiteness still demands individuation: when was the last time a white man was allowed to speak for all white men, or even all American white men? Yet long since *we* ceased giving over the power of voicing the body politic to king or president, there persists a disturbance in representation/representativeness by which black people—*the* racial and, I would add, sexual other(s)—are somehow fixed as slates upon which "whiteness" (an absent or *understood* adjective for American individualism) can be written in almost invisible chalk. Here one of Brooks's formulas, from *Primer for Blacks*, intervenes to help us read *Maud Martha*:

> The conscious shout
> of all that is white is
> "It's Great to be white."
> The conscious shout
> of the slack in Black is
> "Its Great to be white."
> Thus all that is white
> has white strength and yours.
>
> (*PB*, 9)

In a discussion of the "Great" or Emersonian tradition of American literature and scholarship (exemplified by "The American Scholar"), Toni Morrison hints something of the threat that African American (read Brooks's BLACK?) questioning or wrenching of individualism and self-determination, the very lynchpins of American man- or personhood, can have. Morrison says:

[A]utonomy, authority, newness and difference, absolute power not only become the major themes and presumptions of American literature, but . . . each one is made possible by, shaped by, activated by a complex awareness and employment of a constituted savagery, that provided the staging ground and arena for the elaboration of the quintessential American identity.[10]

The self constituted as and by Maud Martha, one of the ordinary "kitchenette people," is made—and assertively remakes herself—not from savagery but from (black) submission and other undistinguished maternal and female matter. Here and in other instances, Brooks manages at least to tweak the system to which Morrison refers—and, further, one might add, to work this revolution surgically within tight lyric confines. At moments, her destructive meditations are not wholly unlike Dickinson's persistently private explosions. But Brooks is always aware of "the People" and her public; that is, of race, of being racialized, and of the need to seize the power and tools of representation.

It is, I should think, customary enough for black academics and poets to be called upon—usually from "above"—to represent *their* race. Brooks reassigns this honor, or curse, to Maud Martha. Her novelistic/ autobiographical answer, painted in miniature from the inside of Maud Martha's experience as this very difference in persona, at once recalls Du Bois's prerogative (setting aside for work his cultivated representative status) of determining the level of his social interactions with whites.[11] But Brooks also subtly undresses and redresses the dynamics of rhetorical power differentials by making a young white male classmate who calls on Maud intrude into a community that, he is made to assume, can only feel blessed by his presence and/or whiteness. We readers are thus ironically privy to—and, in some cases, the butt of the dramatic irony of— Maud Martha's educated perspective on race matters:

> though she liked Charles, though she admired Charles, it was only at the high school that she wanted to see Charles.
> This was no Willie or Richard or Sylvester coming to call on her. Neither was she Charles's Sally or Joan. She was the whole "colored" race, and Charles was the personalization of the entire Caucasian plan. . . .
> What was this she was feeling now? Not fear, not fear. A sort of gratitude! It sickened her to realize it. As though Charles, in coming, gave her a gift.
> Recipient and benefactor.
> It's so good of you.
> You're being so good. (*MM*, 17–18).

If one can safely assume that the readership of *Maud Martha* included a large number of white integrationists of several stripes, Brooks has brilliantly diagnosed, announced, and reversed a disturbance in representation by which white folks are accustomed, as discrete individuals, to identifying individuals who can stand for the group—of colored, Negro, black, other folk(s).[12] Brooks stages, with ironic equanimity (as against Maud's expected Negro gratitude or feminine reserve) a practical encounter that tests liberal notions of accommodation: "Here was the theory of racial equality about to be put into practice, and she only hoped she would be equal to being equal" (*MM*, 17).

If in 1953 Brooks was content to have Maud Martha analytically voice the options open to an ordinary woman—even an "old black gal" (*MM*, 34)—she was audacious enough to create a character who could create herself within the limits of her male-identified world of marital banality:

> To create—a role, a poem, picture, music, a rapture in stone: great but not for her.
> What was wanted was to donate to the world a good Maud Martha. That was the offering, the bit of art, that could not come from any other.
> She would polish and hone that. (*MM*, 22) [13]

Brooks's 1967 announcement of a different public role for herself as poet, along with her embrace of the evolving role of New Black, might have been impossible and surely would not have been very forceful if she had not threaded a consistent meditation on racial and artistic self-construction—and reconstructions of racial and sexual otherness—through her work.

Brooks has always addressed and continues to address difficult issues, including those often decorously silent intimate traumas of abortion, color caste, domestic abuse, alienation, and motherhood in poverty. Defiant in the face of a painful history of racist lies and false consciousness that refuses to yield a "useable past," she has actively fashioned models of personal and communal dignity as poetic blueprints for cultural survival. An early poem like "the mother" (*A Street in Bronzeville*, 1945) adumbrates her later focus on rejected, imperiled, and criminalized urban youth, even as it admits of wildly different ethos and messages: from an anti-abortion plea to a manifesto of women's choice and self-determination. This poem in particular continues to garner classroom and critical response for its complex deconstruction(s) of subjectivity and/or the androcentric lyric tradition. As Barbara Johnson has noted, Brooks bends the genre of apostrophe by addressing the literally doubly victimized, the imaginatively doubly redeemed, and inextricably compounds nonmother and unborn as agent and object of abortion.[14] Brooks manages to convey the force of desire, regret and affirmation without sentimentalizing the role of mother or erasing the horrors of unrealized pasts and futures:

ABORTIONS will not let you forget.
You remember the children you got that you did not get,
The damp small pulps with a little or with no hair,
The singers and workers that never handled the air.
You will never neglect or beat
Them, or silence or buy with a sweet.

(*WGB*, 5)

After that first stanza, which complicates the ontological and epistemological categories generically fixed by personal lyric and the address of
apostrophe, the subject—and here both positions of aborted relationships share objecthood and agency—switches from the general or collo-
quial "you" to an only more apparently fixed "I" that promises but fails
to represent a single point of view or viable position, if only because it is
addressed both to the unborn and the unknowing audience. Characteristically, Brooks both invites and inhibits identification as well as easy
judgment from above and outside:

Believe that even in my deliberateness I was not deliberate.
Though why should I whine,
Whine that the crime was other than mine?
Since anyhow you are dead.
Or rather, or instead,
You were never made.

(*WGB*, 5–6)

If Brooks there achieves in an exemplary fashion the virtually impossible task of at once humanizing and equivocating over victim and
agent—of making present, speaking as and to, those who definitively
never were—she elsewhere works a similarly undecidable agency into
the public arena of city streets and community. In fundamental ways, she
has come increasingly to violate fixed definitions of gender and race
roles as well as systems of representation and cultural reproduction. Perhaps an extreme case, *Riot: A Poem in Three Parts* (1969), gives life to the
humor and horror of needs denied and escape routes blocked. I can only
skim the first poem, which is, granted, a long cry from the second, "The
Third Sermon on the Warpland," with its phoenix rise of "A woman is
dead. / Motherwoman. / She lies among the boxes . . ." (*TD*, 12). Still,
the sequence's beginning, beginning with the source and thrust of its
epigraph, indicates the range of Brooks's irony and her complex identification with the rioters:

> A riot is the language of the unheard.
> —Martin Luther King, Jr.

John Cabot, out of Wilma, once a Wycliffe,
all whitebluerose below his golden hair,
wrapped richly in right linen and right wool,
almost forgot his Jaguar and Lake Bluff;

. . . .

Because the "Negroes" were coming down the street.

Because the Poor were sweaty and unpretty
(not like Two Dainty Negroes in Winnetka)
and they were coming toward him in rough ranks.
In seas. In windsweep. They were black and loud.
And not detainable. And not discreet.

. . . .

John Cabot went down in the smoke and fire
and broken glass and blood, and he cried "Lord!
Forgive these nigguhs that know now that they do."
(*TD,* 5–6)

Long before *Riot,* and before the events therein ironically recorded from within and without the virtual reality of an old negritude, which marks its fall from grace by its dialect apostrophe to "nigguhs," was swept over by a wave of unaccommodating black victims-turned-agents of potentially constructive destruction, Brooks's poetry had italicized and complicated b/Blackness. She had always been hard on Negroes with class pretensions, those who would marry or buy their way into whiteness. She did not abandon the intellectual or literal neighborhood of working-class blacks for the suburbs of academic or other prestige. And beyond the empirics of such community identification, her works explicitly warn of the various temptations to escape or explain away the racism that some black bourgeois, not to mention the intellectuals, refuse to acknowledge. Again, a set piece from *Maud Martha* is particularly revelatory. Maud, at the beauty parlor, thinks she has heard Miss Ingram, a cosmetics saleswoman (about whom Maud "wondered if . . . she knew that in the 'Negro group' there were complexions whiter than her own"), say, "I work like a nigger to earn a few pennies." Seeing no reaction, Maud thinks she must have been wrong. As it turns out, Sonia Johnson, the beautician, failed to react because *she* was certainly not a "nigger," and *she* knew what the word meant:

these words like "nigger" don't mean to some of these here white people what our people *think* they mean. Now, "nigger," for instance, means to them something bad, or slavey-like, or low. They don't mean anything against me. I'm a Negro, not a "nigger." Now, a white man can be a "nigger," according to their meaning for the word, just like a colored man can. So why should I go getting all stepped up about a thing like that? (*MM*, 141) [15]

Therein, Brooks not only underscores the sometimes illusory power of renaming, she insists on a solidarity that will later manifest itself in a refusal to condemn the New Blackness of the sixties that the author behind Maud—who was, after all, a "plain ol' black gal"—might have been expected to reject. But, really only those who failed to read the bold code could have expected that!

Before the 1967 official D Day—or *b*/Black day—her poetry had more than once occasioned the negative commentary of white critics and, in at least one hilarious—or is it scary?—case, broadcasters, who found her language assaultive and her subject matter too frank. Indeed, Brooks's famed "ordinary Negroes" were extraordinarily aware of being positioned within and without their poetic sketches and larger historical and literary traditions. One incident on the road to her ultimate declaration of independence from mainstream aesthetic strictures and white bourgeois values is worth noting. It too is a reflection and public opening on her earlier work. I have in mind the controversial half-life and musical resurrection of "of De Witt Williams on his way to Lincoln Cemetery" (*A Street in Bronzeville*, 1945; *SP*).

In 1962 a Chicago radio station, WNEW, on which Brooks had decades earlier read her poem, banned Oscar Brown Jr.'s musical rendering of "Elegy of a Plain Black Boy" on the grounds that the recurrent phrase "a plain black boy," echoed in and from Brooks's poem, would offend Negroes and violate strictures against mixing politics into art.[16] Of her twenty-year-old poem, updated with a direct address to the new ban on "black," she submitted the assaultive defense that explains her repositioned writing Subject and subject matter; thus: " 'the life and death of a pitiful yet proud and lip-out-thrusting, chest announcing youth.' " [17] Recall for a moment De Witt Williams, as he visits in death the haunts of a youth that, after Brooks's treatment cannot remain simply ill-spent. There is no small freight of literariness in the parody of the interstate journey of Lincoln's bier recorded in Whitman's "When Lilacs Last in the Dooryard Bloomed" and the skewed identification effected by the substitution of "Nothing but a plain black boy" for "Coming for to carry *me* home" of the spiritual's second line:

He was born in Alabama.
He was bred in Illinois.

He was nothing but a
Plain black boy.

Swing low swing low sweet sweet chariot.
Nothing but a plain black boy.

Drive him past the Pool Hall.
Drive him past the Show.
Blind within his casket,
But maybe he will know.

                              (*WGB*, 23)

I do not mean to diminish the history and changes of political position and identification that intervene between the Brooks(es) of the forties, early sixties, and the near past; surely her poetry and programmatic prose would not permit such easy moves. Nevertheless, her interrogations of race, class, and gender remain both complex and in revisionary conversation with several traditions of which she has become part. At one point, Brooks characterizes her post-1967 work as a change of ethos and attitude, from supplication to self-possession:

> Much of the work that preceded the days of considerable black fire belongs in a category I call "condition literature." You remember, in "Song of Myself," Walt Whitman loves animals because they do not tirelessly "whine about their condition." A good many of us who preceded the pioneering influence of Baraka did a lot of poetic, dramatic, and fictional whining. And a lot of that was addressed to white people. We sensed ourselves crying "UP" to them. "Help us," we seemed to cry. We were fascinated by the sickness of the black condition. (*CC*, 5)

I would qualify Brooks's self-corrective dismissal, in that a great deal of what she did involved more than whining or satisfying the guilt, curiosity, imagination of a white audience.[18] But, she does not need me to save or choose her most effective work. It has had impact and influence, and she herself has revisited it in later poems and anthologies.

Even in the most declarative or rhetorical mood, her poems remain, according to her announced non-Western poetics of change and ad hoc utility, in-process and revisionary in their focus on youth and popular misconceptions about inner-city blight. Perhaps the occasional or instructive poems titled or subtitled "Sermon," "Dedication," "Preachment" do not so much conceal as proclaim the irony and distance out of which she configures an identification with, and encouragement of, what are now generations of energetically self-destructive but infinitely promising inner-city young people. If literary allusions and artful oscillations between third-person narrative and internal monologue are more pronounced in *Annie Allen, Maud Martha,* and peak in *In the Mecca,* such poems as "Primer for Blacks" and "To Those of My Sisters Who Kept Their Naturals" (*Primer for Blacks—Three Preachments,* 1991) and the pair "The Chicago Picasso" (one of *Two Dedications,* 1967) and "The Chicago Picasso, 1986" at once recall her earlier performances (sometimes directly citing and renewing earlier poems) and bear witness to New Black consciousness. "Requiem Before Renewal," the Third Preachment in *Primer for Blacks,* names her prospective yet revisionary strategy. In this vein, "The Black Stone Rangers, I, As Seen by Disciplines" [not disciples] (1968) asserts faith in black self-determination:

> There they are.
> Thirty at the corner.
> Black, raw, ready.
> Sores in the city
> that do not want to heal.
>   (*WGB,* 416)

If the Blackstone Rangers were her special link to an allegedly "sick" or stagnant pool of alienated youth talent, the occasional poems Brooks has written as poet laureate of Illinois (named so after Carl Sandburg, in 1968) and for Mayor Harold Washington and Chicago elaborate the general empowerment that comes from an unblinking recognition of potential behind the bleakest facades. "A Hymn to Chicago," in the self-published pamphlet *Mayor Harold Washington and Chicago the "I Will" City* (1983), locates strength and beauty even as it "italicizes" a harsher truth:

> This city mixes garbage and stars. This city seems able
> to make a carol out of what has been obscure. . . .
> . . . This city,
> for all its age, is alive with youth-music and youth-fragrance,
> the music and green and fragrance youth knows how to
> manufacture for itself, cannot give to others, cannot describe.
> Need I italicize our truth
> that this city
> is imperfect, that within it
> crime, race injustice, and cunning prowl and have prowled
>
> · · · · · · · · · — · · · · · · · · · · ·
> Italics emphasize. They do not commend
> rejection of all that surrounds
>   (*MHW,* 7)

Indeed, it seems to me—*pace* editors like Haki Madhubuti who would make her post-1967 position univocally freeze in heroic portraits of male revolutionary race heroes (including his former self, Don L. Lee, and the Rangers who made up her first workshop gang) and mostly feminist critics who lament this alleged fixity—that Brooks remains open to change and self-re-creation. Haki Madhubuti's Third World Press, which recently reissued the out-of-print *Maud Martha*, publishes an extensive and somewhat self-duplicating list of Brooks's poems, whose reprints are often subtle recastings, to which I refer you for proof of Brooks's range and coherence of vision.[19] Perhaps her consciousness, evident in her poetic penetration of the more-than-victim *versus* assailant attitude of young gangsters and other marginalized black urban youth, is not the unification or overcoming of Du Bois's "double consciousness" in a monolithic and potentially obsolete Black Power pose, but a long unfolding of the contradictory interpellation of blackness, an open call, if you will, from poet to people that continues to mark internal differences, mock the mastering white (if not also the male) gaze, and celebrate the ironies that empower the disempowered by a chiding celebration of the honorific name, the Black Magic, that used to be a curse.[20] Again, I will not quote, but I suggest you read, the full text of this short "Preachment"; the following excerpt from the first, third, and eighth (final) stanzas of "Primer for Blacks" suggests Brooks's inclusiveness and her strategic separatism:

Blackness
is a title,
is a preoccupation,
is a commitment Blacks
are to comprehend—
and in which you are
to perceive your Glory.

. . . .
The word Black
has geographic power,
pulls everybody in:
Blacks here—
Blacks there—
Blacks wherever they may be.
And remember, you Blacks, what they told you—
remember your Education:
"one Drop—one Drop
maketh a brand new Black."
Oh mighty Drop.

—And because they have given us kindly
so many more of our people

 . . . .

All of you—
you COLORED ones,
you NEGRO ones,
those of you who proudly cry
"I'm half INDian"—
those of you who proudly screech
"I'VE got the blood of George WASHington in
   MY veins—
ALL of you—
      you proper Blacks,
you half-Blacks,
you wish-I-weren't Blacks,
Niggeroes and Niggerenes.

You.

                    (*PB*, 9–11) [21]

As we shall see, more than her verse form or topics, Brooks decisively changed the force of her irony against the political and cultural status quo that quite systematically dictates standards and undervalues black accomplishment—except when the "natural," blues, rap, or Harlem enjoy temporary renaissance. Consonant with the changing literary and literal politics of the young writers and activists of the Black Arts Movement, in particular the position expressed and the scene captured in Larry Neal's and LeRoi Jones's *Black Fire* (1968), Brooks deliberately changed the composition, site, and invited response of her audience. After the uprisings of the mid-sixties and in the wake of an increasingly elitist or accommodationist civil rights movement, Brooks adopted certain practices and principles from her younger radical colleagues; she also began publishing at small black presses and working with groups of younger and almost exclusively black inner-city young people. Exemplary here is *Jump Bad: A New Chicago Anthology* (Broadside Press, 1971), the anthology of poetry, short prose pieces, and programmatic criticism edited or "presented" by Brooks. This book grew out of the community poetry workshops, formal and informal, Brooks *led*—a word she avers in this context—in Chicago beginning in 1967. Brooks's introduction tells something of her own conversion experience as well as the composition of her audience. Again, though, "audience" is also not quite right, since she is auditor as much as speaker; pupil as well as teacher of a group of young poets and performers from the "literary-minded among the Blackstone Rangers," "teen 'Gangsters,'" whom she met at "the First Presbyterian Church on the South Side" (*JB*, 10). None of the irony of her position is lost on Brooks: middle-aged Lady Pulitzer up against the first members of Kuumba (founded by Val Gray Ward), who were some *Baaad* young folks, including Don L. Lee,"who had already published 'Think Black'" (*JB*, 10), and Sonia Sanchez, whose poem "We a BadDDD People" and anthology *We Be Word Sorcerers* (1973) intertextually and nominally honor Brooks's first broadside for Broadside Press, "We Real Cool," a poem to which we shall return.[22]

It is with an understanding of her own story, even here subsumed to black *history*, that Brooks delineates the position, predisposition, and even the grammatical prepositions that define her "New Black" poets, and herself as a (new) black poet:

> With the arrival of these people my neatly-paced life altered almost with a jerk. Never did they tell me to "change" my hair to "natural." But soon I did. Never did they tell me to open my eyes to look about me. But soon I did. Never did they tell me to find them sane, serious, substantial, superseding. But soon I did. . . .
>
> Incidentally, the question of my status, my position, (was I or was I not a Teacher, a Workshop Ruler?) was soon a gentle joke. I "taught" nothing. I told them, almost timidly, what I knew, what I had learned from European models (well, Langston Hughes too!) And they told me without telling me that the European "thing" was not what they were about. . . .
>
> Many of these black writers are now involved in an exciting labor, a challenging labor. . . . They are blackening English. Some of the results are effective and stirring. Watch for them.
>
> True black writers speak *as* blacks, *about* blacks, *to* blacks. (*JB*, 11–12)

Brooks describes her first encounter with the "New Black[ness]" of such young black poets and playwrights as LeRoi Jones and Ron Milner at the Writers' Conference at Fisk University in 1967 as her full public transformation from Negro to a Black: "It frightens me to realize that, if I had died before the age of fifty, I would have died a 'Negro' fraction" (*RFPO*, 45). Rather than gloat or despair about her distance and irrelevance from the young who would just barely respect anyone's mainstream credentials, she listened and began bridging the "generation gap," which, Brooks came to insist, never (should have) existed among blacks. Her account of this event is worth revisiting at some length, if only because *we* might wish to heed her cautionary note about appropriation embedded in her own self-effacing enthusiasm for the male revolutionary poet-heroes performing in Nashville:

> Until 1967 my own blackness did not confront me with a shrill spelling of itself. I knew that I was what most people were still calling a "Negro." . . .
>
> Suddenly there was New Black to meet. . . . I had been "loved" at South Dakota

State College. Here I was coldly Respected. . . . Imamu Amiri Baraka, then "LeRoi Jones," was expected. He arrived in the middle of my own offering, and when I called attention to his presence there was jubilee in Jubilee Hall. . . .

Up against the wall, white man! was the substance of the Baraka shout, at the evening reading he shared with fierce Ron Milner among intoxicating drumbeats, heady incense and organic underhumming. Up against the wall! And a pensive (until that moment) white man of thirty or thirty three abruptly shot himself into the heavy air, screaming "Yeah! *Yeah!* Up against the wall, Brother! KILL 'EM ALL! KILL 'EM ALL!"

I thought that was interesting.

There is indeed a new black today. He is different from any the world has known. He's a tall-walker. Almost firm. By many of his own *brothers* he is not understood. And he is understood by *no* white. Not the wise white; not the Schooled white; not the Kind white. Your *least* pre-requisite toward an understanding of the new black is an exceptional Doctorate which can be conferred only upon those with the proper properties of bitter birth and intrinsic sorrow. I know this is infuriating, especially to those professional Negro-understanders. (*RFPO*, 84–85)

Brooks's poems as well as their means of publication and distribution changed from styles acceptable to the big New York commercial houses to those possible only in workshops, readings, and small press anthologies. In the sixties, the lines of black (and perhaps not only b/Black) poetic communication were strong and strongly interwoven among many community and political organizations and movements.[23] The circuit Brooks entered was at least circumjacent to the work and workers of SNCC (Student Nonviolent Coordinating Committee), SCLC (Southern Christian Leadership Conference), the Black Panther Party, and other groups that had been literal and figurative fellow travelers on freedom marches and voter registration drives. I do not mean to project sixties nostalgia onto a complex scene whose coalitions were sometimes rather costly, but black and/or revolutionary unity during that period has been nearly erased by interested revisionary histories from several sides.[24] Further, not to expose any secrets that Brooks and more than one black public intellectual continue to reveal, the easy flow of artists and information from performance venues as varied as black colleges (whether traditionally Negro Southern colleges or inner-city state community colleges and universities), organized or informal youth groups (even "gangs"), churches and prisons, and public commemorative occasions (especially in cities with black leaders) continues. Such networks are always somewhat fragile, as capable of excluding members on account of revolutionary purity or Puritanism as being co-opted by critics in search of authenticity, the academic descendants, perhaps, of "professional Negro-understanders." [25]

In any case, consistent with Brooks's 1967 embrace of "New Black," she offered *Report from Part One*, her autobiography-in-process, long awaited by Harper and Row, to Dudley Randall's Broadside Press. In *Broadside Memories: Poets I Have Known* (1975), his memoir and celebratory program of the press's first ten years, Dudley Randall's account of her association with Broadside Press neatly indicates the range and redirection of her work enabled by this change of publisher and audience:

After the assassination of Martin Luther King, she told me she was doing a little book and wished to donate it to Broadside Press. Titled *Riot*, it was published in 1969. All proceeds from the book go to Broadside. It was followed by *Family Pictures*, and *Aloneness*, a children's book.

One day she called me and said she wanted her autobiography to be published by Broadside. Thinking of her welfare, I declined. . . . Upon publication *Report From Part One* was greeted with an enthusiastic review by Toni Cade Bambara on page one of the *New York Times Book Review*.[26]

Her latest book is *Beckonings*, where she tries a style simple and direct enough to reach all Black people, yet rich and deep.[27]

Broadside began by issuing famous poets' broadside poems with original art but soon moved to single book and group anthology publications of new poets. Created by Dudley Randall's vision and with little funding, publishing an impressive roster of black poets and scholars, Broadside surely needed Brooks's prominence and sales potential.[28] But there was much more than that, for Brooks had found both herself and/or a new role as an activist artist, even as she was helping to found a community of poets. Brooks's first Broadside broadside, "We Real Cool," whose title and refrain, borrowed from black English street argot, became something of an anthem, has an interesting history that makes Brooks a leader *avant la révolution*, if you will. Dudley Randall tells it, thus:

In May 1966, I attended the first Writers' Conference at Fisk University, and obtained permission from Robert Hayden, Melvin B. Tolson, and Margaret Walker, who were there, to use their poems. . . . I wrote to Gwendolyn Brooks and obtained her permission to use "We Real Cool." This first group of six Broadsides [is] called "Poems of the Negro Revolt."[29]

Differently presented and received seven years after its publication in the collection *The Bean Eaters* (1960), Randall's broadside of Brooks's "We Real Cool" "was lettered white on black by Cledie Taylor to simulate scrawls on a blackboard," in keeping with the care he took to "harmonize . . . the poem, in paper, color, and typography." This is to say that Brooks's poem was afforded a place of distinction, if not literally a space on many a wall. This poem continues to generate interest, and, if only because I was at least surprised to see it treated to an apparently gratuitous dismissal in a recent issue of *Callaloo*, I would like to spend a few moments over it. Before rival readings, the poem, unfortunately *sans* graphics:

We Real Cool

>   The Pool Players.
>   Seven at the Golden Shovel.

We real cool.   We
Left school.   We

Lurk late.   We
Strike straight.   We

Sing sin.   We
Thin gin.   We

Jazz June.   We
Die soon.

>   (*WGB*, 315)

Of this poem Hortense Spillers, praising the "wealth of implication" in this "[l]ess than lean poem," says it is "no nonsense at all." Finding original artistry, in-crowd and in-race code, and a full range of traditional poetic techniques in Brooks's poem, Spillers say that Brooks's players "subvert the romance of sociological pathos" and, quite comfortably, she has them read Brooks's lines, thus:

They make no excuse for themselves and apparently invite no one else to do so. The poem is their situation as *they* see it. In eight [could be nonstop] lines, here is their total destiny. Perhaps comic geniuses, they could well drink to this poem, making it a drinking/revelry song.[30]

I would like to bring Helen Vendler's recent mention of Brooks into conversation with Spillers's earlier tribute. Speaking with the well-earned authority of her position as a major reader of *the* Western canon and an influential critic of new poet candidates to that tradition, Vendler writes about the new national poet laureate in *Callaloo*, the most important wider-than-academic journal of black and Third World poetry. She generously praises and candidly corrects (explicitly *not* in the sense of "political correctness") the "Identity Markers" Rita Dove marshals to "confront . . . the enraging fact that the inescapable accusation of blackness becomes, too early for the child to resist it, a strong element of inner self-definition." At one point, Vendler economically dismisses Brooks in questioning one of Dove's "relatively unsuccessful historical excursions in a lyric time-machine." Not to make too much of a few lines, I quote her dismissal in full: "This [Dove's early 'odyssey'] may owe something to Gwendolyn Brooks's 'We Real Cool,' but it avoids the prudishness of

Brooks's judgmental monologue, which though it is ostensibly spoken by adolescents, barely conceals its adult reproach of their behavior."[31]

Even though Vendler indicates that Brooks's poem is not properly addressed to the white critical tradition, her response does not fail to register, however unwittingly, Brooks's double movement at once to narrow and to expand the usual distance readers of poetry traverse in becoming—or resisting becoming—"We," whether *real cool* or not. By making Brooks admonish the adolescents, Vendler makes pretty clear who isn't *We*—not to say who "We" isn't. It seems that, however fallen, Brooks, the poet, simply must share the critic's position above those pool players. Curiously, from their different aesthetic and experiential positions, Vendler and Spillers both give valid readings of the poem, and it is no accident that they fix on the pronoun that hangs out there like the prepositions from William Carlos Williams's famous wheelbarrow.

Not to dwell overlong on the ethos or impact of the very different constructions invited by Brooks's "We," I add Brooks's own commentary on the poem, which is delivered as stage directions for her public readings:

First of all, let me tell you how that's ["We Real Cool"] supposed to be said, because there's a reason why I set it out as I did. These are people who are essentially saying, "Kilroy is here. We *are*." But they're a little uncertain of the strength of their identity. The "We"—you're supposed to stop after the "we" and think about *validity*; of course, there's no way for you to tell whether it should be said softly or not, I suppose, but I say it rather softly because I want to represent their basic uncertainty. (*RFPO*, 155–56)

Characteristically, Brooks invites both identification with and objectification of the young men—depending, perhaps on such categories as the race, gender, age of her/their audience. There is something cunning and deceptive both about the openness of Brooks's "We" and her variable distance from both the pool players to whom it refers and the people—at least since its Broadside republication—it seems to rename. Rather like the young white man who, in Brooks's story about Baraka, heeded a call not intended for him, or the "You" of "Primer for Blacks," that shifty pronoun works a critique on audience overidentification and poet's supposed representativeness. After all, isn't *she* supposed to correct the young punks, not to follow them as new leaders? But which *she*? The writer of "We Real Cool," *The Bean Eaters* (1960)? Or the writer of the 1967 broadside, "We Real Cool"? And should the differences of context and thus of content be *fixed*—either in the sense of "healed" or "halted"? Brooks put(s) her readers, specifically a black audience that is not limited to the no-longer-New Blacks of the sixties, to work on such questions.

Rather than stand as the highly decorated, proper, and representative lady and/or poet for her race (the "lady 'negro poet'"), Brooks chose to transform a black audience into poets or, as William Blake might say, prophets. Brooks's address is wider than Whitman's mutual embrace of writer and his people. More literal, literary, and liberating are her encouragement and publicity in favor of young poets than the hope that one day, perhaps crossing to Brooklyn on a ferry, one might think her thoughts. Indeed, it might be that her greatest offense against the literary and academic establishment(s)—the refusal to rest on her (canonical) laurels and apparent dismissal of the capital "P" of Poetry, which is also her refusal to repeat the talented-tenth or exclusive single, sanctioned post of (non-)representative poet, such as Hughes in the Harlem Renaissance—encrypts her most direct engagement of literary history.

Despite a fair amount of thunder and fire, her statement is no "No in thunder," but a generous "Yes" to those systematically excluded from the academic and elitist poetic apparatus. Let me digress for a moment, moving from black to Blake, if you will. Indeed, there is something Blakean, revolutionary yet (re-)visionary, in Brooks's poetic address or ethos that jibes with Blake's ironic assault on Milton and literary canonizations that would create and define both "a fit audience though few" and "justify the ways of God to Man"—not to mention Western Truth for all time readable in a certain poetic genealogy and line. Let me remind you just how economical Blake can be, when he quotes a few words of the biblical Moses at the end of his preface to *Milton*.[32] Moses prevented his servant from forbidding unsanctioned competing men from prophesying with the words "Would to God that all the Lord's people were prophets" (Numbers 11:29). With this epigraph, standing as it does at the beginning of his poem against limits placed on the religion and politics of his time, Blake takes aim against the one Holy and Apostolic Church that English poetry was becoming—ironically, under the name of Milton, erstwhile radical Protestant.

Like Blake, Brooks subsumes and revises the conventional role of poet. Sometimes she critiques the old by celebrating and enacting her new position within poems. "The Wall," for instance, records and comprises Brooks's poetic dedication of "the mural of black dignity" painted on a slum wall at Forty-third and Langley in Chicago. In a *mise-en-scène* that depicts the poet—"She our sister is" ("The Wall," 11. 33–34)—who rises to the podium in order to celebrate and, with the other "Women in wool hair chant their poetry," to take poetry from off shelves and paintings down from walls to this Wall. She is but one of the celebrants, one with the graffiti artists, also an organic cultural critic, celebrating her own history and promise. With one stroke, she helps deface the ugliness of the slum, while together poet and multimedia artists worship, make "yea" and "announcement," "chant," and "sing." Thus, with the African ornaments of sixties costumes and the figures of high art, Brooks at once very precisely locates in time, space, and with the proper names of some participants, the occasion of this celebration of perpetual movement as an assertion of human dignity:

> THE WALL
> August 27, 1967. . . .
>
> A drumdrumdrum.
> Humbly we come.
> South of success and east of gloss and glass are
> sandals;
> flowercloth;
> grave hoops of wood or gold, pendant
> from black ears, brown ears, reddish brown
> and ivory ears
>
>   .   .   .   .   .
> . . . In front of me
> hundreds of faces, red-brown, brown, black, ivory,
> yield me hot trust, their yea and their Announcement
> that they are ready to rile the high-flung ground.
> Behind me, Paint.
> Heroes.
> No child has defiled
>
> The Heroes of this Wall this serious Appointment
> this still Wing
> this Scald this Flute this heavy Light this Hinge.
>
> An emphasis is paroled.
> The old decapitations are revised,
> The dispossessions beakless.
>
> And we sing.
>
>   (*WGB*, 414–15)

In order to sing prophetic poetry with her young people, Brooks had further to go than Blake, since she had not only to reject and replace one precursor, but she had also to renounce the monumentalization of Western art and her own assigned position(s) therein: "First," "Negro," "Woman," "Poet(ess)," and so on. Just so, with reference to Larry Neal and LeRoi Jones's *Black Fire* (1968), her own contribution to *A Capsule*

Course in Black Poetry Writing (1975) prizes the utility as well as the perpetual revolution and resistance of the Black Art she had first embraced, as such and by her own account, in 1967 at the Second Black Writers' Conference at Fisk. In her "Course" she is, again, pupil of the young and poet-in-process; thus:

> The new feeling, among the *earnest* new young black creators, was that concern for the long-lastingness was western and was wrong. One created a piece of art for the enrichment, the instruction, the extension of one's own people. Its usefulness may or may not be exhausted in a day, a week, a month, a year. There was no prayerful compulsion—*among the earnest*—for its idle survival into the centuries. The word went down: we must chase out Western measures, rules, models. (*CC,* 5) [33]

Directly, as a poet consciously and publicly revising both her own image and the poet's representative function, Brooks, in the appendix/ marginalia to *Report from Part One,* opens both person and category "Poet and/or G.B." to change and public interaction and construction. She is conscious of writing at, to, within the limits of a topical tribute to the changes wrought in her by—young and mostly male—revolutionary heroes. She is conscious, too, of future (r)evolutions from poets, prophets, and just plain people she will address and support. Ironically, her secure fame and position enable her to renounce the poet's traditional aesthetic distance:

> My aim, in my next future, is to write poems that will somehow successfully "call" (see Imamu Baraka's "SOS" [*Black Fire*]) all black people: black people in taverns, black people in gutters, schools, offices, factories, prisons, the consulate; I wish to reach black people in pulpits, black people in mines, on farms, on thrones, *not* always to "teach"—I shall wish often to entertain, to illumine. My newish voice will not be an imitation of the contemporary young black voice, which I so admire, but an extending adaptation of today's G. B. voice. (*RFPO,* 183)

Let me make clear that Brooks does not see what I am calling her shift in intended audience (also a shift from general poetic and academic to specifically black community venues) as renunciation of, say, prestige for virtue. She announces a new, provisional yet prophetic writing in the terms of a new (black) consciousness and the affirmation of the beauty of her own dark skin; from the first, we might remember, her poems remarked the self-hatred imposed by color caste and versions of white beauty. And, while her apparent adoption of such roles as queen and mother to poets might seem, from a certain perspective, to recapitulate the old virgin-whore construction, Brooks doesn't end with that rebeginning:

> I—who have "gone the gamut" from an almost angry rejection of my dark skin by some of my brainwashed brothers and sisters to a surprised queenhood in the

black sun—am qualified to enter at least the kindergarten of new consciousness now. New consciousness and trudge-toward-progress.

I have hopes for myself. (*RFPO*, 86)

Notes

Frequently cited works by Gwendolyn Brooks have been identified with the following abbreviations:

CC   *A Capsule Course in Black Poetry Writing.* Gwendolyn Brooks with Keorapetse Kgositsile, Haki R. Madhubuti, and Dudley Randall. Detroit: Broadside Press, 1975.

JB   *Jump Bad: A New Chicago Anthology.* Gwendolyn Brooks, ed. Detroit: Broadside Press, 1971.

MHW *Mayor Harold Washington and Chicago the "I Will" City.* Chicago: Brooks Press, 1983.

MM   *Maud Martha.* New York: Harper and Row, 1953. Repr., Chicago: Third World Press, 1993.

PB   *Primer for Blacks.* Chicago: Third World Press, 1991.

RFPO *Report from Part One,* with prefaces by Don L. Lee and George Kent. Detroit: Broadside Press, 1972.

SP   *Selected Poems.* New York: Harper & Row, 1963.

TD   *To Disembark.* Chicago: Third World Press, 1981.

WGB *The World of Gwendolyn Brooks.* New York: Harper and Row, 1971.

1. Radically different as are the politics of racist fascist Ezra Pound and black feminist Gwendolyn Brooks, they share public and pedagogic address to their audiences. By historical fluke, as right and left are sometimes wont to diverge over the same issue, Pound and Brooks were the two most popular write-in candidates for the Illinois laureateship. Let me share part of the "Collage" of oddments she appended to her autobiography. "From Whit Burnett, regarding his greatest-living-authors anthology *This Is My Best*: 'It may be of particular interest to you that your name was inadvertently left off the ballot sent to six thousand readers, critics, etc., but you and Ezra Pound, another omitted, received the highest number of write-in votes'" (*RFPO*, 212).

2. In "The Occult of True Black Womanhood: Critical Demeanor and Black Feminist Studies" (*Signs: Journal of Women in Culture and Society* 19, no. 3 [Spring 1994]), Ann du Cille attends to Alice Walker's and Toni Morrison's (the second and third, Brooks being the first, black women Pulitzer Prize winners) recuperation and canonizations of and within her "sacred text" of black women's writing and experience. Confessing to having been led to the "sacred text" of black women in graduate school, she does not even mention Brooks, who, from a doubly marginal position as popular and public (as opposed to autobiographical or confessional) poet, might well complicate the picture du Cille draws of questionable black male critical and dubious white female personal appropriations. Brooks's relative neglect by academic feminists, which is not quite matched by that of black women poets, might well be overdetermined by her embrace of populist values and venues as well as by the embrace of a sixties solidarity that diminishes gender before race issues. Brooks has not felt compelled to renounce an earlier strategy of race and class affiliation, by which "Black women, like all women, certainly want and are entitled to equal pay and 'privileges.' But black

women have a second 'twoness.' Today's black men, increasingly assertive and proud, need their black women beside them not organizing against them" (*RFPO*, 199).

3. If Brooks sometimes fails to escape the very trap her writings delineate, it seems clear, especially in light of the outcome of the (Anita Hill and) Clarence Thomas hearings (he being a Supreme Court justice for life), that race matters are gendered "male." This condition hardly means that black solidarity evades manipulation.

4. The Black Arts Movement, uniting more diverse writers and styles than its various official histories suggest, continues to be revived and revised by, among others, Haki Madhubuti, formerly don l. lee, author of *Think Black* (Detroit: Broadside, 1968) and, most recently, *Black Men: Obsolete, Single, Dangerous?* (Chicago: Third World Press, 1990), *Why L. A. Happened* (Chicago: Third World Press, 1993). Madhubuti, a.k.a. Third World Press, is still Brooks's editor and publisher; in many introductions and prefaces he explains her work, his position, and the way the latter continues to inform Brooks's poetry. Anything approaching a full treatment of Madhubuti's work exceeds the scope of this essay, but it is clear that his poetry and politics, which are especially at odds with black feminist and lesbian work (and, for that matter, deliberately not addressed to THEM/us), are not to be discounted.

5. While Madhubuti, in the introduction to Brooks's autobiography (*RFPO*, 22) and elsewhere, tends to mark 1967 as a radical shift in Brooks's work and *In the Mecca* (New York: Harper and Row, 1968) as pivotal but still freighted with old poetic values, George E. Kent, with a slightly different emphasis, sees *In the Mecca* as the stylistic epitome and thematic sublation of Brooks's public and private (women's) work (*A Life of Gwendolyn Brooks* [Lexington: University of Kentucky Press, 1989], 98).

6. By Brooks's account, Johnson was rather formal when he spoke at their church, while Hughes, who later became friend, editor, and colleague, was more than open to the sixteen-year-old poet-would-be, when he "came to the Metropolitan Community Church . . . my mother had brought a whole pack of my stuff, and we showed it to him. He read it right there; he said that I was talented and must go on writing. He was really an inspiration" (*RFPO*, 173–74).

7. Langston Hughes, "The Negro Artist and the Racial Mountain," *The Nation* (1926), repr. in *On Being Black: Writings by Afro-Americans from Fredrick Douglass to the Present*, ed. Charles T. Davis and Daniel Walden (New York: Fawcett, 1970), 161. This is something of an addendum to the classic debate over how and by whom the (New) Negro should be represented that took place on the pages of Du Bois's *Crisis* "Seminars" of 1926.

8. Madhubuti (as don l. lee) deprecates *Annie Allen* and the Brooks of that moment on the grounds that complex style and tentative persona were addressed to, and only understood by, whites: "At best she was a 'new negro' becoming black. Her view of history was that of the traditional American history and had not been challenged by anyone of black substance. In her next book the focus was not on history or tradition, but poetic style. *Annie Allen* (1949), important? Yes. Read by blacks? No. *Annie Allen* more so than *A Street in Bronzeville* seems to have been written for whites. For instance, 'The Anniad' requires unusual concentrated study" (*RFPO*, 17).

9. About the genre of her "autobiographical novel" Brooks offers a metaphoric but useful definition, "nuanceful, allowing. There's fact-meat in the soup, among the chunks of fancy; but, generally, definite identification will be difficult"

(*RFPO*, 190–91). One can take "identification" in at least two senses: audience empathy and historical or biographical accuracy.

10. Toni Morrison, *Playing in the Dark: Whiteness and the Literary Imagination* (Cambridge, Mass.: Harvard University Press, 1992), 44.

11. In various autobiographical statements, Du Bois makes clear that, rather than simply suffering from "double consciousness," he deliberately presents himself on one side or another of the "color line." Moreover, despite charges of accommodationism and special race privileges due to his light color, Du Bois clearly sought race pride and solidarity, in for example "On Being Ashamed of Oneself: An Essay on Race Pride," *Crisis* 40, no. 3 (March 1933), and "Color Caste in the United States," *Crisis* 40, no. 9 (September 1933).

12. In "Nuance and the Novella" Barbara Christian notes that *Maud Martha* (1953), published the same year as, and almost totally eclipsed by, *Go Tell It on the Mountain* and one year after the hugely popular *Invisible Man*, is a founding text, if something of a well kept secret, for black women writers and critics. Interested to recover Brooks for a feminist attack upon racism, Christian praises *Maud Martha*'s refusal of the victim and/or race representative roles prescribed by white and black men for "the Negro novel": "Brooks replaced intense drama or pedestrian portrayal of character with a careful rendering of the rituals, the patterns, of the ordinary life, where racism is experienced in sharp nibbles rather than screams and where making do is continually juxtaposed with small but significant dreams." "Nuance and the Novella: A Study of Gwendolyn Brooks's *Maud Martha*," in *A Life Distilled: Gwendolyn Brooks, Her Poetry and Fiction*, ed. Marla K. Mootry and Gary Smith (Urbana: University of Illinois Press, 1987), 241.

13. In " 'An Order of Constancy': Notes on Brooks and the Feminine," *Centennial Review* 29, no. 2 (Spring 1985), Hortense J. Spillers uses Kenneth Burke's notion of "literature as equipment for living" to elaborate Brooks's "feminine consciousness." She notes that, while remaining "male-identified" *Maud Martha* negotiates "feminist mandates" and "patriarchal modes of power" (225) in constructing before our eyes a separate self that might vie with mythic male individualism (*vide* Morrison) as a force toward human freedom. Spillers captures some of the complexity—confusion?—of Brooks's subjective objectification, if you will, that forces the reader "to confront Maud Martha as the primary and central consciousness of the work, its subject *and* object of gazing" so that "[d]espite her blackness, her femaleness, her poverty-line income, and perhaps, because of these unalterable 'facts' of social status and mensuration, Maud Martha is permitted to have her own 'moment of being' and the narrative itself is its record. . . . The demonstration, I believe, of woman-freedom is the text itself which has no centrality, no force, no sticking point other than the imaginative nuances of the subject's consciousness" (242).

14. Attending both to epistemological and ontological quandaries that Brooks's style puts subtly into play, Johnson says that Brooks "is explicitly rewriting the male lyric tradition, textually placing aborted children in the spot formerly occupied by all the dead, inanimate, or absent entities previously addressed by the lyric. . . . The poem can no more distinguish between 'I' and 'you' than it can come up with a proper definition of life.' " Barbara Johnson, "Apostrophe, Animation, and Abortion," *Diacritics* 16, no. 1 (Spring 1986): 32. Similarly, Marcellus Blount notes of the sonnets from *Annie Allen* and *The Bean Eaters* that Brooks "writes herself into the canon of Western literary history by 'seizing' a poetic form steeped in male conquest and political struggle, then progressively remakes its racial and gender associations as her career as a poet develops. . . .

[S]he stakes her claim to female authority based upon female subjectivity."
"Caged Birds: Race and Gender in the Sonnet," in *Engendering Men: The Question of Male Feminist Criticism* (New York: Routledge, 1980), 236.

15. Brooks's satiric point can be translated as an endorsement of Du Bois's response to writers who thought *Nigger Heaven* was not dangerous or directed at real Harlemites. However, as her career and her fame and popularity with white audiences progressed, Brooks could not have been moved farther from Du Bois's solution to the problem of debasing representations.

16. This amusing story of the belated ban on Brooks's early use of "black" shows her currency with young black musicians and artists as well as the surprising new thrust of the word and concept "black" to reigning definitions of Negro self-presentations. Oscar Brown Jr., composer of the offending musical rendering of Brooks's work, who was working with them on a musical, first introduced Brooks to the Blackstone Rangers. See D. H. Melhem, *Gwendolyn Brooks: Poetry and the Heroic Voice* (Lexington: University of Kentucky Press, 1987), 31, and Brooks's introduction to *Jump Bad*.

17. Melhem, *Gwendolyn Brooks*, 131. Brooks's offered this revised De Witt Williams, no longer a "plain black boy" but a representative of the new radicals around her, on a radio broadcast in February 1962.

18. With reference to Adorno's injunction against poetry after Auschwitz, Addison Gayle Jr.'s "Gwendolyn Brooks: Poet of the Whirlwind," in *Black Women Writers 1950–1980: A Critical Evaluation*, ed. Mary Evans (Garden City, N.Y.: Doubleday, Doran and Co., 1984), records the heroic voices and attitudes that take Brooks beyond "whining," the stage that he defines in Brooks's own word, to resistance and exultation.

19. In addition to *The World of Gwendolyn Brooks*, the big mainstream anthology that ends with *In the Mecca* but gathers all her previous books, see *BLACKS* (1987), the Third World Press anthology intended to supersede the Harper and Row volume. Madhubuti's collection reprints the same earlier material and, as the brochure advertising *Classic Black Literature from Gwendolyn Brooks* suggests, "Relevant poems are excerpted from *Primer for Blacks, Beckonings, To Disembark*, and *The Near Johannesburg Boy and Other Poems*." It has been a while since I have seen "relevant" used without an object, but title and description convey the sense that Brooks represents, not herself or women or poetry, but *blacks*, one race, essentialized, unified, and unmodified by other categories like class and gender.

20. I am aware of such important and thoughtful statements as Larry Neal's (Fanon and pan-Africanist informed) call for a New Black consciousness to overcome Du Bois's "double consciousness" in a unified identity and group solidarity. Such an overcoming might seem to abolish the irony and positionality (also the "feminist" and "subaltern" subjectivity) that I have privileged. Nevertheless, in attempting to reconcile Marcus Garvey and Du Bois, Neal's "And Shine Swam On," revises Garvey in such a way that consciousness and positions multiply and become flexible enough to subsume "double consciousness as a fixture of Black life." Neal shows Garvey "attempting the destruction of that very tension [double consciousness] which had plagued all of Du Bois's professional career. It involved knowing and deciding who and what we are. . . . Garvey was more emotionally cohesive than Du Bois, and not as intellectually fragmented. Du Bois, for all of his commitment, was a somewhat stuffy intellectual with middle-class hangups, for which Garvey constantly attacked him. The people to whom Garvey appealed could never have understood Du Bois. But Garvey understood them, and the life-force within him was very fundamental to them" (in *Black Fire: An Anthology of*

Afro-American Writing, ed. LeRoi Jones and Larry Neal [New York: William Morrow, 1968], 643).

21. In an interested explication of her handy *Webster's New World Dictionary*, Brooks unpacks the "assumptions behind "black" and "white"; simply reproducing all the evil and negative connotations of "black" and contrasting them to the positives accruing to "white," she focuses on the first two usages: black, "1. opposite to white: see color. . . . white, 1. having the color of pure snow or milk." Extrapolating her conclusion (that "we do not find that 'white' is 'opposite of black.' That would lift black to the importance level of white" [*RFPO*, 83]), we can begin to get a sense of what is at stake in refusing self and group definitions ("You") measured by acceptance, denial, or simple reversals of the terms of white identity and of white identifications of blackness.

22. Sonia Sanchez's poem and the contributions of many other Kuumba Player affiliates who participated in a poetic tribute in Chicago in 1969 were edited by don l. lee as *To Gwen with Love*, representing the wide range of poets touched by Brooks. Given present critical configurations of the poetry, identity, and/or gender wars, it might be surprising to see Sanchez, nikki giovanni, Margaret Danner, Margaret Walker, alongside lee, Larry Neal, and Walter Bradford, and Dudley Randall in celebration of Brooks.

23. Black writers of the sixties were united in celebration and conversation as well as in crisis. Langston Hughes was but one tireless promoter and consolidator of the new voices. While rooting around for early pieces of several black beat/surrealist/noncanonical poets (such as Bob Kaufman, Ted Joans, and Ray Durem), I was struck by the diversity of experiment and power of commitment recorded in Hughes's *New Negro Poets, USA* (Bloomington: Indiana University, 1964), which is introduced by none other than Gwendolyn Brooks.

24. Brooks seems to have dropped from the picture as dedicatee or introducer of many of the poets from the Chicago and Detroit scene of the sixties and early seventies. Just as she is absent from Ann Du Cille's genealogy, her name is erased from the lists of radical women writers, disappearing, perhaps, as Whitman says the best poet/teacher should, into the words of her "People"? Or has she been dismissed for being not the New Negro but a frozen image of the New Black or both? In fact, she is still there, as a mother figure in stylistic traces and in conversations behind the scene.

25. Work on such projects as the anthology *The Poetry of the Negro, 1746–1970*, co-written children's stories, and joint performance and promotion ventures are recorded in the recently published correspondence of Arna Bontemps and Langston Hughes (*Letters, 1925–1967*, selected and edited by Charles H. Nichols [New York: Dodd, Mead, 1980]). This volume indicates their continued engagement with new artists. Along these lines, and in anticipation, perhaps, of the recent high cultural and critical embrace of hip-hop, Langston Hughes's *Black Magic: A Pictorial History of the Negro in American Entertainment* (Englewood Cliffs, N.J.: Prentice-Hall, 1967) and Amiri Baraka's *In Our Terribleness (Some Elements of Meaning in Black Style)* (Indianapolis: Bobbs Merrill, 1970) pay visual and personal tribute to the mutual inspiration of black artists across media; they exhibit a special openness to young street kids and other often unrecognized stylists.

26. Toni Cade Bambara also wrote a foreword to *This Bridge Called My Back: Writings of Radical Women of Color* (ed. Cherrie Moraga and Gloria Anzaldua [Watertown, Mass.: Persephone Press, 1981]), which reopens feminist writing and identity politics in a productive way: "[t]his Bridge documents particular rites of passage. Coming of age and coming to terms with community—race, group,

class, gender, self—its expectations, supports, and lessons. And coming to grips with its perversions—racism, prejudice, elitism, misogyny, homophobia, and murder. . . . And coming to grips with those false awakenings too that give use [*sic*] ease as we substitute a militant mouth for a radical politic" (vii). The issues raised in this volume, especially by "A Black Feminist Statement: Combahee River Collective" (210–18), enjoy academic or theoretical currency, but they also project a praxis that, as a continuation and expansion of liberation movements of the sixties, grows out of "the need to develop a politics that [is] antiracist, unlike those of white women, and antisexist, unlike those of Black and white men" (211).

27. Dudley Randall, *Broadside Memories: Poets I Have Known* (Detroit: Broadside Press, 1975), 8. This pamphlet/book, which includes the program of Broadside Press's tenth anniversary banquet emceed by Val Gray Ward, records his work with and for established writers (Brooks, Hoyt W. Fuller, Margaret Danner) as well as younger poets (including Audre Lorde, Etheridge Knight, Haki Madhubuti, nikki giovanni) who were to go on to fame and, in several cases, to open their own small publishing houses.

28. Melba Joyce Boyd's "Out of the Poetry Ghetto: The Life/Art Struggle of Small Black Publishing Houses," *The Black Scholar* (July–August 1985): 12–24, which affords poet-publisher-critic Dudley Randall, who, like Arna Bontemps, had been a librarian committed to the preservation and expansion of African American culture, deserved laurels as the astute yet selfless founder and friend of the black small press poetry scene. Before Randall was forced to suspend operations in 1975, he had encouraged other little houses, including Madhubuti's Third World Press and Naomi Madgett's Lotus Press.

29. Randall, *Broadside Memories*, 23.

30. Hortense J. Spillers, "Gwendolyn the Terrible: Propositions on Eleven Poems," in Mootry and Smith, *A Life Distilled*, 225. Focusing her own meditation on "American Identities" on Brooks, about whom she has written at greater length than most literary theorists and current black feminists, Spillers finds that "for more than three decades now, Gwendolyn Brooks has been writing poetry that reflects a particular historical order, often close to the heart of the public event, but the dialectic that is engendered between the event and her reception of it is, perhaps, one of the more subtle confrontations of criticism" (225).

31. Helen Vendler, "Rita Dove: Identity Markers," *Callaloo* 17, no. 2 (Summer 1994): 384.

32. Blake's ironic call to a revisionary truth is as baffling as the differentially repeated announcements of new American identities, which include, dictate, or enable New Negro and New Black and African American identities. *Milton*'s revisionary ratios, by which Blake causes poetry, politics, and religion to mutually correct and destroy each other in the texts and reputations of the great English poet, are unstoppable. While such flexibility of position and interpretation are a lot easier for and among dead poets than on the street, and might seem frivolous in a discussion of Brooks as black feminist, identity politics that polices the other and frees oneself to change at will, which has been the prerogative of masters, offers strategic advantages to oppressed peoples.

33. The essay from which Brooks takes her non-Western/Africanist notion of the use value of art is James T. Stewart's "The Development of the Black Revolutionary Artist," in Jones and Neal, *Black Fire*, 3–10. There he assigns particular value to a general non-Western (which encompasses Japan and the African diaspora) equation of creativity and change; for example,

The work [African mud architecture and Japanese rice paper drawings] is fragile, destructible; in other words, there is a total disregard for the perpetuation of the product, the picture, the statue, the temple. Is this ignorance? . . . The white researcher, the white scholar, would have us believe that he "rescues" these "valuable" pieces. He "saves" them from their creators, those "ignorant" colored people who merely destroy them. Those people who do not know their value. What an audacious presumption! . . . We know, all non-whites know that man cannot create *a* forever, but he can create forever. But he can only create if he creates as change. Creation is itself perpetuation and change in being. (4)

Contributors

DIANNE CHISHOLM is an associate professor of English at the University of Alberta, Edmonton, and the author of *H. D.'s Freudian Poetics: Psychoanalysis in Translation* (1992).

SUZANNE CLARK is an associate professor of English at the University of Oregon and the author of *Sentimental Modernism: Women Writers and the Revolution of the Word* (1991).

KATE DANIELS teaches creative writing at Vanderbilt University and is a member of the creative writing graduate faculty at Bennington College. She is a poet working on a biography of Muriel Rukeyser.

MARGARET DICKIE is the Helen S. Lanier Distinguished Professor of English at the University of Georgia and the author of *Hart Crane: The Patterns of His Poetry* (1974), *Sylvia Plath & Ted Hughes* (1979), *On the Modernist Long Poem* (1986), and *Lyric Contingencies: Emily Dickinson and Wallace Stevens* (1991).

RICHARD FLYNN is an associate professor of English at Georgia Southern University and the author of *Randall Jarrell and the Lost World of Childhood* (1990) and a collection of poetry, *The Age of Reason* (1993).

JEANNE HEUVING is an associate professor of English at the University of Washington at Bothell and the author of *Omissions Are Not Accidents: Gender in the Art of Marianne Moore* (1992).

CASSANDRA LAITY is an assistant professor of English at Drew University and the editor of H. D.'s *Paint It Today* (1992), as well as the author of the forthcoming *H. D. and Victorian Fin de Siècle: Gender, Decadence, Modernism.*

KATHRYNE V. LINDBERG is an associate professor of English at Wayne State University and the author of *Reading Pound Reading: Modernism after Nietzsche* (1987) and the forthcoming *The Forbidden "Subject" of American Fascism: The Repressed Politics of the 30s.*

MARY LOEFFELHOLZ is an associate professor of English at Northeastern University and the author of *Dickinson and the Boundaries of Feminist*

Theory (1991) and *Experimental Lives: Women & Literature, 1900–1945* (1992).

ROBIN GAIL SCHULZE is an assistant professor at the Pennsylvania State University and the author of the forthcoming *"The Web of Friendship": Marianne Moore and Wallace Stevens.*

LISA STEINMAN is Kenan Professor of English at Reed College and the author of *Made in America: Science, Technology, and American Modernist Poetry* (1987), *Lost Poems* (1976), *All That Comes to Light* (1989), and *A Book of Other Days* (1993).

THOMAS TRAVISANO is Babcock Professor of English at Hartwick College and the author of *Elizabeth Bishop: Her Artistic Development* (1988) and the editor of *The Elizabeth Bishop Bulletin.* He is completing a developmental study of three contemporaries: Robert Lowell, Randall Jarrell, and John Berryman.

CHERYL WALKER is Richard Armour Professor of English at Scripps College and the author of *Anne Bradstreet* (1979), *The Nightingale's Burden: Women Poets and American Culture Before 1900* (1983), *Masks Outrageous and Austere: Culture, Psyche, and Persona in Modern Women Poets* (1992).

Index